The Sounds of Language

LEARNING ABOUT LANGUAGE

General Editors:
Geoffrey Leech and Mick Short, Lancaster University

Already published:

Analysing Sentences (2nd edition) Noel Burton-Roberts

Words and Their Meaning Howard Jackson

An Introduction to Phonology Francis Katamba

Grammar and Meaning Howard Jackson

An Introduction to Sociolinguistics Janet Holmes

Realms of Meaning: An Introduction to Semantics Th. R. Hofmann

An Introduction to Psycholinguistics Danny D. Steinberg

An Introduction to Spoken Interaction Anna-Brita Stenström

Watching English Change Laurie Bauer

Meaning in Interaction: An Introduction to Pragmatics Jenny Thomas

An Introduction to Cognitive Linguistics Friedrich Ungerer and Hans-Jörg Schmid

Exploring the Language of Poems, Plays and Prose Mick Short

Contemporary Linguistics: An Introduction William O'Grady, Michael Dobrovolsky and Francis Katamba

Analysing Sentences Noel Burton-Roberts

An Introduction to Natural Language Processing Through Prolog Clive Matthews

An Introduction to Child Language Development Susan Foster-Cohen

The Sounds of Language: An Introduction to Phonetics Henry Rogers

The Sounds of Language

An Introduction to Phonetics

Henry Rogers

LONDON AND NEW YORK

First published 2000 by Pearson Education Limited

Published 2013 by Routledge
2 Park Square, Milton Park, Abingdon, Oxon OX14 4RN
711 Third Avenue, New York, NY 10017, USA

Routledge is an imprint of the Taylor & Francis Group, an informa business

ISBN 13: 978-0-582-38182-7 (pbk)

British Library Cataloguing-in-Publication Data
A catalogue record for this book is available from the British Library

Library of Congress Cataloging-in-Publication Data
Rogers, Henry, 1940–
The sounds of language : an introduction to phonetics / Henry Rogers.
p. cm. — (Learning about language)
Includes bibliographical references and index.
ISBN 0–582–38182–7 (pbk.)
1. English language—Phonetics. 2. Phonetics. I. Title. II. Series.
PE1135.R64 2000
421′.5—dc21 99–089810

Typeset by 35 in 10/12.5pt Palatino

Διονυσίῳ

Contents

Preface

Most people have little idea about phonetics. Commonly it is confused with phonics, a system for teaching children to read. In buying this book, obviously you have some interest in the subject. So what are you in for?

Phonetics is the scientific study of sounds used in language. Since you must be familiar with English to use this book at all, we begin our study with English. We will consider the two most influential accents in English: one from Britain and one from the United States. In particular, we are interested in how the sounds of English are made. What do we do with our bodies to produce each different sound? After examining the sounds of English in Chapters 1–5, we look at various other dialects of English from around the world in Chapter 6. In Chapters 7 and 8, we turn to how sound can be studied in the laboratory. We will look at acoustic notions such as sound waves and spectrograms. With a good grip on English and on acoustics, we then broaden our scope to include any language (Chapters 9–14). Obviously, we cannot examine all the 5,000 or so languages in the world, but we will be looking at a wide variety of languages from all parts of the globe.

The components of phonetics are interconnected. By looking at English first, we get a general overview of the field of phonetics. Then, when we look at other languages, we have a framework in which to place new information and ideas.

Phonetics uses a large number of technical terms. When these occur, they are in **bold face**. Each chapter has a list of technical terms at the end, and they are all collected and defined in the Glossary (Appendix B).

Appendix A on consonant allophones relates to Chapter 3. Appendix C on Calligraphy shows you how to write symbols in a way that others can recognise. Appendix D is a discussion of the principles and problems in devising a transcription system for English vowels.

The International Phonetic Alphabet (IPA) is used in this book and is widely used by phoneticians, linguists, and speech pathologists around the world. The latest version (1996) is included in Appendix E.

An important feature of this book is the importance it lays on developing the practical skills of learning to produce various sounds. Every chapter contains extensive exercises at the end. These are divided into two parts: basic and advanced. The basic exercises help you learn to produce the sounds just covered in the chapter. The advanced exercises are cumulative, developing your ability to produce new sounds in combination with ones you already know, and they are more difficult, pushing you towards ever greater phonetic dexterity.

The exercises of Chapter 1 give some general advice on how to practise making sounds. Throughout the book, hints and tips are given that have helped others learn to pronounce the various sounds. No book can really teach you practical phonetics. Only close listening and practice can do that. This book will, however, help you do the things necessary for improving your phonetic ability.

Phonetics is for many people a fascinating subject in its own right. Most people who study phonetics, however, do so for its theoretical and practical value. Students of linguistics have to understand how language is spoken, and they have to be reasonably proficient at producing a wide variety of sounds. In speech pathology and audiology, phonetics is crucial. Before a person with a speech problem can be helped, we have to be able to pinpoint what is going wrong in that person's pronunciation and what steps can be taken for improvement. These tasks clearly require a good understanding of phonetics.

The usefulness of phonetics in studying another language is obvious. In my experience, people with a background in phonetics have a clear advantage over others in language classes. For example, if you read that 'in Chinese, retroflex approximants are unrounded', you can translate this to 'smile when you say an [ɹ]' and accordingly sound better than your fellow students. Phonetics is also useful for actors, who need to be able to reproduce various accents. They will find Chapter 6, which examines English of various accents, useful, as well as the exercises that give examples of how English was spoken in the past – by Chaucer, Shakespeare, and Sir Walter Scott.

The aim of this book is to give you a thorough grounding in the theory of phonetics and to help you develop the practical ability to use that theoretical knowledge. I hope that you will find the study of phonetics as enjoyable as I do and as useful as my students have found it over the years.

A great many people have helped me in writing this book. I am very grateful to them all: to Jack Chambers, Bill Cowan, Michael Dobrovolsky, Suzanne Belanger, Dennis Helm, Wanis Khouri, Greg Kondrak, Ed Burstynsky, Pierre Léon, Keren Rice, and Yves Roberge who read various chapters; and to my students for their patience and inspiration.

Linguists are sometimes a bit awkward socially. After listening to someone's learned dinner-table disquisition on current and eternal verities, we are apt, quite innocently, to say 'What an interesting vowel you have there!' I would not wish to create social difficulties for anyone, but I do hope that this book conveys some of the charm, fun, and intellectual intrigue that are to be found in thinking about how we humans talk.

Publisher's Acknowledgements

We are indebted to the following for permission to reproduce copyright material:

International Phonetic Association for *Chart of the International Phonetic Alphabet*, (International Phonetic Association website: *http://www.arts.gla.ac.uk/IPA/ipa.html*); Karin Rada on behalf of the estate of Mrs Signe Östlind for extracts from *A Guide to Chaucer's Pronunciation* by Helge Kökeritz, and Yale University Press for extracts from *Shakespeare's Pronunciation* by Helge Kökeritz, © Yale University Press 1953.

Chapter 1

Introduction

Every day we hear many types of sounds: bells ringing, machinery clunking, dogs barking, leaves rustling, people talking. The science of **acoustics** studies sounds in general, and **phonetics** studies the sounds used in human language. Phonetics is part of the wider field of **linguistics**, which studies language as a whole.

Phonetics is concerned with the sounds we make in speech: how we produce them, how these sounds are transferred from the speaker to the hearer as sound waves, and how we hear and perceive them. Several thousand languages are spoken in the world; obviously we cannot look at the sounds of each one of them. We will examine English in detail first because it is the language that you are all familiar with; this will be followed by an introduction to acoustics. Finally we will survey the kinds of sounds found in languages all over the world.

In this chapter you will learn about:

- the basic fields of phonetics;
- the anatomy of the parts of the body used in making sounds;
- how to determine where in your mouth a sound is made.

At the end of each chapter you will find exercises which will enable you to practise producing sounds. The first portion of the exercises is basic and allows you to practise the sounds which have just been presented in that chapter. The advanced exercises include more difficult material, and they are cumulative, reviewing sounds already studied and incorporating the new material.

Phonetics involves a large number of technical terms. As new terms are discussed, they are shown in **bold type**. At the end of each chapter is a list of technical terms, and Appendix B presents a complete glossary of technical terms. These terms are essential to being able to talk about phonetics. Later work will go much more easily if you make a point of learning each term as it occurs.

The study of phonetics

Branches of phonetics

Articulatory phonetics

The branch of phonetics dealing with the production of sounds is called **articulatory phonetics**. In speech, air passes through a complex passage-way consisting of the lungs, the windpipe, the vocal folds, the throat, the mouth, and the nose. In order to describe how sounds are made, we must become familiar with the various parts of our anatomy which are involved in speech production. We will also learn how we change the shape of the vocal organs to make different sounds.

Acoustic phonetics

From physics, we know that sound is transmitted by vibrations in the air. **Acoustic phonetics** studies the vibrations of speech sounds. With instruments in the laboratory, we can observe and measure various aspects of sound. In Chapters 7 and 8, we will learn how these measurements and observations can be used to widen our understanding of human speech.

Auditory phonetics

Auditory phonetics is the study of how sounds are heard and perceived. This area of phonetics generally falls outside the coverage of this book.

Articulatory phonetics

We begin our study of articulatory phonetics with an examination of the **vocal organs**, the parts of the body used in producing speech (Figure 1.1). The lungs start the process of speech production by pushing air upwards. The vocal folds, which are located in the larynx behind the adam's apple, may vibrate, causing the air that flows between them to vibrate as well. The vibrating airstream is then modified according to the shape of the **vocal tract** – the throat, mouth, and nasal cavity. By moving our tongue and lips, we can produce a large number of modifications on the vibrating air stream, and thus, a wide variety of sounds.

A bicycle horn provides a simple model of how speech sounds are produced. In the bicycle horn, air is pushed out when the bulb is squeezed. The air then passes across the reed, located just past the bulb, which sets it in vibration. Finally, the air passes through the flared tube, the 'horn' proper,

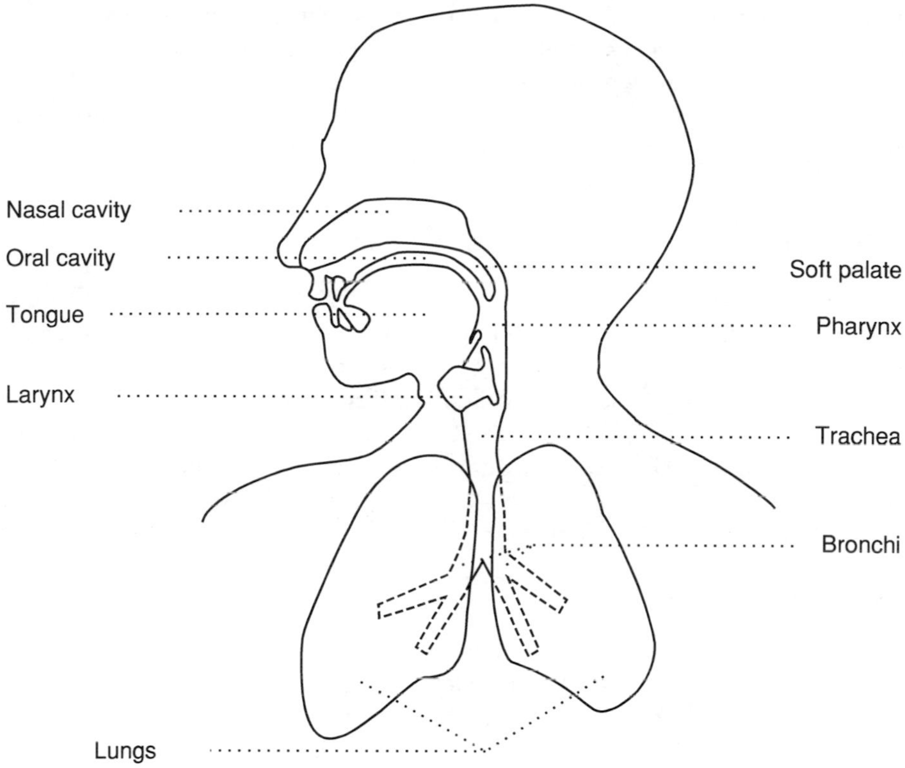

Figure 1.1 The primary vocal organs

which gives a certain quality to the sound. In our body, the lungs are the bulb, pushing the air out. The vocal folds in the larynx are the reed, setting the air in vibration. The vocal tract is the 'horn' giving speech its particular quality. One important difference is that the bicycle horn can produce only one sound. The human vocal tract can be altered in many ways to produce a large variety of sounds.

We will now look at the various parts of the vocal organs. In a number of cases, the Latin or Greek name is normally used in phonetics. These terms are given as they are needed. We need to become familiar with the anatomy and terminology of the vocal mechanism. This is basic information which will be used throughout the book.

Lungs

The **lungs** are cone-shaped structures in the chest composed of spongy, elastic material. The lungs consist of small air sacs, or **alveoli**, where oxygen from the fresh air is exchanged for carbon dioxide in the blood. When the lungs are expanded, air is drawn in; when they are compressed, air is expelled. We have a considerable amount of control over the rate of breathing. When speaking, we breathe in fairly quickly and then expel the air more slowly. In English, all speech is made as the air flows out of the body; that is, English speakers do not ordinarily talk while breathing in.

Trachea

The small tubes of the lungs merge with each other, repeatedly forming larger tubes, until they form two large tubes called **bronchi**, one bronchus coming from the left lung and one from the right lung. The two bronchi merge into a single vertical tube called the **trachea** or windpipe. The top of the trachea is just behind the notch at the top of the breastbone. In speech, the bronchi and trachea function simply as tubes to carry the air in and out of the lungs.

Larynx

The **larynx** is a structure made of several cartilages held together by ligaments and supporting several muscles; it is roughly cylindrical in shape and rests on top of the trachea. The front part of the larynx, known as the **adam's apple**, sticks out in front. The **vocal folds** lie inside the larynx, just behind the point of the adam's apple. They are two horizontal bands of ligament and muscle, lying across the air passage; they can open and close, acting as a valve for air coming from the lungs. The opening between the vocal folds is called the **glottis**; the word **glottal** is used to describe activities of the vocal folds. (The adjective for larynx is **laryngeal**.) The portion below the vocal folds is called **subglottal**; the portion above the larynx is called **supralaryngeal**.

The vocal folds can be adjusted in various ways to give different acoustic effects. When you hold your breath with your mouth open, you close your vocal folds, thus preventing air from leaving or entering the lungs. In phonetics, this act is called a **glottal stop**.

Many sounds in speech are made with the vocal folds separated. As air passes through the opening between the separated vocal folds, a slight friction-like noise is heard. If you make a long /h/— /hhhhhhhhhh/, you will hear this noise. This glottal adjustment is called **voiceless**. Many sounds in English are made with the vocal folds in the voiceless position.

Another adjustment of the vocal folds is also quite common. Try saying a vowel sound such as *ah*. Say it out loud in a relaxed fashion; don't whisper. Your vocal folds are close enough that the air passing between them causes them to vibrate by opening and closing rapidly in succession. While you are making the vowel, place your fingers lightly on your adam's apple. You will feel a vibration known as **voicing**. Try saying the vowel again, but this time with both of your hands over your ears. Now you will hear the voicing as a buzzing sound. When you say the vowel, your vocal folds are vibrating. In English, all vowels and several consonants are made with voicing and are thus called **voiced**. Try saying a long /sssssss/ and then a long /zzzzzzz/. With your hands over your ears, you can hear that the /zzzzzzz/ has the buzz of voicing; the /ssssss/ does not have this buzz and is thus voiceless. Try the same experiment with /fffffff/ and /vvvvvvv/.

Pharynx

The **pharynx** is the technical name for the throat, a vertical tube leading up from the larynx. From Figure 1.2, you can see that the pharynx goes up from the larynx past the mouth to the nasal cavity. If you look in the mirror, lower your tongue, and say *ah*, you can see the back of your throat or **pharyngeal wall**. The pharynx serves primarily as a tube connecting the larynx with the oral and nasal cavities. It can be divided into three parts as

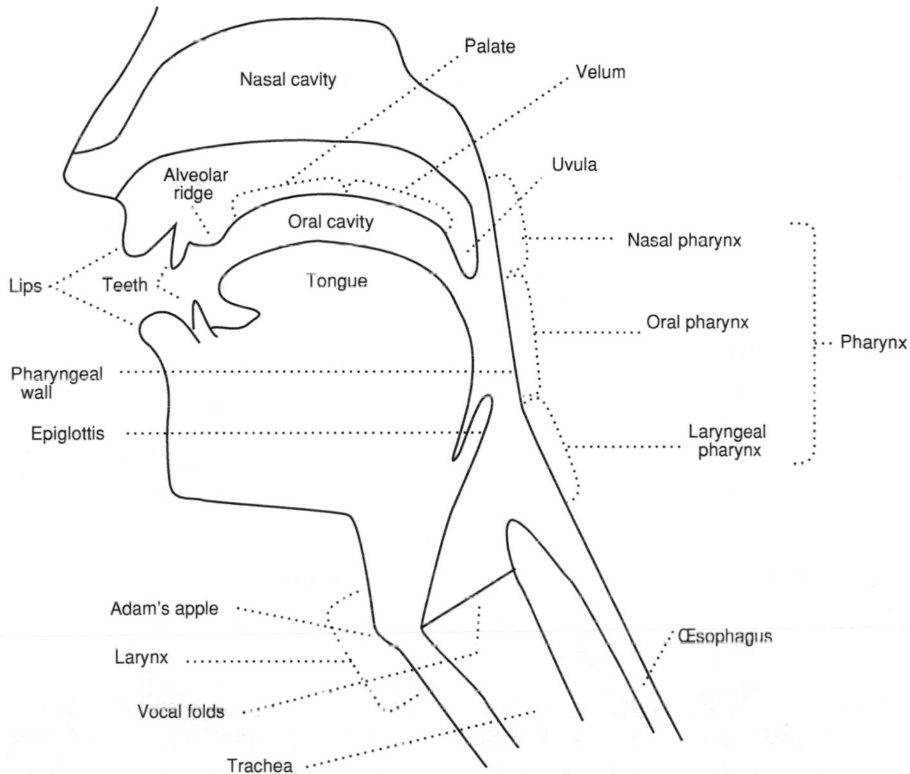

Figure 1.2 The vocal tract

shown in Figure 1.2: the **oral pharynx**, at the back of the mouth, the **nasal pharynx**, leading into the nasal cavity, and the **laryngeal pharynx**, just above the vocal folds. The **œsophagus** is a tube, behind the trachea, which leads to the stomach.

Oral cavity

The **mouth**, or **oral cavity**, is extremely important in the production of speech sounds. By altering the shape of the mouth, we can produce a large number of different sounds. The various points in the oral cavity are referred to as **articulators**. The **upper articulators** are the upper lip, upper teeth, the upper surface of the mouth, and the pharyngeal wall. The **lower articulators** are the lower lip, lower teeth, and tongue. A lower articulator **articulates** with an upper articulator when it is positioned so as to form an obstruction to the air passage. The kind of drawing we use which shows the inside of the head as though it were split down the middle from front to back is called a **sagittal section**.

Lips

The outermost articulators are the **lips**. They commonly articulate with each other to form **bilabial** sounds (Figure 1.3). Another common articulation occurs when the lower lip articulates with the upper teeth to form **labiodental** sounds (Figure 1.4). In English, the initial sounds in *pea, bee,* and *me* are bilabial consonants; the initial sounds in *fee* and *vow* are labiodental consonants.

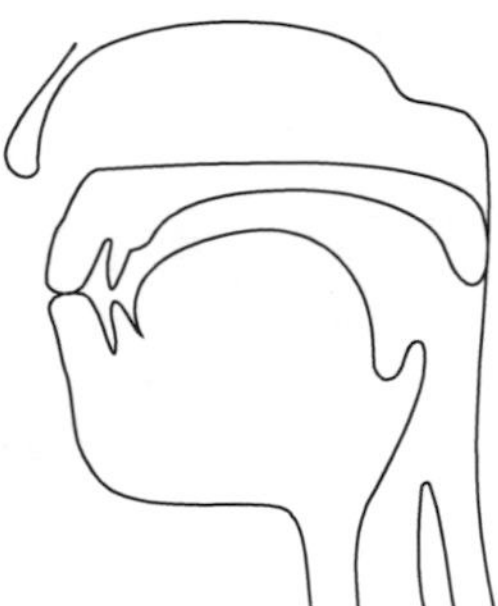

Figure 1.3 Bilabial

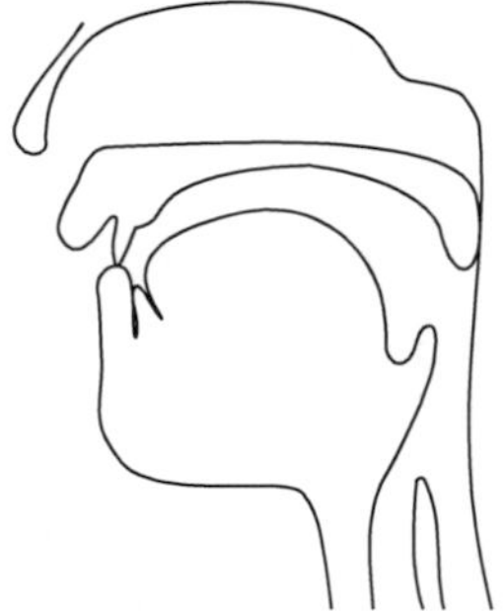

Figure 1.4 Labiodental

Teeth

Sounds which are made with the forward part of the tongue articulating with the upper teeth are called **dental** (Figure 1.5). In English, *thin* and *then* begin with dental consonants.

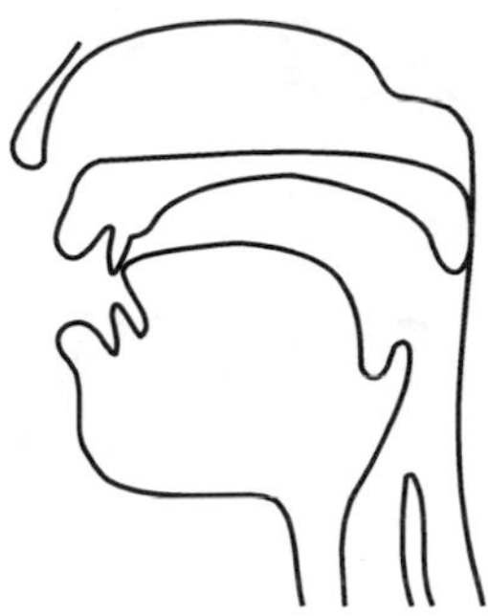

Figure 1.5 Dental

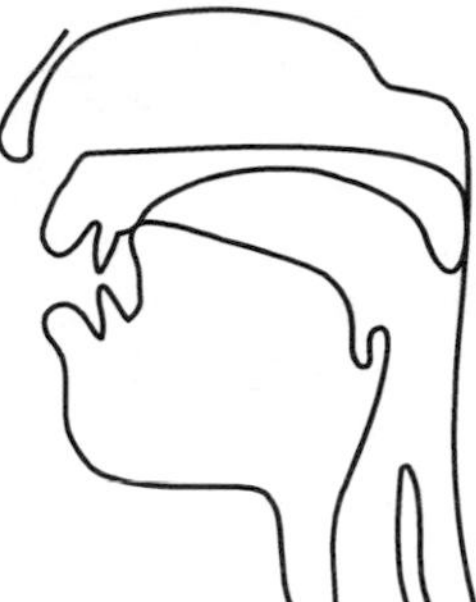

Figure 1.6 Alveolar

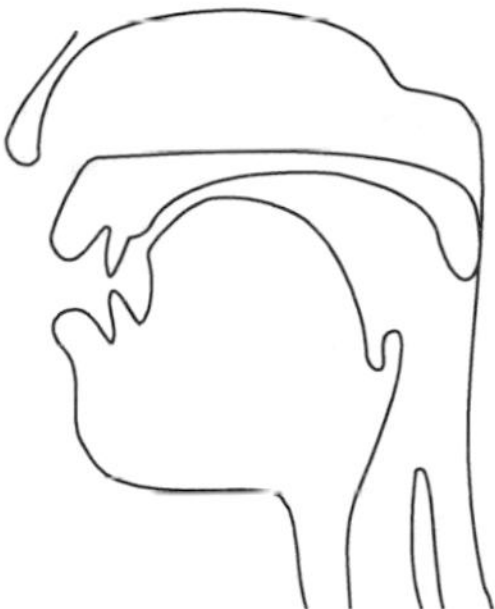

Figure 1.7 Postalveolar

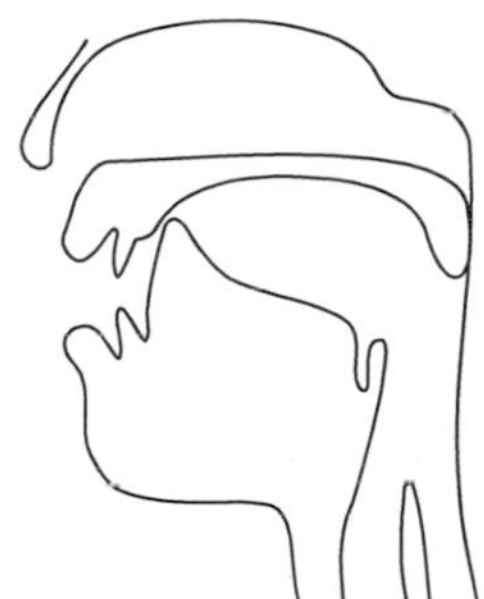

Figure 1.8 Retroflex

Alveolar ridge

Just behind the upper teeth, there is a bumpy area known as the **alveolar ridge**. Put the tip of your tongue against your upper teeth and pull it slowly back. You will likely feel the alveolar ridge between the teeth and the hard palate although a few people do not have a noticeable ridge. Sounds made here are called **alveolar** (Figure 1.6). In English, *doe, toe, no, so, zoo,* and *low* begin with alveolar consonants.

Other sounds in this area are possible. **Postalveolar** sounds (Figure 1.7) are made with the blade of the tongue articulating at the back of the alveolar ridge and the front of the tongue raised towards the palate. (These parts of the tongue are shown in detail in Figure 1.12.) In English, *she, cheese,* and *judge,* begin with postalveolar consonants; also, the middle sound in *pleasure* is postalveolar. **Retroflex** (Figure 1.8) sounds are made with the tip of the tongue curled back to articulate with the area at the back of the alveolar ridge; in English, *red* begins with a retroflex consonant for many speakers.

Palate

The hard palate is a thinly covered bony structure forming the forward part of the roof of the mouth. In phonetics, the hard palate is normally referred to simply as the **palate**. It extends from the alveolar ridge to the soft palate (velum). Sounds made in this area with the front of the tongue are called **palatal** (Figure 1.9). In English, *yes* begins with a palatal sound.

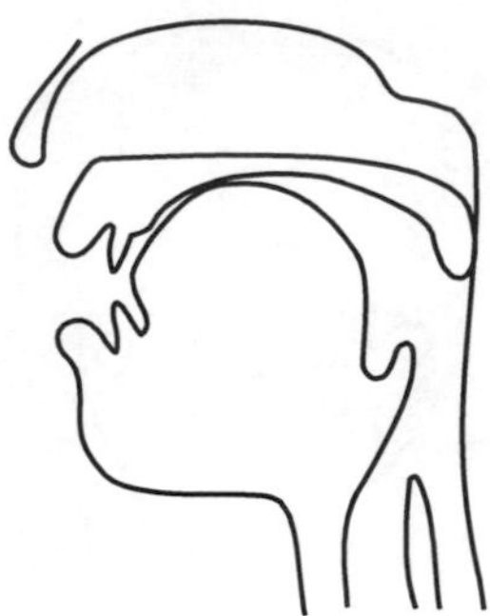

Figure 1.9 Palatal

Velum

The soft palate is the rear portion of the roof of the mouth unsupported by bone. If you move your tongue along the hard palate towards the back of your mouth, the texture suddenly becomes soft where the bone ends; this soft area is the soft palate. In phonetics it is normally referred to as the **velum**. This is short for the longer Latin phrase *velum palati* 'the veil of the palate'. Sounds using the lower surface of the velum as the upper articulator are called **velar** (Figure 1.10). In English, *luck, lug,* and *lung* all end in different velar consonants.

Figure 1.10 Velar

Uvula

At the rear of the mouth, the velum narrows to a long, thin structure known as the **uvula**. If you look in a mirror and open your mouth wide, you can see the uvula hanging down from the velum. Try snoring; you will feel the uvula flapping against the pharyngeal wall. Sounds made with the uvula are called **uvular** (Figure 1.11). English does not use uvular sounds.

Figure 1.11 Uvular

Tongue

The **tongue** is a large, muscular organ which is involved in almost every sound we make. The surface of the tongue is, of course, continuous, but phoneticians find it convenient to divide it into five parts (Figure 1.12).

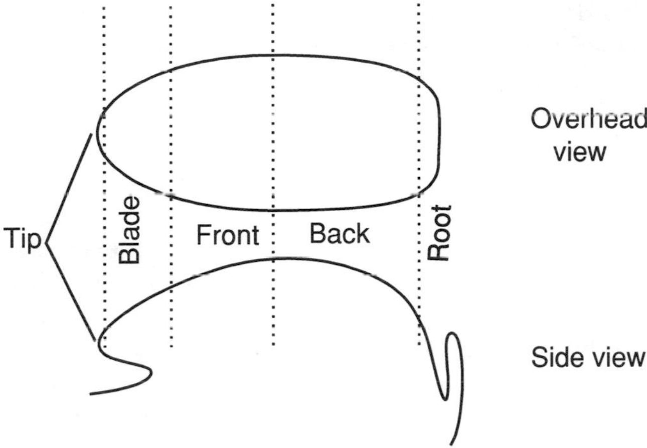

Figure 1.12 Parts of the tongue

The **tip**, or **apex**, of the tongue is its foremost part. Sounds made with the tip of the tongue are called **apical**. **Apico-dentals** are made with the tip articulating with the upper teeth, as in *thin, then*. **Apico-alveolars** are made with the tip of the tongue articulating with the alveolar ridge. In English, apico-alveolars are common, as in *toe, dead, nun*.

Lying just behind the tip of the tongue is a small surface called the **blade**, or **lamina**. Sounds made with the blade are called **laminal**. In English, the initial sounds in *ship* and *shoe* are usually postalveolars, the blade of the tongue being near the back of the alveolar ridge.

The **front** of the tongue has a misleading name. It is not at the front of the tongue, but behind the tip and the blade. Fortunately, we do not need to refer to it that often. The front of the tongue articulates against the palate; such sounds are simply called **palatal**. The initial sound in English of *yes* is palatal, made with the front of the tongue raised towards the palate.

The hindmost part of the horizontal surface of the tongue is called the **back** or **dorsum** (the adjective is **dorsal**). It articulates against the velum to form **dorso-velar** sounds. Be careful not to confuse the *back* of the tongue with the *root*. In English, the final sounds in the words *tick, dog,* and *sang* are all dorso-velar.

The **root** of the tongue is its rear vertical surface facing the pharyngeal wall. The root is not important in English, and we will not need to talk about it until Chapter 10.

Epiglottis

The **epiglottis** is a spoon-shaped cartilage which extends up and back from the larynx. The epiglottis is like the appendix: no one is absolutely sure why we have one. It may have some function in preventing food from going into the larynx, but this is disputed. For phoneticians, its position is a nuisance in that it hangs over the larynx, making the larynx difficult to observe. Recent research has shown that the epiglottis may be of some linguistic importance in a very few languages (see Chapter 10).

Nasal cavity

The pharynx opens upwards into the **nasal cavity**. We have no control over the shape of this cavity; however, the velum can be raised and lowered to open and close the opening from the pharynx to the nasal cavity. When the velum is lowered, air can escape out through the nose. If the velum is raised, air cannot escape through the nose. The upper surface of the velum is called the **velic** surface. Thus we can refer to **velic opening** and **velic closure**. Sounds made with velic opening are called **nasal** or **nasalised**; sounds made with velic closure are called **oral** (Figure 1.13). The words *ram, ran, rang* all end in a nasal consonant. Note that *velic* refers to the upper surface of the velum which moves against the pharyngeal wall, whereas *velar* refers to the lower surface of the velum which articulates with the back of the tongue.

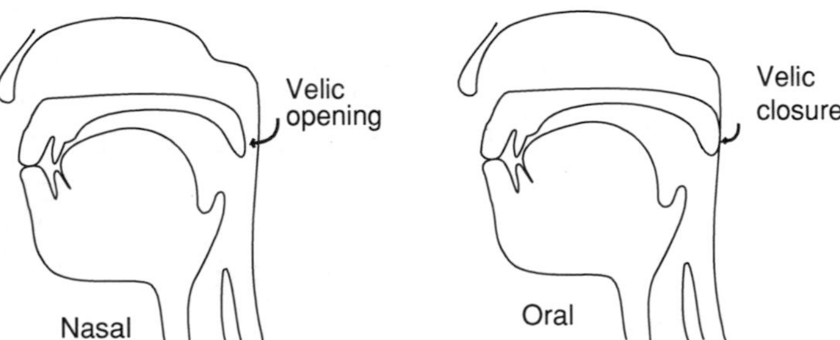

Figure 1.13 A bilabial nasal is shown on the left with a velic opening allowing air to pass out through the nose. On the right, the same bilabial sound is shown, but with a velic closure preventing air from passing out through the nose

If you are familiar with French, you know that a word like *un* 'a, an, one' has a nasalised vowel, but a word like *eux* 'them' has an oral vowel. Practise saying these two words to feel the velum going up and down. It should go down for *un* and up for *eux*.

English places of articulation

Table 1.1 English places of articulation for consonants. The portions of the terms in parentheses are optional. The upper articulators are shown across the top of the chart. The lower articulators are shown down the left. Each cell contains the name of the sound produced by the combination of lower and upper articulators

				upper articulators			
		lip	**teeth**	**alveolar ridge**	**back of alveolar ridge**	**palate**	**velum**
lower articulators	**lip**	bilabial	labiodental				
	tip		(apico-)dental	(apico-)alveolar	retroflex		
	blade				postalveolar		
	front					palatal	
	back						(dorso-)velar

Technical terms

The following technical terms have been introduced in this chapter. Although the list is fairly long, many of the terms are familiar ones. Use this list and the others found at the end of each chapter as a checklist to make sure that you are familiar with each before going on.

acoustic phonetics
adam's apple
alveolar
alveolar ridge
apex
apical
apico-dental
articulate
articulator
back
bilabial
blade
dental
dorsal
dorso-velar
dorsum
epiglottis
front
glottal
glottal stop
glottis
labiodental
lamina
laminal
laryngeal
larynx
lips
lungs
mouth
nasal
nasal cavity
œsophagus
oral
oral cavity
palatal
palate
pharyngeal
pharynx
postalveolar
retroflex
root
sagittal section
subglottal
supralaryngeal
teeth
tip
tongue
trachea
velar
velic
velum
vocal folds
vocal tract
voiced
voiceless
voicing

Exercises

Basic

No book can really teach you practical phonetics. Only close listening and practice can do that. However, by following the suggestions presented in the exercise portions of each chapter, you will be able to make significant improvement in your ability to make a large variety of speech sounds.

1 The following exercises will help you become familiar with the parts of your body used in producing sounds. We will be taking a short tour of the vocal organs. The important point here is to transfer your knowledge of anatomy from a chart to your own body. A few anatomical features not mentioned in the main part of the chapter are presented here. You may be interested in learning these, but they are not essential for understanding this part of the book.

a. Your adam's apple is the point jutting out below your chin. With your thumb and forefinger, feel the V-shaped plates which come together to form the point of the adam's apple; the plates are made of cartilage forming the front of the larynx. Immediately behind the adam's apple lie the vocal folds.

b. Now, let's examine the mouth. Your upper and lower lips are easy to see. With the tip of your tongue, feel the rear surface of your upper teeth. Now pull your tongue slowly back until you feel the bumpy ridge lying behind the teeth; this is the **alveolar ridge**. Look at Figure 1.2, and relate the position of the alveolar ridge on the drawing to what you feel with your tongue. For some people, the alveolar ridge is not very prominent.

From the alveolar ridge, move your tongue back across the hard **palate**, a hard slightly curved surface. People vary considerably in how far they can reach with the tip of the tongue, but most can reach the back edge of the hard palate with their tongue tip and can just feel the forward part of the soft palate or **velum**. Relate what you feel to the corresponding part of Figure 1.2.

c. Now with a mirror, look straight into your mouth. A small flashlight may help. Compare what you see with Figure 1.14. Stick out your tongue, and identify the **tip**, **blade**, **front**, and **back** of your tongue.

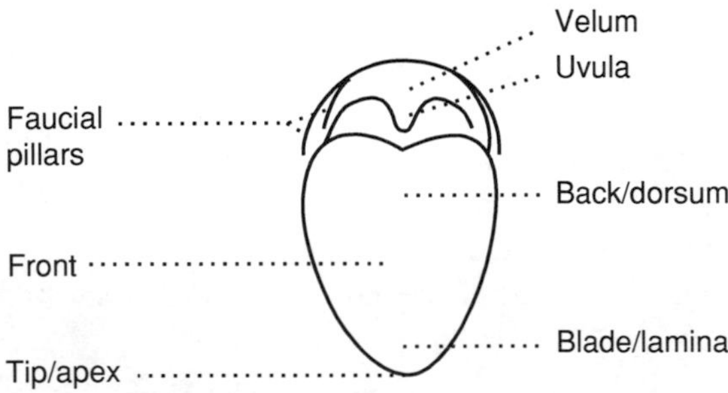

Figure 1.14 The oral cavity

Looking at the roof of your mouth in the mirror, identify the **palate**, the **velum**, and the **uvula**. Between your uvula and your tongue, you can see a portion of the rear **pharyngeal** wall. There are two vertical folds at the sides, called the **faucial pillars**. At the base of these, you may find your tonsils, if they have not been extracted.

2 Figure 1.15 is for you to fill in the names of the important parts of the vocal organs. You may want to make several photocopies of this page for practice work.

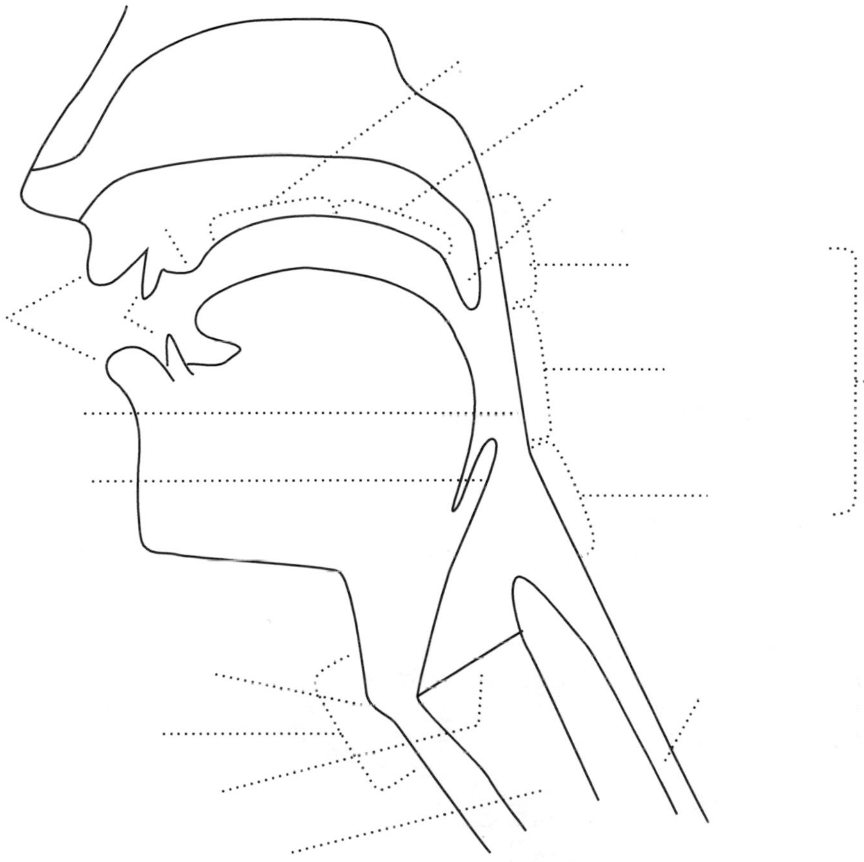

Figure 1.15

Advanced

3 The following sentences are intended to help you develop a feel for various types of sounds. As you say each one over a few times, try to feel which articulators are forming most of the sounds. For each place of articulation, look at the appropriate drawing and visualise your mouth forming that shape as you read each sentence.

bilabial: Peter Brown picked a bushel of Burpee's peppers.
labiodental: Verna found five very fine vines.
dental: Ethel thinks that this other thin thing is their thread.
alveolar: Ed edited it, didn't he – or did Ted do it?
dorso-velar: King Carl quickly kissed the Greek queen.

4 **a.** Circle all the words below that have a nasal as their final sound:

pin tab tame sings sign lamb

b. Circle all the words below that begin with an alveolar sound:

fin sin dumb great thought
just lest church ten nest

c. Circle all the words below that have a velar sound:

care lick sing that
boss jug ridge mice

5 **a.** Say the word *helps,* and feel how each sound is made. In the chart below, some terms are given, complete the rest of the chart for each of the consonants [l p s] at the end of the word.

Table 1.2

	l	p	s
upper articulator		*upper lip*	
lower articulator	*apex*		
voiced or **voiceless**			*voiceless*
oral or **nasal**			

b. Make a similar chart, and fill in the blanks for the [n d] of *sand.*

6 Complete the diagrams below showing the position of the vocal organs during the production of the first consonant of the word indicated. If the sound is voiced, draw a wavy line at the position of the larynx; if voiceless, use a straight line. The initial [m] in *mow* is given as an illustration. Use a pen or pencil which contrasts with the printed lines.

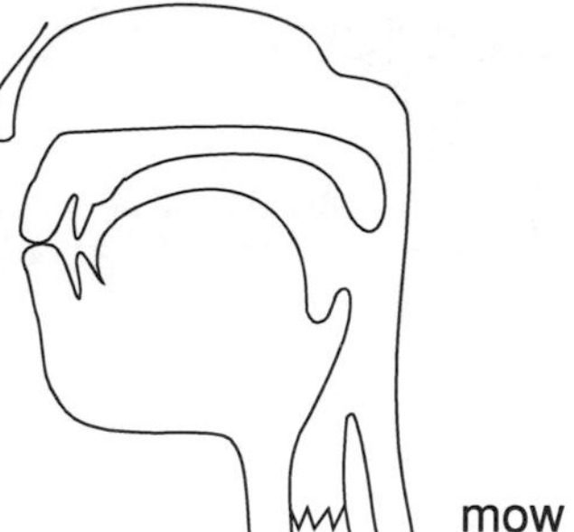

Figure 1.16

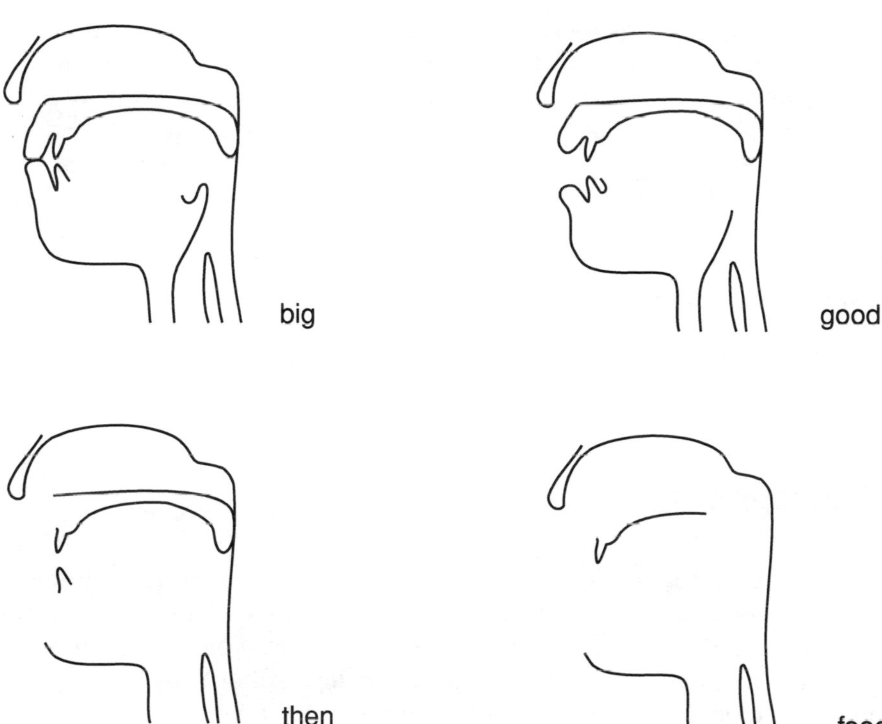

Figure 1.17

Chapter 2

The basic sounds of English

Phoneticians divide sounds into two basic categories: **segments** and **suprasegmentals**. Segments comprise **vowels** and **consonants**. Vowels include things like the sounds in the words *oh, eye, ooh, ah;* they are made with no major obstruction in the vocal tract so that air passes through the mouth fairly easily. Consonants, such as /p n g s l/, involve some type of obstruction in the vocal tract. When you make a /p/, for example, your lips are closed, thereby completely preventing air from leaving through the mouth. Suprasegmentals involve sound components other than consonants and vowels. These include a variety of things such as stress, pitch, intonation, and length. You will have a clearer idea about these when we can discuss them in detail later in this chapter.

In this chapter you will learn about:

- the basic sounds of English;
- symbols for the basic sounds.

Transcription

The ordinary **orthography**, or spelling, of English is often quite different from the phonetic transcription. Frequently, words that sound quite different are written similarly; compare the pronunciation and spelling of the words *tough, though, trough, through, thorough.* All of these words have the letters *ough,* yet, each of them is pronounced differently. On the other hand, words that sound just alike are sometimes written differently; compare *sew, sow, so; to, two, too; led, lead; you, ewe, U, yew.* Clearly, for phonetic purposes, we want a way of writing things down that avoids this sort of ambiguity.

Transcription is the use of phonetic **symbols** to write down the way an **utterance** (a stretch of speech) is pronounced. One obvious goal of phonetics is to be able to **transcribe** accurately any utterance in any language. Achieving this goal is in fact rather more complex than you might think at first. To get started, we will investigate English. Each sound that we discuss in this chapter will be given a symbol. It is important to spend some time now becoming proficient at transcribing English. In many ways, transcription is like typing: the more you do it, the more automatic it becomes. Appendix C shows how to write phonetic symbols.

The symbols used in this book follow the usage recommended by the **International Phonetic Association**. This system, popularly known as the **International Phonetic Alphabet**, is the most widely used set of symbols. Both the Association and the Alphabet are known as the **IPA**.

Quite apart from the choice of symbols is the way in which they are used to form a transcription system for a particular language. Actually, there are a number of systems which have been used for transcribing English. I should make it clear at the outset that, although I believe the transcription system presented here is a good one and suitable to our purposes, it is by no means universally used. In other books on phonetics or linguistics, you may well encounter other systems. Appendix D compares various transcription systems for English.

Although we usually think of speech consisting of a string of sounds, one after the other, phoneticians have discovered that **segmentation**, or the division of a stretch of speech into a string of discrete consonants and vowels, is not a straightforward task. You can easily observe that in most utterances, the tongue is constantly in motion. In a word like *as*, the tongue rises from low in the mouth for the vowel up to the alveolar ridge, but it is difficult to know exactly at what precise point the vowel ends and the consonant begins. We will continue to represent speech as a series of segments, but it is important to keep in mind that speech is produced by a complexly sequenced interaction of several moving organs.

Accents of English

English is spoken as a native language by over 377 million people around the world. Like other languages, English shows a considerable amount of geographic and social variation. Such variation forms different **dialects**. When we speak of **accents**, we mean only the features of the dialect regarding pronunciation. In Chapters 1–5, we will focus on two important accents: one British and one North American. Later, in Chapter 6, we will examine other accents of English.

Around 1400, the accent of the royal court emerged as the prestige accent of English. This accent was essentially the speech of upper-class London. A modern-day descendant of this accent continues as the prestige accent of England, and to a lesser degree of Scotland, Wales, and Ireland as well. It is the accent not only of the royal family and the nobility, but of the upper and upper-middle classes generally. It is the accent commonly used by announcers for the BBC. This accent is known to linguists by the name **Received Pronunciation (RP)**, where the term *received* is used in the nineteenth-century sense of 'correct, proper'. Although RP is spoken by individuals scattered throughout Britain, it has little regional variation; it is spoken as a native accent only by 3–5% of the population.

RP is the British accent usually taught to foreigners. Even by people who do not speak it, RP is widely regarded as 'correct'. Linguists, of course, do not describe an accent as 'correct' or not; rather, they say that it is spoken by certain social classes, here by the upper classes and, in addition, by many of the well-educated.

The United States is a very large area with considerable accent variation, although not nearly so much as in Britain. The east of the US, having been settled longer, shows greater variation than the central and western areas. Very roughly, we can speak of an Eastern accent, spoken in New England; a southern accent, spoken in the south-east; and **General American (GA)** spoken in the central and western areas. The latter is the American accent presented here. Unlike Britain, there is no single prestige accent for the entire country; rather, each geographic region has a certain amount of social variation, although generally less than in Britain. GA is perhaps most familiar as the accent generally used by radio and television announcers for the national American networks. Like RP, GA is the accent usually used in teaching an American accent of English to foreigners. GA is less uniform than RP; some of the variations within GA will be pointed out as we proceed.

In Chapters 2–5, we will be presenting the sound systems of both RP and GA. Sections which apply to only one accent will be labelled accordingly. Note that accents can differ in two ways. They can have different systems; for example, we will soon see that RP has a vowel /ɒ/ not found in GA. On the other hand, two accents can have the same system, but a specific word may have different sounds in each. For example, both RP and GA have the two vowels /ɑ/ and /æ/; however, the word *fast* has the vowel /ɑ/ in RP, but /æ/ in GA. Note that with *fast,* speakers of RP and GA can both produce the other pronunciation with no difficulty. Both accents have words with /æ/ and /ɑ/; it just happens that *fast* has different vowels in the two accents. With /ɒ/, however, GA speakers generally have trouble in reproducing the RP vowel /ɒ/ correctly. Similarly, RP speakers usually have trouble imitating the GA pronunciation of the /t/ in *city* accurately. In thinking about English accents, readers should bear in mind that most of the differences among English accents lie in the vowels, rather than in the consonants.

Keep in mind that in Chapters 2–5, our main goal is to understand phonetics, not to become specialists in English accents. We will overlook many details although some will be discussed in Chapter 6.

Consonants

Consonants are sounds that involve a major obstruction or constriction of the vocal tract; **vowels** are made with a very open vocal tract. If you say the vowel *ee* as in *bee*, you can feel that the air flows out of the mouth fairly freely. Now say a long /z/: /zzzzzzz/. Now start with the vowel *ee*, and move to a /z/, as in the word *ease*. You will feel your tongue move closer to the alveolar ridge for the /z/, making a partial closure causing the hissing noise which characterises /z/. On the other hand, if you go from a /z/ to an *ee* sound, as in the word *zeal*, you can feel your tongue pulling away a bit, allowing the air to pass out more freely. From this simple experiment, you can understand the basic difference between a consonant and a vowel.

Consonants are usually classified along three dimensions: voicing, place of articulation, and manner of articulation. In Chapter 1, we learned that voiceless sounds, such as /f s/, are made with the vocal folds apart, whereas voiced sounds, such as /v z/, are made with the vocal folds close together and vibrating. For each consonant that we discuss, we will note whether it is voiced or voiceless.

The place of articulation describes where the obstruction of the consonant is made, and the manner of articulation describes the nature of the obstruction. Each of the places and manners of articulation has a technical name; you will find phonetics much easier if you spend the time now to become familiar with these terms. Some of these have already been given in Chapter 1; others are described in detail below.

Place of articulation

The **place of articulation** is the description of where the obstruction occurs in the vocal tract. To describe the place of articulation of a consonant, we need to state which of the lower articulators articulates with which of the upper articulators. For example, for a /d/, the tip of the tongue is against the alveolar ridge, but for a /ɡ/, the back of the tongue is against the velum. We have already discussed places of articulation generally in Chapter 1. Refer to the drawings there to see how the vocal tract is shaped for each place of articulation. Now the symbols for English sounds are introduced; Appendix C, at the back of the book, shows you how to write any unfamiliar symbols.

Bilabial

The bilabial sounds of English include /p b m/, as in the initial sounds of the words *pea, bee, me*. The lower lip articulates against the upper lip.

The sounds /p b m/ are made by completely closing the lips. The sound /p/ is voiceless; /b m/ are voiced. The sound /w/, as in *we*, simultaneously involves both labial and velar articulations; it is discussed below under labial-velar.

/p/ *pea, creepy, loop*
/b/ *bee, lobby, rub*
/m/ *moo, summer, loam*

Labiodental

We have two **labiodental** sounds in English: /f v/, as in the initial sounds of the words *feel, veal*. When you make these, you will notice that your lower lip articulates against your upper teeth; /f/ is voiceless, and /v/ is voiced. The term **labial** is used to include both bilabial and labiodental sounds.

/f/ *fun, daffy, laugh*
/v/ *veal, movie, glove*

Dental

Two **dental** sounds occur in English; both are normally written with the letters *th*. Say the words *thin* and *then* while you feel your adam's apple. You will feel the vocal folds vibrating for *then*, but not for *thin*. The initial sound of *thin* is voiceless /θ/, but the corresponding one of *then* is voiced /ð/.

The sounds /θ/ and /ð/ are **apical**, that is, the tip of the tongue is near or just barely touching the rear surface of the teeth. Air passes out with a soft hissing noise.

/θ/ (called *theta*) *thin, ether, health*
/ð/ (called *eth*) *then, either, loathe*

Alveolar

The **alveolars** include more consonants in English than any other place of articulation: /t d s z n l/. If you say the sentence *Ed edited it*, you will feel the tip of your tongue repeatedly hitting the alveolar ridge. Most English speakers make alveolars apically, but some speakers make them with a laminal articulation.

/t/ *top, return, missed*
/d/ *done, sudden, loved*
/s/ *see, messy, police*
/z/ *zap, lousy, please*

/n/ *gnaw, any, done*
/l/ *loaf, relief, dull*

Postalveolar

Postalveolar refers to the area at the rear of the alveolar ridge, bordering on the palate. The tongue is arched with the blade near the postalveolar area. English has four sounds in this area; /ʃ/ is the initial sound in the word *shoe;* it is usually spelled *sh.* The voiced variety of this sound is found in the middle of the word *measure;* it is symbolised as /ʒ/. Traditional English orthography has no standard way of writing this sound. Try making these two sounds. Different people make them in slightly different ways, but generally there is an obstruction in the postalveolar region. With /s z/, you will feel the air hitting the back of your upper teeth; with /ʃ ʒ/, the air is directed more at the lower teeth. Two other sounds are postalveolar: the initial sound in the word *chop,* transcribed /tʃ/, and the initial sound in *gem,* transcribed /dʒ/. If you say *etching* slowly, you can probably feel the two separate sounds /t/ and /ʃ/ – and also the /d/ and /ʒ/ of *edgy.* These are called affricates and are described in more detail below.

/ʃ/	(called *esh*)	*shelf, assure, mesh*
/ʒ/	(called *ezh*)	*treasure, vision, rouge*
/tʃ/		*chin, etching, roach*
/dʒ/		*jam, edgy, ridge*

Instead of IPA symbols, some authors use [š, ž, č, ǰ] for [ʃ, ʒ, tʃ, dʒ], respectively.

Retroflex

The initial sound in *red* is called **retroflex**. This name is used because many people produce it by curling the tip of the tongue up and back towards the rear edge of the alveolar ridge. In making this sound the tip of the tongue does not actually touch the back of the alveolar ridge, but approaches it. Many people, however, make the sound /ɹ/ in a quite different manner (Delattre and Freeman, 1968). They make a **bunched /ɹ/** with the tip of the tongue down, pulling the body of the tongue up and back; the articulation is between the rear portion of the blade and the alveolar ridge. We will use retroflex as the name for the place of articulation for both kinds of English /ɹ/. Whichever kind of /ɹ/ you normally make, try to make the other kind. The upside-down /ɹ/ is the IPA symbol for this English sound. Later on, we will find a use for the right-side-up symbol [r], which represents a trill.

/ɹ/ *run, airy*

Palatal

Palatals are made with the front of the tongue articulating against the palate. In practising palatal sounds, you will find it helpful to anchor the tip of your tongue against the lower teeth. Doing this is not necessary in making palatals, but it helps prevent mistakes.

The only palatal in English is the sound /j/, the initial sound in *yes*. It is often written *y*, but it is also found in words such as *eunuch, use, few, and ewe*. To avoid any confusion between the sound /j/ and the letter *j*, I would recommend calling the phonetic symbol /j/ by the name *yod*.

/j/	(called *yod*)	*yell, onion, fuse*

Velar

Velar sounds are **dorso-velar**, with the back of the tongue articulating against the velum. In English the velars are /k ɡ ŋ/. These are the final consonants in the words *sick, egg,* and *sing.*

/k/		*kiss, locker, sock*
/ɡ/		*gun, rugger, sag*
/ŋ/	(called *eng*)	*singer, bang*

Most people do not have a well-developed **kinæsthetic** feel for velars. **Kinæsthesia** is the ability to perceive the muscle movements of one's own body. It is important to be able to relate a sound to the position of the organs of the vocal tract which produce that sound. The exercises at the end of this chapter provide material to help you develop this ability.

Glottal

The **glottal** place of articulation is somewhat different from the others we have discussed so far. Up to now, all the points of articulation have been in the oral cavity. The glottal stop /ʔ/, however, is made in the larynx by holding the vocal folds tightly together so that no air escapes. If you hold your breath with your mouth open, you will make a glottal stop. Try this a few times to get a kinæsthetic feeling for a glottal stop. Many English speakers use a glottal stop in saying *uh-oh*: [ʔʌʔow].

Labial-velar

The sound /w/ has a double place of articulation **labial-velar**, being both labial and velar. You can easily observe that the lips are rounded when making a /w/; this lip-rounding makes it labial. At the same time, with a little experimenting, you can feel that the back of the tongue is raised towards the velum; thus, it is velar as well.

/w/ *wet, anyway*

GA, but not RP, has a voiceless labial-velar sound /ʍ/.

/ʍ/ *whet, anywhere*

Manner of articulation

The **manner of articulation** is the degree and kind of constriction in the vocal tract. For example, in making a /t/, the tongue is raised to the alveolar ridge and momentarily seals off the vocal tract so that no air passes out. By contrast, during an /s/, we leave a gap between the articulators so that air continues to pass out. Notice that you can make a long, continuous /ssssss/, but not a long /tttttt/.

Stops

A **stop** involves a complete closure such that no air passes out of the mouth. In English /p t k b d g/ are stops. In making each of these, a complete closure is made, at the lips, the alveolar ridge, or the velum, such that no air can escape through the mouth. The nasal stops /m n ŋ/ are a special kind of stop considered below.

Fricatives

Fricatives are sounds made with a small opening, allowing the air to escape with some friction. The escaping air is turbulent and produces a noisy friction-like sound, called **frication**. The fricatives in English are /f v θ ð s z ʃ ʒ ʍ/. Here, the lower articulator is close to the upper articulator, but not so close that air cannot escape, creating frication. The essential components of a fricative are obstructed air-flow with frication.

Approximants

Approximants are consonants with a greater opening in the vocal tract than fricatives. Frication is absent with approximants. In English, this category comprises /l ɹ w j/. These are the initial sounds in *loot, rule, wood,* and *use.* All approximants in English are voiced. Both fricatives and approximants are **continuants**.

The approximant /ɹ/ has already been described as a retroflex consonant. The approximant /l/ is an alveolar lateral. **Laterals** are sounds that are made with only the mid part of the articulators touching. Try making a long /l/: /llllllllllllll/. You will be able to feel the tip of your tongue touching the alveolar ridge. Both sides of the tongue, however, are pulled down slightly from the roof of the mouth so that air escapes around the sides of the tongue. A sound which is not lateral can be called **central**, although this term is usually omitted.

The **glides** /w j/ are considered approximants as well. Although glides function as consonants, phonetically they are moving vowels. They are discussed more fully with the vowels later in this chapter.

Affricates

Affricates are sequences of stop plus fricative. The English sounds /tʃ dʒ/ are postalveolar affricates. These are the sounds in *church* and *judge*, both at the beginning and the end of these words. In the initial part of /tʃ dʒ/, the tip of the tongue is at the rear of the alveolar ridge, somewhat back of its position in words like *did*. In the second part of the affricate, the tongue pulls away slightly from the roof of the mouth to form a fricative. The affricate /tʃ/ is regularly spelled *ch* or *tch* as in words like *church, child,* and *hitch*; /dʒ/ is usually spelled *j, g,* or *dg* as in *joke, gem,* and *trudge*. Make sure that you do not write /j/ when you mean /dʒ/, or /c/ or /ch/ when you mean /tʃ/. Note that although an affricate is a phonetic sequence, it functions as a single unit in English.

Nasals

The sounds /m n ŋ/ are called **nasals** or **nasal stops**. For these three sounds, there is a velic opening, allowing air to pass out through the nose. Usually the term **nasal** is sufficient, but if we need to be explicit, we can call /m n ŋ/ **nasal stops** and /p t k b d g/ **oral stops**. For a nasal sound, the velum is lowered, allowing air to pass out through the nasal passage. Note that nasals are stops in that no air passes out of the mouth; there is a complete closure in the oral cavity. For nasal stops, air escapes through the nose, but not through the mouth; for oral stops, on the other hand, no air escapes through the nose or through the mouth.

Other terms

The term **obstruent** includes oral stops, fricatives, and affricates. Non-obstruents are called **sonorants**; they include nasal stops, approximants, glides, and vowels. Obstruents involve an obstruction in the vocal tract sufficient to cause frication; with sonorants, the vocal tract is more open with a freer air-flow. The sounds /s/ and /z/ are often referred to as **sibilants**. Sibilants may include /ʃ/ and /ʒ/ as well. **Liquids** comprise laterals and r-like sounds. In English, these are /l ɹ/. This grouping is useful because of the acoustic similarity of these sounds.

The glottal stop [ʔ] is optional in English. Although the sound /h/ functions as a consonant, its production is more easily discussed with the vowels later in this chapter.

Summary of English consonants

Table 2.1 English consonants

	bilabial	labiodental	dental	alveolar	postalveolar
stop	p b			t d	
fricative		f v	θ ð	s z	ʃ ʒ
affricate					tʃ dʒ
nasal	m			n	
approximant				l	

	retroflex	palatal	velar	labial-velar
stop			k g	
fricative				ʍ*
affricate				
nasal			ŋ	
approximant	ɹ	j		w

Note: * only in GA

Line drawings

A useful way of visualising the different, but often simultaneous, activities going on in the vocal tract during the production of consonants is with **line drawings**. Figure 2.1 (overleaf) shows the activities for a simple stop [b]. During the stop, we note three stages, the **onset**, the **hold**, and the **release**; these are respectively the coming together of the lips, the period when they remain closed, and their opening. The drawing shows time going from left to right. The two lines are separate during the vowel, and together during the stop; this drawing thus mimics the activities of the lips during the pronunciation of [ɑbɑ].

To illustrate [ɑdɑ], we need a separate line for the alveolar activities. We will call this line **coronal**; coronal is a cover term for places of articulation involving the tip or blade of the tongue: that is, dental, alveolar, postalveolar, retroflex. The activities shown on this line in Figure 2.2 (overleaf) are parallel

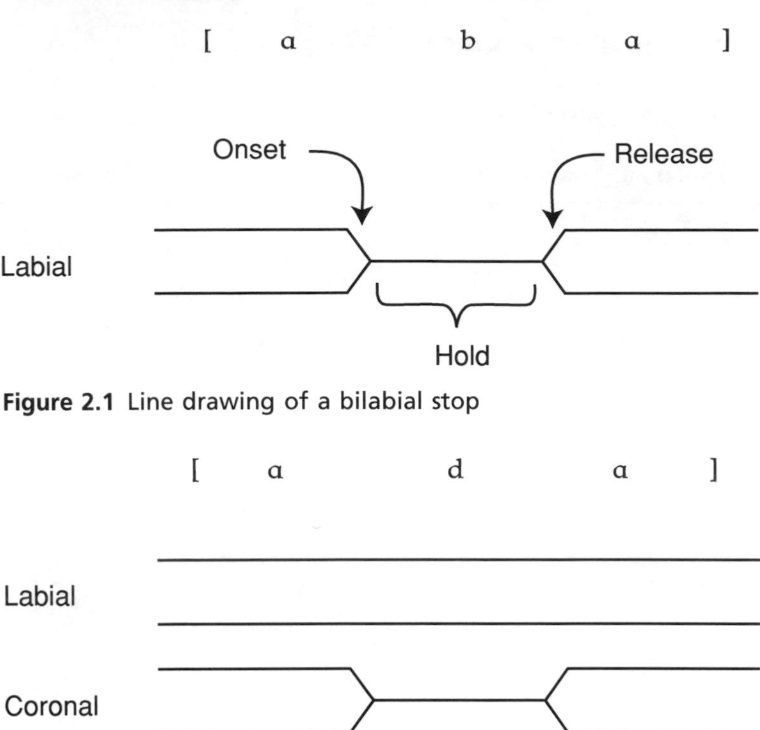

Figure 2.1 Line drawing of a bilabial stop

Figure 2.2 Line drawing of a coronal stop

to the previous example: the separate lines show that the vocal tract is open, the single line shows that the articulators are closed for the stop. During [ɑdɑ], the lips do not close at all, so that the two labial lines remain apart throughout.

To account for all the sounds of English, we need three lines showing place of articulation: **labial**, **coronal**, **dorsal**; every consonant (except a glottal stop) will show some kind of narrowing on one of these three lines.

labial:	bilabial, labiodental
coronal:	dental, alveolar, postalveolar, retroflex
dorsal:	palatal, velar

The degree of stricture is shown by the separation of the two lines; fully open when there is no consonantal activity, slightly closed for an approximant /ɹ l w j/, almost closed for a fricative, and a single line for a stop. Lateral should be marked *lat* above the stricture; dental, postalveolar, and retroflex can be distinguished by writing *den*, *p-a*, *ret* above the stricture, with alveolar left unmarked. We also need a line to show nasal activity. Note particularly that a single nasal line shows that velic closure occurs and that the sound is not nasal; a nasal sound involves velic opening and is shown by a divided line. We have also added a line called glottal to show the state of the glottis; a jagged line for voiced, and a straight line for voiceless. Figure 2.3 shows /ɑsɑ/ with a fricative stricture for the /s/ on the coronal line and also that the /s/ is voiceless on the glottal line with a straight line.

Figure 2.4 shows the words *belts*, and *grump*. Study these carefully. Note how the sequence /lts/ appears on the coronal line in *belts*, whereas the /mp/ transition in *grump* appears on the velic line.

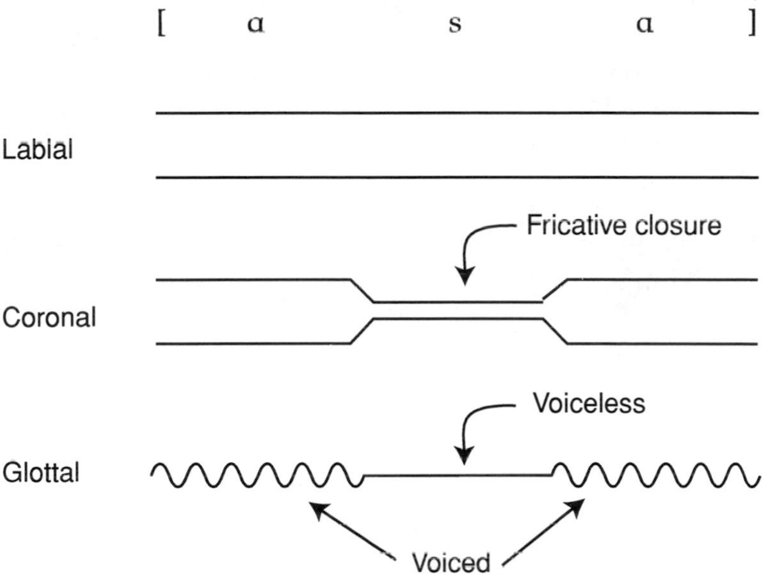

Figure 2.3 Line drawing of a voiceless coronal fricative

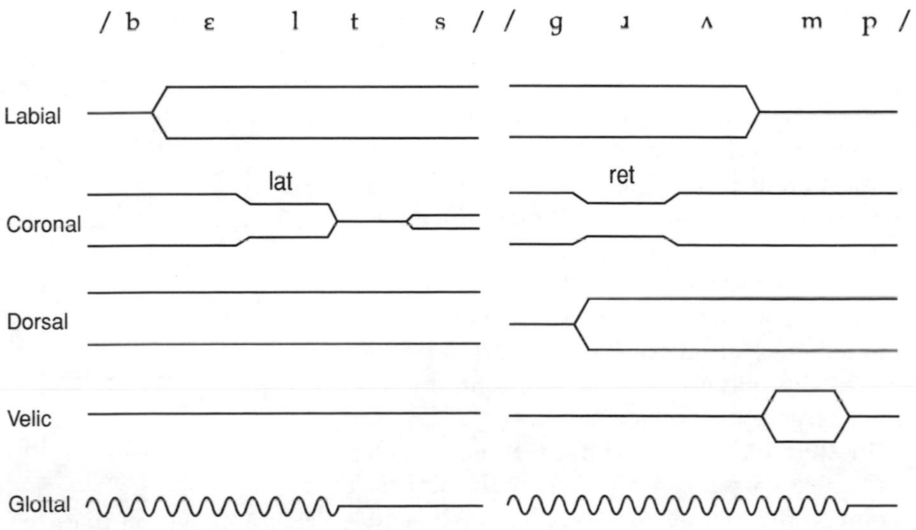

Figure 2.4 Line drawings of *belts* and *grump*

Vowels

How vowels are made

In making vowels, the vocal tract is more open than it is for consonants. Two elements are primarily involved in making different vowels: the shape and position of the tongue in the mouth and the shape of the lips. To get started, we will look at some of the vowels of English.

Try making the vowel in the word *he*; extend the vowel and say *heeeeee*. You can feel that the front of the tongue is fairly close to the forward part of the palate. (The *front* of the tongue, recall, is behind the tip and the blade.) This vowel is described as a high front vowel, transcribed /i/. Now, try making the vowel in *ah*, the one you make for the doctor to see your throat. This is described as a low back vowel, transcribed /ɑ/. Go back and forth between these two vowels (/i/ and /ɑ/), feeling the difference between high front and low back vowels.

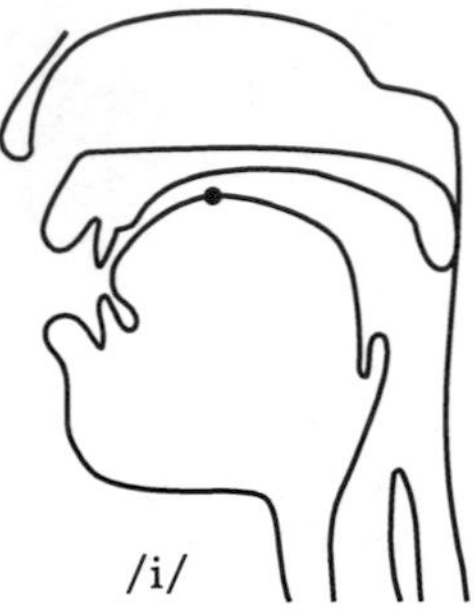

Figure 2.5 The shape of the tongue for the English vowels /i/ and /ɑ/. The dot shows the highest point of the tongue for each vowel

We see then that the shape of the tongue is a primary factor in determining the quality of a vowel. Because of the difficulty of describing the shape of the entire tongue, phoneticians have often described vowels by the location of the highest point of the tongue as shown by the dots in Figure 2.5.

Figure 2.6 shows a chart used to plot vowel positions, in this case, the same vowels [i] and [ɑ], as in Figure 2.5. In such a chart, we plot the position of the highest point of the tongue; we always put front vowels on the left and back vowels on the right. Every vowel that we can make can be plotted either inside the vowel chart or on its edge. The internal lines are present simply for reference purposes.

In studying vowels, consult a chart, such as Figure 2.6, which shows where the highest point of the tongue is, make the vowel, and try to feel how your own tongue is shaped.

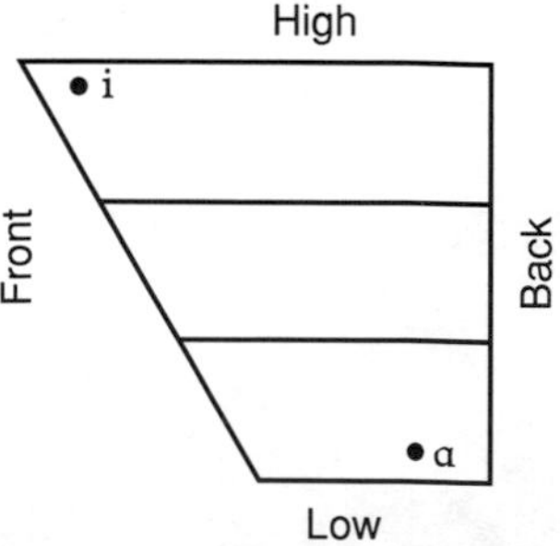

Figure 2.6 Vowel chart for [i] and [ɑ]

In this way, you will develop a kinæsthetic feeling for making vowels and relating the sound to phonetic diagrams.

We will examine in detail the three basic articulatory qualities of vowels: **height**, **backness**, and **rounding**.

Height

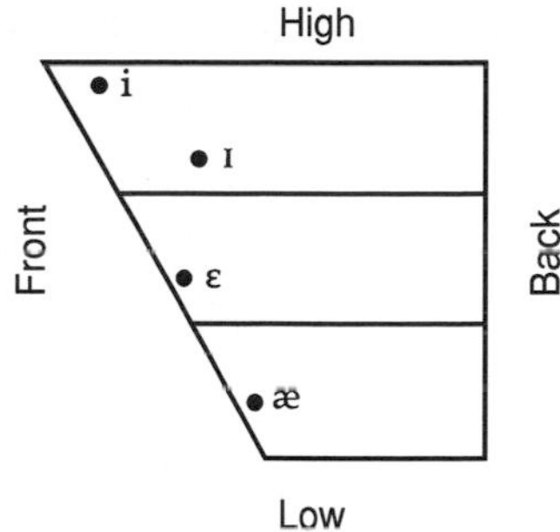

Figure 2.7 Front vowels [i ɪ ɛ æ]

Try saying the words *peat*, *pit*, *pet*, *pat*. You will probably notice that your jaw moves down as you go through the list; with each vowel, your mouth is a little bit more open, and the highest point of the tongue is a little bit lower (Figure 2.7). This variation is what we mean by vowel height. X-ray pictures taken of English speakers uttering these vowels show that the tongue is quite high for /i/, lower for /ɪ/, and progressively lower until we get to /æ/.

We say that /i/ is a **high** vowel; that /æ/ is a **low** vowel; that /ɪ/ is higher than /ɛ/; and that /ɛ/ is higher than /æ/. The vowels in the middle range between high and low, such as /ɛ/, are called **mid** vowels.

Backness

Try saying the vowels in *pan* and *palm*. The symbols for these are /æ/ and /ɑ/. Be sure to write the back vowel as /ɑ/, and not as /a/. Try to say them alone without any consonants: /æ æ æ æ ɑ ɑ ɑ ɑ ɑ/. Although both of these vowels are low vowels, you will feel your tongue change shape as you go from one vowel to the other (Figure 2.8). The high point of the tongue for /æ/ is in the front of the mouth, and the high point for /ɑ/ is in the back of the mouth (Figure 2.9). Just as we can make high and low vowels, so we also can make **front** and **back** vowels.

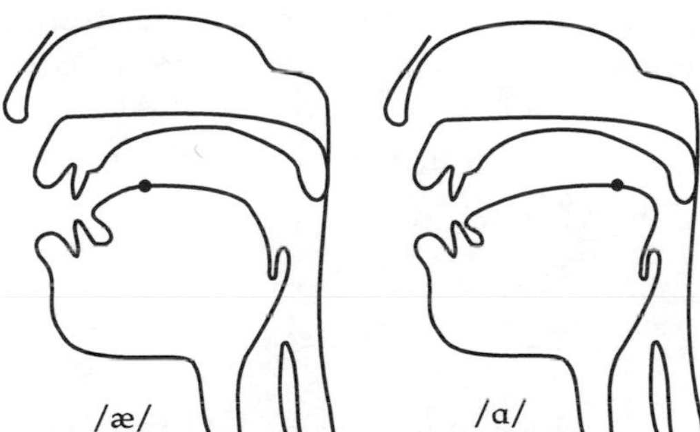

Figure 2.8 Tongue position for low vowels [æ ɑ]

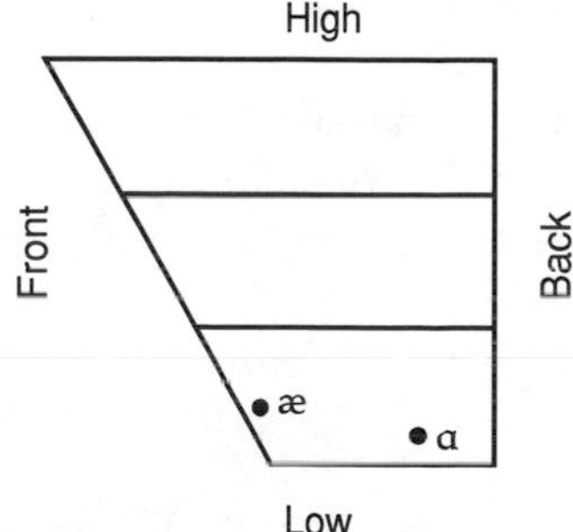

Figure 2.9 Vowel chart showing [æ] and [ɑ]

Rounding

Height and backness are not the only dimensions for vowels. Try saying /i/ and /u/ – the vowels for *key* and *coo*. You will note that your lips are rounded for /u/, but not for /i/ (Figure 2.10). For each vowel, we specify whether it is **rounded** or **unrounded**.

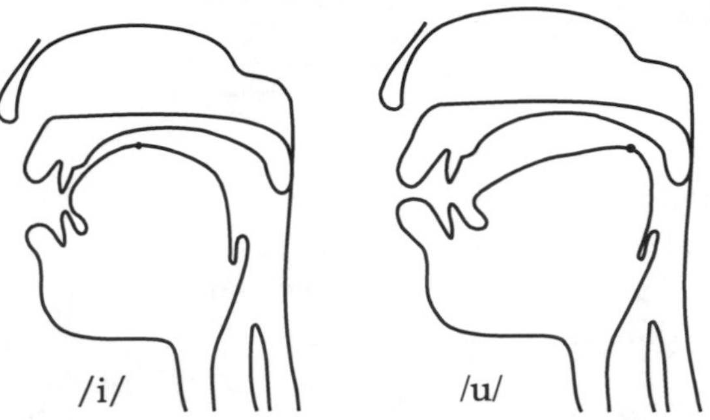

Figure 2.10 Tongue and lip position for [i] and [u]

Glides

Glides are moving vowels; they move rapidly from one vowel position to another; vowels, on the other hand, have a relatively steady articulation. Although phonetically similar to vowels, glides function either as consonants before a vowel or as the final portion of a syllable nucleus after a vowel.

The glide /j/ moves to or from a high front unrounded position. In a word like *yell* /jɛl/, the tongue starts at a high front unrounded position – approximately the position for /i/ – and then moves to the lower /ɛ/ position. The glide /w/ is similar, except that it moves either to or from a high, back rounded position; a word like *well,* starts at a high, back rounded position – like the position for /u/ – and moves to an /ɛ/ position. In *yell* and *wet,* the glides precede the vowel; glides which follow vowels are illustrated in the section below on diphthongs.

/j/ *yell, you, yawn*
/w/ *well, wit, wand*

In Figure 2.11, arrows show the directions of movements. A thicker line shows slower speed of tongue movement and thus greater prominence.

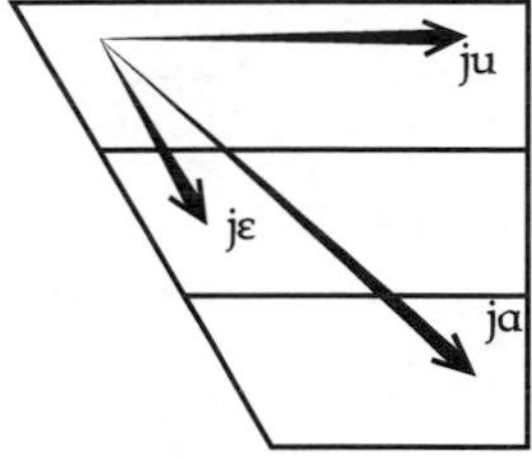

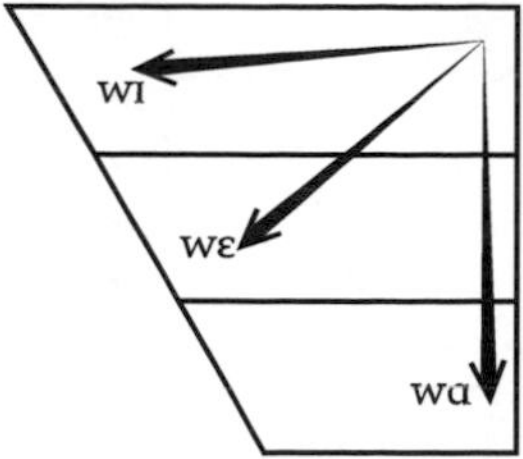

Figure 2.11 The glides /j/ and /w/ preceding vowels

Diphthongs

A **diphthong** can be defined for the time being as a sequence of a simple vowel and a glide. (Note especially the spelling and pronunciation of *diphthong* – RP /ˈdɪfˌθɒŋ/ GA /ˈdɪfˌθɔŋ/; there is no /p/ sound.) Try saying the word *cow* slowly. Disregarding the /k/ at the beginning, if you listen carefully, you will hear that there are two parts to the rest of this word. It starts off with a low vowel; then it moves upwards to a vowel sound something like a /u/. The first portion is between /ɑ/ and /æ/; we will transcribe it as /a/ (a different symbol from /ɑ/). The second portion moves and is therefore a glide. It moves to a high front unrounded position like /u/, and we thus symbolise it as /w/. Thus, the word *how* is transcribed /haw/. Figure 2.12 shows the diphthong /aw/. The thicker part of the arrow shows the slower vowel part of the diphthong, and the thinner part with the arrowhead shows the end of the glide.

We will now consider the vowel systems of RP and GA separately, and then compare the two systems.

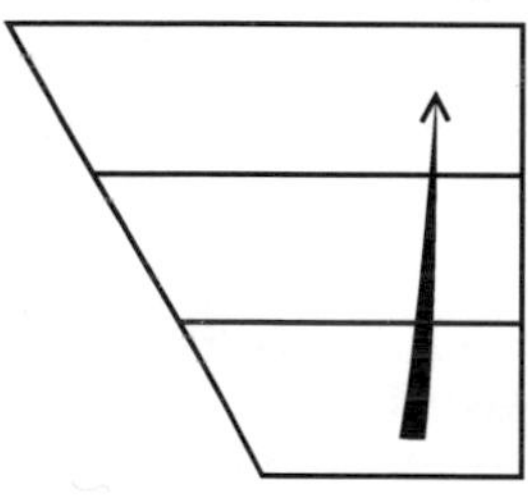

Figure 2.12 The diphthong /aw/

The RP vowel system

RP has the following vowels:

i		u	ɪə	ʊə
ɪ	ɜ	ʊ	ɛə	
ej	ə	əw		
ɛ	θ	ɔ		ɔj
æ	ʌ	ɑ,ɒ	aj	aw

beat	i			*boot*	u				
bit	ɪ			*put*	ʊ				
bait	ej	*hurt*	ɜ	*boat*	əw	*peer*	iə	*jury*	ʊə
bet	ɛ	*sofa*	ə	*bought*	ɔ	*pear*	ɛə		
bat	æ	*but*	ʌ	*pot*	ɒ			*boy*	ɔj
				bath	ɑ	*bite*	aj	*bout*	aw

RP simple vowels

/i/ *beat, see, these, piece*
/ɪ/ *bit, myth, ring, happy*
/ɛ/ *bet, bread, said*
/æ/ *bat, land, sang*
/ɜ/ *purr, stern, heard, fir*
/ʌ/ *putt, love, lung*
/u/ *boot, cube, view*
/ʊ/ *put, wood, should*
/ɔ/ *bought, jaw, chalk*
/ɒ/ *pot, rob, box*
/ɑ/ *palm, father, far*

Our last simple vowel is a mid central unrounded vowel, slightly lower than /ɜ/ (Figure 2.13); it has the special name **schwa** and is written /ə/. In RP schwa occurs only in unstressed syllables. Listen to the second vowel in *sofa*. This is a schwa; you may find it hard to hear because it is so short. If you slow down your pronunciation of *sofa* in an attempt to focus on the schwa more clearly, you are likely to distort its pronunciation.

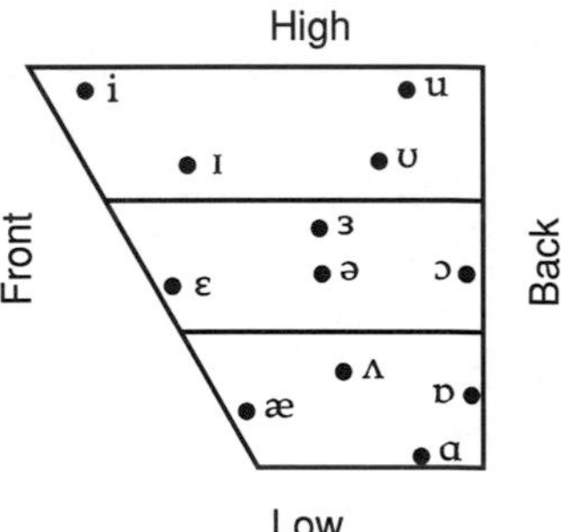

Figure 2.13 RP simple vowels

/ə/ *ago, open, enough, receive, vodka, character, paper, teacher, metre, anchor, colour, martyr*

RP diphthongs

The diphthongs /aw aj ɔj/ (Figure 2.14) all start with low vowels and have long glides, either to a high front or high back position. The vowel /a/ represents a low front vowel; this is the position where the /aj/ and /aw/ diphthongs begin (Figure 2.14). The starting point for /aw/ is a little farther back than for /aj/. Note that the vowel in the diphthong is written /a/, not /ɑ/.

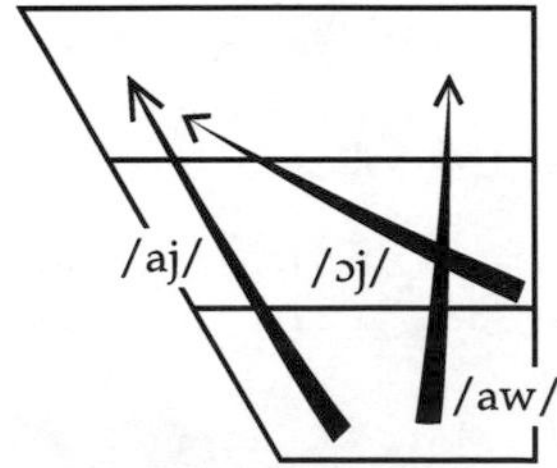

Figure 2.14 RP low diphthongs

/aj/	*my, sigh, write, I*
/aw/	*cow, mouth, renown*
/ɔj/	*joy, noise, employ*

The diphthongs /ej əw/ (Figure 2.15) both start from a mid vowel with glides shorter than with the low diphthongs. Notice how the lip rounding increases as you go from /ə/ to the rounded glide /w/. The reverse happens with /ɔj/; the lips are rounded for the /ɔ/ and become less so for the /j/.

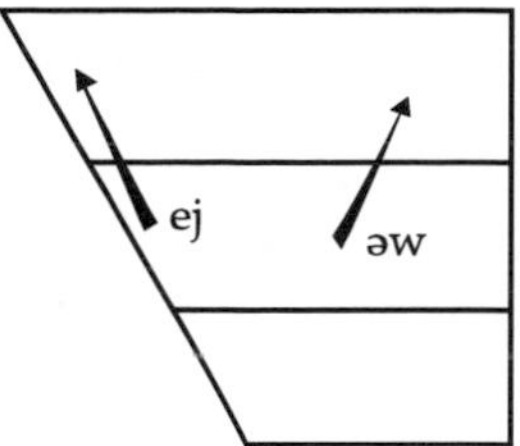

Figure 2.15
RP mid diphthongs

/ej/	*pay, made, break*
/əw/	*go, note, road*

Three diphthongs are the historic result of the loss of /ɹ/. With these, rather than the /ɹ/ simply disappearing, it became a glide towards a /ə/ position (Figure 2.16). Since the glide moves towards a central position, we can call these the **centring diphthongs**.

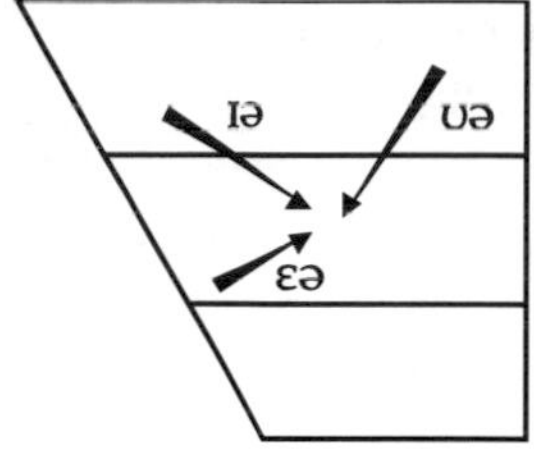

Figure 2.16
RP centring diphthongs

/ɪə/	*beer, here, hearing, idea, real*
/ɛə/	*bare, hair, their, Mary*
/ʊə/	*cure, moor, dour, mural, jury*

In these diphthongs, the schwa should properly be written with a subscript diacritic [ə̯] to show that it is a glide, not a vowel (see Chapter 9). For the present, however, the diacritic is omitted for simplicity's sake. Note that in many words, some RP speakers have /ɔ/ instead of /ʊə/: /kjɔ/ *cure*, /mɔ/ *moor*.

The GA vowel system

GA has the following vowels:

i		u		
ɪ		ʊ		
ej	ə	ow		
ɛ	ɵ	ɔ		ɔj
æ	ʌ	ɑ	aj	aw

beat	i			*boot*	u				
bit	ɪ			*put*	ʊ				
bait	ej	*sofa*	ə	*boat*	ow				
bet	ɛ	*but*	ʌ	*bought*	ɔ			*boy*	ɔj
bat	æ			*palm*	ɑ	*bite*	aj	*bout*	aw

GA simple vowels

/i/	*beat, see, these, piece, city*	/ʊ/	*put, wood, should*
/ɪ/	*bit, myth, ring*	/ɔ/	*bought, jaw, chalk*
/ɛ/	*bet, bread, said*	/ʌ/	*putt, love, lung*
/æ/	*bat, land, sang*	/ɑ/	*palm, father, far, pot, rob, box*
/u/	*boot, cube, view*		

Our last simple vowel is a mid central unrounded vowel (Figure 2.17); it has the special name **schwa** and is written /ə/. In GA, schwa occurs only in unstressed syllables and before /ɹ/. Listen to the second vowel in *sofa*. This is a schwa; you may find it hard to hear because it is so short. If you slow down your pronunciation of *sofa* in an attempt to focus on the schwa more clearly, you are likely to distort its pronunciation.

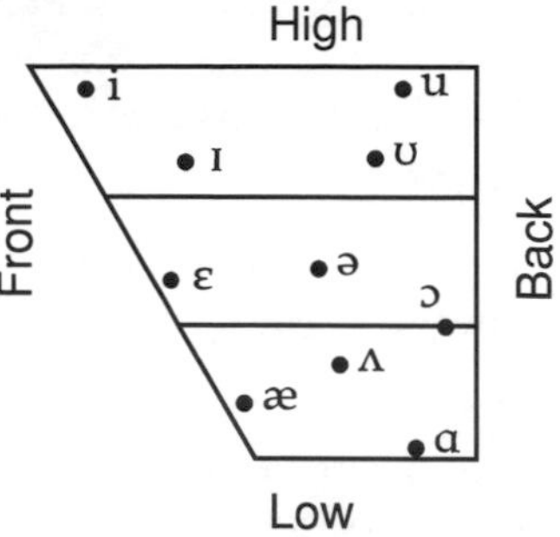

Figure 2.17 GA simple vowels

/ə/ *ago, open, enough, receive, vodka, character, purr, fir, heard, paper, teacher*

The diphthongs /aw aj ɔj/ (Figure 2.18) all start with low vowels and have long glides, either to a high front or high back position. The vowel /a/ represents a low front vowel; this is the position where the /aj/ and /aw/ diphthongs begin as shown in Figure 2.18. Note that the vowel in the diphthong is written /a/, not /ɑ/.

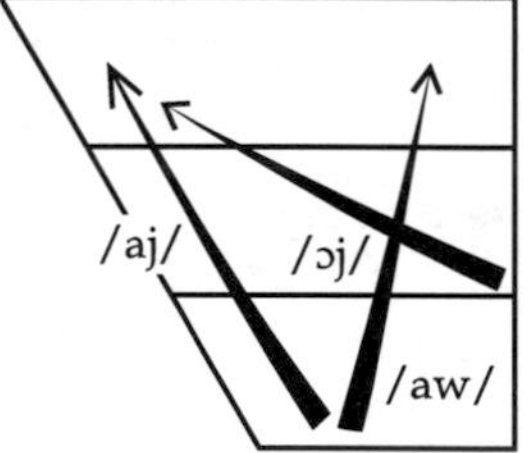

Figure 2.18 GA low diphthongs

/aj/	*my, sigh, write, I*
/aw/	*cow, mouth, ouch, renown*
/ɔj/	*joy, noise, employ, foist*

The diphthongs /ej ow/ (Figure 2.19) both start from a mid vowel with glides shorter than with the low diphthongs. Notice how the lip rounding increases as you go from the lower /o/ to the higher glide /w/. The reverse happens with /ɔj/; the lips are rounded for the /ɔ/ and become unrounded for the /j/.

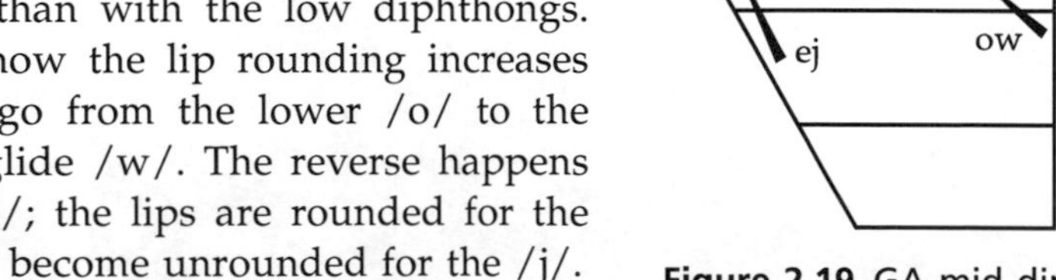

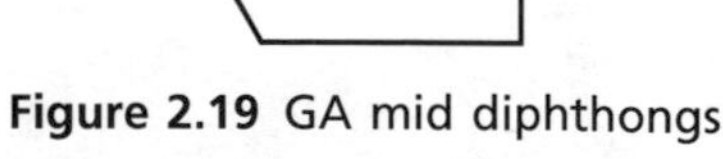

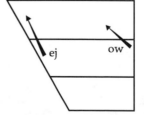

Figure 2.19 GA mid diphthongs

/ej/	*pay, made, break*
/ow/	*go, note, road*

RP and GA: /h/

Phonetically, /h/ is ordinarily realised as a voiceless vowel – just like the following vowel, except that the vocal folds are in a voiceless position. Although /h/ is a voiceless vowel in terms of its production, it functions as a consonant, occurring only at the beginning of a syllable. Thus the /h/ of *he* sounds like a voiceless /i/; the /h/ of *head* sounds like a voiceless /ɛ/; the /h/ of *who* sounds like a voiceless /u/, etc. Most often, /h/ occurs at the beginning of a word; it never occurs at the end of a syllable. It is rather rare in the middle of a word.

/h/   *he, hay, head, who, ahead, anyhow, overhaul*

Line drawings for vowels and glides

On line drawings (Figure 2.20), vowels are shown with open strictures. Glides are shown with the partial stricture of approximants. The palatal glide /j/ is shown on the dorsal line; the labial-velar glide /w/ (and /ʍ/ in GA) is shown on both the labial and the dorsal lines. Vowels are marked only as voiced. The phoneme /h/ is shown as a voiceless vowel.

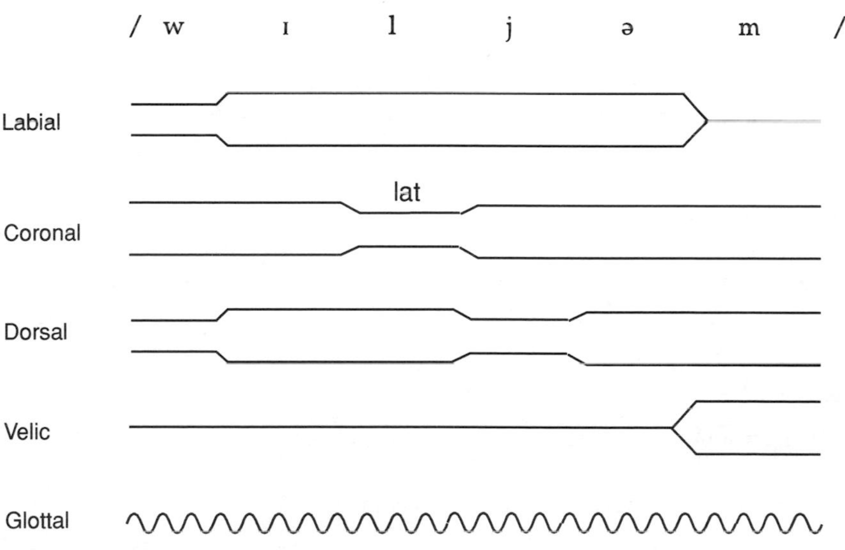

Figure 2.20 Line drawing of *William*

Stress

Say the words *sofa, appear, lady,* and *recover* one after the other. Now, hum them, saying something like *mm* for each syllable. You will notice that some syllables seem more prominent than others; we will say that the prominent syllables have a **primary stress** and that the other syllables are **unstressed**. The first syllables of *sofa* and *lady* have primary stress; whereas the primary stress falls on the second syllable of *appear* and *recover*. Primary stress is shown by a superscript vertical mark placed before the stressed syllable. The other syllables are unstressed and written with no special mark.

RP /ˈsəwfə əˈpɪə ˈlejdi ɹɪˈkʌvə/ *sofa, appear, lady, recover*

GA /ˈsowfə əˈpɪɹ ˈlejdi ɹɪˈkʌvəɹ/

Stress in English is manifested by a combination of three phonetic elements: greater loudness, higher pitch, and longer duration. Stress is an extremely important element in English. Consider the word *survey,* as a noun and as a verb. (We will discuss the vowel alternations in Chapter 4; for now just note the stress differences.)

	RP	GA
To build the road, we'll need a new ***survey.***	/ˈsɜvej/	/ˈsəɹvej/
This is the site we need to ***survey.***	/səˈvej/	/səɹˈvej/

Notice that in the noun the first syllable has primary stress, whereas in the verb the second syllable has primary stress. This pattern, although subtle, is fairly common in English. Consider the words: *produce, subject, convert, convict.* Most native speakers of English will pronounce these differently as nouns and as verbs, placing the stress on different syllables.

Now try saying the words *helicopter, appetising, operator.* These words have primary stress on the first syllable. However, the third syllable in all of them seems to have some degree of stress as well. Say the words again to test this. For these syllables, we need a third level of stress, intermediate between primary stress and unstressed, which we can call **secondary stress**, marking it with a subscript vertical line before the appropriate syllable.

RP	GA	
/ˈhɛlɪˌkɒptə/	/ˈhɛlɪˌkɑptəɹ/	*helicopter*
/ˈæpɪˌtajzɪŋ/	/ˈæpɪˌtajzɪŋ/	*appetising*
/ˈɒpəˌɹejtə/	/ˈɑpəˌɹejtəɹ/	*operator*

Secondary stress, by the way, is not limited to the third syllable. It also falls on other syllables, as the following examples show.

RP	GA	
/ˌəwˈpejk/	/ˌowˈpejk/	*opaque*
/ˈblækˌbɜd/	/ˈblækˌbəɹd/	*blackbird*
/əˌsəwsɪˈejʃən/	/əˌsowsiˈejʃən/	*association*
/əˈnjuməˌɹejt/	/əˈnjuməˌɹejt/	*enumerate*

Marking the levels of stress accurately requires some practice. The exercises at the end of this chapter will get you started. We will look at stress in greater detail in Chapter 5. For now, assume that every phrase has one and only one primary stress and possibly one or more secondary stresses. In word lists, if a word has only one syllable, we usually do not mark the primary stress since it is predictable.

Comparison of RP and GA

Inventory

With the consonants, the most obvious difference between RP and GA is the loss of /ɹ/ in RP at the ends of syllables: RP /kɑ/ GA /kɑɹ/ 'car'. This loss has affected the vowel system. The RP vowel /ɜ/ usually corresponds to GA /əɹ/, and the schwa-diphthongs /ɪə ɛə ʊə/ usually correspond to GA /ɪɹ ɛɹ ʊɹ/: *near, hair, cure.*

GA has retained the older voiceless /ʍ/ in words such as *which, where, whine*; in RP, this sound has merged with /w/.

In addition, RP has the low back rounded vowel [ɒ] which is missing in GA. Note also that the RP [ɔ] is made somewhat higher than the GA [ɔ].

Distribution

For the most part, the vowel corresponding to RP [ɒ] became unrounded in GA, thus merging with [ɑ]. However, in some GA words [ɒ] merged with [ɔ] and thus remained rounded. As a result, we have two sets of correspondences for RP [ɒ].

RP	GA	
/ɒ/	/ɑ/	*cot, knob, box, Tom, swan, watch, knowledge*
/ɒ/	/ɔ/	*moth, moss, long, coffee, Boston, sausage, origin, horrible, sorrow, Laurence.*

Note that there is considerable variation in GA between the two vowels, especially before a following velar: *fog, dog, log, mock, long.*

Generally, words with RP /æɹ ɛɹ ɛəɹ/ have all merged into GA /ɛɹ/.

RP	GA	
/ˈmɛɹi/	/ˈmɛɹi/	*merry, sherry, very, Kerry, herald*
/ˈmæɹi/	/ˈmɛɹi/	*marry, Harry, Larry, carry, Harold*
/ˈmɛəɹi/	/ˈmɛɹi/	*Mary, hairy, vary, Carey, airy,*

RP and GA have the same stress system although occasionally the assignment of stress may be different. Different stresses often change the vowel; this will be discussed in Chapter 4.

RP	GA	
/ˈbæˌtɒn/	/bəˈtɑn/	*baton*
/ləˈbɒɹətɹi/	/ˈlæbɹəˌtɔri/	*laboratory*
/ˌlækˈtejt/	/ˈlækˌtejt/	*lactate*
/ˌpɹɪnˈsɛs/	/ˈpɹɪnsɪs/	*princess*

The following is a short list giving examples of words which have different pronunciations in RP and GA but which do not fit into regular classes. This list could easily be considerably extended. Frequently, both RP and GA have minority pronunciations corresponding to the other accent; that is some RP speakers say /ˈvajtəmɪn/, and some GA speakers say /ˈæntɪ-/.

RP	GA	
/ˈæntəni/	/ˈænθəni/	*Anthony*
/ˈænti-/	/ˈantaj-/	*anti-*
/ɛt/	/ejt/	*ate*
/bin/	/bɪn/	*been* (stressed form)
/ˈbʊfej/	/bəˈfej/	*buffet*
/klɑk/	/kləɹk/	*clerk*
/ˈkɒmˌpɒst/	/ˈkɑmˌpowst/	*compost*
/ˈkʊˌku/	/ˈkuˌku/	*cuckoo*
/ˌfɔˈtin/	/ˌfɔɹtˈtin/	*fourteen*
/ˈfɪgə/	/ˈfɪgjəɹ/	*figure*
/hɜb/	/əɹb/	*herb*
/ˌajˈzajə/	/ˌajˈzejə/	*Isaiah*
/ˈlɛʒə/	/ˈliʒəɹ/	*leisure*
/ˈlivə/	/ˈlɛvəɹ/	*lever*
/ˌlɛfˈtɛnənt/	/ˌluˈtɛnənt/	*lieutenant* (army)
/ˈmɪsˌajl/	/ˈmɪsəl/	*missile*
/ˈpɹajmə/	/ˈpɹɪməɹ/	*primer* (introductory book)
/ˈpɹɪvəsi/	/ˈpɹajvəsi/	*privacy*
/ˈʃɛdˌjul/	/ˈskɛˌdʒul/	*schedule*
/ʃɒn/	/ʃown/	*shone*
/ˈsɒldə/	/ˈsɑdəɹ/	*solder*
/səˈdʒɛst/	/səgˌdʒɛst/	*suggest*
/ˈstɪɹəp/	/ˈstəɹəp/	*stirrup*
/ˌθɜˈtin/	/ˌθəɹtˈtin/	*thirteen*
/təˈmɑtəw/	/təˈmejtow/	*tomato*
/tɹəˈkiə/	/ˈtɹejkiə/	*trachea*
/ˈvɪtəmɪn/	/ˈvajtəmɪn/	*vitamin*

Technical terms

accent
affricate
alveolar
apical
  apico-alveolar
  apico-dental
approximant
back
  backness
bilabial
bunched /ɹ/
central
consonant
continuant
coronal
dental
diphthong
  centring diphthong
dorsal
  dorso-velar
frication
fricative
front
GA/General American
glide
glottal
height
  high
hold
interdental
International Phonetic Association/Alphabet/IPA
labial-velar
kinæsthesia
  kinæsthetic
labial
labiodental
lamino-alveolar
  lamino-dental
lateral
line drawing
liquid
low
manner of articulation
mid
nasal
  nasal stop
obstruent
onset
oral stop
orthography
palatal
place of articulation
postalveolar
release
retroflex
  retroflexed /ɹ/
rounding
  rounded
  unrounded
RP/Received Pronunciation
schwa
segment
  segmentation
sibilant
sonorant
stop
stress
  primary stress
  secondary stress
suprasegmental
symbol
transcription
  transcribe
unstressed
utterance
velar
vowel

Symbols

The following list gives the names for the phonetic symbols that we have used which are not ordinary letters of the alphabet.

[ɪ]	**small cap i**	[ʊ]	**small cap u**	[ʔ]	**glottal stop**
[ɛ]	**epsilon**	[ə]	**schwa**	[j]	**yod**
[æ]	**ash**	[ə̯]	**schwa glide**	[ɹ]	**upside-down r**
[a]	**front a**	[θ]	**theta**	[ŋ]	**eng**
[ɑ]	**back a**	[ð]	**eth**	[ˈ]	**primary stress**
[ɒ]	**turned a**	[ʃ]	**esh**	[ˌ]	**secondary stress**
[ɔ]	**open o**	[ʒ]	**ezh**		

Exercises

Basic

Exercises focusing solely on one of the accents will be so labelled.

1 a. The paragraph below describes the actions made during the consonant at the end of the word *sang*. Fill in the blanks, using the terms given in Chapter 1.

At the end of the vowel, the soft palate <u>(is lowered)</u> so that the air flows out the <u>(nasal passage)</u>. At the same time, the __________ of the tongue rises to articulate with the __________ , preventing air from escaping through the __________. The lips remain __________. The vocal folds continue to __________.

b. Draw a sagittal section showing the consonant described in question 1a. Indicate voicing with a wavy line at the larynx and voicelessness with a straight line.

2 a. Consider the consonant at the beginning of the word *bat*. In a fashion similar to question 1a above, describe the actions of the vocal organs in producing this consonant.

b. Draw a sagittal section showing the consonant described in question 2a. Indicate voicing with a wavy line at the larynx and voicelessness with a straight line.

3 Read the following. Some of the symbols are not explained until Chapter 3, but you can probably guess the words.

RP	GA
/ðə ˈwɒz ə jʌŋ ˈmæn fɹəm kælˈkʌtə	/ðɛɹ ˈwɑz ə jʌŋ ˈlejdi nejmd ˈpəɹkɪnz
hu ˈkəwtɪd ɪz ˈtɒnsɪlz wɪð ˈbʌtə	hu wəz ɪkˈstɹimli ˈfɑnd əv gɹin ˈgəɹkɪnz
ən ˈɔltəd ɪz ˈsnɔ	wʌn ˈdej ət əɹ ˈti
fɹəm ə ˈsɒnəɹəs ˈɹɔ	ʃi ˈejt twɛɾ̃i ˈθɹi
tu ə ˈsɒft əwliˈædʒɪnəs ˈmʌtə/	ən pikl̩d əɹ ˈɪntəɹnl̩ ˈwəɹkɪŋz/

4 The following words all have the vowel /i/. Transcribe these words, paying attention to the consonants. Remember to listen to the sounds. English spelling can be quite misleading.

be	*seek*	*leaks*	*scene*
neat	*piece*	*deal*	*keys*

5 The following words all have the vowel /ɪ/, but some of the consonant sounds have special symbols: /ŋ/, as in song; /ɹ/, as in are; and /ʃ/, as in wash. Note that /ŋ/ is a single sound, although usually written with two letters –ng.

sing	*trick*	*ship*	*wick*
rid	*wring*	*nicked*	*squish*

6 Practise transcribing the following words with /ɑ i u/:

calm	*seed*	*rude*	*balm*
me	*moo*	*heat*	*through*
moon	*soothe*	*sue*	*peas*
do	*these*	*lose*	*loose*

7 Now try a few more with other vowels:

lip	*set*	*gnat*	*sick*	*seek*
rose	*bad*	*debt*	*ring*	*note*
his	*hiss*	*bang*	*fret*	*freight*

8 Practise transcribing these words which have /ʊ/, as in *put*; or /ʌ/, as in *putt*:

book	*nut*	*foot*	*lug*
buck	*good*	*mud*	*should*

9 Transcribe these words, which have various vowels:

love	*push*	*dumb*	*zinc*	*mash*
reign	*splat*	*reach*	*look*	*said*

10 Pronounce:

sæg	pʌg	zɛn	pʊt	mejt	mɪl
ʃɪm	læs	wʌn	væt	kʌd	kʊd

11 Transcribe. RP: pay attention to /ɑ ɒ ɔ/; GA: pay attention to /ɑ ɔ/.

cat	*cart*	*caught*	*dock*	*dark*	*yacht*
lodge	*large*	*cough*	*cod*	*card*	*was*
Don	*dawn*	*darn*	*stark*	*stalk*	*stock*

12 Note the difference in voicing between the initial consonants of *thin* /θ/, and *then* /ð/. Transcribe the following words:

that	*thus*	*myth*	*three*	*thee*
thumb	*tenth*	*thwart*	*thought*	*though*

13 Transcribe the affricates /tʃ/ and /dʒ/ in the following words. Be sure not to confuse them with /ʃ/ and /ʒ/:

hutch	*gem*	*jump*	*chump*
jaw	*witch*	*Scotch*	*judge*
gel	*butch*	*Jew*	*botch*

14 Each of the following items is the transcription for more than one word. How many different words can you find for each item?

e.g.:	/dow/	*dough, doe*			
blu	si	lɛd	huz	tu	flu
plejn	wejst	pɹej	mit	lut	sajt

15 Correct these transcriptions:

glue	/glju/	*gouge*	/gawz/
knives	/knajvz/	*wealth*	/wɛlð/
reef	/ɹɪf/	*bloom*	/blʊm/
shoot	/sut/	*done*	/dəwn/
chew	/cu/	*Roy*	/ɹoj/
yes	/yɛs/	*says*	/sez/
jump	/jʌmp/	*lamb*	/læmb/

16 Try the following words with the diphthongs /aj aw ɔj/. Note that the first two use the symbol /a/, not /ɑ/:

ride	*boys*	*loud*	*dies*
lines	*soiled*	*spine*	*rouse*

17 Transcribe the following words which have various diphthongs:

sliced *down* *joist* *coins* *signs*

18 Pay attention to /ə/ (and /ɜ/ for RP):

upon	*fathom*	*her*	*sir*	*afire*	*fern*
wallaby	*deeper*	*blurt*	*fur*	*enough*	*surprise*

19 The following words show some accent variation; that is, they are pronounced differently by people from different places. Transcribe these the way you ordinarily say them. Then compare your transcription with friends, particularly with someone from a different part of the English-speaking world.

fast	*aunt*	*with*	*either*	*hearth*	*hover*
garage	*due*	*pen*	*schism*	*brooch*	*figure*

20 Draw sagittal sections showing the consonants /b s ŋ/. Make sure that the articulators are in the correct position and that you have the proper velic position. For a voiced sound, draw a wavy line at the glottis; for a voiceless sound, draw a straight line.

21 Draw sagittal sections for each sound in the words *top, six, scream, eighth.*

Advanced

The instructions are transcribed in RP to give you practice in reading phonetic transcriptions. If you speak with another accent, you should still be able to figure them out.

21 /ˌwi həv ˈnaw ˌkʌvəd ˌɒl ðə ˈbejsɪk ˌsawndz əv ˌɪŋglɪʃ. ðə ˈfɒləwɪŋ ˌɛksəˌsajzɪz pɹəˈzɛnt məˌtɪəɹɪəl əv ɪŋˈkɹisɪŋ ˌdɪfɪˌkʌlti. bi ˌʃɔ tə ˌpej əˈtɛnʃən tə ˌwɒt ju ˈsej, ˈnɒt tə ðə ˌspɛlɪŋ. wɪð ˌwɜdz əv ˌmɔ ðən ˌwʌn ˈsɪləbl, ˌʃəw ˈpɹajməɹi ˌstɹɛs./

a.	*have*	*halve*	*eggs*	*voiced*	*what*
	why	*jazz*	*cloths*	*clothes*	*breath*
	breathe	*foiled*	*sense*	*cents*	*wash*

b. /ˌmɑk ˈpɹajməɹi ˌstɹɛs ɪn wɜdz əv mɔ ðən ˌwʌn ˈsɪləbl/

machine	*ocean*	*seizure*	*anxious*	*finger*
wringer	*longer*	*danger*	*sudden*	*courage*
sadness	*ginger*	*pleasure*	*either*	*ether*
fissure	*ensign*	*resource*	*colonel*	*fossils*
victuals	*marquis*	*valet*	*helm*	*tough*
though	*through*	*thorough*	*cupboard*	*hiccough*

c.	*scours*	*heart*	*mirth*	*tired*	*fourth*
	roar	*spark*	*spearing*	*chair*	*poured*

d.	*jealous*	*spank*	*south*	*southern*
	pooch	*poach*	*idea*	*wow*
	boiler	*higher*	*English*	*French*

e. /ɪn ðə ˈfɒləwɪŋ ˌwɜdz, ˌɪndɪˌkejt ˌbəwθ ˈpɹajməɹi ən ˌsɛkəndəɹi ˈstɹɛs./

tranquility	*epilepsy*	*sassafras*	*logarithm*
diplomatic	*ineptitude*	*architecture*	*loquacious*
salacious	*silversmith*	*greengrocer*	*ironmonger*

Chapter 3

English consonants

In Chapter 2 we listed all the segments of English. In this chapter, we will look at the various consonants in more detail. We will discover that a consonant may be pronounced differently in different situations.

Put your hand about three inches in front of your mouth. In a normal speaking voice, say the English words *pie* and *spy*. You will feel a puff of air with the /p/ of *pie*, but not with the /p/ of *spy*. This puff of air is called **aspiration**. Try the same thing with *tie* and *sty;* and again with *cool* and *school*.

This experiment confirms the point just made that a consonant may be pronounced differently in different situations. In each case when a voiceless stop /p t k/ is at the very beginning of the word as in *pie, tie,* and *cool*, the stop is aspirated. When the stop is preceded by /s/, there is no aspiration, as in *spy, sty,* and *school*. We will transcribe aspiration with a small raised *h;* the consonants of *pie, tie, cool* can thus be transcribed as [pʰ tʰ kʰ]. An addition to a symbol such as the small raised *h* used to transcribe aspiration is called a **diacritic**. Unaspirated consonants will be transcribed without a diacritic.

In this chapter you will learn about:

- allophones and phonemes;
- broad and narrow transcription;
- variations in English consonants.

Note: From here on, where the RP and GA forms differ only slightly, examples will be given in RP transcription in full, followed by the GA portion which is different: e.g., *pleasure* [ˈplɛʒə] GA [-ʒəɹ].

Allophones and phonemes

The experiment in the previous section presents us with a theoretical dilemma. On the one hand, English has a single /p/. Ask someone on the street how many /p/-sounds there are in English. To the layperson, the question does not quite make sense because the answer is so obviously 'one'. Despite this general perception, however, we have just seen that English indeed does have two [p]-sounds.

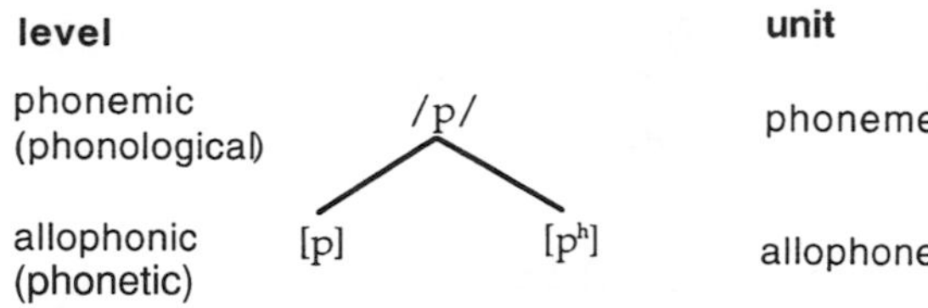

Figure 3.1 Levels

Linguists deal with this problem by positing two different levels for representing sounds (Figure 3.1). At one level, there is one /p/; at the other level, there are two – [p] and [pʰ]. The level of the single /p/ is called **phonemic** or **phonological**. The level of the two [p]-sounds is called **phonetic** or **allophonic**. **Phonology** is the area of linguistics that deals with this sort of issue extensively. We will concern ourselves here only with the basic notions of these two levels. Note that from now on, phonemic transcriptions are enclosed in slant lines, called **solidi**, whereas allophonic transcriptions are enclosed in **square brackets**. This convention is simply to keep the reader informed as to which level is being described. Units at the phonemic level are called **phonemes**. Units at the allophonic level are called **allophones**. Appendix A contains an extensive survey of the consonantal allophones in English.

Phonemes **contrast** with each other: that is, if we substitute one phoneme for another, we get another word. For example, if we substitute the phoneme /v/ for /f/ in *fat* /fæt/, we get a different word – *vat* /væt/. Allophones of the same phoneme, such as [p pʰ], do not contrast with each other: that is, if we exchange them, we do not get different words – e.g., [spʰɪt] [pɪt]. These pronunciations just sound odd; the exchange does not form new words.

The **environment** of a sound is the phonetic context in which the sound occurs, that is, the adjacent sounds. The environment of [m] in *camp* is 'after initial [kʰæ] and before final [p]'. We can symbolise this environment as [kʰæ–p], where the dash shows the position of the sound in question. Sounds which occur in the same environment and create different words are said to contrast and to belong to different phonemes. Thus, in English, the allophones [pʰ] and [kʰ] belong to the different phonemes /p/ and /k/ because both occur in the same environment [–ɪt], as in the two words *pit* and *kit*. We say that *pit* and *kit* form a **minimal pair** in that they are different words which differ in only one sound. A minimal pair always shows that two sounds contrast. We can also note that the allophones [p] and [pʰ] do not contrast as they do not occur in the same environment creating different words; we can never find a minimal pair with [p] and [pʰ] as the differing sounds.

Rules are commonly used to express the relationship between phonemes and allophones. For example, aspiration of /p/ could be expressed as:

/p/ → [pʰ] / initially in a stressed syllable

This rule is read as 'the phoneme /p/ is realised as the allophone aspirated [pʰ] when it occurs initially in a stressed syllable'. The arrow is read 'is realised as' or 'becomes', and the single slant line introduces the environment. The following rule is more general.

[voiceless stop] → [aspirated] / initially in a stressed syllable

It applies to all voiceless stops /p t k/ and shows that any one of them is aspirated when it occurs initially in a stressed syllable.

Occasionally, two sounds occur in the same environment without causing a difference in meaning. Such sounds are not considered contrastive but are said to be in **free variation**. In English, both [p] and [pʰ] occur in word-final position. The word *sip* may be heard as [sɪp] or as [sɪpʰ]. This alternation does not create different words and is thus not contrastive; rather, [p] and [pʰ] are in free variation and are allophones of the same phoneme /p/.

In Chapter 2, we said that the English affricates [tʃ] and [dʒ] are both sequences and single units. We can now see that at the phonetic level, they are sequences of a stop and a fricative. At the phonological level, however, they are single units, contrasting with other single consonants: *chill, Jill, pill, bill, dill, kill, mill.*

Broad and narrow transcription

For the purpose of transcription, the phonemic–allophonic difference can be viewed as a continuum. A transcription at the phonemic end of the continuum is known as a **broad** transcription; it uses fewer symbols to represent the utterance and shows little phonetic detail. At the allophonic end, a **narrow** transcription shows more non-contrastive, phonetic detail. Transcriptions may be more or less broad or narrow. A completely broad transcription is a phonemic transcription using the minimum number of symbols, one for each phoneme; such transcriptions are very useful. A completely narrow transcription would show all phonetic detail. In practice, however, this is impossible, and such a transcription would probably be useless as we would be smothered in detail. The sentence *Small birds fly quickly* is transcribed below in broad and narrow transcription.

	RP	GA
broad:	/ˈsmɔl ˌbɜdz ˌflaj ˈkwɪkli/	/ˈsmɔl ˌbəɹdz ˌflaj ˈkwɪkli/
narrow:	[ˈsmɔːɫ ˌbɜːdz ˌflaˑj ˈk̠ʰwɪk̟li]	[ˈsmɔːɫ ˌbɚˑdz ˌflaˑj ˈk̠ʰwɪk̟li]

Transcriptions in this book are usually rather broad although we often use narrow transcriptions to illustrate a particular point. In doing so, the relevant parts of the form may be in narrow transcription, but the remainder of the form may be transcribed more broadly. This makes it easier to focus on the question at hand. For example, if we were discussing dental consonants, we might transcribe *tenth* as [tɛn̪θ], rather than as [tʰɛn̪θ], not showing the aspiration of the [t], since it is irrelevant to our concerns at the moment.

Morphology

Phonemes are meaningless units of language. The individual phonemes /b/, /ʊ/, /k/, and /s/ have no meaning by themselves although in combination /bʊks/ does have a meaning. In fact, the word *books* /bʊks/ can be divided into two parts, each with meaning: /bʊk/ is a 'bound piece of writing', and /s/ indicates 'plural'. These meaningful parts are called **morphemes**. (Note that in our example, /s/ happens to be both a meaningless phoneme and a meaningful morpheme.) We will occasionally use these terms although **morphology**, 'the study of word-structure', is a separate field of linguistics.

Voicing

Although we classify English consonants as phonemically voiced and voiceless, when we look more closely, we usually find that the so-called voiced obstruents, the stops, fricatives, and affricates, are partially voiceless when they occur at the beginning or end of a word. We are not ordinarily aware of this short bit of voicelessness; however, if we listen carefully to a word such as *buy*, spoken in a slow but casual style, we may be able to notice that voicing does not begin until a bit after the lips close to form the stop. In examining your own speech, be careful to keep it casual. One characteristic of careful speech for many people is to exaggerate various aspects, such as the amount of voicing. We will have more to say about voicing under *aspiration* later in this chapter.

Length

Length refers simply to the duration of a sound. In RP and GA, neither consonants nor vowels are distinguished from each other solely by length. There is, however, a considerable amount of allophonic variation of length for both consonants and vowels.

Obviously, if you are speaking very quickly, you will make shorter sounds than if you are speaking slowly. We are not interested in the absolute length of sounds, but in the length of sounds relative to each other. For example, we are interested in knowing whether the initial [k] and final [k] in *kick* have the same length or not. Phoneticians have made detailed observations about consonant length in English (Crystal and House, 1988a), and have discovered that consonants at the end of a word are in fact slightly longer than at the beginning: *kick* [kɪk·], *lull* [lʌl·], *seen* [sin·]. Here a raised dot [·] indicates a slightly longer sound.

Place of articulation

All sounds are affected by their environment to some extent. A common tendency, for example, is for a sound to become more like its neighbouring sounds. Some sounds seem more susceptible to this sort of variation than others. On the other hand, some sounds seem to exert greater influence upon their neighbours than do other sounds.

Labials

The labial place of articulation does not exhibit very much allophonic variation except for the assimilation of homorganic nasals, which is discussed below.

Coronals

When an alveolar sound precedes a dental /θ ð/, the alveolar sound usually becomes dental as well. Say the word *ten,* and feel where the tip of your tongue is during the /n/. It is on the alveolar ridge. Now try saying the word *tenth,* and feel where the tip of your tongue is for the /n/. You will find it against the teeth instead of in its usual position at the alveolar ridge. The /n/ of *tenth* is a dental [n̪]. Rather than make an alveolar [n] and then move the tongue forward to make a dental /θ/, we anticipate the dental articulation of the /θ/ and make the /n/ dental as well.

We can say that in *tenth,* the alveolar [n] **assimilates** to the dental place of articulation of the following [θ]. **Assimilation** is the **process** by which one sound becomes more like another sound. Assimilation is a very common phonological process.

Instead of creating totally new symbols for dentals, we write the alveolar symbol with a diacritic [̪] beneath it: e.g., [t̪ d̪ n̪ l̪], as in *width* [wɪd̪θ] or [wɪt̪θ], *tenth* [tɛn̪θ], *filth* [fɪl̪θ].

Note that dental assimilation often occurs across word boundaries: *at three* [ˌæt̪ ˈθɹi], *read these* [ˌɹid̪ ˈðiz], *in the book* [ɪn̪ ðə ˈbʊk], *Will this do?* [ˌwɪl̪ ˌðɪs ˈdu].

In GA, there is a different example of assimilation where an alveolar assimilates slightly to the retroflexed position after an /ɹ/. **Retroflexion** is indicated by special symbols which are like the alveolar symbols, but with a subscript hook to the right: [ʈ ɖ ɳ ʂ ʐ ɭ]: *hurt* [həɹʈ], *bird* [bəɹɖ], *barn* [bɑɹɳ].

Commonly in RP, and usually in GA, the postalveolars /tʃ dʒ ʃ ʒ/ and the retroflex /ɹ/ have inherent rounding which is independent of the context. If you say *cheat, jack, shell, Giles,* and *red,* you will likely see that these are pronounced with lip rounding, even before an unrounded vowel. We indicate this lip rounding with the diacritic [ʷ]: [tʃʷit dʒʷæk ʃʷɛl ʒʷil ɹʷɛd]. When we tell someone to be quiet with a long [ʃʷʃʷʃʷʃʷʃʷʃʷ] *shhh!,* the rounding is often quite apparent.

Dorsals

The velar stops /k g/ are particularly sensitive to the nature of the vowels following them in the same syllable. If the following vowel is a front vowel, the closure for /k/ or /g/ is made quite far forward on the velar surface, almost into the palatal area. On the other hand, if the vowel is a back vowel – particularly a low one – the closure is made much farther back.

Try saying *key* /ki/ and *calm* /kɑm/. You can easily feel that, before /i/, the stop is made much farther forward than the stop of *caw* (Figure 3.2). With intermediate vowels, the closure is accordingly made at an intermediate point on the velar surface. If we regard the back variety as basic, we can transcribe the fronted variety with a diacritic [˖], a subscript plus sign; this diacritic means that the sound is articulated a bit more forward than usual. Thus, [k̟] is appropriate for a narrow transcription of /k/ in *key* [k̟i] or *kid* [k̟ɪd]. The same variations are found with /g/: *geese* [g̟is], *gill* [g̟ɪl].

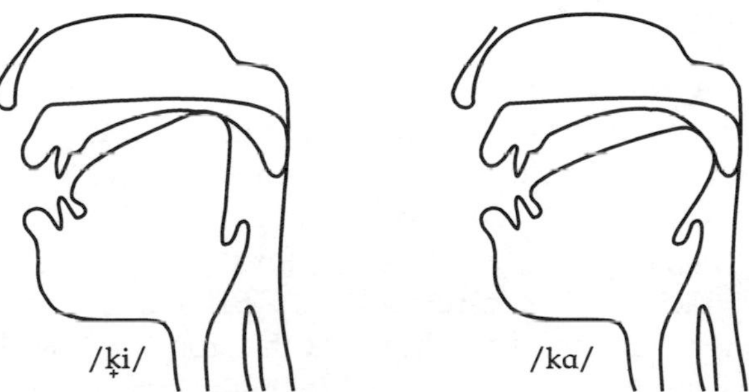

Figure 3.2 Allophones of /k/ before /i/ and /ɑ/

Homorganic nasals

As we learned with *tenth* above, nasals preceding a consonant, particularly in the same syllable, commonly assimilate to the place of articulation of the following consonant. Not only do we find dental clusters such as [n̪θ] in [tɛn̪θ], but we also find a tendency for nasals generally to assimilate to the place of articulation of the following consonant. Such a nasal is called

homorganic, that is, made with the same organs. The morpheme *syn-* illustrates homorganic nasal assimilation:

RP	GA	
[ˈsɪmpəθi]	[ˈsɪmpəθi]	*sympathy*
[ˈsɪɱfəni]	[ˈsɪɱfəni]	*symphony*
[ˌsɪn̪ˈθəsɪs]	[ˌsɪn̪ˈθəsɪs]	*synthesis*
[ˈsɪnˌtæks]	[ˈsɪnˌtæks]	*syntax*
[ˈsɪŋkəpi]	[ˈsɪŋkəpi]	*syncope*

The symbol [ɱ] is used for a labiodental nasal. Homorganic nasal assimilation over a word boundary is not unusual particularly in casual speech,: *in five* [ˌɪɱ ˈfajv], *ten pieces* [ˌtɛm ˈpisɪz], *on board* [ˌɒm ˈbɔd] GA [ˌɑm ˈbɔɹd], *and that* [ˌæn̪ ˈðæt], *in case* [ˌɪŋ ˈkejs], *in gear* [ˌɪŋ ˈgɪə] GA [ˌɪŋ ˈgɪɹ]. Note that homorganic nasal assimilation is not always required in English: *Paddington* [ˈpædɪŋtən].

Manner of articulation

Stops

Aspiration

Voiceless stops are aspirated at the beginning of a stressed syllable: *pull* [ˈpʰʊl], *talk* [tʰɔk], *can* [kʰæn], *impel* [ɪmˈpʰɛl], *retard* [ɹɪˈtʰɑd] GA [-ˈtɑɹd], *incur* [ɪŋˈkʰɜ] [-kəɹ]. However, after a syllable-initial /s/ or at the beginning of an unstressed syllable, voiceless stops are not aspirated: *spy* [ˈspaj], *stem* [ˈstɛm], *scan* [ˈskæn], *super* [ˈsupə] GA [-pəɹ], *looking* [ˈlʊkɪŋ].

Aspiration involves a delay in the onset of voicing; that is, in the segment following the aspirated stop, voicing does not begin immediately, but is delayed slightly. During voicelessness, the vocal folds are separated; air continues to pass through the glottis while the closure for the stop is being made higher in the vocal tract. Air pressure builds up behind the stops closure and is responsible for the 'puff of air' heard as the stop is released. Note that aspiration affects not only the voicing of following vowels, but also the voicing of following sonorants /l ɹ j w/. We use a small circle under the sonorants to show that they are voiceless.

tip	[tʰɪp]
plum	[pʰl̥ʌm]
queen	[kʰw̥in]

Figure 3.3 is a line drawing showing the timing of voicing for three situations: an initial voiced stop, a voiceless stop, and a voiceless aspirated stop. At the beginning of the [d], the alveolar opening closes to become a stop; this is shown by the merger of the two lines into a single line. At the

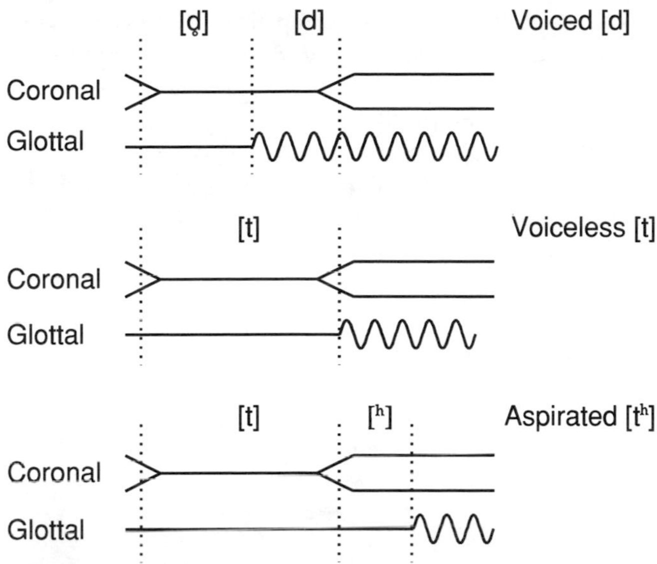

Figure 3.3 The timing of the alveolar closure in relation to voicing, shown for voiced, voiceless, and voiceless aspirated stops

beginning to the stop, the vocal folds are in a voiceless position; this portion is transcribed [d̥]. Part way through the stop, the vocal folds begin to vibrate in voicing.

In the voiceless unaspirated stop [t], the onset of voicing is simultaneous with the release of the stop. Thus, the stop is completely voiceless, and the vowel is completely voiced. (Note that [d̥] and [t] are equivalent notations.)

The bottom portion of Figure 3.3 shows an aspirated stop [tʰ]. Here the voicelessness of the stop continues part way into the vowel after the stop is released.

Thus we see that in initial position all alveolar stops have some voicelessness; [d] has the least, and [tʰ], the most.

Coarticulation

Although we say that in a word such as *peck* the sounds occur in the sequence /p – ɛ – k/, in fact the tongue moves to a position for /ɛ/ before the lips part at the end of the [p]. Likewise, the back of the tongue is moving upwards getting ready for the /k/ before the end of the /ɛ/. **Coarticulation** refers to the fact that the gestures of one sound are not completely discrete as to timing from those of its neighbours.

Many allophonic variations can be explained by coarticulation. Most consonants are rounded to some degree before a rounded vowel: e.g., *two* [tʷu], *noose* [nʷus]. This rounding is explained as due to the fact that the lips assume a rounded position in advance of the vowel itself.

A particular type of coarticulation, called **overlapping**, that occurs with stops is shown in words such as *apt*. Phonemically, the word is /æpt/ with a simple sequence of /p/ followed by /t/. Phonetically, however, the /t/ is formed before the /p/ is released (Figure 3.4). Try saying *apt;* now, say it again, but stop half-way through, during the /p/. You will probably feel the tip of your tongue already at the alveolar ridge before the /p/ is released. There is a short period when the closures for /p/ and /t/ overlap. We do not hear the release of the /p/ when the lips part because the tongue has already made a closure for the /t/. For this reason, we say that in a sequence of two overlapping stops, the first is released silently (Henderson and Repp, 1982); we can show this as [p͡t]. We do not hear the release of the /p/ or the onset of the /t/.

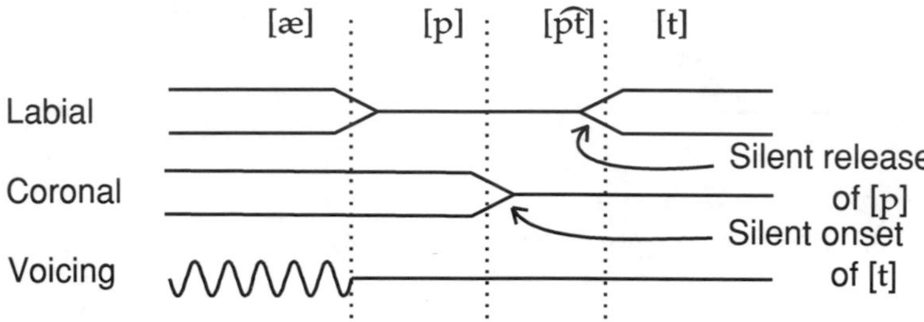

Figure 3.4 Overlapping in *apt*. The timing of the labial closure is shown in relation to the alveolar closure

Release

Phonemic voiced stops are usually phonetically somewhat voiceless at the end of a word or phrase, and may be entirely voiceless: [bɛdd̥] or [bɛd̥]. It may seem odd to say that *voiced* sounds are *voiceless,* but remember that we are dealing with different linguistic levels; stops which are considered voiced at the phonemic level may be voiceless at the phonetic level. In word-initial position, the crucial phonetic distinction is aspiration.

Stops at the end of a phrase may be released immediately or held for some time so that the release is **inaudible**. The raised corner [˺] is used to show stops with inaudible release: *lab* [læb̥ ~ læb̥˺ ~ læbb̥ ~ læbb̥˺]. The allophones of /b/ – [b̥ b̥˺ bb̥ bb̥˺] – are thus in free variation with each other: i.e., a final stop may be released audibly or not with no difference in meaning, and it may be completely voiceless or partially voiceless, again with no difference in meaning. There are similar allophones in free variation for /d/ and /g/.

Phonemically voiceless stops at the end of a word or phrase are also phonetically voiceless. They may be plain, aspirated, or inaudibly released. Like the final allophones of the voiced stops, these three allophones are also in free variation: *hip* [hɪp] ~ [hɪpʰ] ~ [hɪp˺], *put* [pʰʊt] ~ [pʰʊtʰ] ~ [pʰʊt˺], *sick* [sɪk] ~ [sɪkʰ] ~ [sɪk˺].

In ordinary speech, when two stops with the same place of articulation occur together, the cluster is heard as one long stop, with no release at all after the first stop. In phrases like *black cat* and *black goose*, there is no release after the first /k/. We can use [k˺] to symbolise either no release, or inaudible release: [ˌblæk˺ˈkæt], [ˌblæk˺ˈgus]. The release of consonants in clusters with different places of articulation is discussed in the following section.

Voiced and voiceless stops in English

We have pointed out that phonemically 'voiced' stops of English are often phonetically voiceless. Table 3.1 shows that the phonetic realisation for these English stops varies according to where they occur in the word. Note that it is important here to distinguish phonemically voiced (contrasting phonemically with voiceless) from phonetically voiced (the vocal folds are vibrating).

Table 3.1 Typical phonetic manifestation of phonemically voiced and voiceless stops in English in different environments

Position in word	Phonemically voiced	Phonemically voiceless
Initial	unaspirated (partially) voiceless	aspirated voiceless
Medial	shorter closure duration longer preceding vowel	longer closure duration shorter preceding vowel
Final	longer preceding vowel (partially) voiceless	shorter preceding vowel voiceless

We can see that in English, there is no single phonetic feature which characterises the phonemic distinction of voiced–voiceless. Note that with /sp st sk/, the stops are unaspirated; there are no contrasting sequences /sb sd sg/ in English. Recall also that voiceless stops in final position can be unaspirated, aspirated, or unreleased; voiced stops can be released or unreleased. In initial position, the first part of a phonemically voiced stop may be voiceless; in final position, the last part of a phonemically voiced stop may be voiceless.

GA: Taps

In GA, the /t/ in a word like *city* is pronounced quite differently from the /t/ of *top*. Say these words aloud: *city, butter, matter, lettuce.* If you listen carefully, you will notice that the /t/-sound in these words is voiced (feel your vocal folds); you can also note that this sound is made very quickly. This sound is a voiced, alveolar **tap**. In *ladder,* with an ordinary stop [d], the tongue movement seems much more deliberate; in *latter,* the feeling is that the tongue is thrown against the alveolar ridge striking it only momentarily and generally moving faster.

The difference between stops and taps can be compared to that between guided and ballistic missiles. Guided missiles are under control from start to finish. Their course can be altered in mid-flight. With ballistic missiles, such as a rifle bullet, the course cannot be altered once the missile has been fired. Stops are like guided missiles. The course of the action of the articulators is in the control of the nervous system throughout the production of the stop. Taps, on the other hand, are like ballistic missiles in that once the action starts, they are no longer controlled.

The voiced alveolar tap which occurs in English is transcribed with the symbol [ɾ]; it looks like an [r] with the top serif missing. The tap occurs as an allophone of /t/ at the beginning of a non-initial unstressed syllable: [ˈsɪɾi] *city*, [ˈbɛɾi] *Betty*, [ˈlɛɾəɹ] *letter*, [ˈɛɾɪkət] *etiquette*, [ˈɛkwɪɾi] *equity*.

The accent described here is quite common in North America, but some speakers use a [d] instead of a tap: [ˈlædəɹ] 'latter', [ˈlæˑdəɹ] 'ladder'. Others use a tap for both the /t/ and /d/: [ˈlæɾəɹ] 'latter', [ˈlæˑɾəɹ] 'ladder'. In these accents, the longer vowel before /d/ distinguishes it from /t/ (see Chapter 4 on vowel length). Taps, or one of the variations just described, are a distinctive characteristic of North American English; only in New York City is it common to find speakers who have a stop [t].

Many speakers also have a nasal tap in words such as *winter* [ˈwɪɾ̃əɹ]. Here, the velum is down allowing air to flow out through the nose. The diacritic, a **tilde**, indicates nasality. In such a word, the consonants form a sequence /nt/ at the phonemic level, but a single segment [ɾ̃] at the phonetic level.

Yod dropping and yod coalescence

In stressed syllables with a coronal consonant followed by /ju/, English has generally had a tendency to lose the /j/; this loss, known as **yod dropping** is quite variable and has been more widespread in GA than in RP. After /ɹ/, /j/ is normally lost everywhere; after /θ s z l/, it is always lost in GA, and variably so in RP. The list below shows the commoner forms; note that Wells (1990) gives RP /sju/ *sue*, but /sut/ *suit*.

RP	GA	
/tjun/	/tjun, tun/	*tune*
/djun/	/djun, dun/	*dune*
/nju/	/nju, nu/	*new*
/sju, su/	/su/	*sue*
/ɹɪˈzjum, ɹɪˈzum/	/ɹɪˈzum/	*resume*
/ɛnˈθjuziæzm̩, /ɛnˈθuziæzm̩/	/ɛnˈθuziæzm̩/	*enthusiasm*
/lut, ljut/	/lut/	*lute*
/ɹud/	/ɹud/	*rude*

After /t d n/, /j/ has always been retained in RP. In the US, it is lost more often as one travels west. In this book /j/ is transcribed for GA after /t d n/, but the reader must understand that there is a great deal of individual variation. Interestingly, in East Anglia, /j/ after consonants has been lost generally, giving forms such as *music* [ˈmuzɪk], *beautiful* [ˈbutɪfəl], *cute* [kut].

Across word boundaries in GA, the sequences /t#j/ and /d#j/ are often realised as [tʃj] and [dʒj] (where /#/ indicates a word boundary), particularly in casual speech. This process is referred to as **yod coalescence**. Like /t#j/ and /d#j/, the sequences /s#j/ and /z#j/ are also often realised as [ʃ] and [ʒ].

I'll hit you	[ˌajl ˈhɪtʃʊ]
She fed you	[ˌʃi ˈfɛdʒʊ]
I'll miss you	[ˌajl ˈmɪʃʊ]
I'll buzz you	[ˌajl ˈbʌʒʊ]

Yod coalescence is not so common in casual RP speech, although casual forms such as *did you* [ˈdɪdʒʊ] and *would you* [ˈwʊdʒʊ] are normal in English everywhere.

Retroflex affricates

The sequences /tɹ/ and /dɹ/ are sometimes realised as rounded retroflexed postalveolar affricates, shown here as [ʈʂʷ ɖʐʷ]; [ʂ] is a voiceless retroflex fricative, and [ʐ] is the voiced equivalent: *tree* [ʈʂʷɹi], *trap* [ʈʂʷɹæp], *dream* [ɖʐʷɹim], *drew* [ɖʐʷɹu]. With this type of palatalisation, different speakers vary considerably, even in their own pronunciations; it seems most common before /i/, as in *tree, dream.*

RP: glottalisation

Among younger speakers of RP, [t] is commonly accompanied by a glottal stop in medial and final positions. Thus we find *pit, sitting, quite likely, button, bottle* [pʰɪʔ͡t ˈsɪʔ͡tɪŋ ˌkwajʔ͡tˈlajkli ˈbʌʔ͡tn̩ ˈbɒʔ͡tl̩]. The raised arch [͡] is used over two symbols, as in [ʔ͡p], to indicate that they are pronounced simultaneously. The timing of the glottal stop generally overlaps the [t], but the glottal stop may precede slightly. In non-RP accents, particularly in south-eastern and northern England, and in Scotland, glottalisation is even more common, occurring with /p/ and /k/ as well, in some cases replacing the oral stop entirely. In North America, glottalisation is relatively uncommon, occurring mostly before syllabic /n/ as in *button* [ˈbʌʔ͡tn̩], but not commonly elsewhere: *bottle* [ˈbɑɾl̩]. For the stroke under the [n], see 'Syllabic consonants' below, p. 59.

Fricatives

In non-initial position, phonemically voiced fricatives often show considerable voicelessness. They can nevertheless be distinguished from the corresponding phonemically voiceless fricative by the length of the preceding vowel (see Chapter 4). Thus we sometimes find *safe* /sejf/ [sejf], *save* /sejv/ [se·jf]. The labiodentals /f/ and /v/ do not exhibit major allophonic variations other than the devoicing just mentioned.

The dental fricatives exhibit some individual variation as to whether the tip or the blade of the tongue is used. We can label these variations **apico-dentals** and **lamino-dentals**. With a little practice, you should be able to make both varieties. Dentals also vary with individuals as to whether the tongue is behind the teeth or partly protrudes between the teeth. The latter are referred to as **interdentals**. These are more common in loud or very careful speech.

There is a certain amount of variation in the way /s/ or /z/ is produced. Various tongue positions produce the same sound. Typically, the tip of the tongue is near the alveolar ridge with only a very narrow opening. Air passes through this gap, striking the rear surface of the upper teeth, and makes a hissing noise. Some speakers make the gap more with the blade of the tongue, with the tip pointing down. A common speech problem is the substitution of [θ ð] for [s z]. This is a kind of **lisp**, a general term for the use of an inappropriate coronal fricative.

Note that with [s z], the central position of the tongue is lower than the sides, forming a central groove for the air-flow. In Figure 3.5, the dotted line shows the surface of the central portion of the tongue and the solid line shows the tongue edge. The groove is not present in [ʃ ʒ].

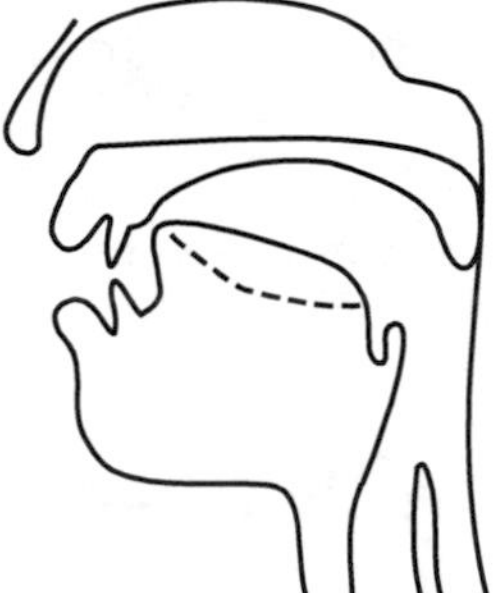

Figure 3.5 In /s/, the central portion of the tongue, shown by the dotted line, is lower than the sides, forming a groove from front to back

The postalveolar fricatives [ʃ ʒ] are made with a broader surface of the tongue than are the alveolar fricatives. Individuals show considerable variation in producing postalveolars but typically direct the air-flow against the lower teeth. There may be an arching of the tongue so that the laminal surface articulates with the alveolar ridge and the forward part of the palate. Alternatively, the tip of the tongue may be raised or even curled slightly back as for retroflex sounds.

In Chapter 2, we saw that at the beginning of a word, /h/ is a voiceless vowel. Note that some books describe [h] as a glottal fricative because of the fricative-like noise as the air comes through the vocal folds. In the middle of a word, however, such as in *ahoy* or *ahead*, the /h/ is neither voiced nor voiceless. It is made with another adjustment of the vocal folds, called **breathy voice**. We will discuss breathy voice more fully in Chapter 12. For the time being, use [ɦ] for the narrow transcription of /h/ in the middle of words: [əˈɦɔj əˈɦɛd]. Breathy voiced [ɦ] also occurs in a stressed syllable at the beginning of a word if the preceding sound is an unstressed vowel in the same phrase: [ə ˈɦɛd] *a head*, [ðə ˈɦajˌwʌn] *the high one.*

The initial cluster /hj/ is found in words like *hew, huge, human*. We treat this phonemically as a cluster /hj/ although phonetically it is a single segment – a voiceless palatal glide [j̥]: [j̥u j̥udʒ ˈj̥umən] *hew, huge, human.* Note that the cluster /hj/ only occurs before the vowel /u/.

Nasals

The allophonic alternation of homorganic nasals has already been noted above. The sound /n/ is regularly dental [n̪] before [θ ð] and frequently labiodental [ɱ] before /f v/. The velar nasal /ŋ/ occurs only **postvocalically** (after a vowel) in a syllable: *singing* [ˈsɪŋɪŋ]. Velar /ŋ/ is common before /g/ or /k/; otherwise, it is found only at the end of a morpheme; the only exception I know is *hangar* [ˈhæŋə] GA [-ŋəɹ]. In transcribing /ŋ/, note that the spelling *ng* sometimes includes a [g]-sound, and sometimes not: *finger* [ˈfɪŋgə], *wringer* [ˈɹɪŋə] GA [ˈfɪŋgəɹ] [ˈɹɪŋəɹ]. In parts of northern England and for some speakers in New York City, words written with *ng* are all pronounced with [ŋg].

Nasal onset and release

When a nasal occurs before a homorganic stop, that is one with the same place of articulation, the transition between nasal and stop is called **nasal onset** and is marked by the minimum articulatory change. For example, in *send* [sɛnd], during the [n], the vocal folds are vibrating, the nasal passage is open allowing air to escape through the nose, and the tip of the tongue is touching the alveolar ridge stopping air from escaping through the mouth. The only difference between an [n] and a [d] is that there is velic opening for the [n]. Thus, the transition from [n] to [d] is marked only by raising the velum. Taking the stop as primary, we say that it has a nasal onset. Figure 3.6 (overleaf) shows the relative timing for the alveolar closure and the velic closure in nasal onset in *send.*

In a word like *Rodney* [ˈɹɒdni] GA [ˈɹɑdni] (Figure 3.6), the same transition between stop and nasal occurs except in the reverse order. Here the stop has **nasal release** marked by a lowering of the velum allowing air to escape through the nose. In careful pronunciation, a word such as *kindness* [ˈkajndnɪs] exhibits both nasal onset and nasal release; in more casual speech, the [d] is lost and there is a long [n]: [ˈkajnnɪs].

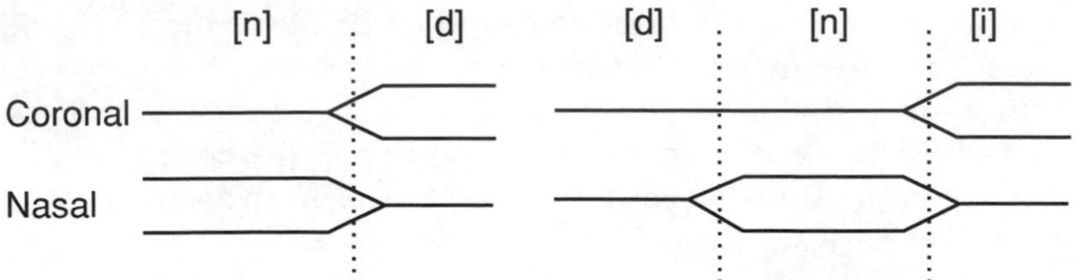

Figure 3.6 Nasal onset and release. On the left, [nd] as in *send*; on the right, [dni] as in *Rodney*. The timing relationships of the stop and nasal are shown

Approximants

Lateral approximant

The lateral approximant /l/ has two allophones: **clear [l]**, with the back of the tongue relatively low in the mouth (Figure 3.7); and **dark [ɫ]**, with the back of the tongue raised. Clear [l] occurs before vowels *let* [lɛt], *lawd* [lawd]; and dark [ɫ] occurs at the end of a syllable *bell* [bɛɫ], *built* [bɪɫt], *people* [ˈpipɫ̩]. The difference between the two kinds of /l/ is greater in RP than in GA.

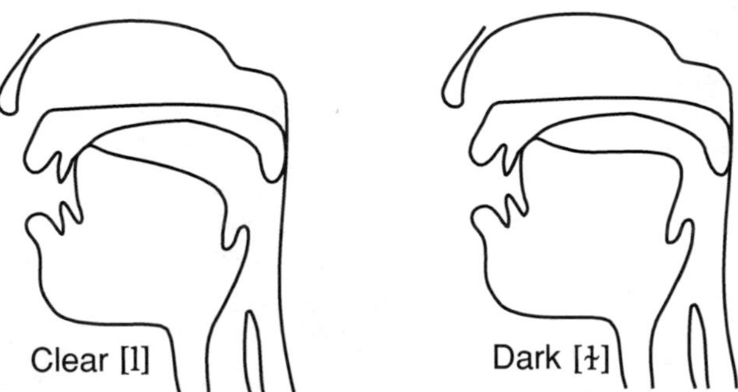

Figure 3.7 Clear and dark /l/

Lateral onset and release

Lateral onset and **release** are parallel to nasal onset and release. The transition is from a lateral articulation to a central one, or vice versa. In going between /l/ and /d/, the only change is that the sides of the tongue rise or fall.

Lateral onset occurs in *build*. During the /l/, the tip of the tongue is touching the alveolar ridge, but the sides of the tongue are down allowing air to pass out laterally. At the beginning of the /d/, the sides of the tongue come up to form a complete closure, thus producing a /d/. Lateral onset is shown

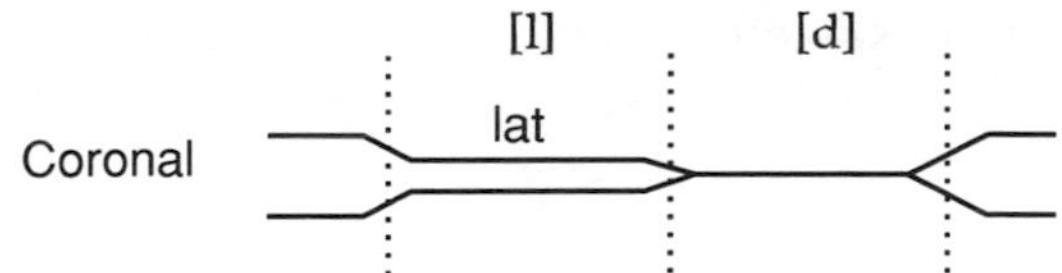

Figure 3.8 Lateral onset in *build*. The timing relationship of the lateral and the alveolar stop is shown

in Figure 3.8 where the narrowing of the lines indicates the partial closure for the /l/, followed by a complete closure for the /d/. In lateral release, as in *fiddler*, the events occur in the reverse order.

Syllabic consonants

Ordinarily every syllable contains a vowel as its central part. Sometimes, however, a syllable contains a sonorant nasal or liquid instead of a vowel. Pronounce the word *sudden* [ˈsʌdn̩] at an ordinary rate. You will notice that there is nasal release between the /d/ and the /n/, that is the tongue stays at the alveolar ridge throughout the /d/ and /n/. Thus, there can be no intervening vowel. The /n/ itself forms a syllable; we call it a **syllabic** nasal, transcribed [n̩], with a short subscript stroke as the diacritic to indicate **syllabicity**.

In like manner, you can observe that the final sonorant in *ladle* can be pronounced with a syllabic consonant: [ˈlejdɫ̩]. Words which have syllabic consonants, can alternatively be pronounced with a vowel: [ˈsʌdən], [ˈledəɫ]. However, such pronunciations with the vowel are typical of very careful, slow speech and may sound stilted and artificial; the pronunciations with the syllabic consonant are much more common. Syllabic consonants also occur occasionally after fricatives: *prison* [ˈpɹɪzn̩], *prism* [ˈpɹɪzm̩], *rhythm* [ˈɹɪðm̩]. In rapid speech, further combinations may occur: [ˈbekŋ̍] *bacon*, [ˈbʌmpm̩] *bump 'em*, [ˈɹɪbm̩] *ribbon*. In GA, syllabic [m̩] is normal after /t/ (= [ɾ]): *bottom* [ˈbɑɾm̩]. The test for a syllabic consonant is whether or not a vowel intervenes; a syllabic consonant is never next to a vowel. In a word like *gambolling* [ˈgæm bl̩ lɪŋ], note that the syllabic consonant is in the second syllable, and the third syllable begins with an [l].

Rhotic approximant

In initial position, /ɹ/ may be pronounced in either of two ways: with the tongue tip up (retroflexed), or with the tip pointing down and the tongue bunched. The retroflexed version seems commoner in Britain, and the bunched version commoner in the US; however, there is little acoustic difference between the two sounds. Speakers who ordinarily make /ɹ/ with the tongue tip up may find that they use a 'bunched [ɹ]' after velars: *crate*, *green*. Conversely, speakers with a 'bunched /ɹ/' may keep the tongue tip up after alveolar stops: *tree, drain*. In RP commonly and in GA normally, initial /ɹ/ is rounded [ɹʷ]: *red* [ɹʷɛd]. In emphatic speech, particularly in RP, after initial /θ/, /ɹ/ is occasionally pronounced as an alveolar tap, as in *three* [θɾi].

In the GA phonemic sequence /əɹ/, the /ɹ/ is normally pronounced simultaneously with the schwa, that is the schwa is retroflexed or **rhotic**. Thus, a two-segment phonemic sequence /əɹ/ is realised as a single phonetic segment. This rhotic schwa has a special symbol [ɚ]. The body of the tongue is in position for a [ə], and the tip of the tongue is retroflexed back to the postalveolar region. To some degree all vowels preceding /ɹ/ are rhotic: e.g., *beer, care, far, door, cure*. However, the temporal overlapping is much more complete in the case of /ə/.

We have called this sound a rhotic schwa and transcribed it as [ɚ]. We could just as well have called it a syllabic /ɹ/ and transcribed it as [ɹ̩]. The first way conceptualises it as the vowel /ə/ with rhotic properties; the second way thinks of it as the consonant /ɹ/ with syllabic properties. There is no difference in the sound produced, no matter how we conceptualise it. I will use [ɚ] in narrow transcriptions, and /əɹ/ in broad.

Accents such as GA which preserve historic /ɹ/ after vowels are called **rhotic**; those that have lost it, like RP, are called **non-rhotic**. We will examine the consequences of this loss in more detail in Chapter 4.

Technical terms

affricated
allophone
allophonic
apico-alveolar
  apico-dentals
approximant
aspiration
assimilate
  assimilation
breathy voice
broad
centisecond
central
clear [l]
coarticulation
contrast
dark [ɫ]
diacritic
environment
free variation
fricative
homorganic
inaudible release
interdental
laminoalveolar
  laminodentals
lateral onset
  lateral release
length
lisp
minimal pair
morphology
  morpheme
narrow
nasal onset
  nasal release
overlapping
palatalisation
phonology
  phoneme
  phonemic
  phonetic
  phonological
postvocalic
process
retroflexion
rhotic
rule
slant lines
solidi
square brackets
stops
syllabic
  syllabicity
tap
tilde
vowel colour

Symbols

	Name	Use
[ɱ]	**m with tail**	labiodental nasal
[ɦ]	**hooktop h**	breathy voiced h
[ɫ]		dark l
[ɾ]		tap
[ː]	**colon**	extra length
[ˑ]	**raised dot**	slight extra length
[̥]	**subscript ring**	voiceless
[̪]	**subscript bridge**	dental
[ʰ]	**superscript h**	aspiration
[ʷ]	**superscript w**	rounded
[̟]	**subscript plus**	advanced
[̠]	**subscript minus**	retracted
[̩]	**subscript stroke**	syllabic
[͡]	**superscript arch**	simultaneous pronunciation
[̚]	**superscript corner**	inaudible release
[̃]	**tilde**	nasalisation

Exercises

Basic

1 Complete the following proportions (solve for the value of X) on the basis of your knowledge of features (labial, voiced, nasal, etc.). Circle the correct answer.

a. [p : m] as [t : X] X = [k ŋ ð tʃ n]
b. [n : s] as [n̪ : X] X = [ɱ n θ z ð]
c. [p : k] as [m : X] X = [ɡ t ŋ n θ]
d. [b : p] as [n : X] X = [n̥ n̩ m m̥ n]
e. [u : w] as [i : X] X = [j y ɪ ǰ ʊ]
f. [i : ɪ] as [u : X] X = [ɛ æ ʌ o ʊ]
g. [f : v] as [ʃ : X] X = [z ʒ ʃ tʃ θ]

2 Transcribe each of the following words, and make line drawings for the consonants:

	[*bit*]	[*piece*]
labial		
coronal		
dorsal		
glottal		
velic		

	[*etch*]	[*hind*]
labial		
coronal		
dorsal		
glottal		
velic		

	[*coughed*]	[*maiden* (use syllabic nasal)]
labial		
coronal		
dorsal		
glottal		
velic		

	[*belt*]	[*petty*]
labial		
coronal		
dorsal		
glottal		
velic		

3 Transcribe each of the following words, showing aspiration and overlapping. Make line drawings, showing carefully the timing of aspiration and overlapping.

	[*scan*]	[*can*]
labial		
coronal		
dorsal		
glottal		
velic		

	[*peptic*]	[*world*]
labial		
coronal		
dorsal		
glottal		
velic		

4 In each word, place a raised stroke [ˈ] at the beginning of the syllable with the primary stress.

a. antique
b. profile
c. afternoon
d. relation
e. unimportant
f. caterpillar
g. aquamarine
h. objectivity
i. catholicism
j. autobiographic
k. electrification
l. unreliability

5 a. Make a broad transcription of the following words.

b. Then make a narrow transcription showing the details of only the consonants (i.e., leave the vowels in a broad transcription). Mark primary stress throughout.

	[a]	**[b]**
saddle		
skipped		
anthem		
purity		

6 a. Pronounce the following English words written in a broad transcription. Write them out in ordinary English orthography:

stɹɪp θɹɪps ɹʌŋz gɑd θætʃt plɪnθ
jɛld θɪŋ ðʌs kædʒ ʃɹʌgd θɹɛd

b. Transcribe the following in a broad transcription.

thin *lung* *gin* *then* *yen* *stretch*
shin *chin* *death* *bait* *blind* *feed*
shoal *don* *ground* *join* *moon* *mew*
blue *through* *sigh* *feud* *tough* *coat*
food *though* *bleed* *flood* *sew* *shade*
stealth *thwack* *chugged* *push* *than* *yelp*
myths *groaned* *thanks* *plunge* *fling* *rubbed*

Florence *Kate* *Priscilla* *Stuart* *Nancy* *Ida*
Edwin *Basil* *Veronica* *Ethel* *Xavier* *Jerome*
Aaron *Clarissa* *Dennis* *Leroy* *Euphemia* *Quincy*
Maria *Randolph* *Timothy* *Gertrude* *Yolanda* *Oliver*
Heather *Zacharias* *Winifred* *Theodore* *Sean* *Augusta*

7 Say *hat.* Stretch out the [h]: [hhhhhæt]. Now, say just the [h] alone: [hhhhhhhhh]. In English, /h/ does not occur at the end of a word. One way of improving your phonetic ability is to learn to say a sound in positions where it does not occur in English. In the following exercises, practise saying [h] at the end of the word. Start slowly, [mɛhhhhh], stretching out the [h]. Then gradually shorten it to [mɛh].

mɛh lɪh kɪh lɛh mæh bʊh

8 [ŋ]. Transcribe:

bang *lung* *gangs* *sinks* *singing* *dunking*

The sound [ŋ] does not occur at the beginning of words in English. Try the following hints to learn to say [ŋ] at the beginning of a word.

a. Try saying [ŋŋŋŋŋŋ], and then shorten it gradually to just [ŋ].

b. If this seems not to work, try saying *sing* [sɪŋ], then [ɪŋ], then [ɪŋŋŋŋ]. Gradually lengthen the [ŋ] until you can say it without any vowel. Now try saying *sing it.* Start with [sɪŋɪt], then say [ɪŋɪt], then [ŋɪt].

Try these nonsense words to learn to pronounce [ŋ] in initial position:

ŋɪt ŋæk ŋɛd ŋʌbd ŋɪks ŋʊlb

9 Aspiration. This exercise will first help you to become aware of aspiration and then to control it.

a. Put the open palm of your hand close to your mouth and say *pit – spit.* You will notice a stronger puff of air with the [p] of *pit* than with *spit.* Try the same experiment with your hand with the words *tool – stool* and *cool – school*. In English, voiceless stops /p t k/ are aspirated at the beginning of a stressed syllable, but not when the stop is preceded by /s/.

b. In the following exercise, pronounce the words normally, and then try to pronounce aspirated stops after /s/. If you have difficulty, try sounding emphatic.

step	stɛp	st^{h}ɛp	*spun*	spʌn	sp^{h}ʌn
skid	skɪd	sk^{h}ɪd	*stool*	stul	st^{h}ul

Try these:

sp^{h}ɹejn   st^{h}ʌmp   sk^{h}ɪn   sp^{h}lin   st^{h}ɹɛtʃ   sk^{h}wɪd

c. To make an initial unaspirated stop, try the following exercise. Start with [stɛp]; lengthen the [s] to [ssssstɛp]. Now make a short pause between the [s] and the [t] without aspirating the [t]: [sssss tɛp]. It helps to try to relax your mouth. From [sssss tɛp], try to lengthen the pause, and then do away with the [s] altogether. It may help to articulate softly when working on unaspirated stops at first.

d. Some people use a special kind of English when speaking to babies. They delete initial preconsonantal /s/ leaving an unaspirated consonant at the beginning:

e.g.: *spit* [spɪt] → [pɪt]

RP	GA	
[ˌpɪt ɪt ˈawt]	[ˌpɪɾ ɪɾ ˈawt]	*spit it out*
[ˈtɒp ɪt]	[ˈtɑp ɪt]	*stop it*
[ˈɡəw tə ˈkul]	[ˌɡow ɾə ˈkul]	*go to school*

Try saying:

RP	GA	
[ˌpɪt awt ðə ˈp^{h}ɪt]	[ˌpɪɾ awt ðə ˈp^{h}ɪt]	*spit out the pit*
[ˌɪts ˌk^{h}ul ɪŋ ˈkul]	[ˌɪts ˌk^{h}ul ɪŋ ˈkul]	*it's cool in school*
[ˌtɒp ðə ˈt^{h}ɒp]	[ˌtɑp ðə ˈt^{h}ɑp]	*stop the top*

f. Now try both aspirated and unaspirated stops at the beginning of a word:

RP	GA		RP	GA	
t^{h}ʌb	tʌb	*tub*	k^{h}ʌp	kʌp	*cup*
p^{h}ʊt	pʊt	*put*	t^{h}əɹn	təɹn	*turn*

10 Practise saying the following, first normally, and then making all the voiceless stops unaspirated:

Tiny Teddy Tucker tripped his two-toed, timid twin, Toto.
Pushy Patty Potter paid the punky, pompous parson for the puny pumpkin pie.
Queen Catherine kissed her crotchety cousin and complimented her kinky colleague King Carl the Cute.
Tanned Poppy MacLeod paid quite close attention to her customer's pleasant trill.

11 Pronounce, then transcribe, the following words using [ʒ] for the sound shown in bold type:

rouge	*lesion*	*azure*	*garage*	*usual*
erosion	*measure*	*vision*	*seizure*	*casual*

12 These words have more than one pronunciation. For each transcribe as many pronunciations as possible.

bow *read* *sow* *lead* *mow*

13 GA: the symbol [ɚ] is used for the sound in *fur, brother,* or *dirtier.*

a. Pronounce:

kɚ tʃɚtʃ ˈɚmə ɪnˈfɚ pɚˈvɚt flɚt

b. Transcribe each of the following phonemically and phonetically:

ladder *summer* *irksome* *surfer* *murder* *murderer*

14 In English, alveolar [n t d l] occurring immediately before a dental [θ] are regularly changed to a dental [n̪ t̪ d̪ l̪]. The diacritic [̪] is used to change the symbol for an alveolar sound to that of a dental.

Pronounce *ten* [tɛn] and *tenth* [tɛn̪θ]. Note that the place of articulation of the nasal of *ten* is alveolar whereas the nasal of *tenth* is dental.

Pronounce the following: ejt̪θ fɪl̪θ ˈsɛvən̪θ
Transcribe: *wealthy* *tenths* *width*

Try saying the following first with alveolars and then replace them with dentals.

Ed edited a tiny titillating trilogy on dental trills.
Daniel doted on Dotty's tantalising titbits.

15 GA: taps. Pronounce, then transcribe, the following words, noting the tap:

city	*mutter*	*writing*	*latter*	*knitting*
water	*witty*	*weighty*	*hated*	*matted*

Accents with [ɾ] generally distinguish it from [d], a voiced alveolar stop, that is they contrast *latter* [ˈlæɾəɹ] and *ladder* [ˈlædəɹ]. Some accents, however, merge the two and pronounce *both* with [ɾ] or [d].

Pronounce the following words first with [ɾ], then with [d], and then with [t]:

e.g.: *city* [ˈsɪɾi – ˈsɪdi – ˈsɪti]
Betty *writing* *better* *metal* *cut it* *at a glance*

The following words normally have [tʰ]; pronounce them with [ɾ]:

e.g.: *hotel* [howˈtʰɛl] [howˈɾɛl]
eternal *retire* *deter*

For the *t* of the following words substitute in turn [tʰ t ɾ d]:

e.g.:	*return*	[ɹɪˈtʰɚn – ɹɪˈtɚn – ɹɪˈɾɚn – ɹɪˈdɚn]	
	cutter	*bat*	*town*

16 RP: glottalisation. Pronounce the following words with a glottalised [ˀ͡t] and with a plain [t]:

e.g.:	*let*	[lɛˀ͡t lɛt]		
cut	*hit*	*sat*	*fight*	*sent*
cutting	*hitting*	*matted*	*nightlight*	*rented*
cotton	*meeting*	*bottom*	*rattle*	*matter*

Pronounce the following with glottalised stops and with plain stops:

e.g.:	*sip*	[sɪˀ͡p sɪp]	*licking*	[ˈlɪˀ͡kɪŋ ˈlɪkɪŋ]
cap	*tack*	*lamp*	*aunt*	*capped*
rattrap	*knapsack*	*campsite*	*apple*	*buckle*

Go back, and try all these words with a glottal stop only: [kʌˀ hɪˀ . . .].

17 In the sequence of consonants at the end of the word *plants*, we can describe the actions of the vocal tract as:

> For the /n/ the tip of the tongue rises to touch the alveolar ridge, the vocal folds continue to vibrate, there is velic opening. For the /t/, the vocal folds stop vibrating, and there is velic closure. For the /s/ the tip of the tongue moves slightly away from the alveolar ridge.

Notice that this description only mentions the changes: for example, the fact that the tip of the tongue remains at the alveolar ridge for the /t/ is not mentioned.

Make similar descriptions of the activities of the vocal tract for the final consonant clusters in:

page *rubs* *world* *pests* *kitten*

Make descriptions of the activities of the vocal tract for the initial consonant clusters in:

spend *blue* *grin* *thwart* *strip*

Advanced

The instructions are transcribed in GA for practice.

18 /ˈɹid əˌlawd/:

> GA: /ˌwɪð əz ˌlɪɾl̩ ˌɛnəɹˌdʒi ənd əz ˌmʌtʃ ˌfɔls ˈhowp əz ə ˌlɑbstəɹ ˌkɛpt əˈlajv ɪn ə ˌɹɛstəˌɹɑnt ˈwɪnˌdow, ˈpitəɹ ˌɹɪtʃəɹdz əˈwowk ən dɪd hɪz ˌfju ˌsmɔl ˌminɪŋlɪs ˈɛksəɹˌsajzɪz/

19 [ˈpɹæktɪs ˌsejɪŋ ðə ˌfalowɪŋ ˌwəɹdz, ˈfəɹst wɪð ə ˌfajnl̥ ˌkansənənt, ˈðɛn wɪð ə ˌfajnl̥ ˌejtʃ, ən ˈðɛn ˌwɪð ˈnow ˌkansənənt əˈtɔl]

e.g.:	lɪk	lɪh	lɪ		
fɛg	wʌŋ	væm	dæb	lʊd	zʌð
fʊn	kɛs	tɪʒ	mɛl	gʊf	bʌk

20 [sɪlˈæbɪk ˌkansənənts ər ˌmejd wɪðˌawt ə ˌvawəl. ˌtrænˈskrajb ðə ˌfalowɪŋ wɪð ə sɪˈlæbɪk ˌkansənənt. ˈpɹæktɪs ˌsejɪŋ ðm̩ ˌbowθ ˈwɪð ə ˌvawəl ən ˌwɪð ə sɪˌlæbɪk ˈkansənənt.]

e.g.: *sudden* [ˈsʌdən] [ˈsʌdn̩]
sodden *hidden* *laden* *leaden* *wooden*

[ɪn ˌwəɹdz ˌlajk ˈbʌtn̩, wi ˌgɛɾ ə vəˈɹajəɾi əv pɹəˌnʌnsiˌejʃn̩z/: [ˈbʌtn̩ ˈbʌʔn ˈbʌʔtn̩ [wɛɹ] [ʔt] [ˌɹɛpɹəˌzn̩ts ə ˌsajml̩ˈtejniəs ˌglaɾl̩ ˌstap ən ˈti. ˌtɹænsˌkɹajb ˈjʊɹ pɹəˌnʌnsiˌejʃn̩ əv ˈðə ˈfalowɪŋ]:

button *kitten* *rotten* *batten*

[ˈlɪsn̩ ˌklowsli n̩ ˌtɹænsˌkɹajb ˈjʊɹ pɹəˌnʌnsiˌejʃn̩ əv ðə ˈfalowɪŋ]:

bottom *item* *atom* *datum*

[ˈnaw ˌsej ˌðiz ˌwəɹdz, ˈfəɹst wɪð ə ˌvawəl ˌplʌs ˌnejzl̩, ən ˈðɛn wɪð ə sɪˌlæbɪk ˌnejzl̩]

e.g.: *button* [ˈbʌtən] [ˈbʌtn̩]
kitten *rotten* *satan* *tighten*

[də ju ˌhæv sɪˈlæbɪk ˌnejzl̩z ɪn] *prison? prism?*

[ˌtɹænsˌkɹajb ðə ˈfalowɪŋ, ˈjuzɪŋ ə sɪˌlæbɪk ˌnejzl̩ ʍənˌɛvəɹ ˈpasɪbl̩]:

e.g.: *blacken* [ˈblækŋ̍]
bacon *Fagan* *Hogan* *ship 'em* *stab 'em* *happen*

[ˌtɹænˌskɹajb ðə ˈfalowɪŋ]

idle *ripple* *trickle* *dangle* *nickel* *saddle*

21 Inaudible release. At the end of a word a voiceless stop in English has three alternative forms in free variation with each other: aspirated, unaspirated, or inaudibly released. Thus *lip* can be pronounced [lɪpʰ – lɪp – lɪp˺].

Try the following words with all three types of final voiceless stop:

gnat *neck* *rap* *hurt* *belt* *nest*

22 Overlapping. Pronounce these words first so that the stops do not overlap, even put a short /ə/ between them; then pronounce them so that the second stop is formed before the first ends.

e.g.: *acting* [ˈækᵊtɪŋ] – [ˈæktɪŋ] – [ˈæk͡tɪŋ]
napped *lactate* *reptile* *deadbeat* *Pitcairn*

Transcribe the following according to your own pronunciation, paying attention to overlapping and also to whether the stops are aspirated, unaspirated, or inaudibly released. Write out alternative transcriptions where more than one type is possible. Practise pronouncing all possibilities.

stopping	*stopped*	*topped*	*nightcall*	*steak knife*	*feckless*
misplaced	*report*	*restart*	*ignite*	*ripcord*	*laptop*

23 [ˈvɔjsɪŋ ˌpɹæktɪs. wi ˌhæv ə ˈnʌmbəɹ əv ˌsawndz ʍɪtʃ ˌfɔɹm ˈvɔjslɪs-ˈvɔjst ˌpɛɹz.]
[ˈtɹaj ðə fˌɑlowɪŋ, ˌɹidɪŋ əˈkɹɔs]

s s s s s   z z z z z   f f f f f   v v v v
θ θ θ θ θ   ð ð ð ð   ʃ ʃ ʃ ʃ ʃ   ʒ ʒ ʒ ʒ ʒ

[ˌʍajl ˈsejɪŋ ˌðiz, ˈplejs jəɹ ˌfɪŋgəɹz ˈowvəɹ jəɹ ˌædəmz ˌæpl̩ ən ˈfil ðə ˌvowkl̩ ˌfowldz ˈvajbrejt ˌdjʊɹɪŋ ˌvɔjsɪŋ. ˈpɹæktɪs ˌɔltəɹˌnejɾɪŋ bɪˌtwin ˈvɔjst n̩ ˌvɔjslɪs ənˌtɪl jʊ hæv ə ˌsɛns əv kənˌtɹowl ˌowvəɹ ˈvɔjsɪŋ.]

s z s z s z s z   f v f v f v f v   θ ð θ ð θ ð θ ð   ʃ ʒ ʃ ʒ ʃ ʒ ʃ ʒ

[ðə sawndz] [m n l ɹ] [ˌjuʒuəli əˌkəɹ ˈvɔjst ɪn ˌɪŋglɪʃ; ðɛɹ ˈvɔjslɪs ˌkawr̃əɹˌpɑɹts əɹ ˌɹɪtn̩ wɪð ə ˌdajəˈkɹɪɾɪk] [̥] – [m̥ n̥ l̥ r̥]. [ˈmɛni ˌpipl̩ ˌhæv ə ˌfɔɹm tə ˌʃow əˌgɹimn̩t] [ʔmˈm̥] [wɪð ðə ˈsɛkn̩d ˌsɪləbl̩ ˌvɔjslɪs. ˈsej ˌðɪs n̩ ˈfil ðə ˌvɔjslɪsnɪs əv] [m̥] [ətʃəɹ ˈædm̩z ˌæpl̩]:

m m m m m m̥ m̥ m̥ m̥ m̥   l l l l l l̥ l̥ l̥ l̥ l̥   n n n n n n̥ n̥ n̥ n̥ n̥   ɹ ɹ ɹ ɹ ɹ ɹ̥ ɹ̥ ɹ̥ ɹ̥ ɹ̥
m m̥ m m̥ m   l l̥ l l̥ l   n n̥ n n̥ n   ɹ ɹ̥ ɹ ɹ̥ ɹ

non̥ɛ	m̥ɑmæ	lɒl̥u	nɑŋ̊ɛ	ɹ̥ʌɹɛ	l̥æɹ̥ɑ
noɹ̥ʊ	m̥ʊm	ŋum̥o	n̥oɹ̥ʊ	ɪnm̥ɛ	ɹ̥ilu

24 [ˌˈvɔjslɪs ˈsownəɹənts. ʍɛn ən ˌæspɪˌɹejɾɪd ˈstɑp pɹɪˌsidz] [l ɹ w j] [ɪn ˈɪŋglɪʃ, ðə ˌsownəɹənt ɪz ˌjuʒjəli ˈvɔjslɪs].
[ˌˈtɹænsˌkɹajb ðə ˈfɑlowɪŋ]

pray	*cram*	*tray*	*cute*	*puny*	*twin*
pure	*quince*	*clay*	*plump*	*plough*	*prince*
tune	*nude*	*cleanse*	*twice*	*cream*	*pueblo*

[pɹəˌnawns ˈitʃ əv ðə ˌpɹiˈsidɪŋ ˌwəɹdz ˈlɪsn̩ɪŋ tə ðə ˌvɔjslɪs ˌsownəɹənt. ˈæftəɹ sejɪŋ ˌitʃ ˌwʌn, ɹəˈpiɾ ɪt wɪðˌawt ði ɪˈnɪʃl̩ ˌstɑp, bət ˌlivɪŋ ðə ˌsownəɹənt ˈvɔjslɪs]:

e.g.: *pray* [pɹ̥ej – ɹ̥ej]   *cram* [kɹ̥æm – ɹ̥æm]

[ˈnaw ˌpɹaktɪs sejɪŋ ðiz ˌwəɹdz wɪð ən ˈʌnˌæspɪˌɹeɾɪd ˌstɑp n̩d ə ˈvɔjst ˌsownəɹənt]:

pɹe   kɹæm   tɹej   *etc.*

25 [ˈtæps]. [ˈpɹæktɪs ˈðiz ˈfɔɹmz wɪð ˌɪr̃əɹˌvowˈkælɪk] [ɾ]:

ɑɾɑ   ˈiɾi   ˈɛɾu   ˈuɾə   ˈɪɾʊ   ˈʌɾə

[ˈnaw ˌtɹaj pɹəˈnawnsɪŋ ðiz ˌfɔɹmz wɪð ɹ̩nɪʃəl] [ɾ]:

ˈɾɑɾɑ ˈɾiɾi ˈɾɛɾu ɾəˈɾɔ ɾɪˈɾej ˈɾɔɾɪ

[ˈtɹaj ðəˈfɑlowɪŋ ˌɡɹædʒuəl ˈtʃendʒɪz, ɹ̩idɪŋ ˈdawn. ˌdownt ˈɹʌʃ.]

ˈdɪɾædu doˈdedu
ˈdɪɾæɾu doˈɾedu
ˈɾɪɾæɾu doˈɾeɾu
ˈɾɪdæɾu ɾoˈɾeɾu
ˈɾɪdædu ɾoˈdeɾu

26 GA: [ɪn ˈɪŋɡlɪʃ ˌwəɹðz sʌtʃ əz] *winter*, [ˈmɛni ˌnɔɹθ əˌmɛɹɪkn̩z həv ə ˌnezl̩ ˈtæp; ˌðɪs kn̩ bi ˌtɹænˈskɹajbd əz]: [ɾ̃] – [ˈwɪɾ̃əɹ]. [ɪn ˈdʒɛnɹəl], [ɾ̃] [ˌɹɛpɹəˈzn̩ts] /nt/.
[ˌtɹænsˌkɹajb ðə ˈfɑlowɪŋ]:

plenty *resented* *Monty* *flinty* *cantor* *scented*

[də ˌju ˌdɪsˈtɪŋɡwɪs] *winter* [ən] *winner* [ɪn ˌkɛɹfəl ˌspitʃ? ɪn kəˈlowkwiəl ˌspitʃ?]
[ˌtɹaj ɹɪˈplejsɪŋ ðə] [ɾ̃] [əv ðə ˈpɹiviəs ɪɡˌzæmpl̩z wɪð] [n]: [ˈplɛni], [ɹəˈzɛnɪd], etc.

27 [pɹəˌnawns ˈðiz ˌnɑnˌsɛns ˌwəɹdz]:

ˈbɪmpʌv	zʊdˈsæl	ˈfɛpɡɪk	ˈnʊlwɪf	vʌnˈtɛl	mæpˈwʌɡ
ˈwʊbkɪm	ˈlʌvkɛz	stɛks	slʊnts	znʌɡz	mlɪbd
bdækt	ktɪmpt	dzɛtp	zblɪndɡ	ˈvzɛdn̩s	mbʊdɡd

Chapter 4

English vowels

In Chapter 2, we introduced the vowel phonemes; now we will examine them in greater detail.

In this chapter we will learn about:

- which vowels occur in which environments;
- the differences between tense and lax vowels;
- the allophonic details of English vowels.

Distributional restrictions

Not all vowels occur in all possible environments. For example, /bi/ and /bej/ are possible monosyllabic words in English, whereas /bɪ/ and /bɛ/ are not. The description of the distributional possibilities of sounds is called **phonotactics**.

Tense and lax

For phonotactic reasons, English vowels are commonly divided into two categories: **tense** and **lax**. You must be careful not to read too much into these terms. In English, the tense vowels are longer than the lax ones, usually produced a little higher and a little more to the periphery of the vowel area than the corresponding lax vowels; however, the muscles of the vocal tract are not necessarily in a state of greater tension during the production of tense vowels. Instead of thinking of the terms **tense** and **lax** as descriptions of the muscle activity, you should consider them simply as arbitrary names for two categories of vowels, categories which are based on the environments in which they occur. As we will see, schwa is anomalous and does not fit well into the tense–lax classification; we will list it as a special case of the lax vowels.

Open and closed syllables

Word-finally, the lax vowel /ɛ/ occurs only in a **closed syllable**, that is one ending in a consonant; i.e., we have /pɛt/ *pet*, but there is no possible word in English of the shape /pɛ/. We can state the generalisation that in English lax vowels do not occur in word-final open syllables. An **open syllable** is one which ends in a vowel or glide with no final consonant. Tense vowels, however, occur in both open and closed syllables: *saw, sawed.*

English accents differ most noticeably in their vowel systems. For this reason, we will first present the basic structure of RP and GA separately. This approach will involve some duplication if you read both descriptions, but it allows each system to be presented more coherently.

The vowel phonemes of RP

We find twenty different vowel **nuclei** in RP. A **nucleus** is the **vocalic**, or vowel part of a syllable.

/i/	*dean, see, peel*	/u/	*dune, sue, pool*
/ɪ/	*din, pill, sing*	/ʊ/	*wood, pull*
/ej/	*deign, say, pail*	/əw/	*tone, sew, pole*
/ɛ/	*den, bell*	/ɔ/	*dawn, saw, pall*
/æ/	*Dan, pal, sang*	/ʌ/	*done, gull, sung*
		/ɒ/	*don, doll, song*
/ɜ/	*turn, fir, curl*	/ɑ/	*calm, mar*
/ə/	***a**bout, sof**a**, ladd**er***		
/aj/	*dine, sigh, pile, mire*	/ɪə/	*mere, weird, id**ea***
/aw/	*down, now, cowl, hour*	/ɛə/	*mare, cared, S**a**rah*
/ɔj/	*coin, soy, boil, coir*	/ʊə/	*moor, cure, c**u**rious, j**u**ry*

Twelve of these vowels are **monophthongs**, that is simple nuclei, written with only one vowel symbol; the other eight are diphthongs. We will see later that phonetically, some of the tense monophthong phonemes are in fact phonetically diphthongs. Six of the vowels are lax, all monophthongs. Thirteen are tense; of these, five are monophthong, eight diphthongs. Schwa is classed as a special lax monophthong.

lax:	Monophthongs	/ɪ ɛ æ ʊ ʌ ɒ/ /ə/
tense:	Monophthongs	/i ɜ ɑ ɔ u/
	Diphthongs	/ej əw aj aw ɔj ɪə ɛə ʊə/

As we have just noted, the lax vowels only occur in closed syllables: *pit, pet, pat, put, putt, pot.* Schwa is not a typical lax vowel in that it occurs in both open and closed syllables: /ˈvɒdkə əˈpil/ *vodka, appeal.* The tense vowels occur in both open and closed syllables: *pea, peat; purr, purred; car, card; saw, sawed; shoe, move; pay, pate; go, goat; lie, line; cow, cowl; boy, coin; beer, weird; pair, dared; moor, moored.*

RP vowel allophones

The tense vowels are allophonically longer than the lax vowels. For the diphthongs, this length is already symbolised in the use of two symbols. For the tense monophthongs /ɜ ɑ ɔ/, we can show length by a length diacritic [ˑ]: [ɜˑ ɑˑ ɔˑ]. The vowel nuclei /i/ and /u/ contain very short glides; that is phonetically they are very short diphthongs [ij] and [uw] (Figure 4.1).

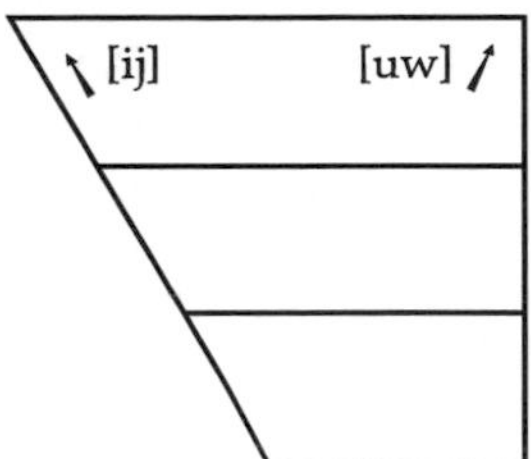

Figure 4.1 RP: diphthongal quality of /i/ and /u/

The vowel portion of the diphthong /aw/ is farther back than that of /aj/ (Figure 4.2). It could be transcribed in a narrow transcription as [ɑw]: cf. *high* [haj], *how* [hɑw].

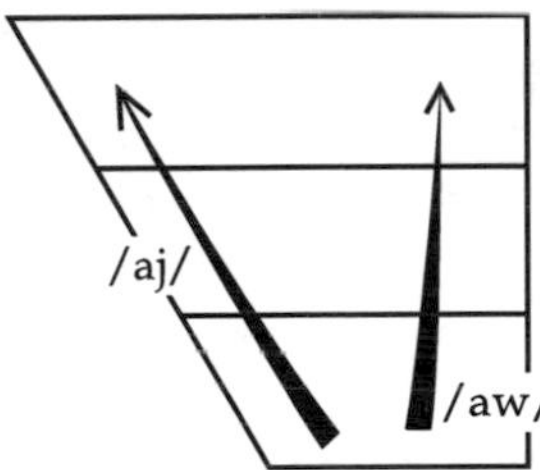

Figure 4.2 RP: /aj/ and /aw/ diphthongs

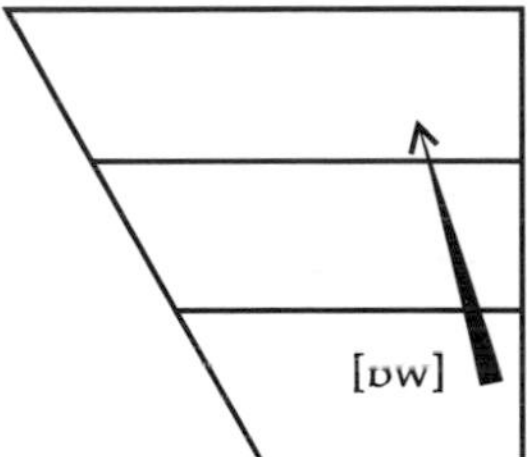

Figure 4.3 [ɒw] variant of /əw/

Before [ɫ], a common variant of /əw/ is [ɒw] (Figure 4.3): *coal* [kɒwɫ], *fold* [fɒwɫd]. This variant is common in Britain, although not usually used by RP speakers.

The diphthong /ʊə/ seems to be disappearing. Above I listed *moor, cure, curious, jury* as examples; however, many speakers may have other vowels in these words. In monosyllables, /ʊə/ has merged with /ɔ/ for many speakers, resulting in considerable neutralisation: *moor, more, maw* /mɔ/; *poor, pour, paw* /pɔ/; *sure, shore, Shaw* /ʃɔ/.

Smoothing

The diphthongs /aj aw ɔj ej əw/ occur before /ə/: *fire, hour, joyous, player, slower*. In careful speech, these are pronounced with the full diphthong. In casual or rapid RP, the original glide is often lost and schwa becomes a glide, a process known as **smoothing**. Smoothing is more common with /ajə/ and /awə/. Some RP speakers use smoothing in all but the most formal and careful styles of speech.

fire	/ˈfajə/	[fa·ə]
hour	/ˈawə/	[ɑ·ə]
joyous	/ˈdʒɔjəs/	[dʒɔ·əs]
player	/ˈplejə/	[plɛ·ə]
slower	/ˈsləwə/	[slɜ·]

Note that smoothing tends to reduce two syllables to one, lengthening the vowel. Also, certain small phonetic changes in vowel quality take place. With the loss of the glide, one might expect that *tyre* and *tower* would merge. For some speakers, this is the case; however, the allophonic back quality of the vowel in *tower* [tɑə] remains, distinguishing it from *tyre* [taə]. The /ej/ vowel is lowered to [ɛ] in [plɛ·ə]. With /əwə/, the two schwas merge as [ɜ·]. Some speakers may completely merge forms such as *shire, shower, shah* as [ʃɑ·]; such pronunciations are, however, sometimes viewed as affected.

Linking /ɹ/

In the eighteenth century in southern England, /ɹ/ was lost at the end of a phrase or before a consonant. Thus, in the phrase *very far*, the /ɹ/ of *very* remained, but the /ɹ/ of *far* was lost at the end of the phrase: /ˌvɛɹɪˈfɑ/. However, in the phrase *far away*, the /ɹ/ of *far* was not lost since it was not at the end of the phrase: /ˌfɑɹəˈwej/. At first, we could say that the underlying form of *far* was /fɑɹ/ and explain its loss by the rule just mentioned. In the course of time, however, the situation has been reconceptualised. For RP speakers today, the underlying form of *far* is /fɑ/, and the /ɹ/ in /ˌfɑɹəˈwej/ is now inserted by a rule, known as **linking /ɹ/**. The present-day rule is that /ɹ/ is inserted between morphemes where the preceding morpheme ends in a non-high vowel and the following morpheme begins with a vowel:

Ø → /ɹ/ / [–high V] # – V, where # is a morpheme boundary.

In addition to inserting /ɹ/ in phrases such as *far away*, many speakers now insert /ɹ/ where it never existed historically.

Emma /ɹ/ is	*Korea /ɹ/ and Japan*
the idea /ɹ/ of it	*put a comma /ɹ/ at the end*

even sometimes

I saw /ɹ/ it	*draw /ɹ/ ing*

Many speakers, however, look down on the insertion of /ɹ/ where it does not appear in the spelling. The former prime minister, Margaret Thatcher, who acquired an RP accent as an adult, was joshingly referred to as 'Laura Norder' because she used the phrase 'law and order' so frequently with an inserted /ɹ/. Wells (1982) notes that the complete absence of linking /ɹ/ is a mark of acquired RP, and according to van Buuren (1988), Lady Thatcher did not in general learn to apply the rule consistently.

The vowel phonemes of GA

We find fifteen different vowel **nuclei** in GA. A **nucleus** is the **vocalic**, or vowel part of a syllable.

/i/	*dean, see, peel*	/u/	*dune, sue, pool*
/ɪ/	*din, pill, sing, mere*	/ʊ/	*wood, pull, moor*
/ej/	*deign, say, pail*	/ow/	*tone, sew, pole*
/ɛ/	*den, bell, mare*	/ɔ/	*dawn, saw, pall, more*
/æ/	*Dan, pal, sang*	/ʌ/	*done, gull, sung*
		/ɑ/	*calm, la (note in singing), mar, don, doll, song*
/ə/	***a**bout, sof**a**, turn, ladder*		
/aj/	*dine, sigh, pile, mire*		
/aw/	*down, now, cowl, hour*		
/ɔj/	*coin, soy, boil, coir*		

Ten of these vowels are **monophthongs**, that is simple nuclei, written with only one vowel symbol. The other five are diphthongs. We will see later that phonetically, some of the tense monophthong phonemes are in fact phonetically diphthongs. Five of the vowels are lax, all monophthongs. Nine are tense; of these, four are monophthongs, and five diphthongs. Schwa is classed as a special lax monophthong.

lax:	monophthongs	/ɪ ɛ æ ʊ ʌ/ /ə/
tense:	monophthongs	/i ɑ ɔ u/
	diphthongs	/ej ow aj aw ɔj/

As we have just noted, the lax vowels only occur in closed syllables: *pit, pet, pat, put, putt.* Schwa is not a typical lax vowel in that it occurs in both open and closed syllables. The tense vowels occur in both open and closed syllables: *pea, peat; la, pod; paw, pawed; few, feud; pay, pate; go, goat; lie, line; cow, cowl; boy, coin.*

GA vowel allophones

The tense vowels are allophonically longer than the lax vowels. For the diphthongs, this length is already symbolised in the use of two symbols. For the tense monophthongs /ɑ ɔ/, we can show length by a length diacritic [ˑ]: [ɑˑ ɔˑ]. The vowel nuclei /i/ and /u/ contain very short glides, that is phonetically they are very short diphthongs [ij] and [uw] (Figure 4.4).

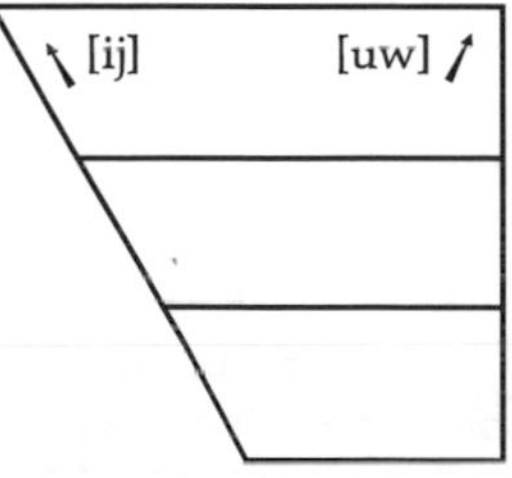

Figure 4.4
GA: diphthongal quality of /i/ and /u/

In parts of the GA area, particularly in the northern Midwest, and also in most of Canada, the vowels /ɔ/ and /ɑ/ have merged: *cot caught* /kɑt/; *dawn Don* /dɑn/. This change appears to be spreading westwards.

In the south-east, outside the GA area proper, /ɛ/ has become /ɪ/ before all nasals: *ten, tin* /tɪn/, *gym, gem* /dʒɪm/. This change appears to be spreading to other areas. Note that all English accents have /ɪ/ in *English* /ˈɪŋglɪʃ/ although not in *strength* or *length*.

For many GA speakers, there is no difference in vowel quality between /ʌ/ and /ə/: *cut* /kət/, *butter* /ˈbətəɹ/.

GA: Before /ɹ/

In GA, only some vowels occur before /ɹ/. Note particularly /əɹ/; this is the only situation in which /ə/ occurs in a stressed syllable. The vowels /i ej æ ʌ oj u/ do not occur before /ɹ/ (Figure 4.5).

/ɪ/	fear, cheery
/ɛ/	fair, carriage
/ɑ/	far, starring
/ɔ/	for, gory
/ʊ/	pure, mooring
/ə/	fir, courage, butter
/aj/	fire, diary
/aw/	flour, dowry
/ɔj/	coir, Moira

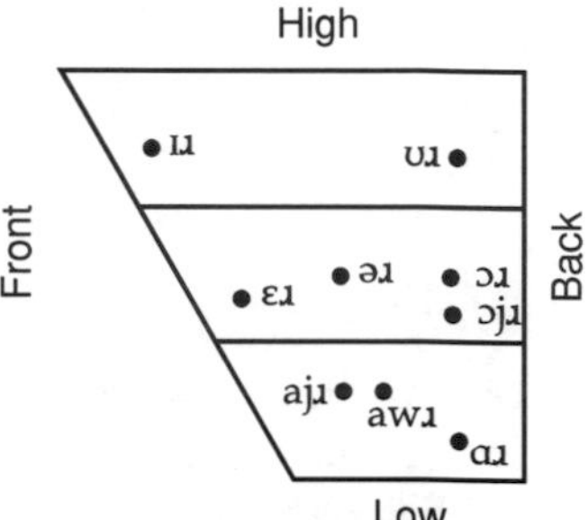

Figure 4.5 GA: vowels before /ɹ/

RP and GA vowels

Before /ʃ ŋ/

In both RP and GA, lax, but not tense vowels occur before /ʃ/ or /ŋ/. A few exceptions to this statement exist. The words *leash, quiche,* and (*micro-*)*fiche* have a tense /i/ before /ʃ/; *gauche* has a tense /əw/ GA /ow/; and *douche* has a tense /u/. These words are all borrowed from French. *Quiche, fiche, gauche,* and *douche* are exceptions to the rule because they have only come into English fairly recently, and their French form has not been adapted to conform to the general tense–lax distribution. *Leash,* on the other hand, although originally borrowed from French, has been around in English for several hundred years; I do not know why it is an exception.

Words like *oink, boing,* and *boink* disobey the constraint in having tense /ɔj/ before /ŋ/; words like this are not felt to be ordinary words and often do not agree with regular phonotactic constraints.

In GA, other exceptions with tense vowels before /ʃ/ and /ŋ/ are words such as *wash, slosh, long,* and *wrong,* with tense /ɑ/ before /ʃ/ and /ŋ/. Earlier, these vowels had a lax vowel still found in RP, and thus conformed to the general rule of vowels before /ʃ/ and /ŋ/. Subsequently, in GA, this vowel merged with [ɑ], a tense vowel, creating exceptions to the general rule.

Students occasionally have difficulty in identifying /æ/ as the vowel before /ŋ/ as in *sang, rang, fang, hang.*

RP: Summary of vowel phonotactics in words of one syllable

Table 4.1

	Closed syllables	Open syllables	–ʃ	–ŋ
Tense vowels				
/i/	peat	pea	(leash)	—
/ej/	bait	pay	—	—
/ɑ/	palm	bar	—	—
/ɜ/	burn	purr	—	—
/əw]	boat	dough	(gauche)	—
/u/	boot	sue	(douche)	—
/aj/	bite	buy	—	—
/aw/	pout	cow	—	—
/ɔj/	voice	toy	—	—
/ɪə/	reared	peer	—	—
/ʊə/	lured	cure	—	—
/ɛə/	cared	pear	—	—
Lax vowels				
/ɪ/	pit	—	dish	ring
/ɛ/	pet	—	mesh	length
/æ/	pat	—	lash	rang
/ɒ/	pot	—	wash	long
/ʌ/	putt	—	hush	rung
/ʊ/	put	—	push	—
/ə/	*—	—	—	—

* only occurs in unstressed syllables

GA: Summary of vowel phonotactics in words of one syllable

Table 4.2

	Closed syllables	Open syllables	–ʃ	–ŋ	–ɹ
Tense vowels					
/i/	peat	pea	(leash)	—	—
/ej/	bait	pay	—	—	—
/ɑ/	pot	la	(wash)	—	car
/ɔ/	bought	paw	—	(long)	more
/ow/	boat	dough	(gauche)	—	—
/u/	boot	sue	(douche)	—	—
/aj/	bite	buy	—	—	fire
/aw/	pout	cow	—	—	hour
/ɔj/	voice	toy	—	(oink)	coir
Lax vowels					
/ɪ/	pit	—	dish	ring	peer
/ɛ/	pet	—	mesh	length	pear
/æ/	pat	—	lash	rang	—
/ʌ/	putt	—	hush	rung	—
/ʊ/	put	—	push	—	cure
/ə/	—	—	—	—	purr

Allophonic variation of both RP and GA

Some variation is inherent; some is conditioned by the environment. The conditioned variation of vowels is usually determined by the shape of the syllable, the neighbouring consonants, or stress.

Length

As we have seen above, the tense vowels are slightly longer than the lax vowels. This length, which is independent of context, is called **inherent length**. For example, the tense vowel /ɑ/ is pronounced longer than the lax vowel [ɪ] in the same context: [kɑ·m kɪm] *calm, Kim*.

In addition to inherent length, there is **contextual length**. Try saying the pairs: *beet – bead, rick – rig, luff – love*. Say them aloud in a relaxed fashion. You will probably be able to notice that the vowel in *bead* is longer than the vowel in *beet*. Similarly, the vowels of *rig* and *love* are longer than those of *rick* and *luff*. The general rule in English is that vowels are longer before a voiced sound than before a voiceless sound. Now try saying the pair *bee – beat*, and you will be able to hear that the vowel in an open syllable is also longer than before the voiceless consonant. In diphthongs before voiced consonants, the vowel portion is lengthened, not the glide – [a·j a·w ɔ·j]. For /ɑ/ in this context, the transcription [ɑ:] shows a length somewhat longer than that shown by the raised dot alone [·], combining the inherent and the contextual length: [kɑ:d – kɑ·t] RP *card–cart* GA *cod–cot*. A raised dot [·] shows length, and a colon [:] shows even greater length.

Crystal and House (1988b) report that in connected speech tense vowels are about 1.5 times as long when stressed as when unstressed, and that lax vowels are about two times as long when stressed as when unstressed.

Vowels and stress

In Chapter 2, we distinguished three levels of stress: primary, secondary, and unstressed. The vowels we have been describing so far are the ones which occur with primary stress. As we mentioned above, the tense–lax distinction is found only in syllables with primary or secondary stress.

In unstressed syllables, the only common vowels are /ə ɪ/. Unstressed [ʊ] is sometimes found in RP; in GA, /u/ or /ə/ may be found instead.

	about	[əˈbawt]	*effect*	[əˈfɛkt]
	lightest	[ˈlajtɪst]	*village*	[ˈvɪlɪdʒ]
RP	*influence*	[ˈɪnflʊəns]	*educate*	[ˈɛdjʊˌkejt]
GA	*influence*	[ˈɪnˌfluəns]	*educate*	[ˈɛdʒəˌkejt, ˈɛdˌʒuˌkejt]

The distribution of unstressed vowels is complex. Sometimes /ɪ/ and /ə/ contrast in unstressed syllables: e.g., *roses* /ˈɹəwzɪz/ GA /ˈɹowzɪz/ and *Rosa's* /ˈɹəwzəz/ GA /ˈɹowzəz/. More often, however, they are in free variation in unstressed syllables. Different speakers may use different vowels: e.g., *goodness* /ˈgʊdnəs/ or /ˈgʊdnɪs/. Individual speakers may in fact use one vowel sometimes and the other at other times. Unstressed syllables are usually quite short.

Final /i/

At the end of a word, both RP and GA have an unstressed /i/ even though the syllable is open: /ˈhæpi/ *happy*, /ˈhæpɪli/ *happily*. Like other final vowels, this final /i/ is often a bit longer than other unstressed vowels. Older RP, some non-RP British accents, and some accents in the south-east of the US have [ɪ] in this position: /ˈhæpɪ/ *happy*, /ˈlɪlɪ/ *lily*.

Before /l/

Before /l/ the vowels /i u/ frequently have a schwa glide, symbolised here as [ə̯]: [piə̯ɫ] *peel*, [puə̯ɫ] *pool*. The vowel /ej/ sometimes becomes a diphthong with the same glide [eə̯]: [peə̯ɫ] *pail* (Figure 4.6).

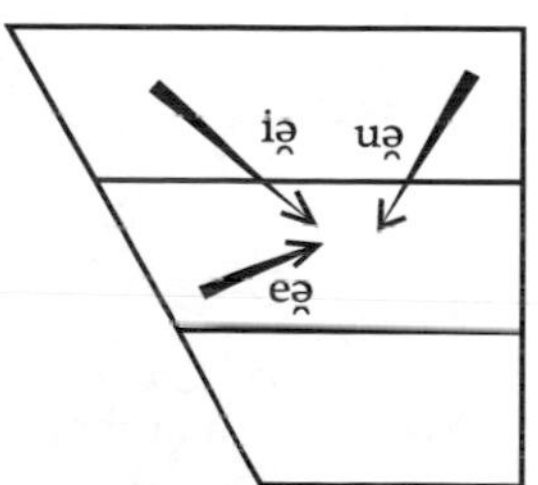

Figure 4.6
Glides before /l/

Nasalised vowels

Vowels occurring next to a nasal consonant /m n ŋ/ are frequently nasalised. This occurs when the movement of the velum does not coincide precisely with the boundaries of the nasal. In a word like *me* [mĩ], where the nasal precedes the vowel, the velum is down for the /m/ and is not raised until after the vowel has begun. The result is that the vowel following the /m/ is **nasalised**, that is while the vowel is being made, air is simultaneously flowing out through the nasal cavity. **Nasalisation** is shown by a **tilde** [˜] above the vowel.

In a word such as *ran* [ɹæ̃n], where the nasal follows the vowel, the velum is lowered during the vowel in anticipation of the following nasal consonant. In *man* [mæ̃n], where the vowel is both preceded and followed by nasal consonant, the entire vowel may be nasalised.

Technical terms

closed syllable
contextual length
inherent length
lax
linking /ɹ/
monophthong
nasalised
  nasalisation
nucleus
open syllable
phonotactics
rhotic
smoothing
tense
tilde
vocalic

Symbols

ː	**colon**	length
ˑ	**raised dot**	half length
˜	**superscript tilde**	nasalisation
ə̯		schwa glide

Exercises

Basic

1 Make broad and narrow transcriptions of the following words. Mark primary and secondary stress. For the narrow transcription, focus on the consonants: release, assimilation, dark /l/, taps, syllabic consonants.

	[broad]	[narrow]
pool-table		
millilitre		
nettle		
sliced		
wealthier		

2 Each of the following words is pronounced in more than one way by native speakers of English. For each, show two pronunciations, transcribed broadly, and underline the one that you yourself use. Be sure to mark primary stress.

either e.g.: /ˈajðəɹ/ /ˈiðəɹ/	*width*
arctic	*lieutenant*
lever	*ration*
shone	*falcon*

3 Find five words each using a different allophone of the phoneme /t/. Do not use the examples in Appendix A. For each word, write it in ordinary spelling, then phonetically in broad transcription, but showing the allophone of /t/ in narrow transcription.

4 Transcribe (broadly) the following sentences, and make a line drawing of each.

Jim set it down.

Rachel took a catnap.

She can go to Toronto tonight.

Betty didn't bite the back bacon. (Main stress on *back*)

5 Transcribe each of the following words, showing aspiration and overlapping. Make a line drawing for each, carefully showing the timing for the aspiration and overlapping.

print *scraped* *Atkins*

6 Read the following broad transcriptions:

fud dʌn bejk kiʃ mɪks ɹust
najf bɹɛd lɔ fɹaj mɔjst pɑt
kʊk lin mæʃ bɹawn najvz ti

7 Transcribe the following words broadly:

web *dig* *melt* *gnat* *puff* *bins*
come *soot* *dull* *pull* *dipped* *wealth*
loop *knead* *loud* *toyed* *tied* *psalm*
wipe *rogue* *nude* *waist* *combed* *louse*

8 Transcribe, using a narrow transcription for the consonants:

lift *dread* *splat* *tuft* *could* *tank*
wing *stunk* *plugs* *clam* *woods* *tap*
cud *stab* *scum* *twitch* *bunched* *tenth*

9 Tense and lax. For each of the following words, identify whether the vowel is tense or lax.

sound *air* *out* *this* *can* *said*
drink *sung* *cod* *put* *move* *write*
foist *rang* *world* *wipe* *fudge* *bathes*

10 For the following words, make a broad transcription marking stress:

loading *conveyor* *resident* *ginger* *retire*
elegy *resistance* *hospital* *coffin* *business*

11 With the following words, practise making short, medium, and long vowels. Be careful to keep your tongue steady so as not to produce a diphthong.

e.g.: *mad* [mæd mæˑd mæːd]
bed *bit* *foot* *lad* *cup* *look*

The following words have diphthongs. Pronounce each making the vowel portion of the diphthong first short, then long:

e.g.: *loud* [lawd laˑwd].
so *fine* *rhyme* *died* *coy* *bee* *do*
teak *wave* *sigh* *coo* *doe* *pay* *joys*

12 GA: This exercise is to give you practice in making the [ɒ] vowel of RP which GA lacks. First say [ɑ] as in *father*. Now saying [ɑ], slowly round your lips without changing the position of your tongue. If nothing else changes you should be saying [ɒ]. Practise the following combinations of [ɑ ɒ o].

ɑ	ɒ	o	ɒ	ɑ	ɒ
mɑmɒ	momɒ	sɒsɑ	sɒso	lɑdo	nɑfɒ
dɒso	gɒnɑ	mɑmɒmɑ	dɒdodɒ	kɒmɒdɑ	lomɒvo
pɒmɑdo	pomɑdɒ	pɑmɒdɑ	pomɒdɑ	sɑzɒnɑ	fɒbovɒ

Now try distinguishing [ɒ] and [ɔ]:

ɒ	ɔ	ɒ	ɔ		
mɒ	mɔ	mɒmɒ	mɔmɔ	mɒmɔ	mɔmɒ
lɔlɒ	lɒlɔ	sɔnɒ	sɒnɔ	dɔgɒ	pɒzɔ

Finally, try the following words with all three [ɑ ɒ ɔ]:

dɑ	sɔ	lɒ	ɑm	ɔg	ɒz
ɹɑfɔ	pɒnɔ	hɑtɒ	sɔdɒ	fɒkɑ	gɒlɔ
ɔvɒ	ɔmɒ	ɑbɔθɑ	ɑʃɒðɑ	jɔŋɒʒɔ	lɒdɔɹɒ

13 Say the word *my* [maj]. Now make the vowel part of the diphthong long [maaaaaaj]. Try to remove the [j] without changing the vowel: [maaaaa]. Practise the same steps with these words.

lie *sigh* *ride* *guide* *sign* *lime*

14 Try the same technique with *how* [haw]. Lengthen the diphthong to [haaaaaw], and then try to remove the glide: [haaaaa]. Practise with the following words:

cow *now* *sow* *town* *house (v.)* *gouge*

15 The GA vowels in *bay* and *go* phonetically are diphthongs [bej] and [gow]. Many languages have similar monophthongal vowels: [e o]. It is useful to learn to make these without any glide. If you have [əw] in *go*, try to imitate an American pronunciation [ow].

a. First, exaggerate the diphthongal quality of *bay* by stretching it out: [beeeeeejjj].

b. Now, focus on stretching out the vowel portion: [eeeeeeej]

c. Try again, keeping your mouth and tongue quite steady during the [e] portion.

d. Start over. Say a long [eeeeeej], but before you get to the glide, abruptly put in a glottal stop [ʔ] (i.e., hold your breath with your mouth open): [eeeeee?]. Make the glottal stop suddenly, trying not to anticipate it.

e. Now try saying [eeeeee] without the glottal stop and without any glide.

f. If you have difficulty with the preceding steps, try saying *Graham* [ˈɡɹe–əm]. The [e] here often has very little glide. Hold the first vowel steady and drop the second syllable, ending up with [ɡɹeeee].

g. Try the same procedures to say [o]. Start with [oooooow], then cut off the glide with a glottal stop [oooooo?], then just [oooooo].

For [o] it is useful to practise in front of a mirror. The [o] has moderate lip rounding, but the [w] glide has considerably more lip rounding; thus to get rid of [w], make sure that you are not changing the lip rounding.

h. English as spoken in northern England and Scotland has monophthongs [e:] and [o:] rather than [ej] and [ow]. Try imitating this type of accent.

Practise the following. First exaggerate the glides and use glottal stops to get rid of them. Then speed up slightly, and try to omit the glottal stop.

ejkej	ejke?	e?ke?	eke?	eke
owfow	owfo?	o?fo?	ofo?	ofo
nejsow	nejso?	ne?so?	neso?	neso
gowlej	gowle?	go?le?	gole?	gole
owkow	owko?	o?ko?	oko?	oko
ejmow	ejmo?	e?mo?	emo?	emo

Try the following, first with the diphthongs [ej ow], and then with monophthongs [e o].

The rain in Spain stays mainly in the plain.
Joe's folks hoped that most of the old blokes would go home.

16 GA: Vowels before /ɹ/. Make a narrow transcription of the following.

nurse	*care*	*bar*	*war*	*cork*	*fear*
sport	*dare*	*fire*	*sour*	*roar*	*cure*
fir	*fur*	*fern*	*mere*	*sure*	*bear*
hearth	*lure*	*sore*	*sire*	*north*	*lurch*

17 Vowels before /l/. Make a narrow transcription of the following.

dill	*sole*	*sell*	*aisles*	*doll*	*cull*
real	*cowl*	*full*	*fool*	*nails*	*Al*
oil	*ruled*	*kneel*	*foul*	*ghoul*	*dial*

18 Make a narrow transcription of the following, showing stress.

It was a dark and stormy night; the rain fell in torrents – except at occasional intervals, when it was checked by a violent gust of wind which swept up the streets (for it is in London that our scene lies), rattling along the housetops, and fiercely agitating the scanty flame of the lamps that struggled against the darkness.

Advanced

The instructions are given in RP.

19 /pɹəˈnawns/:

pʰik	kʰʊf	mæb	tʰɪŋ	vʌtʰ	gæ
wɪl	ŋæm	kʰæn	stʊ	splændz	twɛŋks
plʊmb	sklʌps	tlɛŋz	klʌŋgz	dlɪmbz	tʌd
skʰʌŋ	spʰlɪŋ	pædɪ	kɛgz	ŋʌfs	tʊpf

20 /ˌpɹæktɪs ˌsejɪŋ ðə ˈfɒləwɪŋ ˌwɜdz ɪn ˌswɑˈhili, ə ˌlæŋgwɪdʒ ˌspəwkən ˈwajdli ɪn ˌistən ˈæfɹɪkə; ˈpej əˌtɛnʃən tə ˌæspiˈrejʃən/:

/pɑ/	*roof*	/pʰɑ/	*gazelle*
/tɑndo/	*fungus*	/tʰɑndo/	*swarm*
/tʃuŋgu/	*cooking pot*	/tʃʰuŋgu/	*black ant*
/pʰembe/	*horn*	/pembe/	*big horn*
/tʰundu/	*hole*	/tundu/	*big hole*
/tʃʰupɑ/	*bottle*	/tʃupɑ/	*demijohn*
/kʰutɑ/	*walls*	/kutɑ/	*large walls*

21 /ˌpɹæktɪs wɪð ðə ˈfɒləwɪŋ ˌləw ˌbæk ˈvawəlz/:

dɑ	dɒ	sɔ	sɒ	gɔ	gɒ
ɑnɔ	ɒnɒ	ɑnɒ	bɔbɑ	bɒbɑ	bɒbɔ
gɔbɑ	zɒvɑ	lɔpɒ	ɹɒdɒ	mɒg	sɔk
dɒl	dɔl	mɑŋ	wɒŋ	θwɔd	glɒp

22 /ɪn ˌɛksəˌsajz ˈtɛn, jʊ ˌlɜnd tə ˈmejk ðə ˌsɪmpl̩ ˈvawəl/ [o] /wɪðˌawt ə ˈglajd. ˌpɹæktɪs ˈɔltəˌnejtɪŋ/ [ɔ o].

ɔ	o	ɔ	o		
nɔ	no	nonɔ	kɔko	fɔfo	tɔtɔ

23 /ðə ˌglɒtl̩ ˈstɒp/ [ʔ] /ɪz ˌfawnd ɪn ˈɪŋglɪʃ ɪn ə ˈkæʒʊəl ˌwej əv ˈsejɪŋ/ 'no' [ˈʔm̩ʔm̩] and in *uh-oh* [ˈʔʌˌʔəw].
/hɪnts/:

a. /ˈtejk ə ˌbɹɛθ, ˌkip jʊ ˈmawθ ˌəwpən, ˈsej/ [ɑ], /ən ˈsʌdn̩li ˌhəwld jʊ ˌbɹɛθ. ðə ˈslajt kætʃ ɪz ə glɒ]tl̩ ˈstɒp/

b. /pɹɪˌtɛnd tə ˈhɪˌkʌp, bət wɪð ɪnˈhejld ˌɛə. ˌju wɪl ˈstɒp ði ˌɪnwəd ˌfləw əv ˌɛə wɪð ə glɒtl̩ ˌstɒp. ˌtɹaj fə ðə ˈsejm ˌsawnd wɪð ˈɛksˌhejld ˌɛə/

c. /ˈtɹaj ˌsejɪŋ/ [ʔɑʔ], /ˈðɛn/ [ʔɑʔɑ], /ˈðɛn/ [ʔɑʔɑʔɑʔɑ].

d. /ˈnaw ˌtraj tə dɪsˈtɪŋgwɪʃ/ [sɑ – sɑʔ].

/ˈpɹæktɪs/:

fɑ	fɑʔ	li	liʔ	du	duʔ
mɛ	mɛʔ	dʒæ	dʒæʔ	θʌ	θʌʔ

/ˌtraj tə dɪsˈtɪŋgwɪʃ ə ˌvawəl ˈwɪð ən wɪðˈawt ə ˌglɒtḷ ˌstɒp ət ðə bəˈgɪnɪŋ/:

ɑ	ʔɑ	ɑʔ	ʔɛ	ɛ	ɛʔ	ʔi	i	iʔ
i	ʔi	iʔ	ʔi	ʔiʔi	iʔ	uʔ	u	ʔu

/ˌtɹaj ˈðiz/:

ko	koʔ	ʔok	bik	bi	biʔ	lʊʔ	lʊ	lʊʔ
ne	neʔ	neʔɑ	eʔ	eʔe	ʔeʔ	keʔ	ʔek	ke
ajˈdiə	ʔajˈdiə	ʔajˈdiʔə	ʔajˈdiə	ajˈdiə	ajˈdiəʔ			

24 /nejzḷ vawəlz. ði ˌɪŋlɪʃ sawnd əv səˈpɹajz, ɹɪtṇ/ *huh,* /ɪz ˌjuʒuəli ˈspəwkən wɪð ə ˈnezḷ vawəl/ [hʌ̃ʔ]. /ˌsej ˌðɪs ə ˈfju ˌtajmz tə ˌgɛt ðə ˈfil əv ə ˈ nezḷ ˌvawəl. ˌnaw ˌsej ə ˈlɒŋ/ [ʌ̃ʌ̃ʌ̃ʌ̃]. /ˌju ˌmej ˈfajnd ðət ɪt ˈhɛlps tə ˌgɛt ˈkwajt ɹɪˌlækst, ˌlɛt ju ˌhɛd ˈdɹɒp, ən ˌlɛt ði ˌɛə ˌfləw ˈawt əz ˈðəw jʊ wɜ ˈdɛd ˌtajəd./

/ˈtɹaj ˌsejɪŋ/ [ɑ̃ɑ̃ɑ̃ɑ̃]; /ˌðɪs ˌsawnds ˌsʌmθɪŋ ˌlajk ə ˈtʌgˌbəwt ˌhɔn. ˌtɹaj ðɪs wɪð ˈʌðə ˌvawəlz/: [ĩ ɪ̃ ẽ ɛ̃ æ̃ ɑ̃ õ ʊ̃ ũ ɑ̃j̃ ɑ̃w̃ ɔ̃j̃ ə̃].

/sej ðə ˈfɒləwɪŋ ˌsɛntṇsɪz, ˌmejkɪŋ ˌɔl ðə ˌvawəlz ˈnejzəˌlajzd; ju ˌʃʊd ˌtɹaj tə ˈsawnd əbˈnɒkʃəsli ˌwajni./

The rain in Spain stays mainly in the plain.
All my old clothes are already outside on the line.
My maid Mame mends minute moth holes.

/ˌnaw ˌtɹaj ðə ˈsejm ˌsɛntṇsɪz wɪð əz ˌlɪtḷ ˌnejzḷɪˈzejʃən əz jʊ ˈkæn./

25 /ˈbɪldˌʌp/:
[ˈpi tɛ ˈlɑ nɔ ˈfi ʃu]

/tə ˈdu ˌðɪs, ðə ˈfɜst ˌtajm ˈsej/	[ˈpi];
/ðə ˈsɛkənd ˌtajm ˈsej/	[ˈpi tɛ];
/ðə ˈðɜd ˌtajm ˈsej/	[ˈpi tɛ ˈlɑ];
/ðə ˈfɔθ ˌtajm ˈsej/	[ˈpi tɛ ˈlɑ nɔ]; /ˌɛt ˈsɛtəɹə/.

/ˌwɛn jʊ kən pɹəˈnawns ðə ˌhəwl ˈsikwəns, ˈpræktɪs ənˌtɪl jʊ kən ˌsej ɪt ˈkəmfətəbli ˈθɹi ˌtajmz ˌwɪðawt ˈlʊkɪŋ./

/ˈnaw ˌtɹaj səm ˌʌðəz/:

[ˈkɑ wi ˈɹɒ bɪ ˈŋæ mʊ]
[jʌ ˈtʃɔ gɪ ˈθu fʌ ˈvæ]
[ˈjɒ nʊ ŋi ˈðɛ ʒu hɛ]

/dɪd jʊ ˌpej əˈtɛnʃən tə ˌstɹɛs?/

26 /ˌwɜdz ɪn ðə ˈfɒləwɪŋ ˌlɪst ɑ ˌnəwn tə ˌhæv ˌdɪfɹənt pɹəˌnʌnsiˈejʃənz ɪn ˈvɛəɹɪəs ˌdajəˌlɛkts əv ˌɪŋglɪʃ. ˌtɹænˈskɹajb ðəm əˌkɔdɪŋ tə jʊɹ ˈəwn pɹəˌnʌnsiˌejʃən, ən ˈðɛn ˌbi ɒn ðə ˈlʊkˌawt fɔ ˌpipl̩ hɪɪ pɹəˈnawns ðəm ˌdɪfɹn̩tli. ˌtʃɛk ˌwɔt pɹəˌnʌnsiˈejʃn(z) ˈjʊ ˌdɪkʃn̩ɹɪ ˌgɪvz./

either	*lever*	*khaki*	*data*	*with*	*schedule*
lieutenant	*ration*	*shone*	*figure*	*apricot*	*pecan*
suggest	*thirteen*	*hover*	*progress*	*hearth*	*missile*
leisure	*envelope*	*status*	*economic*	*arctic*	*Newfoundland*
often	*path*	*resources*	*garage*	*anti–war*	*programme*

27 /ˌɹid ðə ˌfɒləwɪŋ ˈnɒnsn̩s ˌwɜdz əˈlawd/:

ˈbiʃʌ	tʊˈwej	ˈŋɑɹdʒu	ˈvɔjθawgɛ	ʒæˈtʃaw	hæˈʃelu
ˈhɪpɛpu	noˈlɛsɑ	ʒiˈdɑmʌ	ˈsɔfiŋɛ	wedoˈki	ɑloˈŋu
fʊˈmɔɹɪ	æˈgɹomʌ	ˈzɔðʊlæ	θɑnˈdʊflɛ	ˈskoefɔ	ɛlʒbɪnˈdʌ

28 The following story is one used extensively by the IPA as a standard short text; it has been translated and transcribed in hundreds of languages and dialects. Practise reading the following RP transcription.

[ðə ˈnɔθ ˈwɪnd ən ðə ˈsʌn]

[ðə ˈnɔθ ˈwɪnd ən ðə ˈsʌn wə dɪsˈpjutɪŋ ˈwɪtʃ wəz ðə ˈstɹɒŋgə, wən ə ˈtɹævlə kejm əˈlɒŋ ˈɹæpt ɪn ə ˈwɔm ˈkləwk. ðej əˈgɹid ðət ðə ˈwʌn hu ˈfəst səkˈsidɪd ɪn ˈmejkɪŋ ðə ˈtɹævlə tejk ɪz ˈkləwk ɒf ʃʊd bi kənˈsɪdəd ˈstɹɒŋgə ðən ði ˈʌðə. ˈðɛn ðə ˈnɔθ ˈwɪnd ˈblu əz ˈhɑd əz i ˈkʊd, bət ðə ˈmɔɹ i ˈblu ðə mɔ ˈkləwsli dɪd ðə ˈtɹævlə ˈfəwld ɪz ˈkləwk əˈɹawnd ɪm; ənd ət ˈlɑst ðə ˈnɔθ ˈwɪnd gejv ˈʌp ði əˈtɛmpt. ðɛn ðə ˈsʌn ʃɒn ˈawt ˈwɔmli ənd ɪˈmidjətli ðə ˈtɹævlə tʊk ˈɒf ɪz ˈkləwk. ən ˈsəw ðə ˈnɔθ ˈwɪnd wəz əˈblajdʒd tə kənˈfɛs ðət ðə ˈsʌn wəz ðə ˈstɹɒŋgəɹ əv ðə ˈtɹɪ.]

Chapter 5

English suprasegmentals

Speech consists not merely of a string of consonants and vowels pronounced one after the other. Rather, there are several levels of organisation. The study of **suprasegmentals** involves two different aspects. One is how segments are organised to form larger units, in particular, syllables. The other aspect is the study of phonetic entities which apply to syllables or longer stretches of speech.

In this chapter you will learn about:

- syllables and their structure;
- phonotactics;
- stress;
- intonation;
- rhythm.

Syllables

All languages have syllables. Although linguists are in general agreement as to what a **syllable** is in terms of consonants and vowels, phoneticians have a harder time in describing precisely the articulatory actions that make up a syllable and the actions that divide a string of consonants and vowels into a series of syllables. In Chapter 14 we will look more closely at various attempts to define the syllable.

Structure

The vowel of a syllable, and any following semivowel, is regarded as the **nucleus** or centre of the syllable. The elements before the nucleus are called the **onset**; and the elements after the nucleus are called the **coda**. The nucleus and coda taken together are known as the **rhyme**. Figure 5.1 shows the internal structure of a simple syllable like *pat* /pæt/.

A syllable with an empty coda is called an **open syllable**; one with a filled coda is called a **closed syllable**. Note that the /j/ or /w/ of a diphthong belongs to the nucleus and does not close a syllable.

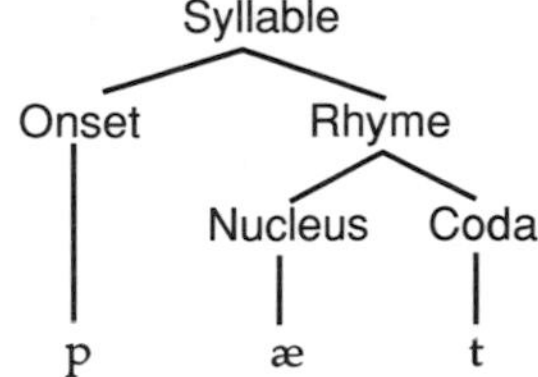

Figure 5.1 Structure of the syllable

open: /gu/ /naw/ /ɛ/ /kʌ/ /mej/
closed: /ʃin/ /ɛg/ /wajps/

Phonotactics

English has a large number of consonant clusters formed of sequences of consonants. Not all sequences of consonants occur. The study of the possible combinations of sounds in a language is called **phonotactics**. In this section, we will examine the phonotactics of the English syllable. We distinguish two types of **gaps** in the language, that is, forms which do not occur. Some combinations, as in /bnɪk/, violate a structural condition of the language; here, /bn/ is not a permitted consonant sequence for the onset. The other type can be illustrated by /lʊt/. I am unaware of any such word in English, although it is clearly a possible word; it is very similar to the words *look* and *foot*. Both /bnɪk/ and /lʊt/ are phonotactic gaps in English. The first type /bnɪk/ is simply not English; it is a **systematic gap**. The second type /lʊt/ is a possible, although unknown, form; it is called an **accidental gap**. Note that a systematic gap is language-specific: that is, although [bnɪk] impossible for English, it may occur in some other language.

Onset

All consonants except /ŋ/ occur as the onset of the syllable. The sound /ʒ/ is found initially in very few words, borrowed from French: *gigue, genre.* The onset may be empty, as in *ice, on, egg.*

Consonant clusters also occur in the onset. Generally, /s/ can precede a voiceless stop, and the approximants /l ɹ w j/ can follow a stop; however, not all of these possibilities actually occur. The following lists show clusters with a stop and another consonant in the onset:

stop + approximant

bl	bɹ	bw	bj	*blow, bray, bwana, beauty*
–	dɹ	dw	dj	*drive, dwell, dune*
gl	gɹ	gw	gj	*glow, green, Gwen, gules*

pl	pɹ	pw	pj	*plough, pry, pueblo, puny*
–	tɹ	tw	tj	*try, twin, tune*
kl	kɹ	kw	kj	*clay, cry, queen, cute*

/s/ + voiceless stop

sp	*spin*
st	*stop*
sk	*skip*

/s/ + voiceless stop + approximant

spl	spɹ	–	spj	*splice, sprint, spume*
–	stɹ	–	stj	*stray, stew*
skl	skɹ	skw	skj	*sclerosis, scrape, squall, skew*

The lists above show certain systematic gaps (/tl dl stl/), certain accidental gaps (/spw stw/), and certain rarities (/pw gj/). In English, the lateral /l/ occurs after /b p g k/ but not after /t/ or /d/: that is there are no words with /tl dl stl/ in the onset. Note that, as the second or third part of the onset, /j/ occurs only before the nucleus /u/. The clusters /pw/ and /bw/ are rare in native words although they occur in borrowed words such as *pueblo, bwana, Buenos (Aires)*. *Gules* /gjulz/ is a rare word used to describe the colour red in heraldry. This is the only example of word-initial /gj/ that I am aware of; however, /gj/ does occur word internally in words such as *ambiguity* or *legume*. Although the clusters /spw/ and /stw/ seem possible, I know of no examples. Clusters with /skl/ are very rare.

In addition to the clusters above, the following ones occur in the onset:

m + j	*mute*
f + l ɹ j	*fly, fry, few*
v + j	*view*
θ + ɹ w	*thrive, thwart*
s + l w f v	*sleep, swim, sphere, svelte*
ʃ + ɹ l	*shrine, schlemiel*
h + j	*huge*

Coda

The consonant /h/ does not occur in the coda; in RP /ɹ/ does not occur in the coda. The coda may be empty in one-syllable words if the nucleus contains a tense vowel. Many clusters occur in the coda; some are described below. Notice that many of the clusters exist only because a suffix (such as 'plural', 'third singular present', or 'past') in /s/ or /z/ is added. In *digs,* the cluster /gz/ is formed by adding the third singular present morpheme /z/ to the final /g/; I am unaware of any single morpheme ending in /gz/. Similarly, many clusters are formed by the addition of the past tense morpheme in /t/ or /d/.

p	+	t θ s	*apt, depth, hops*
t	+	θ s	*eighth, lets*
k	+	t s	*act, axe*
b	+	d z	*rubbed, cobs*
d	+	z	*adze*
g	+	d z	*lagged, digs*
tʃ	+	t	*latched*
dʒ	+	d	*judged*
f	+	t θ s	*miffed, fifth, reefs*
v	+	d z	*moved, leaves*
θ	+	t s	*unearthed, myths*
ð	+	d z	*bathed, wreathes*
s	+	p t k	*lisp, nest, task*
z	+	d	*buzzed*
ʃ	+	t	*hushed*
ʒ	+	d	*rouged*
m	+	p f θ d z	*damp, lymph, warmth, harmed, roams*
n	+	t tʃ θ s d dʒ z	*bent, lunch, tenth, sense, honed, lunge, tons*
ŋ	+	k d z	*bank, ringed, songs*
l	+	p t k d tʃ f v θ s z m n	*help, belt, milk, weld, milch, elf, delve, wealth, else, tells, harm, film, kiln*

GA only

ɹ	+	p t k tʃ f θ s ʃ b d g tʃ v z m n l	*harp, sort, dirk, lurch, wharf, earth, parse, kirsch, curb, mired, morgue, purge, carve, beers, harm, corn, furl*

English has a number of three consonant final clusters as well, and even a few with four consonants. I give only a few examples here.

sps	*lisps*	sts	*lists*
lps	*helps*	tθs	*eighths*
kts	*acts*	lks	*milks*
lvz	*shelves*	ndz	*ends*
lfθ	*twelfth*	lkts	*mulcts*
ksts	*texts*	ksθs	*sixths*

GA only

ɹbd	*absorbed*	ɹldz	*worlds*

In the nasal–fricative transitions /mf mθ ms nθ ns/, as in *lymph, warmth, glimpse, tenth, sense,* it is often difficult to say with certainty whether the nasal and the fricative follow each other directly or whether an intervening stop occurs, that is [lɪmf] (or [lɪɱf]) or [lɪmpf], [sɛns] or [sɛnts]. Some speakers seem to favour one pronunciation, and others favour the other. Some speakers may vary somewhat as well. I have never met a native speaker of English who consistently contrasted words like *cents* – *sense* with the presence or absence of [t]. In pronouncing these two forms, the activities of the vocal organs are the same; the difference is in the timing. In [wɪns] *wince* (Figure 5.2) the release of the stop is simultaneous with the closure of the nasal passage; with the pronunciation /wɪnts/, the alveolar opening follows the velic closure and the onset of voicelessness.

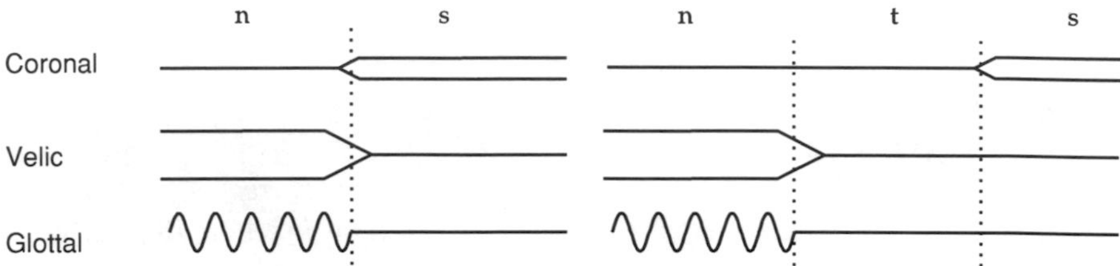

Figure 5.2 Timing of closures for *wince*: /wɪns/ and /wɪnts/

Syllable division

Usually syllables are fairly easy to count. For example, most English speakers can tell us that *intercontinental* has six syllables. On the other hand, it is sometimes difficult to divide a word into syllables. If we first look at just the segments in *dictate,* we can imagine three possible divisions, with /-/ showing the syllable break: *di-ctate, dic-tate, dict-ate* (Figure 5.3). The correct choice is determined by the principle of **maximisation of onsets**. This principle means that we make the onset as large as possible. In the case of *dictate,* the largest onset would be *di-ctate*; however, we note that /kt/ never occurs in English as the onset of the first syllable of a word. Therefore, we try the division *dic-tate*; here, /t/ is a possible onset for a word. The division of *dic-tate* thus results in the largest possible onset. This division agrees with the native intuition of most English speakers.

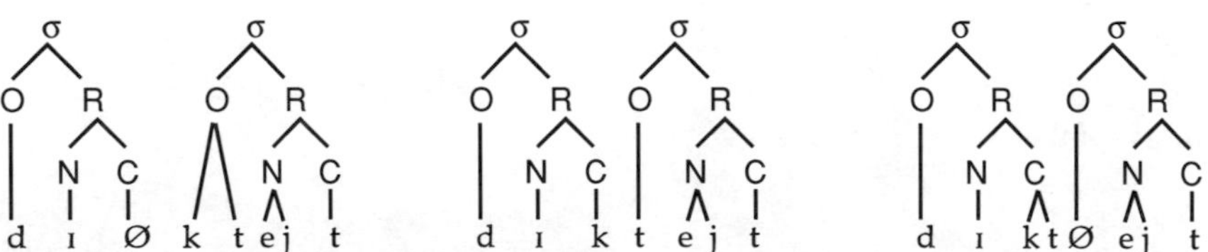

Figure 5.3 Possible syllable structures for *dictate*: *di-ctate, dic-tate, dict-ate*

Speakers of English, however, are less confident whether to divide *seven* as *se-ven* or *sev-en*. Neither one seems completely satisfactory to native speakers. According to the principle of maximisation of onsets, we would expect *se-ven* /ˈsɛ-vən/. This solution, however, produces a syllable /sɛ/ which violates our general principle that lax vowels do not occur in open syllables. We can resolve this problem by invoking a second principle of **ambisyllabicity** (Gussenhoven and Jacobs, 1998). This principle says that in an unstressed syllable, the first consonant of the onset also serves as the coda of the preceding syllable. Since the second syllable of *seven* is unstressed, the /v/ belongs both to the coda of the first syllable and to the onset of the second syllable (Figure 5.4).

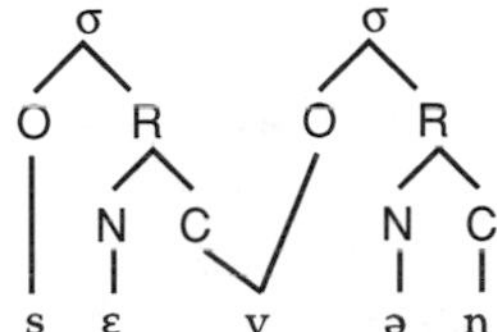

Figure 5.4 Syllable structures for *seven*, showing ambisyllabicity

A word such as *pantry* shows a more complex situation, but one which can still be resolved with the two principles just described. According to maximisation of onsets, the syllable division would be /n-tɹ/: /tɹ/ is a possible onset, but /ntɹ/ is not. According to the ambisyllabicity principle, /t/ is ambisyllabic and thus belongs both to the coda of the first syllable and to the onset of the second syllable (Figure 5.5).

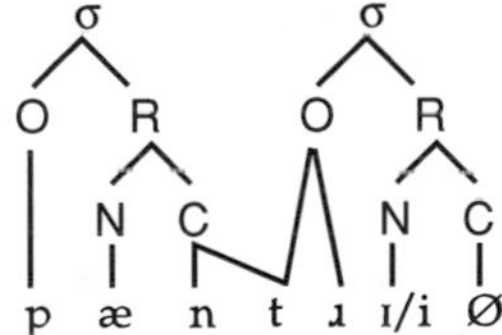

Figure 5.5 Syllabic structure of *pantry*

The notion of ambisyllabic consonants may seem a bit strange at first, but notice that with it, we can describe the rule of t-tapping of GA quite concisely: ambisyllabic /t/ is tapped [ɾ]. In GA *city*, the /t/ is ambisyllabic, and thus the tap is correctly predicted (Figure 5.6).

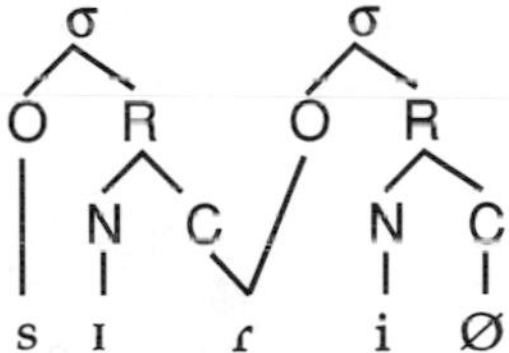

Figure 5.6 GA: syllabic structure of *city*

Stress

Stress is a complex auditory impression which the listener perceives as making one syllable more prominent than its neighbours. A number of different things, either individually, or in combination – greater loudness, higher pitch, greater length – contribute to the perception of stress. A stressed syllable in English often has all three of these characteristics. In other languages, stress may be created by using just one or two of the characteristics.

Levels of stress

A word like *telegram* /ˈtɛləˌɡɹæm/ has three levels of stress. You can easily hear that the first syllable /tɛ/ has the strongest stress. The last syllable /ɡɹæm/ is not so strongly stressed as /tɛ/, but it has stronger stress than the middle syllable /lə/. We mark the strongest or primary stress with a short raised stroke [ˈ], the middle level or secondary stress with a short lowered stroke [ˌ]. These strokes are placed before the onset of the affected syllable. The weakest level of stress, as in the middle syllable, is not marked.

Three levels of stress are adequate for a word like *elevator* /ˈɛləˌvejtə/ GA /ˈɛləˌvejtəɹ/. The second syllable /ə/ and the fourth /tə/ GA /-təɹ/ are both unstressed. The word *operator* /ˈɒpəˌɹejtə/ GA /ˈɑpəˌɹejtəɹ/ has a similar stress pattern. By itself, each of these words exhibits three levels of stress. We can, however, combine them into a single compound word *elevator-operator*. Just combining the transcriptions as /ˈɛləˌvejtəɹ-ˈɒpəˌɹejtə/ GA /ˈɛləˌvejtəɹ-ˈɑpəˌɹejtəɹ/ is not enough in itself. This compound word is ordinarily pronounced with a greater stress on *elevator* than on *operator*. There is a general rule in English that a phrase has only one primary stress. The effect of this rule is that /ˈɛl/ continues to have a primary stress, but the other stresses are reduced by one level: /ˈɛlə‿vejtəɹ-ˌɒpə‿ɹejtə/ GA /ˈɛlə‿vejtəɹ-ˌɑpə‿ɹejtəɹ/. Here, a subscript stroke /ˌ/ continues to show secondary stress, and a lowered arch /‿/ shows a new level of stress, **tertiary stress**. Syllables with the weakest level of prominence are called **unstressed** and are unmarked in the transcription.

We could probably continue this extension of the number of stress levels. In fact, however, it is almost impossible to be certain of the relative level of stress in comparing syllables that are separated by more than a few syllables. Say the sentence *Where did you put the paper I brought home last night?* and try to decide whether the stress levels of *put* and *last* are the same or different.

In our transcriptions of English, we will generally mark only three levels of stress: primary, secondary, unstressed. Tertiary stress will occasionally be marked when it is relevant. In rapid speech, syllables with tertiary, and sometimes even secondary, stress are often reduced to unstressed. In extremely slow or careful speech, syllables normally unstressed may acquire

Table 5.1 Strong and weak forms

	Strong	Weak
and	/ˈænd/	/ənd, ən, n̩/
them	/ˈðɛm/	/ðəm, əm/
as	/ˈæz/	/əz/
the	/ˈði/	/ðə, ðɪ/
a	/ˈej ~ ˈæ/	/ə/
of	/ˈɒv/ GA /ɑv/	/əv, ə/
he	/ˈhi/	/i/
because	/bɪˈkɒz/ GA /bɪˈkɔz/	/bɪkəz/

tertiary or even secondary stress. Generally, every phonetic phrase contains one and only one primary stress.

English stress has been the subject of extensive research in recent years. This work, known as metrical theory, has generally been phonological, even syntactic, in nature, and has been less concerned with the phonetic nature of the syllable. It has emphasised the point that stress is relational, that a certain syllable has stronger or weaker stress than its neighbours. In Chapter 14, we will look at the stress patterns of various languages, comparing them to that of English.

Strong and weak forms

Read the following sentence aloud emphasising the italicised word:

> *That* is the book that I wanted.

You probably pronounced the first *that* as /ˈðæt/, and the second one as /ðət/. Many words in English are pronounced both with and without stress depending on the structure of the sentence. The presence or absence of stress changes the quality of the vowel. With stress, either primary or secondary, we get a full vowel, such as in /ˈðæt/; without stress, we get one of the unstressed vowels /ɪ ə ʊ/, as in /ðət/. The form with stress is called the **strong form**, and the form without stress is called the **weak form**. Generally, it is words such as articles, prepositions, conjunctions, and pronouns which have this alternation; verbs, nouns, and adjectives generally do not. Table 5.1 gives a few common examples.

In weak forms, usually vowels are lost or changed, but with some words, such as *and*, consonants may be lost as well.

A characteristic of formal speech is that it is slower than colloquial speech. In slow speech the phrases are smaller, and thus more words are stressed and fewer are left without stress. Thus, an utterance spoken in a formal style has more strong forms than the same utterance spoken in a colloquial style.

Sometimes people think that the weak forms are 'wrong' or 'inferior'. This is not the case. Native speakers of English from all social classes regularly use weak forms. Not to use weak forms when they are appropriate gives English a stilted, artificial sound. If you are not a native speaker of English, you may find it useful to practise the weak forms, as they are often not taught sufficiently. Gimson (1980: 261–3) has quite an extensive list of weak forms. See also the exercises at the end of this chapter.

It is interesting to note that for some people, the original strong form has been lost and a new one created. The environments which cause prepositions and articles to be stressed are very rare. We use the weak forms most of the time, rarely needing the strong forms. For some people, particularly GA speakers, the strong form of a word such as *of* is so rare that the older strong /ˈɒv/ GA /ˈɑv/ has been lost. In the rare cases where a strong form is needed, the /ə/ of the weak form /əv/ is stressed to the most similar vowel sound of /ʌ/ as in /ˈʌv/. As a result, many GA speakers have /ˈfrʌm/, /ˈðʌ/, and /ˈwʌz/ rather than the older GA /ˈfrɑm/, /ˈði/, and /ˈwɑz/. By contrast, GA speakers do not have a weak form for *my;* some British speakers, however, use /mi/ as the weak form in casual speech, although this is not normal in the RP accent outside a few set phrases.

Pitch and intonation

Pitch is the quality we hear in playing two different notes on the piano. In speech, we control the pitch of an utterance by changing the vibration rate of the vocal folds. The faster they vibrate, the higher the pitch. We will examine this in greater detail in Chapter 14.

Some languages, like Chinese, use pitch to distinguish different words; they are called **tone languages** (see Chapter 14). In such languages a word spoken with a high pitch might be a completely different word from the same segments spoken with a low pitch. English does not work like this; it does, however, distinguish different phrases and sentences with different intonation contours. **Intonation** is the use of pitch in a phonetic phrase.

Each of the two sentences in Figure 5.7 constitutes a single phonetic phrase. They are the same except that one is a statement, and the other a question. The major stress is on *computer*.

The pitch pattern of each sentence is drawn above the sentence. In each utterance, the pitch pattern has two parts. For both utterances, the pitch gradually falls in the first part; the second part of the pitch pattern, however, differs for the two utterances. In the statement, the pitch starts high and falls; in the question, the pitch starts low and rises. The pitch pattern for an utterance is called the **intonation contour**. The intonation system of English is very complex and not completely understood. We will examine a number of typical contours.

Marge has a new com**pu**-ter.

Marge has a new com**pu**-ter?

Figure 5.7 Intonation contours of a statement and a question

Contours

Try saying the sentence in Figure 5.8 with the major stress on *Thursday*.

Nancy bought a new house on **Thurs**-day.

Figure 5.8 Intonation contour for a statement with stress on *Thursday*

You can hear that the pitch starts moderately high and falls slightly. At the stressed syllable of *Thursday*, the first curve stops, and a new contour starts from a high pitch and once again falls. Now, move the major stress to *house* (Figure 5.9).

Nancy bought a new **house** on Thursday.

Figure 5.9 Intonation contour for a statement with stress on *house*

We find two falling contours again, except that the second one starts at the stressed syllable of *house*. Try the same sentence once more with the major stress on *new* (Figure 5.10).

Nancy bought a **new** house on Thursday.

Figure 5.10 Intonation contour for a statement with stress on *new*

Again, we have two contours with the second beginning at the major stressed syllable of the sentence. You can experiment with the intonation when the major stress is on *Nancy*, *bought*, and even *a* or *on*. The intonation contours shown for these examples are by no means the only ones possible for such sentences; they are, nevertheless, commonly used as neutral contours.

Typically, we find that in a simple statement like the sentence above, the intonation contour has two parts with the break between them coming at the beginning of the tonic syllable. The **tonic syllable** is the syllable of the phrase having primary stress. In the example given in this section the tonic syllable is the syllable in the bold word with the primary stress.

You might wonder what would happen if the first syllable of the utterance were the tonic syllable. Try saying the sentence again, stressing *Nancy* (Figure 5.11).

Nancy bought a new house on Thursday.

Figure 5.11 Intonation contour for a statement with stress on first word, *Nancy*

Here, the tonic syllable /ˈnæn/ is at the beginning of the second part of the contour, but the first part of the contour is empty and thus does not occur.

This same intonation contour used for statements is also used for calling someone. Think of yourself calling for children (Figure 5.12).

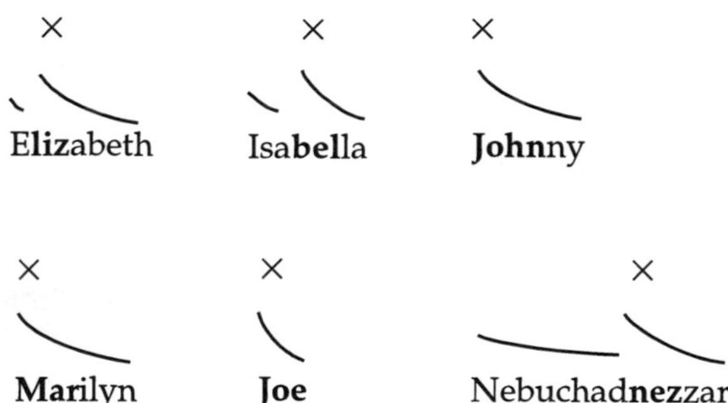

Figure 5.12 Intonation contours for names of varying length. X marks the tonic syllable

The intonation contour is a general shape. We take whatever phonetic material we are given and fit it to the intonation contour, placing the tonic syllable properly. The main break in the contour is determined by the position of the tonic syllable.

To place an intonation curve over an utterance, first mark the tonic syllable with an ×. Next, stretch the right part of the intonation curve to fit over the last part of the utterance beginning at the tonic syllable. Last, stretch the left part of the curve to fit over any remaining part of the utterance to the left of the tonic syllable. As you see in Figure 5.12 with *Johnny, Marilyn,* and *Joe,* this part may be empty.

So far we have focused on one intonation contour. There are, however, a large number of them. We will now examine a few others.

English has three basic types of questions as shown in Table 5.2.

Table 5.2 Types of question in English

Word order	Type	Intonation contour	Example
regular	yes–no	question	*Nancy bought a new computer?*
inverted	yes–no	statement	*Did Nancy buy a new computer?*
inverted	wh-word	statement	*What did Nancy buy?*

In questions with regular word order, the verb follows (here *bought*) the subject; with inverted word order, the verb (here *did*) precedes the subject. **Yes–no questions** require an answer of 'yes' or 'no'. **Wh-questions** contain a wh-word such as *what, who, where, when, why,* or *how* and ask the listener to fill in a blank (e.g., *a new computer*). Where the word order is the same for a statement and a question (e.g., *Nancy bought a computer*), a special intonation contour (Figure 5.13) for questions tells the listener that the utterance

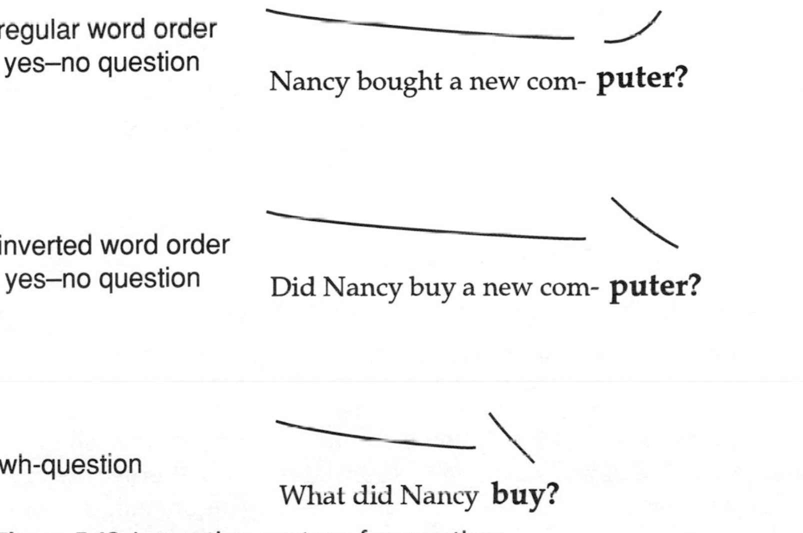
regular word order
yes–no question
Nancy bought a new com- **puter?**
inverted word order
yes–no question
Did Nancy buy a new com- **puter?**
wh-question
What did Nancy **buy?**

Figure 5.13 Intonation contour for questions

is a question, not a statement. In questions with inverted word order, the word order signals the fact that the utterance is a question; as a result, no special intonation contour is required.

It is possible to use a question intonation contour with a wh-question, as in Figure 5.14, but this is usually interpreted as *Did I hear you correctly in saying 'What did Nancy buy?'*

What did Nancy **buy?**

Figure 5.14 Wh-question with rising intonation contour

There are special contours for counting or listing things (Figure 5.15). We use a rising intonation for non-final items, and a falling intonation for the final one.

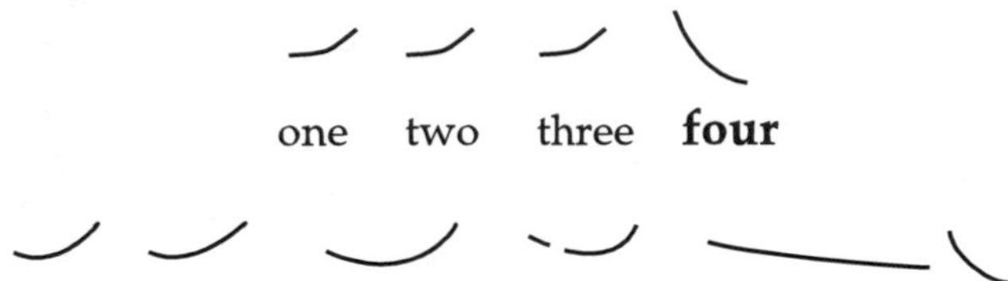

Jane Wilbur Winifred Imelda and Mrs. Ben**oit**

Figure 5.15 Two examples of a list contour

Note that the rising contour shows that the series is not finished. We immediately recognise that the list is over when we hear the falling contour.

Subordinate clauses preceding the main clause typically have a contour with a more level pitch, as in Figure 5.16. The more level pitch on *soon* tells us that the clause is over, but not the sentence.

If he comes **soon**, we will be able to make the **mov**ie.

Figure 5.16 Intonation contour showing a subordinate clause

There is a great variety of intonation contours available in English. Most sentences are capable of being said with several different patterns. The ones shown here are common, but by no means the only intonation contours possible for the sentences illustrated.

Rhythm

English sentences follow certain patterns of **rhythm**. Say the following sentence aloud at a normal speaking rate:

Which is the train to Bath, please?

Leaving aside the difference of primary and secondary stress, the syllables *which, train, Bath, please* all bear greater stress than the other syllables. Now, clap your hands together at even time intervals, like a metronome. While you are doing this, say the sentence again, say *which* just as your hands come together. You will likely find that the stressed syllables also fall on the beat of your hands. We can show this using × for the hand-beat.

×	×	×	×
Which is the	*train to*	*Bath,*	*please?*

The sentence consists of four time units called feet. Each **foot** has one stress, and the stresses come at equal intervals of time. Thus, each foot occupies the same amount of time. The first foot *which is the* has three syllables; the second foot *train to* has two; and the last two feet *Bath* and *please* have only one foot each.

In the sentence *Which is the train to Manchester, please?*, we can see that the three syllables of *Manchester* are spoken more quickly so that they take the same amount of time as the single syllable of *Bath.*

×	×	×	×
Which is the	train to	Manchester,	please?

Note that if a foot has several syllables, the syllables are said faster; however, if a foot has only one syllable, the nucleus is lengthened. This is necessary to equalise the time between stresses.

In the following examples, notice that each phrase constitutes a single foot and takes the same amount of time. As more syllables are added to the first foot, you can hear that the duration of the syllable *speed* /spid/ decreases.

× ×	× ×	× ×
speed demon	speedy demon	speedily driven

The equal timing of feet is a tendency rather than an absolute requirement. Poetry is often written to emphasise this quality and often has very evenly timed feet. Prose offers somewhat more variety. Languages in which stresses come at equivalent intervals, such as English, are called **stressed-timed**. In Chapter 7, we will discover that French is a **syllable-timed** language, with each syllable occurring at equivalent intervals of time.

Technical terms

- ambisyllabicity
- closed syllable
- coda
- foot
- gap
  - accidental gap
  - systematic gap
- intonation
  - intonation contour
- maximisation of onsets
- nucleus
  - nuclei
- onset
- open syllable
- phonotactics
- pitch
- rhyme
- rhythm
- stress
- stressed-timed
- strong form
- suprasegmental
- syllable
- syllable-timed
- tertiary stress
- tone language
- tonic syllable
- unstressed
- weak form
- wh-question
- yes–no question

Symbol

⌢ **lowered arch** tertiary stress

Exercises

Basic

1 For each of the following consonant clusters, find two words with the cluster in the onset of the first syllable. Do not use the examples on pp. 89–90. Use ordinary orthography.

e.g.: pj *pure, putrid*

br kl stɹ θw

2 Transcribe and draw labelled syllable trees for the following words:

plough *lists* *repeat* *comfort* *ready* *rusted*

3 Put an X over the tonic syllable, and apply the following intonation curve to the following words:

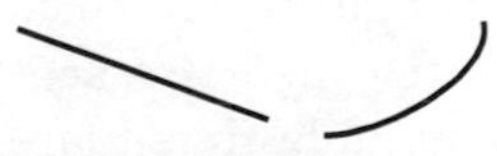

Figure 5.17

trombone *clarinet* *piccolo*

flute *bugle* *piano*

4 Find five words with weak forms. For each, give the strong form for each and as many weak forms as you find.

5 Transcribe casual forms for the following. Put the primary stress on the pronoun:

e.g.: do ˈI /dwaj/
do ˈyou does ˈhe did ˈI did ˈyou did ˈhe

6 Transcribe the following with three degrees of stress: /ˈ/ preceding a syllable with strong stress, /ˌ/ before syllables with secondary stress, and unstressed syllables unmarked. Remember that in English almost all unstressed syllables have one of the vowel nuclei /ə ɪ ʊ/ or a syllabic consonant.

social	*noises*	*human*	*whistle*	*animal*	*creature*
practice	*finger*	*of course*	*the book*	*a hundred*	*redden*

7 Read the following nonsense words aloud. Some are potential English words and some are not. Can you tell which ones could not be English words? Why not?

stɛks	blɪnd	pluθk	ðɑd	ŋæt	flɔjf
plʊθ	tluð	hɪmpks	dwawn	bɹajl	ðʌŋd
pawb	sklʊŋk	lbog	θɹʌtʃ	vlejmb	knujθs

8 Many phrases and words have two stresses. Commonly the secondary stress immediately precedes the strong stress. Transcribe, marking primary and secondary stress.

irate	*produce (v.)*
verbose	*chaotic*
urbane	*outstanding*

9 Transcribe, marking primary and secondary stress:

centimetre	*laboratory*	*fundamental*
the darkest one	*four o'clock*	*at the school*

10 Transcribe the following words. For each word, think of three others which have exactly the same stress pattern:

Chinese	*alone*	*invoice*	*husband*	*understand*	*quantity*
appetite	*tomato*	*remarkable*	*rhinoceros*	*enumerate*	*affiliation*

11 Many words vary in pronunciation, having syllables occurring either as a secondary stress with a full vowel or as unstressed with a weak vowel; the unstressed form occurs more often in casual speech, whereas the full vowel occurs in slower, more formal speech.

Transcribe and pronounce the following using both styles:

e.g.:	*financial*	/ˌfajˈnænʃl̩/	/fɪˈnænʃl̩/
	pronounce	*umbrella*	*subsumed*
	repeat	*Sir William*	*St George*

12 For each of the following words, transcribe how it occurs as a strong form, and then transcribe as many weak forms for each that you can find:

was *them* *at* *for* *to* *her*

13 Transcribe the following, paying particular attention to the vowels in the unstressed syllables:

We watched Oliver Twist *Wednesday evening.*
Incandescent lighting changes the appearance of colours.

14 For each syllable in the following, draw a labelled tree showing the *onset, rhyme, nucleus, and coda*:

not	*at*	*or*	*can*	*roads*	*splint*
flayed	*eyes*	*bookcase*	*twilight*	*clubhouse*	*Norway*
fearful	*olympic*	*adventure*	*marry*	*city*	*representation*
sudden	*idea*	*definition*	*folly*	*citadel*	*alabaster*

15 Find two words beginning with each of clusters /pl bl kl gl/.

e.g.: pl *play, pleonasm*

What other initial clusters have /l/ as the second element? Give two examples for each cluster you can think of.

e.g.: fl *fly, flounder*

16 In each of the following, draw the intonation contour.

Charlotte brought in the last of the corn.	*Is Harold coming?*
When is Harold coming?	*Alpha, beta, gamma, delta, epsilon.*
If Harold is coming, I'm leaving.	*The more, the merrier.*

17 In each of the following utterances, mark the primary stress with a raised stroke [ˈ]. Say them aloud, speaking naturally. Try tapping the intonation of the sentence with a pencil; the syllable with primary stress will be the loudest one. There will be only one primary stress in each utterance.

e.g.:	*at the table* →	*at the ˈtable*
in the kitchen	*good morning*	*I saw a rabbit.*
every Thursday	*each and every book*	*lost and found*

Try pronouncing each phrase by moving the primary stress to the other words. This will often create possible phrases, but ones which would only occur in unusual circumstances:

e.g.: *on the ˈtable* *ˈon the table* *on ˈthe table*

Now go back and listen for secondary phrases. These will sound stronger than other syllables, but not so strong as the syllable with primary stress. Mark them with a lowered stroke [ˌ] (after you have marked the primary stress). Note that a phrase may have more than one secondary stress.

e.g.: *vaˌnilla ˈice ˌcream*

18 In the following sentences, mark the primary stress and as many secondary stresses as you find. Always mark the primary stress first.

The building's falling down.
He hasn't shown up yet.
We bought coffee from the child. (not tea)
The future I've already seen! (i.e., *I have already seen the future.)*
It's not altogether correct.

19 Following the instructions on pp. 98–9, place the intonation curve used in Figure 5.12 on the following words. (Be sure to mark the tonic syllable.)

China	*Canada*	*Australia*
Wales	*Barcelona*	*New York*

Do the same thing with the intonation curve shown in Figure 5.13 for a yes–no question with regular word order. Place this curve on the words just given.

20 Say the following poem aloud, clapping your hands at regular intervals. Mark the stressed syllables with an X. Read it aloud again, timing your reading so that each syllable marked X occurs at the same time as your hands clap.

Ring around the rosie,
Pocket full of posey
Hasha, hasha,
They all fall down.

21 The following poem has two silent beats; that is, if you clap your hands as in Exercise 20, some beats will have no words. Mark all the rhythmical stresses with an X. See if you can discover where the silent beats are. Mark them with an X as well. Try repeating the poem without a break.

Row, row, row your boat,
Gently down the stream,
Merrily, merrily,
Merrily, merrily.
Life is but a dream.

Advanced

Some instructions are in GA.

22 /ˌitʃ əv ðə ˈfɑlowɪŋ ˌwərdz ˌhæz ə ˈstɹɔŋ ˌfɔɹm ənd ət ˈlist ˌwʌn ˈwik ˌfɔɹm. ˌtɹænˈskɹajb ðə ˈstɹɔŋ ˌfɔɹm ənd əz ˈmɛni ˌwik ˌfɔɹmz əz ˌju kən ˌfajnd./

could *them* *at* *Saint* *have* *us*

23 *Syntax* is the study of the structure of sentences; it can be transcribed as /ˈsɪnˌtæks/. The tax on alcohol and tobacco could be called a *sin tax*. Try saying *syntax* and *sin tax*. Some people distinguish these two forms by lengthening the first syllable of *sin tax*, but not of *syntax*.

syntax /ˈsɪnˌtæks/ *sin tax* /ˈsɪnːˌtæks/

Try another example. A *greenhouse* [ˈɡɹinˌhaws] is a 'building for growing plants'. The *Greene house* [ˈɡɹinːˌhaws] is a 'house belonging to the Greene family'. For some speakers at least, this last phrase has a lengthening of the first syllable. Not everyone makes such lengthenings.

/ˌtɹaj ˈðiz əɡˌzæmpl̩z tə ˌsi ɪf ju ˌhæv ðɪs ˈlɛŋθənɪŋ/:

Long Island is a long *island.*	(Contrastive stress on second *long*.)
My suitcase is unpacked.	('I haven't put anything in it yet.')
My suitcase is unpacked.	('I have taken everything out of it.')

In the last pair of sentences, look for lengthening in the syllable *un-*.

24 /ðə ˈfɑlowɪŋ səˌlɛkʃn̩ ɪz fɹəm ˌdʒuljəs ˈsizəɹ, ˌʃowɪŋ haw ɪt wʊd əv bɪn pɹəˈnawnst ɪn ˈʃejkˌspɪɹz ˌdej. ˌpɹæktɪs jʊɹ sɪkstinθ ˌsɛntʃɹi ˈæktɪŋ ˌskɪlz/

Julius Cæsar 3.2.79–86

ˈfrɛnz ˈroːmənz ˈkʌntrɪmən	*Friends, Romans, countrymen,*
ˈlɛnd mi juɹ ˈiːɹz.	*lend me your ears;*
ʌj ˈkʌm tə ˈberɪ ˈseːzəɹ	*I come to bury Cæsar,*
ˈnɒt tʊ ˈpreːz ɪm.	*not to praise him.*
ðɪ ˈiːvɪl ðət ˈmɛn ˈduː	*The evil that men do*
ˈlɪvz ˈæːftəɹ ðəm	*lives after them,*
ðə ˈɡʊd ɪz ˈɔːft ɪnˈtəːrɪd	*The good is oft interred*
wið ðəɹ ˈboːnz	*with their bones;*
ˈsoː let ɪt ˈbiː wiθ ˈseːzəɹ.	*So let it be with Cæsar.*
ðə ˈnoːbl̩ ˈbruːtəs	*The noble Brutus*
əθ ˈtoːld ju	*hath told you*
ˈseːzəɹ wəz æmˈbɪʃɪəs	*Cæsar was ambitious;*
ɪf ɪt ˈwɛːɹ ˈsoː	*If it were so,*
ɪt wɔz ə ˈɡriːvəs ˈfɔːlt	*it was a grievous fault,*
ən ˈɡriːvəslɪ	*And grievously*
əθ ˈseːzəɹ ˈæːnsəɹd ɪt.	*hath Cæsar answer'd it.*

(Adapted from Kökeritz (1953) by permission.)

25 /ˈtɹænˌskɹajb də ˌpæsɪdʒ əv ˌdʒuljəs ˈsizəɹ əz ɪt wəd bi ˌsɛd təˈdej ɪn ˈjʊɹ ˌdajəˌlɛkt. ˌʍat ˈdɪfəɹənsɪz də jʊ ˈfajnd bəˌtwin ˈjʊɹ ˌæksɛnt ən ˈʃejkˌspɪɹz?/

26 The RP version of the story was given at the end of the exercises in Chapter 4. Here is the GA version. Practise reading the transcription. For practice in English accents, you could change this version to RP and vice versa.

[ðə ˈnɔɹθ ˈwɪnd ən ðə ˈsʌn]

[ðə ˌnɔɹθ ˌwɪnd ən ðə ˈsʌn wəɹ dɪsˈpjutɪŋ ˌʍɪtʃ wəz ðə ˈstɹɔŋgəɹ, ˌʍɛn ə ˈtɹævləɹ kejm əˌlɔŋ ˈɹæpt ɪn ə ˌwɔɹm ˌklowk. ðej əˌgɹid ðət ðə ˌwʌn hu ˈfəɹst səkˌsidɪd ɪn ˌmejkɪŋ ðə ˌtɹævləɹ ˌtejk ɪz ˈklowk ˌɔf ʃʊd bi kənˌsɪdəɹd ˈstɹɔŋgəɹ ðən ðɪ ˌʌðəɹ. ˈðɛn ðə ˌnɔɹθ ˌwɪnd ˌblu əz ˈhɑɹd əz i ˌkʊd, bət ðə ˈmɔɹ i ˌblu ðə ˌmɔɹ ˈklowsli dɪd ðə ˌtɹævləɹ ˈfowld ɪz ˌklowk əˌɹawnd ɪm; ənd ət ˈlæst ðə ˌnɔɹθ ˌwɪnd ˌgejv ˈʌp ði əˌtɛmpt. ˌðɛn ðə ˌsʌn ˌʃown ˌawt ˈwɔɹmli ənd ɪˈmidiətli ðə ˈtɹævləɹ ˌtʊk ˌɔf ɪz ˌklowk. ən ˌsow ðə ˈnɔɹθ ˌwɪnd wəz əˌblajdʒd tə kənˈfɛs ðət ðə ˈsʌn wəz ðə ˌstɹɔŋgəɹ əv ðə ˌtu.]

Chapter 6

English accent differences

English is spoken as a native language by some 377 million people around the world (Crystal, 1995). It is spoken on every continent. Like all languages, English varies in the way it is spoken from place to place. These varieties are called **dialects**; we use the term **accent** when referring to only the phonetic aspects of a dialect.

In this chapter you will learn about:

- history of English;
- various English accents.

Background

Two thousand years ago, Britain was inhabited by Celtic-speaking people known as Britons, the ancestors of the present-day Welsh of Wales and Bretons of France. In 55 BC, Julius Caesar visited Britain, and from AD 43 Roman soldiers colonised and ruled southern Britain until the early part of the fifth century when Rome recalled the soldiers to help with difficulties at home. The political vacuum created by the Romans' departure was filled by sizeable settlements of Germanic-speaking people from continental Europe from AD 450. These people are traditionally known as the Angles, Saxons, and Jutes; in Britain they became known as the English (< Angle-ish 'belonging to the Angles'). They established themselves strongly, pushing back the Britons towards the west and also south across the water to Brittany. The English seized and settled all of Britain except for Wales and the north of Scotland. Their early language is known as Anglo-Saxon or Old English.

Old English is very different from Modern English. In addition to internal changes, English was influenced somewhat by the Scandinavians who held much of England in the ninth and tenth centuries, and to a much greater extent in the Middle English period following the conquest of the French-speaking Normans in 1066.

From the beginning, accent differences existed among the English. Certainly there is considerable variation now in the local accents between Scotland in the north and the southern coast of England. The rural accents show the greatest variation, although they seem to be slowly giving way to urban accents. There is less variation in the various accents of the cities, although generally enough to tell where someone comes from.

About the same time as the Germanic speakers invaded Britain (fifth century AD), Gaelic speakers from Ireland conquered much of Scotland. The Anglo-Saxons settled in the lowlands (south and east) of Scotland, and the Gaels in the north-west. Since then, the use of English has gradually increased and pushed Scots Gaelic back to the north-west coastal region. The lowland dialects of English have many interesting features, such as *twa* /twɑ/ for 'two' and *ane* /en/ for 'one'.

In the Gaelic-speaking highlands (the north and west) of Scotland, English was introduced widely in the nineteenth century by teachers speaking middle-class Scottish English. As a result, highland English has standard grammatical features with an urban Scottish accent and few of the features specifically associated with rural lowland speech.

In Wales, English has steadily pushed west over the centuries, gradually eroding the territory where Welsh is spoken. English is the native language of more than 80% of the people of Wales. As in the Scottish highlands, English was introduced in Wales largely through the school system with the result that the grammar of Welsh English is essentially the same as that of standard English although there are differences in pronunciation and vocabulary.

Ireland previously spoke Irish Gaelic, a Celtic language. Since the seventeenth century English has been spoken there, first in Dublin, then spreading out from the capital. The north of Ireland was colonised in the early seventeenth century by English speakers, many of whom had Scottish accents. During the nineteenth century almost the entire country adopted English as its native language.

English reached North America with the British settlers in the early seventeenth century. The earliest settlers were from England, but they were soon joined by English speakers from Scotland and Ireland as well. Much of the West Indies became English speaking; however, its linguistic history is a bit more complicated, as we will see when we look at Jamaican English.

The great colonial enterprise of the nineteenth century saw English become established in South Africa, Australia, and New Zealand as English-speaking peoples settled in those areas. English became the predominant second language in other areas such as India, Singapore, Hong Kong, and much of Africa.

General scheme

In the rest of this chapter, we will be looking at a variety of English accents, comparing them either to RP or GA. First we will look at accents in the British Isles and then overseas. The purpose of these brief descriptions is, on the one hand, to present the variety of English for those interested in English accents, and further to help speakers of accents other than RP or GA understand their own accent. These descriptions are obviously very brief and do not pretend to be complete discussions. Readers seeking more information should turn to general discussions such as Hughes and Trudgill (1996), Trudgill and Hannah (1994), Wells (1982), and Wolfram and Schilling-Estes (1998).

Minor variations exist in the consonants, but most of the variation in English accents is in the vowels which are presented as a list showing a sample word and the vowel used in that word. The list for RP is given in Table 6.1. and for GA in Table 6.12. Note that in the last three words, *baby*, *runner*, and *sofa*, it is the second vowel which is of interest, as shown by the bold print.

Table 6.1 RP vowels

beat	i	*boot*	u	*peer*	ɪə
pit	ɪ	*put*	ʊ	*pear*	ɛə
hate	ej	*boat*	əw	*part*	ɑ
pet	ɛ	*bought*	ɔ	*hurt*	ɜ
pat	æ	*pot*	ɒ	*cure, jury*	ʊə
path	ɑ	*soft*	ɒ	*four*	ɔ
but	ʌ	*palm*	ɑ	*bab**y***	i
bite	aj	*out*	aw	*runn**er***	ə
		choice	ɔj	*sof**a***	ə

This presentation gives reference points to you in figuring out the pronunciation of other words with a fair degree of accuracy. If you want to know how to pronounce a word in a certain accent, find a word on the relevant chart that has the same vowel in RP or GA. For example, if you want to say *plate* with an Australian accent, you will find that the word *hate* is on the Australian list (Table 6.7), and note that it has the vowel /ʌj/. From your own knowledge of English, you should be able to guess that *hate* and *plate* have the same vowel. Therefore, you can make a fairly reliable guess that *plate* also has the vowel /ʌj/ in Australian English. (See Wells (1982: 122–4) for a discussion of this type of presentation.)

The following is a short list of traits which commonly distinguish English accents. If you are investigating someone's accent, you might look first at these features.

1 Presence of non-prevocalic /ɹ/. Accents with this /ɹ/ are called **rhotic**; those without, **non-rhotic**.
2 Distinction of *caught–cot*.
3 Distinction of *but–put*.
4 Final vowel of *baby*: [i] or [ɪ]?

5 Distinction of *pat–path.*
6 Presence of /h/.
7 Vowels of *hate* and *boat*: diphthongs or monophthongs?
8 Presence of /j/ after alveolars.
9 Intervocalic /t/: voiced, tapped, or glottalised.
10 Distinction of *merry, marry, Mary.*
11 Distinction of *which–witch.*

In the description of accents that follow, some or all of these eleven traits are identified as criteria for those accents.

Received Pronunciation (RP) revisited

Although RP is regarded as the standard accent of Britain, it is spoken natively by only a very small proportion of the population. Many people, particularly in the south of England, however, have an accent which is quite similar to RP. Even accents such as Cockney, our first example, although phonetically different from RP, are structurally quite similar to RP.

In terms of the criteria cited above, RP has the following traits:

1 Non-rhotic: *car* [kɑ].
2 *Caught–cot* distinguished: [kɔt kɒt].
3 *But–put* distinguished: [bʌt–pʊt].
4 Final vowel in *baby* [i]: [ˈbejbi]. Older RP had [ɪ]: [ˈbejbɪ].
5 *Pat–path* distinguished: [pæt pɑθ].
6 /h/ present: *half* /hɑf/.
7 *Hate* and *boat* have diphthongs: [hejt bəwt].
8 /j/ present after alveolars: *tune, dune, news* [tjun djun njuz].
9 Intervocalic /t/ glottalised non-finally, especially with younger speakers: *city* [ˈsɪʔ͡ti].
10 *Merry, marry, Mary* all distinguished: [ˈmɛɹi ˈmæɹi ˈmeəɹi].
11 *Which–witch* not distinguished: both [wɪtʃ].

Among younger RP and near-RP speakers, one notices that *poor, pour,* and *paw* are merged as [pɔ]. The phoneme /ɹ/ among these speakers is often a labiodental approximant [ʋ]: *very* [ˈvɛʋi].

Certain words show variability in almost all accents of English, including RP:

again(st)	[əˈgɛn(st)]	[əˈgejn(st)]
either	[ˈajðə]	[ˈiðə]
Sunday (and other days)	[ˈsʌndi]	[ˈsʌnˌdej]
often	[ˈɒfn̩]	[ˈɒftn̩]
kilometre	[kɪˈlɒmɪtə]	[ˌkɪləˈmitə]

Garage is notoriously variable. In RP, [ˈgæɹ̞ɑʒ] and [ˈgæɹ̞ɑdʒ] are both common, as well as [ˈgæɹɪdʒ]. (In GA, [gəˈɹɑʒ] has the greatest prestige, but [gəˈɹɑdʒ] is common. In Canada, [gəˈɹɑʒ] is most commonly heard, but many people say [gəˈɹædʒ] or even monosyllabic [gɹædʒ].)

The accents outside North America are more like RP. In the descriptions in this chapter, they are compared to RP, and the important points where they differ from RP are noted. North American accents are similarly compared to GA.

Note: In this chapter, the variety of sounds presented makes it necessary to introduce some symbols which are not discussed until later in the book.

Cockney

A well-known non-RP, working-class accent of the City of London is **Cockney**, traditionally defined as spoken by someone born within the sound of the Bow Bells. Structurally, Cockney is not very different from RP, but there are a number of phonetic differences.

Table 6.2 Vowels of Cockney

beat	i	*boot*	u	*peer*	iə̯
pit	ɪ	*put*	ʊ	*pear*	ɛə̯
hate	æj	*boat*	æʉ̯	*part*	ɑ
pet	ɛ	*bought*	ɔ	*hurt*	ɜ
pat	ɛ̝, ɛj	*pot*	ɒ	*cure, jury*	ʊə̯
path	ɑ	*soft*	ɒ	*four*	ɔ
but	ʌ	*palm*	ɑ	*bab**y***	i
bite	ɑj	*out*	æə̯	*runn**er***	ə
		choice	ɔj	*sof**a***	ə

1 The phoneme /h/ is lost: *half* [ɑf], *help* [ɛo̯p].
2 Non-final /ɔ/ is realised as [o]; a morpheme-final [ɔ] is kept when a suffix is added. This creates a contrast between words such as *paws* and *pause*.

paw [pɔ] *paws* [pɔz] *pause* [poz]

3 Glottal stop is common before voiceless stops and regularly replaces intervocalic and final /t/: *stop* [stɒˀp], *butter* [ˈbʌˀə].
4 /l/ becomes the glide [o̯] before consonants and at the end of words. This development is spreading to other southern English accents. The [̯] diacritic shows that in *bell* the [o] is a glide: *will* [wɪo̯], *shelf* [ʃɛo̯f].
5 Often, /θ/ and /ð/ are replaced by /f/ and /v/: *Arthur* [ˈɑfə], *other* [ˈʌvə].

6 Initial /t/ is affricated: *tea* [tsi].
7 Specific words: *the* /də/, *they* /ej/, *nothing* /ˈnʌfɪŋk/.

Yorkshire

A West Yorkshire accent is presented here as an example of northern English.

Table 6.3 Vowels of Yorkshire

beat	i	*boot*	u	*peer*	iə̯
pit	ɪ	*put*	ʊ	*pear*	ɛə̯
hate	e	*boat*	o	*part*	ɑ
pet	ɛ	*bought*	ɔ	*hurt*	ɜ
pat	æ	*pot*	ɒ	*cure, jury*	ʊə̯
path	æ	*soft*	ɒ	*four*	ɔə̯
but	ʊ	*palm*	ɑ	*baby*	ɪ
bite	ae̯	*out*	aw	*runn**er***	ə
		choice	ɔj	*sof**a***	ə

1 This accent is non-rhotic.
2 The vowels of *but* and *put* are the same: [bʊt]–[pʊt].
3 Generally /h/ has been lost: *hat* /æʔ/.
4 For some speakers, there are two contrasts:

plate, mate	[e]	*boat, nose*	[o]
weight, eight	[ej]	*knows*	[ow]

5 Final /t/ is often realised as glottal stop: *bite* /bae̯ʔ/.
6 Specific words: *make* [mɛk], *take* [tɛk]

Scotland

Until 1603, Scotland had a separate monarch, and until 1707, was politically independent from England. It is not surprising, then, that it has its own standard accent different from RP, although some Scots do speak RP. Grammatically, standard Scottish English is quite similar to the standard accent of England. Lowland Scotland also has a traditional local accent, known as **Scots** or sometimes **Lallans**, which has maintained a literary presence, as in the poetry of Robert Burns. The accent described here is that of educated speakers of central Scotland.

The transcription [ae̯] represents a diphthong starting at [a] with a following glide to an [e] position.

Table 6.4 Scottish vowels

beat	i	*boot*	ʉ	*peer*	ir
pit	ɪ	*put*	ʉ	*pear*	er
hate	e	*boat*	o	*part*	ar
pet	ɛ	*bought*	ɔ	*hurt*	ər
pat	a	*pot*	ɔ	*cure, jury*	ʉr
path	a	*soft*	ɔ	*four*	or
but	ʌ	*palm*	a	*baby*	e
bite	ae̯, ʌj	*out*	ʌw	*runner*	ər
		choice	ɒj	*sofa*	ʌ

1 Scottish English is rhotic, the *r* is usually a tap [ɾ] or even a trill [r]: note *fern* [fɛɾn], *pearl* [pɛɾl].
2 The RP vowels /ʊ/ and /u/ are merged as /ʉ/ (a high central vowel, pronounced farther forward than the RP /u/: *look, Luke* [lʉk].
3 The RP vowels of words such as *bath* and *hat* are merged, both having a low front vowel (lower than the /æ/ of *hat*).
4 Initial /h/ is retained: *half* [haf].
5 The mid vowels /e o/ are monophthongs.
6 The *which–witch* distinction is maintained: /ʍɪtʃ wɪtʃ/.
7 The unstressed vowel corresponding to schwa is often /ʌ/: *sofa* [ˈsofʌ].
8 Words such as *fir, there, fur* are often distinguished as /fɪr, ðɛr, fʊr/.
9 Length differs in Scottish English from other accents.

a. At the end of a morpheme, vowels, except /ɪ/ and /ʌ/, are long:

row	[ro·]	*rowed*	[ro·d]	*road*	[rod]
agree	[ʌˈgri·]	*agreed*	[ʌˈgri·d]	*greed*	[grid]

In these examples, *row* and *agree* have long vowels at the end of a morpheme. This length is retained when the past tense morpheme is added, producing a contrast with *road* and *greed*, which have short vowels.

b. Vowels, except /ɪ/ and /ʌ/, are long before the consonants /v ð z r/:

move	[mʉ·v]	*seethe*	[si·ð]	*size*	[sa·e̯z]	*pour*	[po·r]

10 The alternations described in 9a. apply to diphthongs as well; for the diphthong of *tie*, there is an alternation of quality as well.

tie	[ta·e̯]	*tied*	[ta·e̯d]	*tide*	[tʌjd]
cow	[kʌ·w]	*cows*	[kʌ·wz]	*loud*	[lʌwd]
toy	[tɒ·j]	*toys*	[tɒ·jz]	*Lloyd*	[lɒjd]

Note that *tied, cows,* and *toys* consist of two morphemes each, whereas *tide, loud,* and *Lloyd* consist of only one.

11 Most Scottish speakers also use a voiceless velar fricative /x/ in words such as *loch* /lɔx/, and in many place names – *Tulloch* /ˈtʌlʌx/.

Belfast

From the seventeenth century onwards, English speakers settled in northern Ireland. The English of Ulster, particularly the northern areas, is still quite similar to Scottish English. Southern Ulster English is more like that of the midlands of England. The modern urban speech of Belfast has elements of both these communities. There are a number of similarities between Ulster English and GA, reflecting the large Ulster settlement in the US.

Table 6.5 Belfast vowels

beat	i	*boot*	ʉ	*peer*	iɹ
pit	ɪ	*put*	ʉ	*pear*	eɹ
hate	ɛə̯	*boat*	o	*part*	a
pet	ɛ	*bought*	ɔ	*hurt*	ɹ̩
pat	a	*pot*	ɒ	*cure, jury*	uɹ
path	a	*soft*	ɒ	*four*	ɔ
but	ʌ	*palm*	ɑ	*baby*	ɪ
bite	ɛj	*out*	æw	*runner*	əɹ
		choice	ɔj	*sofa*	ə

1 This accent is rhotic. The tongue position for [ɹ] is a little farther back than in RP, more as in GA.
2 There is often a *caught–cot* contrast: [kɔt]–[kɒt].
3 The RP vowels of words such as *bath* and *hat* are merged, both having a low front vowel (lower than the /æ/ of *hat*).
4 The phonemes /ʌ/ and /ʊ/ are distinct, but the distribution may be different from that in RP.
5 The phoneme /h/ is present: *hat* [hat].
6 The *which–witch* distinction is maintained: /ʍɪtʃ wɪtʃ/.
7 The lateral /l/ is clear in all environments.
8 Intervocalic /t/ is often voiced or even a tap as in GA.
9 The words *bay, say, day* have the vowel [ɛ].

Dublin

In Eire, English has been spoken since the seventeenth century, and it is often influenced by Irish Gaelic features. The accent shown here represents an educated accent of Dublin.

Table 6.6 Irish vowels

beat	i	*boot*	u	*peer*	iɹ
pit	ɪ	*put*	ʊ	*pear*	eɹ
hate	e	*boat*	o	*part*	aɹ
pet	ɛ	*bought*	ɑˑ	*hurt*	ʌɹ
pat	a	*pot*	ɑ	*cure, jury*	uɹ
path	a	*soft*	ɑ	*four*	oɹ
but	ʌ	*palm*	aˑ	*baby*	i
bite	ɑj	*out*	aw	*runner*	əɹ
		choice	ɔj	*sofa*	ə

1 This accent is rhotic.
2 The RP vowels of words such as *bath* and *hat* are merged, both having a low front vowel (lower than the /æ/ of *hat*).
3 The phoneme /h/ is present.
4 For some speakers, the phonemes /ʌ/ and /ʊ/ are merged as [ʊ].
5 The *which–witch* distinction is maintained: /ʍɪtʃ wɪtʃ/.
6 Words such as *fir, fur, fern* are distinct as [fɪɹ, fʊɹ, fɛɹn].
7 /l/ is clear in all environments.
8 For some speakers, /θ/ and /ð/are commonly realised as dental stops [t̪] and [d̪]. This is a Gaelic influence.

Australia

Australian English is structurally very similar to RP; there are, however, a number of phonetic differences. Within Australia, there is little regional variation, although social variation may be quite marked (Mitchell and Delbridge, 1965).

Table 6.7 Australian vowels

beat	ɨj	*boot*	ʊw	*peer*	i
pit	ɪ	*put*	ʊ	*pear*	e
hate	ʌj	*boat*	ɒw	*part*	a
pet	e	*bought*	ɔ	*hurt*	ə
pat	ɛ	*pot*	ɒ	*cure*	o
path	a	*soft*	ɒ	*four*	ɔ
but	ʌ	*palm*	a	*baby*	i
bite	ɑj	*out*	æw	*runner*	ə
		choice	ɔj	*sofa*	ə

1 Australian English is non-rhotic.
2 The vowel of *path* and *palm* is a front /a/, as is the vowel of *part* and *car*.
3 Initial /h/ is frequently lost: *hat* [æt].
4 Intervocalic /t/ is often voiced: *city* [ˈsɪdi].

5 The vowels of *pet* and *pat* are higher than in RP.
6 Schwa is more frequently used in unstressed syllables than in RP: *stop it* [ˈstɒp ət]. The weak forms of *it* and *at* are both [ət].
7 The lateral /l/ is dark in all positions: *leave* [ɫɨjv].

New Zealand

Table 6.8 The vowels of New Zealand English

beat	ɨj	*boot*	ʉ	*peer*	ɪə̯
pit	ə	*put*	ʊ	*pear*	eə̯
hate	ʌj	*boat*	ʌw	*part*	a
pet	e	*bought*	ɔ	*hurt*	ɵ
pat	ɛ	*pot*	ɒ	*cure, jury*	ʊə̯
path	a	*soft*	ɒ	*four*	ɔ
but	ʌ	*palm*	a	*baby*	i
bite	ɑj	*out*	æw	*runner*	ə
		choice	ɔj	*sofa*	ə

1 The vowel of *kit* is pronounced [ə]; also /ʊ/ after /w/ is pronounced [ə]. Unstressed vowels are normally realised as [ə]. All this has the result that *woman* and *women* are both pronounced [ˈwəmən].
2 For many speakers, there is neutralisation of certain vowels before /l/:

fellow, fallow	[fɛləw]
will, wool	[wəl]

3 Younger speakers are no longer distinguishing *which* and *witch*, pronouncing both as [wɪtʃ].
4 Intervocalic /t/ is sometimes voiced to [ɾ], as in GA.

South Africa

Table 6.9 Vowels of South African English

beat	i	*boot*	u	*peer*	iə̯
pit	ɪ/ə	*put*	ʊ	*pear*	eˑ
hate	əj	*boat*	əw/ʌˑ	*part*	ɑ
pet	e	*bought*	ɔ	*hurt*	ɜ
pat	ɛ	*pot*	ɒ	*cure, jury*	ʊə̯
path	ɑ	*soft*	ɒ	*four*	ɔ
but	ʌ	*palm*	ɑ	*baby*	ɪ
bite	aˑ	*out*	ɑw	*runner*	ə
		choice	ɔj	*sofa*	ə

1 The phoneme /h/ is present.
2 The phoneme /t/ is often voiced or tapped intervocalically: *better* [ˈbeɾə].
3 *Which* and *witch* are both pronounced with [w].
4 The /ɪ/ phoneme has two allophonic realisations: [ɪ] and a more centralised [ɪ̈].

[ɪ] in stressed sylls	next to velars	*lick, big, sing, kit, gift*
	after /h/	*hit*
	word initially	*inn*
	before postalveolars	*fish, ditch, bridge*
[ɪ̈] elsewhere	*bit, lip, tin, slim, minutes, limited* (both sylls)	

5 Consonant clusters as in *doctor, captain* are pronounced without overlap, i.e., with audible release.
6 The voiceless stops /p t k/ are often unaspirated.

West Indies

English in the West Indies is quite varied, although generally British-oriented in its phonology. Some West Indians speak RP or near-RP; almost all speakers there are aware of RP and will tend to shift their accent towards RP in formal social situations. In addition to ordinary English, most of the English-speaking islands have languages which linguists call **creoles**. These are full-fledged languages with a very interesting history. The West Indies also has creoles based on French, Portuguese, and other languages. (For general information about creoles, see Holm, 1988; Romaine, 1988; for details of West Indian English, see Roberts, 1988.) We will use the non-creole English spoken in Jamaica as an example of West Indian English.

Table 6.10 West Indian vowels

beat	i	*boot*	u	*peer*	e
pit	ɪ	*put*	ʊ	*pear*	e
hate	e	*boat*	o	*part*	aˑ
pet	ɛ	*bought*	aˑ	*hurt*	ʌ
pat	a	*pot*	a	*cure*	o
path	a	*soft*	aˑ	*four*	o
but	ʌ	*palm*	aˑ	*bab**y***	ɪ
bite	aj	*out*	ɔw	*runn**er***	a
		choice	aj, ɔj	*sof**a***	a

1 West Indian English is generally non-rhotic; only Barbados is regularly rhotic.

2 Note especially the vowels /a/ and /aˑ/; /a/ corresponds to RP /æ ɒ ə/, and /aˑ/ corresponds to RP /ɑ ɔ/.
3 The consonant /h/ is generally absent.
4 The dental fricatives /θ/ and /ð/ are often pronounced as alveolar stops /t/ and /d/:

this thing /dɪs tɪŋ/ *mother* /mada/

5 Certain consonant clusters are reduced:

fact /fak/ *mask* /maˑs/ *west* /wɛs/

6 The glide /j/ is sometimes found after initial velar stops: *garden* /gjaˑdn̩/, *car* /kjaˑ(ɹ)/

India

English is spoken as a second language by a large number of people in South Asia: Pakistan, India, Bangladesh, and Sri Lanka. It is a native language for some. Although the characteristics of Indian English were originally due to the fact that speakers spoke an Indian language natively, and thus acquired English with an Indian accent, these characteristics have now become established as the norm for Indian English. Nevertheless, RP still serves as a model for educated people. Obviously, there is considerable variation in such a large area, based both on education and on different native languages.

Table 6.11 Vowels of Indian English

beat	i	*boot*	u	*peer*	i
pit	ɪ	*put*	ʊ	*pear*	ɛ
hate	e	*boat*	o	*part*	ɑ
pet	ɛ	*bought*	ɔ	*hurt*	ə
pat	a	*pot*	ɒ	*cure*	ʊ
path	ɑ	*soft*	ɒ	*four*	o
but	ʌ	*palm*	a	*baby*	iː
bite	aj	*out*	aw	*runner*	ə
		choice	ɔj	*sofa*	ə

1 Some speakers may be rhotic.
2 Stops are frequently unaspirated.
3 The fricatives /θ ð/are often realised as [t̪ d̪].
4 The stops /t d/ are often retroflex [ʈ ɖ].
5 The lateral /l/ is clear in all positions.
6 The stress pattern of Indian English is syllable-timed (see Chapter 14).

General American (GA) revisited

Table 6.12 GA vowels

beat	i	*boot*	u	*peer*	ɪɹ
pit	ɪ	*put*	ʊ	*pear*	ɛɹ
hate	ej	*boat*	ow	*part*	ɑɹ
pet	ɛ	*bought*	ɔ	*hurt*	əɹ
pat	æ	*pot*	ɑ	*cure, jury*	ʊɹ
path	æ	*soft*	ɔ	*four*	ɔɹ
but	ʌ	*palm*	ɑ	*bab**y***	i
bite	aj	*out*	aw	*runn**er***	əɹ
		choice	ɔj	*sof**a***	ə

In terms of the criteria cited on pp. 110–11, GA has the following traits:

1 Rhotic: *car* [kɑɹ].
2 *Caught–cot* distinguished: [kɔt kɑt].
3 *But–put* distinguished: [bʌt–pʊt].
4 Final vowel in *baby* [i]: [ˈbejbi].
5 The vowels of *pat–path* are not distinguished: [pæt pæθ].
6 /h/ present: *half* /hæf/.
7 *Hate* and *boat* have diphthongs: [hejt bowt].
8 /j/ variably present after alveolars: *tune, dune, news* [tjun djun njuz]; more often present in eastern areas than in the west.
9 Intervocalic /t/ tapped: *city* [ˈsɪɾi].
10 *Merry, marry, Mary* not distinguished: [ˈmɛɹi ˈmɛɹi ˈmɛɹi].
11 *Which–witch* variably distinguished: [ʍɪtʃ wɪtʃ]. This distinction common in the south-eastern United States, and less so elsewhere.

A change in the vowel pattern for part of the GA area is currently in progress in the urban north central region, known as the **Northern Cities Vowel Shift** (Labov, 1991). It is strongest in cities such as Chicago, Detroit, Buffalo, Rochester, and Syracuse. As shown in Figure 6.1, there is a circular type of change affecting the low vowels. The symbol [ʌ̟] is pronounced farther front than the usual GA [ʌ].

[ɑ] → [æ]	*lock* [læk], *calm* [kæm]
[æ] → [ɛ]	*cat* [kɛt], *can't* [kɛnt]
[ɛ] → [ʌ̟]	*pet* [pʌ̟t], *wreck* [ɹʌ̟k]
[ʌ̟] → [ʌ]	*but* [bʌt]

For some GA speakers, dark [ɫ] is replaced by a glide [ɣ̑] before fricatives, especially before [f v] and sometimes before [s z]; the vowel quality of

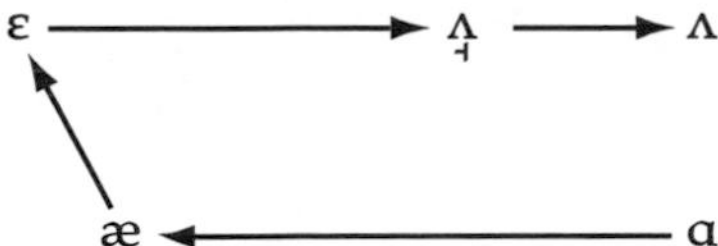

Figure 6.1 GA: Northern cities vowel shift

this glide is like an unrounded [o̜]: *golf* [gɑɤ̯f], *elves* [εɤ̯vz], *else* [εɤ̯s], *wells* [weɤ̯z].

New England

Table 6.13 Vowels of New England

beat	i	*boot*	u	*peer*	ɪə̯
pit	ɪ	*put*	ʊ	*pear*	æə̯
hate	ej	*boat*	ow	*part*	a
pet	ε	*bought*	ɒ	*hurt*	ɜ
pat	æ	*pot*	ɒ	*cure, jury*	ʊə̯
path	a	*soft*	ɒ	*four*	oə̯
but	ə	*palm*	ɑ	*bab**y***	i
bite	aj	*out*	aw	*runn**er***	ə
		choice	ɔj	*sof**a***	ə

The accent of eastern New England has many features different from GA. The accent of most western New England speakers is generally GA.

1. This accent is non-rhotic, with linking [ɹ]; the north-eastern area is, however, rhotic.
2. A rounded central vowel between [ε] and [o] is used by some speakers; it is known as New England Short /o/: [ɵ]: *road, home, stone, coat, whole, smoke, yolk, toad, folks, bone* – cf. *rode* /ow/.
3. Note the vowel in *path*; as in RP, it is distinct from *pat*.
4. *Aunt* is frequently [ɑnt], distinct from *ant* [ænt].

New York City

New York City English has a number of features which are quite distinct from other areas of the US. Many people in New York City speak General American. The accent described here is a traditional one.

Table 6.14 Vowels of New York City

beat	i	*boot*	u	*peer*	ɪə̯
pit	ɪ	*put*	ʊ	*pear*	ɛə̯
hate	ej	*boat*	ow	*part*	ɑə̯
pet	ɛ	*bought*	oə̯	*hurt*	ɜ
pat	ɛə̯	*pot*	ɑə̯	*cure, jury*	ʊə̯
path	ɛə̯	*soft*	ɔə̯	*four*	ɔə̯
but	ʌ	*palm*	ɑə̯	*bab**y***	i
bite	ɑj	*out*	aw	*runn**er***	ə
		choice	ɔj	*sof**a***	ə

1 The accent is non-rhotic.
2 Older speakers have [ɜj] in *hurt.* I recall a lecture given by a professor with an older upper-class New York accent who spoke on *The third person of the Hittite verb* [ðə ˌθɜjd ˌpɜjsən əv ðə ˈhɪˌtajt ˌvɜjb].
3 Note the numerous [ə̯]-glides.
4 Some speakers have [t d] for /θ ð/.
5 The higher vowel in *pat, path* is similar to the change taking place in the Northern Cities Vowel Shift shown in Figure 6.1 above.

US South

The accents of the south-east of the United States are quite diverse; the following comments are only generally true.

Table 6.15 Vowels of southern US English

beat	i	*boot*	u	*peer*	ɪə̯
pit	ɪə	*put*	ʊə	*pear*	ɛə̯
hate	ej	*boat*	ow	*part*	ɑ
pet	ɛə̯	*bought*	ɔ	*hurt*	ɜ
pat	æə̯	*pot*	ɑ	*cure, jury*	ʊə̯
path	æə̯	*soft*	ɔ	*four*	ɔə̯
but	ə	*palm*	ɑ	*bab**y***	ɪ
bite	aj	*out*	aw	*runn**er***	ə
		choice	ɔj	*sof**a***	ə

1 These accents are generally non-rhotic.
2 The diphthong /aj/ is commonly realised as [a]: *I tied my tie* [ˌa ˌtad ma ˈta].
3 The *hoarse–horse* distinction is common:

/oə̯/ *hoarse, pork, borne, four, fore, force, course, cored, ore, oar, ford, port, forge, wore, boarder, oral, mourning*

/ɔ/ *horse, fork, stork, born, for, north, cord, lord, form, or, tort, short, George, war, border, York, aural, morning*

4 Before any nasal, /ɛ/ is realised as [ɪ]: *ten, tin* [tɪn]; *tempo* [ˈtɪmpow].
5 In much of the south, the vowel /ow/ is pronounced [əw], similar to RP. This phenomenon seems to be spreading, even to areas outside the south.
6 In some southern speech, [l] may be lost before consonants, as in *wolf, help*: [wʊə̯f hɛə̯p] or even [wʊf hɛp].
7 Note the common casual forms: *isn't* [ˈɪdn̩t], *wasn't* [ˈwɑdn̩t].

African American Vernacular English

African American Vernacular English (AAVE) originated in the US south but is now spoken widely in urban areas throughout the country. The stronger characteristics of this dialect are grammatical rather than phonological. Interestingly, the phonetic features which distinguish it from the southern accent just discussed are generally consonantal in nature.

Table 6.16 Vowels of African American Vernacular English

beat	i	*boot*	u	*peer*	ɪə̯
pit	ɪə	*put*	ʊə	*pear*	ɛə̯
hate	ej	*boat*	ow	*part*	ɑ
pet	ɛə̯	*bought*	ɔ	*hurt*	ɜ
pat	æə̯	*pot*	ɑ	*cure, jury*	ʊə̯
path	æə̯	*soft*	ɔ	*four*	ɔə̯
but	ə	*palm*	ɑ	*baby*	ɪ
bite	aj	*out*	aw	*runner*	ə
		choice	ɔj	*sof**a***	ə

1 Final stop devoicing: *bid* [bɪt].
2 Consonant cluster reduction: *best* [bɛs], *left* [lɛf].
3 Final /θ/ often becomes /f/: *bath* [bæf].

Canada

Canadian English is very close to GA. In the late eighteenth century large numbers of loyalists settled in Ontario and in the Maritimes. The accent of Ontario was later carried westwards; there is little accent difference in middle-class speech from Halifax to Victoria. The Maritimes show greater differences, and Newfoundland English is different enough to be given a separate treatment below.

Table 6.17 Canadian vowels

beat	i	*boot*	u	*peer*	iɹ
pit	ɪ	*put*	ʊ	*pear*	ɛɹ
hate	ej	*boat*	ow	*part*	ɑɹ
pet	ɛ	*bought*	ɑ	*hurt*	əɹ
pat	æ	*pot*	ɑ	*cure, jury*	ʊɹ
path	æ	*soft*	ɑ	*four*	ɔɹ
but	ʌ	*palm*	ɑ	*bab**y***	i
bite	aj, ʌj	*out*	aw, ʌw	*runn**er***	əɹ
		choice	ɔj	*sof**a***	ə

1 The contextual variation for the diphthongs /aj/ and /aw/ forms a distinctive feature of Canadian English, commonly known as **Canadian Raising**. Before voiceless sounds, the vowel portion of these diphthongs is higher than that used before voiced sounds or at the end of a word. We can symbolise this higher vowel as [ʌ] (Figure 6.2).

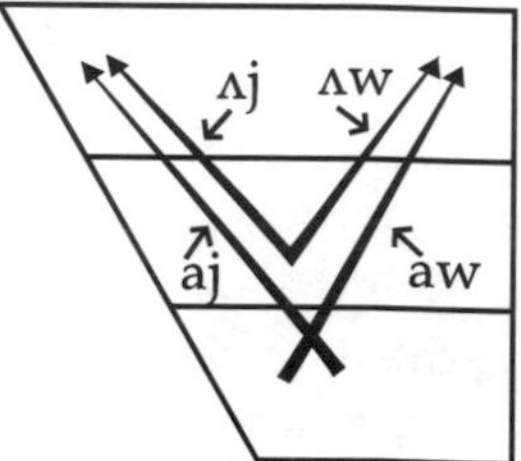

Figure 6.2 The diphthongs of Canadian raising. The lower lines show the unraised [aj aw]; the upper lines show the raised varieties [ʌj ʌw]

ride	[ɹa·jd]	*write*	[ɹʌjt]
lie	[la·j]	*like*	[lʌjk]
wives	[wa·jvz]	*wife*	[wʌjf]
loud	[la·wd]	*lout*	[lʌwt]
how	[ha·w]	*mouth*	[mʌwθ]
house (v.)	[ha·wz]	*house (n.)*	[hʌws]

Notice that because of vowel lengthening before voiced consonants and in open syllables, the unraised vowels are allophonically longer than the raised ones.

2 *Cot–caught* are merged as /ɑ/. In western Canada, some speakers have this vowel as [ɒ] or [ɔ]. Before /l/, /ɑ/ is allophonically [ɒ]: *doll* [dɒl]; *collar, caller* [ˈkɒləɹ].

3 In words such as *borrow, sorrow, orange,* where GA has /ɔ/, some speakers of Canadian English have /o/: /ˈboɹow, ˈsoɹow, ˈoɹɪndʒ/.

4 The vowel /æ/ is pronounced quite low: [æ̞]. Canadian English does not participate in the Northern Cities Vowel Shift found in the US described above.

5 The glide /j/ is lost after coronal consonants /t d n/; e.g., /tun, dun, nu/ *tune, dune, new*. This loss is common in GA, but almost universal in Canadian English.

6 *Which* and *witch* are merged as /wɪtʃ/.

7 The following list shows some irregular differences in pronunciation between Canadian English and GA. In many cases, the Canadian pronunciation is more like the British; frequently the GA pronunciation is also used in Canada.

	Canadian	**GA**	
	ˈænti-	ˈænˌtaj-	*anti-*
	ˈæʃfɒlt	ˈæsfɔlt	*asphalt*
	kəˈɹɒləɹi	ˈkɔɹəˌlɛri	*corollary*
	ˈdɛkl̩	ˈdiˌkæl	*decal*
	ɛɹ	əɹ	*err*
	həɹb	əɹb	*herb*
	ˌlɛfˈtɛnənt	ˌluˈtɛnənt	*lieutenant*
	ˈmɪsajl	ˈmɪsl̩	*missile*
	ˌmʌntɹiˈɒl	ˌmɑntɹiˈɔl	*Montréal*
	ˈɑɾəˌwɑ	ˈɑɾəˌwə	*Ottawa*
	ˈpɹajməɹ	ˈprɪmər	*primer (book)*
	ɹiˈzɔrs	ɹiˈsɔrs	*resource*
	ʃɑn	ʃown	*shone*
(but	ʃown	ʃown	*shown*)
	t(ə)ˈɹɑ̃ow	ˌtowˈɹɑnˌtow	*Toronto*
(in casual Canadian speech often [ˈtɹɑ̃ə] or [ˈtɹɑnə])			
	vɑz, vejz	vejs	*vase*

8 Many words in Canada have /æ/ where GA has /ɑ/: e.g., *pasta* /ˈpæstə/, *drama* /ˈdɹæmə/, *plaza* /ˈplæzə/, *Iran* /ɪˈɹæn/, *Iraq(i)* /ɪˈɹæk(i)/. Note Canadian *Iranian* /ɪˈɹejnɪən/ GA /ɪˈɹɑnɪən/.

9 Pronunciations of *again(st)* /əˈgejn(st)/, *either* /ˈajðəɹ/ and *laboratory* /ləˈbɔɹəˌtɔɹi/ are common in Canada in addition to the typical GA /əˈgɛn(st), ˈiðəɹ, ˈlæbrətɔɹi/.

10 As a strong form, /bin/ *been* is common; a strong form /wɛɹ/ *were* is occasionally heard among older speakers. *Québec* is variably /kwəˈbɛk, kəˈbɛk, ˌkejˈbɛk/. *Newfoundland* is generally /ˌnufn̩ˈlænd/ in Newfoundland, but elsewhere also /ˈnufn̩ˌlænd, ˌnuˈfawndln̩d, ˈnufn̩ln̩d/. *Calgary* is usually /ˈkælgəɹi/, but occasionally /ˈkælˌgɛɹi/. Some Canadians have /ˌajˈzajə/ *Isaiah* for GA /ˌajˈzejə/.

Newfoundland

The accent of Newfoundland is distinct enough from general Canadian English to deserve its own description. This difference is not surprising considering the island's early settlement in the sixteenth century, political independence from Canada until 1949, and large numbers of fairly isolated outport communities. All of these factors have acted to distinguish Newfoundland English from its Maritime neighbours (Clarke, 1997; Paddock, 1981; Shorrocks, 1997). There is considerable accent variation within Newfoundland.

Table 6.18 Newfoundland vowels

beat	i	*boot*	u	*peer*	ɛɹ
pit	ɪ	*put*	ʊ	*pear*	ɛɹ
hate	ɛ˙	*boat*	ɔ̈w	*part*	æɹ
pet	ɛ	*bought*	ɑ	*hurt*	əɹ
pat	æ	*pot*	ɑ	*cure, jury*	ɔ̈ɹ
path	æ	*soft*	ɑ	*four*	ɔ̈ɹ
but	ɔ̈	*palm*	æ	*bab**y***	i
bite	ɔ̈j	*out*	əw	*runn**er***	əɹ
		choice	ɔ̈j	*sof**a***	ə

1 Most of the island is rhotic with quite strong retroflexion although certain communities are non-rhotic.
2 Some accents of Newfoundland have the *cot–caught* distinction as in GA.
3 The vowel /ɔ̈/ is a central vowel with variable rounding, lying between [ɔ] and [œ].
4 Raising is not so common as in the rest of Canada.
5 The dental fricatives are often pronounced as alveolar stops: [t] and [d]. In some areas dental stops are used: [t̪] and [d̪]. Some speakers substitute [f] and [v] for [θ] and [ð].
6 /hj/ appears simply as /j/, in words like *humour* and *human.*
7 Many speakers have a clear [l] in postvocalic position [bɛl, hɛlp], although others have [ɰ], a voiced velar approximant: *bell* [beɰ], *help* [hɛɰp].
8 Initial fricatives are sometimes voiced: [zɪŋk] *sink,* [væn] *fan.*

Technical terms

African American Vernacular English
Cockney
Creole
accent
Lallans
Northern Cities Vowel Shift
rhotic
non-rhotic
Scots

Exercises

Basic

1 Some accents of English replace all final voiceless stops with a glottal stop:

tɑʔ *top* fɪʔ *fit* dʌʔ *duck*

Try imitating such an accent in the following words:

stop *cat* *back* *wit* *tap* *rat* *tack* *stack*

In the following sentence, turn the final consonants into [ʔ].

At eight, that bike sat outside in the dirt on top of the mat.

2 Practice:

ʔe ʔi ʔɑ	ʔeʔi ɑ	ʔe i ɑ	ʔe i ʔɑ	e i ʔɑ
e i ɑ	e ʔi ɑ	e ʔi ʔɑ	e i ɑʔ	ʔe i ɑʔ

3 Many accents of English distinguish voiced and voiceless [w], particularly before unrounded vowels. See if someone you know distinguishes *which* and *witch* /ʍɪtʃ – wɪtʃ/. Try pronouncing the following words on the left with /w/ and those on the right with /ʍ/:

witch	*which*	*wet*	*whet*	*watt*	*what*	*win*	*whim*
we	*whee*	*were*	*whir*	*went*	*when*	*ware*	*where*

4 There is also a distinction of /j – hj/ as in *you–hue*, found in most accents of English, but in only a few words. Transcribe the following according to your own accent:

huge *Hubert* *Hugh* *you* *hew* *Houston* *Hume*

Pronounce the following nonsense pairs:

jow – hjow	jəw – hjəw	wɑ – ʍɑ	ji – hji	je – hje
wo – ʍo	jɒ – hjɒ	jɛ – hjɛ	wu – ʍu	jɔ – hjɔ
wʊ – ʍʊ	wɛ – ʍɛ	wəw – ʍəw	jæ – hjæ	jʌ – hjʌ

5 Many English speakers in North America do not distinguish *do* and *due*, pronouncing them both as /du/. These accents do, however, distinguish /u – ju/ after labials and velars, as in *coot–cute* and *booty–beauty*; after alveolars, however, /ju/ does not occur.

Practise making this distinction with the pairs below. For each set, use /u/ in the words on the left and /ju/ in the words on the right.

/u/	/ju/	/u/	/ju/
do	dew, due	Dooley	duly
too	tune	stooge	student
noose	news	noon	newt

Try pronouncing the following words with /ju/ after the initial consonant:

e.g.: /ljuɹ/

lure *ruse* *sure* *super* *lucid* *runic*

6 Transcribe the vowel in the words below in your accent. Now find a dictionary (as close to your dialect as you can) and look up the sample words below. Write down the dictionary's transcription of the vowel. You now have a conversion key to go back and forth between our transcription system and the dictionary's:

	your accent	**dict-ionary**		**your accent**	**dict-ionary**		**your accent**	**dict-ionary**
beat	_____	_____	*boot*	_____	_____	*peer*	_____	_____
pit	_____	_____	*put*	_____	_____	*pear*	_____	_____
hate	_____	_____	*boat*	_____	_____	*part*	_____	_____
pet	_____	_____	*bought*	_____	_____	*hurt*	_____	_____
pat	_____	_____	*pot*	_____	_____	*cure, **jury***	_____	_____
path	_____	_____	*soft*	_____	_____	*four*	_____	_____
but	_____	_____	*palm*	_____	_____	*bab**y***	_____	_____
bite	_____	_____	*out*	_____	_____	*runn**er***	_____	_____
			choice	_____	_____	*sof**a***	_____	_____

7 Transcribe the following paragraph into your accent:

After thirty years on the force, your gut tells you more than your brain, and when Pete's calm, blood-shot, hound-dog eyes saw the moist, butchered corpse of the world's nicest dolphin, once the most popular animal star on television and now left for the swimming vultures of the gulf to devour, he knew something both sinister and perverted was about.

8 Pick RP or GA (whichever is more different from your native accent). Find a dictionary appropriate for that accent. Using Table 6.1 or Table 6.12, make a conversion key like the one you made in Exercise 6.

9 Now, using the chart you made in Exercise 8, transcribe the paragraph of Exercise 7 into RP or GA (whichever you used in Exercise 8), using our system of transcription.

10 Look up the following words in American and British dictionaries and compare the pronunciations. Show your own pronunciation if it is different.

	[American]	[British]	[Yours]
carry			
hairy			
wary			
staff			
disaster			
aster			
cloth			
cross			
laboratory			
resource			
khaki			
garage			
either			

Advanced

11 Using the information from the main part of the chapter, transcribe the paragraph of Exercise 7 into one of the accents described in this chapter (i.e., not RP or GA). Try to find someone with each of these accents. Ask them to read the passage in a relaxed fashion. Tape record them, if you can, to work on your transcription later. Read the passage to them as you thought it would be pronounced. Ask them to correct where you went wrong. Did you make a mistake or does the person have a different accent from the one described in the book?

12 Find someone who speaks English with an accent different from the ones described in this chapter. Tape record them reading the paragraphs in Exercise 7. Make sure to ask them to speak in a relaxed fashion the way they would speak to friends back home. Transcribe this as narrowly as you can. Transcribe how you expect them to pronounce the words below. Try to mimic their speech. Be sure to make it clear that you are learning from them and not making fun of their accent.

beat	__________	*boot*	__________	*peer*	__________
pit	__________	*put*	__________	*pear*	__________
hate	__________	*boat*	__________	*part*	__________
pet	__________	*bought*	__________	*hurt*	__________
pat	__________	*pot*	__________	*cure*	__________
path	__________	*soft*	__________	*four*	__________
but	__________	*palm*	__________	*bab**y***	__________
bite	__________	*out*	__________	*runn**er***	__________
		choice	__________	*sof**a***	__________

13 In Exercise 24 of Chapter 5, a passage of *Julius Cæsar* was given in Shakespeare's own pronunciation of the sixteenth century. Today Shakespeare is usually presented on the stage in an RP accent, even in North America. Using the information in this chapter, transcribe the passage from *Julius Cæsar* into RP. A British dictionary might be helpful.

14 Pretend that you are Shakespeare listening to a modern performance of your play with the actors using an RP accent. With the transcription from *Julius Cæsar* that you made in Exercise 13 just above, note the points in which RP English would sound odd to you (Shakespeare).

Considering how strange a modern RP accent would have sounded to Shakespeare, why do you think that directors and actors often choose RP as the accent for his plays today?

Chapter 7

Sound waves, spectra, and resonance

Acoustics is the branch of physics dealing with the properties of sound. **Acoustic phonetics** is the sub-branch which focuses on the sounds used in human language. As we know from physics, the sounds we hear are caused by **vibrations** in the air. These vibrations are conveyed through the air in the form of **waves**. This chapter examines the basic properties of these sound waves. Chapter 9 will apply this knowledge in an acoustic description of the sounds of English.

In this chapter you will learn about:

- sine waves and complex waves;
- sound spectra;
- resonance.

Sound waves

In this section we will look at two questions. What are the measurable properties of vibrations in the air caused by speech? And how do these vibrations travel through air?

When we speak, we push a stream of air out of our body. This air stream has a constantly varying pressure. The variations are caused by the many individual actions in the vocal tract. They are conveyed through the air to the listener and are interpreted as speech. To understand these complex variations, we first need to examine simple vibrations, such as those produced by a tuning fork.

A tuning fork is a device constructed with two arms which **oscillate**, that is, swing back and forth in a regular fashion, alternately pushing and pulling the neighbouring air. Figure 7.1 (overleaf) shows the effect of the vibrations of the tuning fork on the air. The dot to the right of the fork represents a molecule of air. At point (a), the fork is at rest. Striking it sets it in motion with the arms moving in opposite directions; when the arm of the fork moves to the right (b), the pressure between the arm and the air molecule is increased and the air molecule is pushed to the right (c). Eventually, the arm of the tuning fork stops moving to the right and begins to move leftwards (d), reducing the pressure between it and the molecule of air. This pulls the molecule of air towards the left. The leftward movement continues until the tuning fork arm reaches the limit of its range (g). Then the movement starts to the right again (h). We can see that the movement of the tuning fork causes a similar movement in the molecule of air.

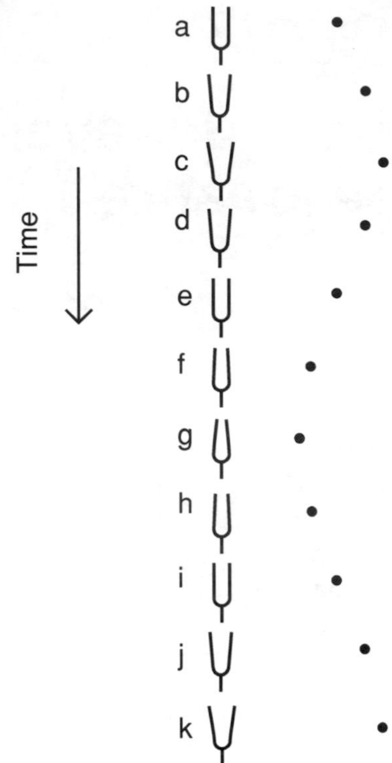

Figure 7.1 Movement of a tuning fork

If we were to fix a pen on to the molecule of air and pull a sheet of paper past the pen, the motion of the air molecule would be recorded as shown in Figure 7.2. The horizontal dimension shows time going from left to right, and the vertical dimension shows the displacement of the molecule of air from its resting place, which is indicated by the horizontal line. The resulting shape is a **waveform** which shows the movement of the air. As the tuning fork moves, the air pressure surrounding the air molecule increases and decreases proportionally to the movement. Since it is relatively easy to measure changes in air pressure and rather hard to observe the movement of a molecule of air, in the laboratory we use variation in air pressure to describe a sound.

The waveform of the pressure variation has the same shape as that of the movement of the air molecule. This pattern of movement is shown in Figure 7.2; it is called a **sine** or **sinusoidal** wave because of certain mathematical properties it has. Physicists can make a number of measurements of such a wave. Sound waves of actual speech are more complex than a sine

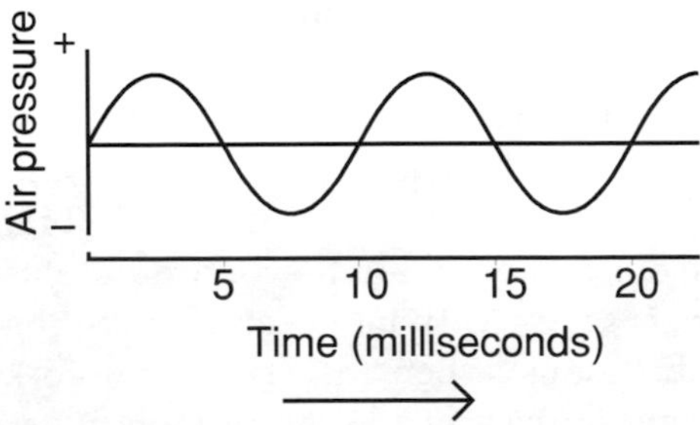

Figure 7.2 Sine wave

wave, but it is easier to understand the basic principles if we start with simple sine waves.

Speech is fairly rapid. We average around seven segments a second. To measure such short units, phoneticians use **milliseconds** (1 ms = 0.001 second). In Figure 7.2 we see that one complete cycle of oscillation takes 10 ms.

Propagation

So far we have been talking about a single molecule of air vibrating as a result of speech. Sound is, however, **propagated** through air. Air comprises some 400 billion billion molecules per cubic inch at ordinary pressures. Air molecules tend to maintain a constant pressure between themselves and thus a constant distance from each other. This distance acts in an elastic fashion. If something pushes the molecules of air closer together than usual, they resist and try to move back to the original position. Likewise, if pulled apart, they resist and try to return to the original position.

A simple analogy is to think of the molecules of air connected to each other by springs. If one molecule moves towards the next, the spring between them is compressed and will try to push them apart. On the other hand, if the molecules are pulled apart, the spring is stretched and will try to pull them back to their original position.

If we take our tuning fork and molecule of air from Figure 7.1 and add several other molecules of air, we can see how vibration is propagated. The tuning fork and molecules of air are connected by springs; thus the movement of one molecule of air causes a corresponding movement on the next one, and so on. Figure 7.3 shows this. Note that the wave motion travels

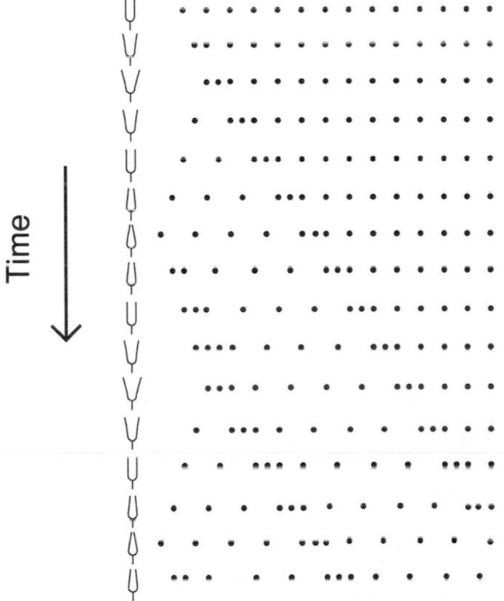

Figure 7.3 The cyclical propagation of waves

away from the source of energy (the tuning fork); however, the individual molecules of air do not move far from their original position.

In our model, the wave would continue for ever. In real life, of course, the tuning fork loses energy and gradually comes to rest. In addition, as the wave spreads out in a circular fashion from the tuning fork, the energy is spread over an increasingly large area, and the wave gradually dissipates.

Amplitude and intensity

The difference of air pressure between its greater value and its neutral value is called its **amplitude**. On a chart of a sine wave, as in Figure 7.4, amplitude is the vertical dimension. Figure 7.4 shows two waves which are the same except that they have different amplitudes. Line a–a′ shows the amplitude of wave A at time 2.5 milliseconds. At the same time, the amplitude of wave B is greater, as shown by the longer line b–b′. At time 8 ms, the amplitudes of the two waves are negative as shown by the lines c–c′ and d–d′. The amplitude of a sine wave as a whole is considered to be its maximum amplitude, that is the distance from the base-line to the highest point of the curve. Thus, wave A would be said to have an amplitude of a′, and wave B would have an amplitude of b′.

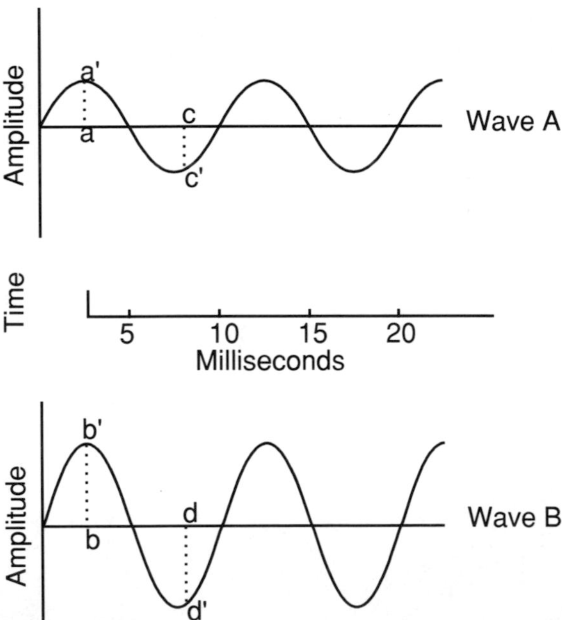

Figure 7.4 Two sine waves with different amplitudes

Perception of loudness

In general, the greater the amplitude, the louder the sound is perceived to be. Frequently amplitude is converted into **intensity**, which describes the power transmitted by a wave, because intensity is more closely related to the psychological property of loudness. Intensity is measured in decibels (dB). Commonly, we measure intensity by comparing the intensity of a particular sound to that of a just audible sound. Note that amplitude and intensity are physical properties whereas loudness is a psychological property. Table 7.1 gives you an idea of a few common intensities.

Table 7.1 Common intensity levels

Intensity (dB)	Sound
130	4-engined jet aircraft, 120 ft
120	Threshold of pain; pneumatic hammer, 3 ft
110	Rock band
100	Car horn, 15 ft; orchestra playing loud
90	Pneumatic hammer, 4 ft
80	Noisy subway train; loud radio music
70	Busy traffic, 70 ft
60	Conversation, 3 ft; car 30 ft
50	Quiet office
40	Residential area, no traffic; subdued conversation
30	Quiet garden; whispered conversation
20	Ticking of watch, at ear; broadcast studio
10	Rustle of leaves
0	Threshold of audibility

The human ear is remarkably sensitive. Under very good conditions, a person with normal hearing can perceive a sound whose amplitude is as small as the diameter of a hydrogen molecule, or about 0.04 nanometres (Laver, 1994).

Frequency

Consider now the sine waves in Figure 7.5 (overleaf). Both have the same intensity but they differ in the frequency of their repetition. One complete repetition of the pattern is called a **cycle**. The **frequency** of a wave is the number of cycles per second. One cycle of wave A, for example, takes 10 ms (0.01 seconds); thus, there would be a total of 100 cycles in a second. One **Hertz** (Hz, named after the nineteenth-century German scientist H. Hertz) equals one cycle per second. Thus, the frequency of this wave is 100 Hz. In wave B, the cycle takes 5 ms (0.005 seconds) giving a frequency of 200 Hz. The frequency in Hz equals 1 divided by the duration of one cycle (measured

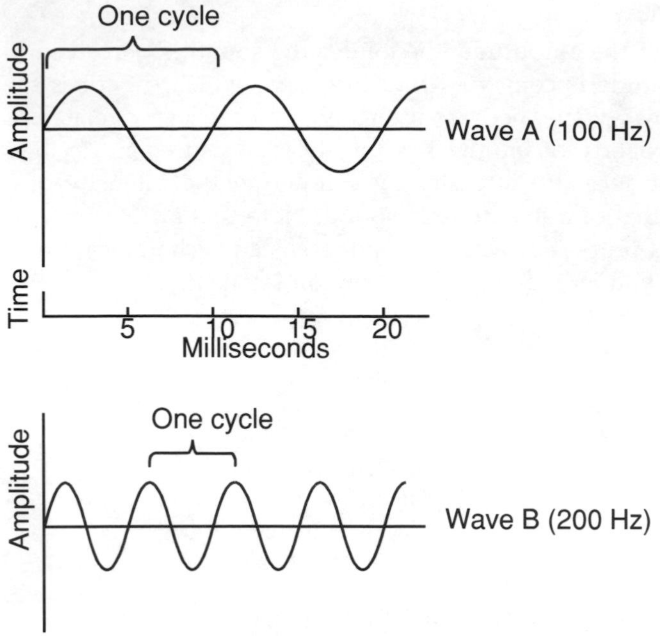

Figure 7.5 Two sine waves with different frequencies

in seconds). If a cycle lasts 0.005 seconds, the frequency equals 1/0.005 seconds or 200 Hz. A cycle can be measured from any point on a wave to the next corresponding point.

Perception of frequency

We perceive frequency as **pitch**. The higher the frequency, the higher the pitch we hear. Remember that pitch and loudness are psychological, perceptual properties, whereas frequency, amplitude, and intensity are physical properties.

The pitch range that an individual can produce varies considerably. The range of pitch found in speech is about 60–500 Hz although we do not usually use the entire range in speaking. Typical average pitches used in speaking are:

Children	265 Hz
Women	225 Hz
Men	120 Hz

We can hear a much wider range of sounds. Our hearing is usually best in our youth when we can hear sounds in the range of about 20–20,000 Hz (provided we haven't listened to very much loud music). A modern piano has a low note of 27.5 Hz and a high note of 3520 Hz. The instruments of an orchestra are tuned so that the A above middle C is 440 Hz.

Pitch and loudness are related in our hearing ability; that is, at some frequencies, the sound must be louder for us to hear it than at other frequencies.

Complex waves

A property of tuning forks is that they produce wave forms that closely approximate sine waves. Most sounds are more complex than sine waves. Figure 7.6 shows the wave of someone producing the vowel [ɑ]. Clearly this is not a sine wave. A wave like this is called a **complex repetitive wave**: complex, because it is not a simple sine wave, and repetitive, because it has a pattern of repeating cycles. Although the cycles of a real sound, as in Figure 7.6, are not exactly the same, we assume in the following discussion that the cycles repeat themselves exactly.

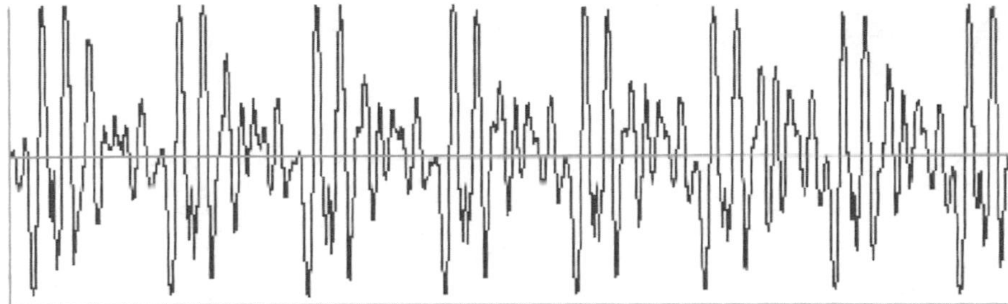

Figure 7.6 A complex repetitive wave

Complex waves as in Figure 7.6 are of limited use to phoneticians. Fortunately, a nineteenth-century French mathematician and Egyptologist, Joseph **Fourier**, formulated an analysis which allows any complex repetitive wave to be analysed as the sum of a series of sine waves.

For example, in Figure 7.7 (overleaf), wave A is a complex wave. Fourier analysis tells us that it can be analysed as the sum of two simple sine waves B and C. To describe a sine wave, we need to know its frequency and amplitude. Wave B has a frequency of 100 Hz, and C has a frequency of 200 Hz.

The mathematical calculations of Fourier analysis to extract waves B and C are formidable, but the reverse observation that sine waves can be added together to form a complex wave is also true, and involves only addition. For example, waves B and C can be added together to produce wave A (Figure 7.7). At any point in time, the amplitude of the complex wave equals the sum of the amplitudes of the components. Thus, at a certain time, the amplitude of B is measured as (b) and the amplitude at the same time for C is measured as (c). The amplitude for the complex wave A, then, at that point in time is (a) which equals (b + c).

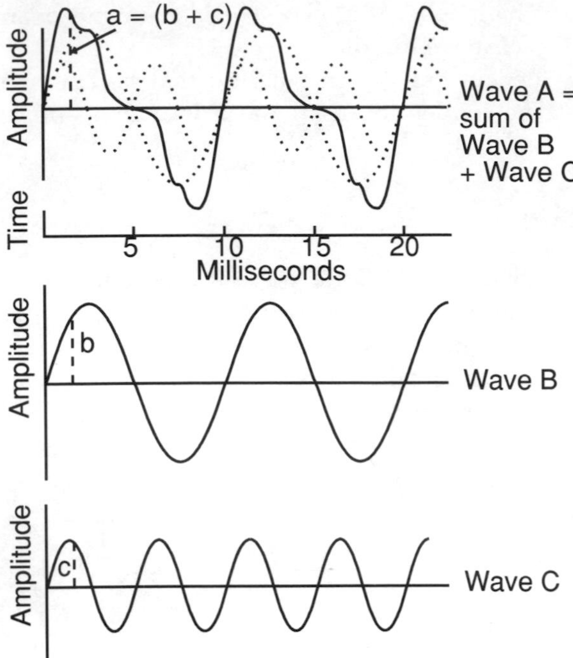

Figure 7.7 The addition of two sine waves to form a complex wave

Figure 7.8 shows the same process for a complex wave A with three components B, C, and D. The frequency and amplitudes are shown in Figure 7.9 on p. 140.

At every point in time, we add the intensity of the 100 Hz wave (B), the 200 Hz wave (C), and the 300 Hz wave (D) to get the intensity of the complex wave (A). In Figure 7.8, wave A shows the amplitude of the complex wave; that is, it is the sum of the amplitudes of the individual waves at every point in time.

Fourier analysis is an extremely important tool in acoustic phonetics. It takes the complex wave and analyses it into a series of sine waves, telling us the frequency and amplitude of the individual components. We believe that the human ear performs an analysis similar to that of Fourier analysis.

Harmonics

In the examples given so far, the complex wave has consisted of two or three component sine waves. The waves of speech sounds, however, consist of a large number of components. The individual components of the complex wave are called **harmonics**. Harmonics are numbered from the lowest upwards: the first harmonic, second harmonic, etc. The first harmonic has

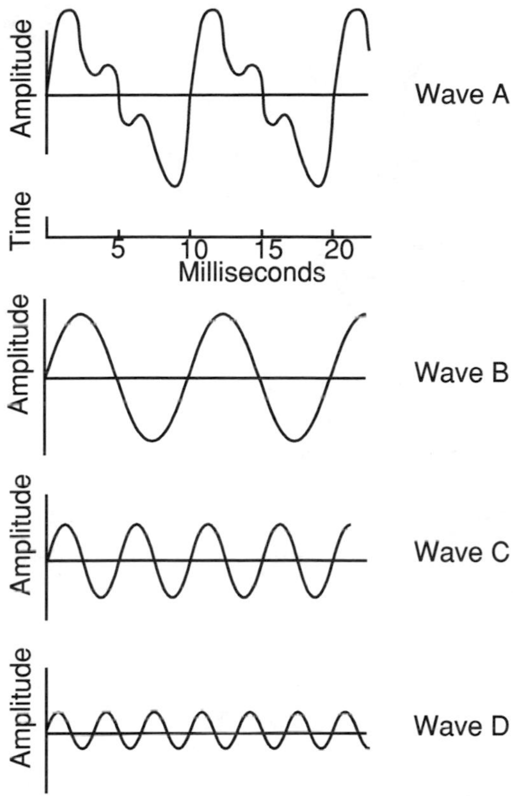

Figure 7.8 The addition of three sine waves to form a complex wave

the special name of **fundamental (harmonic)**; its frequency is called the **fundamental frequency**, often abbreviated $\mathbf{F_0}$ (read 'f-zero').

The frequency of every harmonic is a whole multiple of the frequency of the fundamental; that is, if the fundamental (first) harmonic has a frequency of 70 Hz, the second harmonic has a frequency of 140 Hz, the third of 210 Hz, etc. Note that the frequency of a complex wave is also 70 Hz. The frequency of the repetitive complex wave is always the same as the frequency of its fundamental. Since they are always the same, the pitch we perceive can be described as dependent on the frequency of the fundamental or on the frequency of the whole wave.

Spectrum

A **spectrum** is a display showing the frequency and the intensity (or amplitude) of the harmonic components of a wave. Figure 7.9 shows the spectrum of the wave shown in Figure 7.8. It has three harmonics with

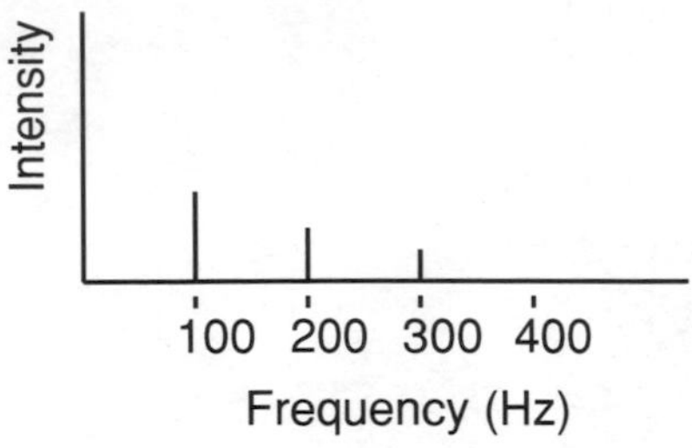

Figure 7.9 Spectrum of the complex wave of Figure 7.8

frequencies at 100 Hz, 200 Hz, and 300 Hz. The three harmonics have different intensities.

A sound **spectrogram** is a visual representation of the spectrum of a sound. Phoneticians generally use three dimensions in talking about the harmonic analysis of an utterance: frequency, intensity, and time. In order to put three dimensions on a two-dimensional piece of paper, the axes of the spectrogram are usually frequency (vertical) and time (horizontal); intensity is shown by darkness.

Figure 7.10 shows a spectrogram of the first part phrase *in union* [ɪn ˈjunjən]. The first harmonic is the lowest horizontal line, the second harmonic is the second lowest line, and so on. In this example, the first harmonic is at about 250 Hz and the second at 500 Hz. The frequencies can be established by referring to the scale at the left.

In the example in Figure 7.10, the first, second, and generally the third harmonics are continuous throughout the utterance; the higher harmonics are broken. In a spectrogram, time moves from left to right. Thus, in this

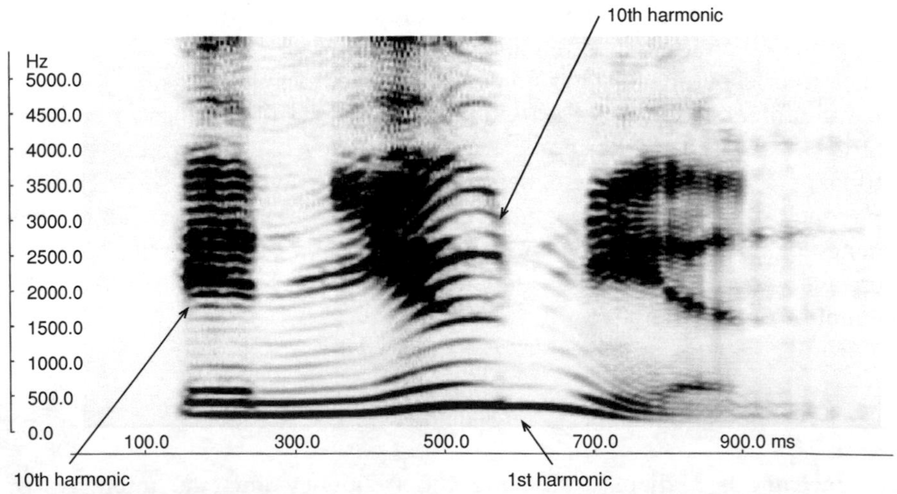

Figure 7.10 Spectrogram of *in union* [ɪn ˈjunjən] with first and tenth harmonics labelled

utterance, we can say that there are three points in time where the higher harmonics are strong, with weaker gaps in between. These darker areas on the spectrogram correspond to greater intensity in the acoustic signal. In this example the areas of greatest intensity correspond to the vowels and glides: from left to right, [ɪ], [ju], [jə].

Note that in Figure 7.10, the 10th harmonic is indicated. Since the frequency of each harmonic is always a whole multiple of the frequency of the fundamental (first) harmonic, the frequency of the 10th harmonic is always 10 times the frequency of the fundamental at that point in time. Often, it is easier to determine the fundamental frequency by determining the frequency of the 10th harmonic and dividing by ten. Thus, at the end of [n] in Figure 7.10, the frequency of the 10th harmonic is about 2500 Hz; therefore, the frequency of the 1st harmonic is 250 Hz. We could use other harmonics, but the 10th is convenient because dividing by 10 only involves moving the decimal point.

In Figure 7.11 we see a spectrogram of [ɑʔɑ], spoken with rising and then falling pitch. The gap in the middle corresponds to the glottal stop. The frequency of the harmonics changes, corresponding to the changes in pitch first with rising harmonics and then falling. Since harmonics are all multiples of the fundamental, if one harmonic changes, they all change. We perceive this as a sound with a rising pitch. In the later part of Figure 7.11, the harmonics fall; we perceive this as a sound with a falling pitch.

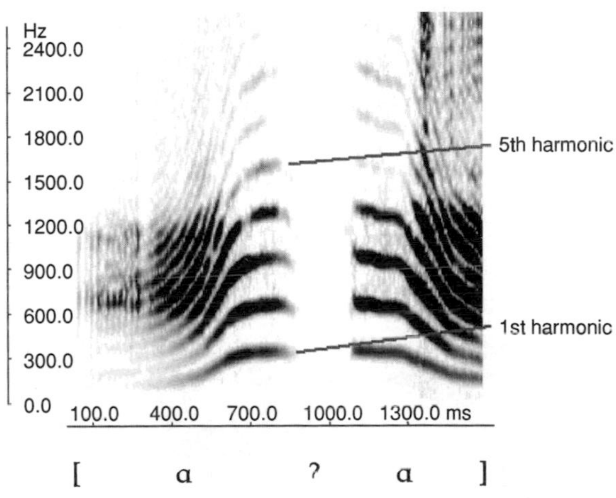

Figure 7.11 Spectrogram of [ɑʔɑ] spoken with rising, then falling pitch

Figure 7.12 (overleaf) shows the diphthong [aj] spoken at a steady pitch. Note that the harmonics stay level, but their intensities change. A level harmonic indicates a steady pitch; changes in their intensity indicate a changing vocalic quality.

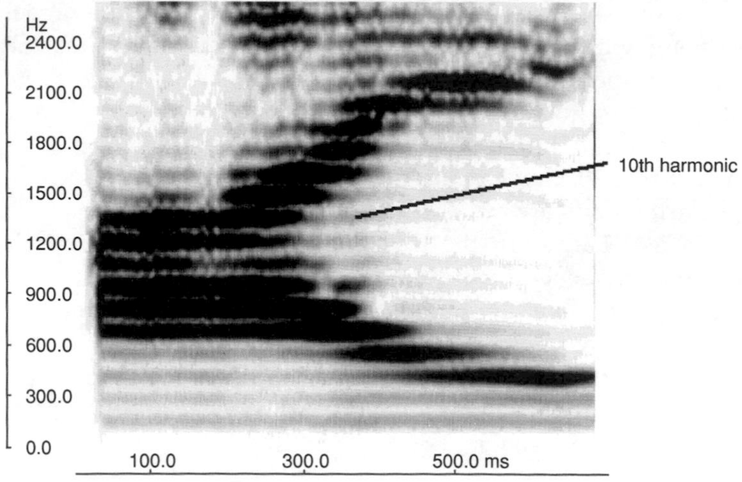

Figure 7.12 Spectrogram of [aj] spoken with a level pitch

Thus, we see that in making a vowel, the pitch and the vowel quality are completely independent. We can easily verify this by singing a tune pronouncing only the vowel [u]. In the same way, we can say different vowels at the same pitch. Remember, pitch depends on the frequency of the fundamental, controlled by the vibration rate of the vocal folds. Vowel quality depends on the shape of the vocal tract.

We hear the fundamental frequency as the pitch of a sound. Generally, we do not hear the individual harmonics as such, although if a harmonic is artificially removed from the wave, we are able to hear the difference in sound quality.

Glottal wave

When the vocal folds are vibrating, the steady flow of air from the lungs is broken up into a series of pressure variations by the repeated opening and closing of the vocal folds. By this mechanism, a glottal wave is formed. Figure 7.13 shows this wave.

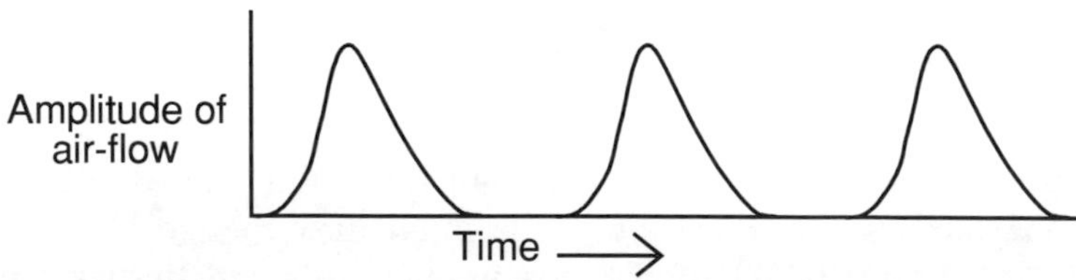

Figure 7.13 Spectrum of the glottal wave

Next we will see how this glottal spectrum is modified as it passes through the vocal tract.

Resonance

An important acoustic property is **resonance**, the natural tendency of a body to vibrate at a certain frequency. You know that if you pluck a string on a violin, it vibrates at a certain frequency. This is because a string has a natural resonating frequency, which depends on its mass, length, and tension. If the string is tightened, its natural resonating frequency is raised. A tube or other cavity also has a resonating frequency. If you blow across the lip of a bottle, the air in the bottle will vibrate at a certain frequency. If the volume of this cavity is changed, the resonating frequency changes as well. If you drink some of the fluid out of the bottle, the air cavity within is enlarged. Now, when you blow across the lip, the resulting pitch is lower than before. The larger the cavity, the lower its resonating frequency.

The top of Figure 7.14 (overleaf) shows the spectrum of the glottal wave given in Figure 7.13. Note that the fundamental is strongest in amplitude with gradually decreasing amplitudes as the harmonics get higher in frequency.

A body resonates not just at a single frequency but over a range of frequencies. The middle of Figure 7.14 shows the **resonance curve** of a certain complex tube. Such a curve shows how strongly the tube will resonate at various frequencies. The tube of Figure 7.14 will resonate strongly at frequencies around 400, 2300, and 3000 Hz, but less strongly at other frequencies. In fact, our vocal tract is a tube with approximately the resonance curve of Figure 7.14 when it is shaped to produce the vowel [i].

Our vocal folds vibrate so as to produce a glottal wave with a spectrum like that in Figure 7.14. Our vocal tract acts as a resonator, modifying the glottal spectrum. The output, after the glottal wave has been modified by the vocal tract, is a sound which we hear as [i], with a spectrum like that shown at the bottom of Figure 7.14. The peaks of intensity shown in Figure 7.14 at 400, 2300, and 3000 Hz are called **formants**. Formants are crucial in distinguishing different sounds.

The frequencies of the fundamental and the harmonics are determined entirely by the vibration of the string, and thus they remain at the same frequencies as before; that is, the spacing of the harmonics in the spectra of the glottal wave and the output wave (Figure 7.14) is the same. Passing the glottal wave through the tube does, however, change the intensities of its harmonics to agree more closely with its resonance curve, producing the formant pattern as in Figure 7.14.

One way of looking at resonance is to consider that a resonating chamber filters the spectrum which it receives. The output spectrum is the result of the filtering action of the resonator. Some frequencies are passed freely;

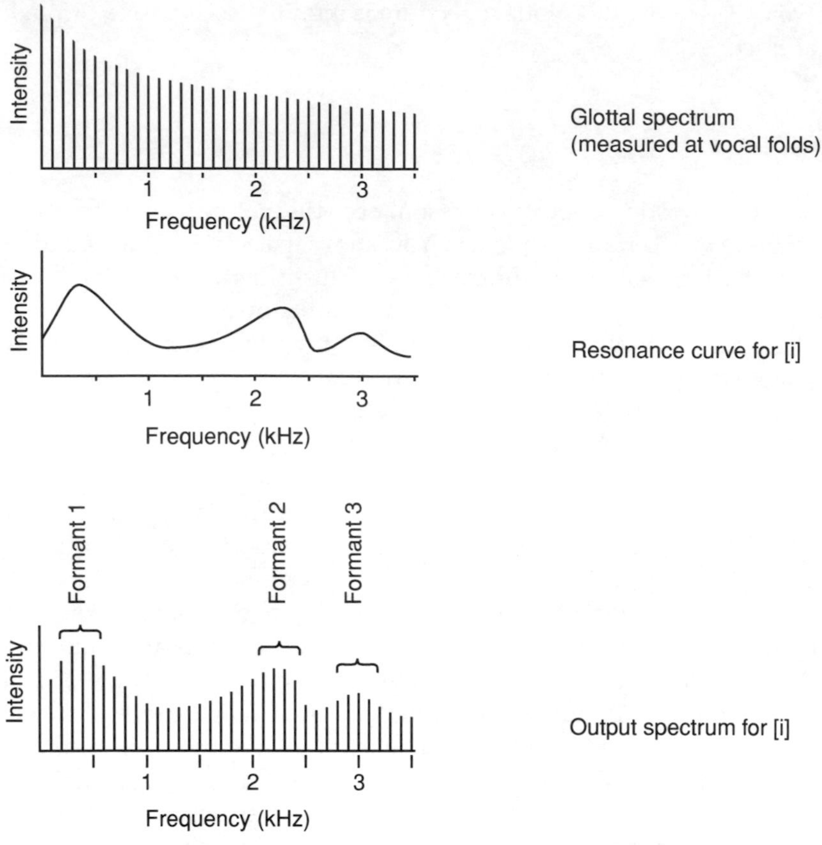

Figure 7.14 Glottal spectrum, resonance curve, and spectrum (after passing though the resonating vocal tract). The vocal tract is shaped for [i]

these are formant frequencies. Other frequencies are filtered out; these frequencies form the valleys in the output spectrum.

We can change the tension of our vocal folds so that they vibrate at a different rate and thus change the fundamental frequency (and consequently the frequencies of the other harmonics). We can also change the shape of our upper vocal tract, by moving our jaw, tongue, lips, etc., producing a great variety of shapes, each with its own resonance curve. We can thus produce a great variety of sounds.

Remember:

- the frequency of the fundamental harmonic determines the pitch we hear;
- the frequencies of the other harmonics are whole multiples of the fundamental;
- the frequencies of the formants determine vowel quality.

Noise

Up to now, all the sounds we have discussed have had a repetitive cyclical wave form. There are, however, certain speech sounds which do not have such wave forms. They exhibit irregular energy called **noise**. In an unconstricted path, air flows in a smooth linear fashion. When the pathway is partially constricted, the constriction causes turbulence in the air-flow. This turbulence produces noise (also known as **frication**); it has the quality of a fricative. If you make a long, strong voiceless [s], you will hear the noise produced by turbulence as air strikes the teeth. On a spectrogram, noise appears as a pattern of random speckles, often referred to as the **random noise pattern**. The energy in noise is not organised into formants as it is in sounds produced by repetitive waveforms, such as vowels. Figure 7.15 shows the waveform and spectrogram of a fricative [s]. Note the irregular waveform and the speckled random noise pattern in the spectrogram. Also note that the energy has a fairly high frequency, starting at about 4500 Hz.

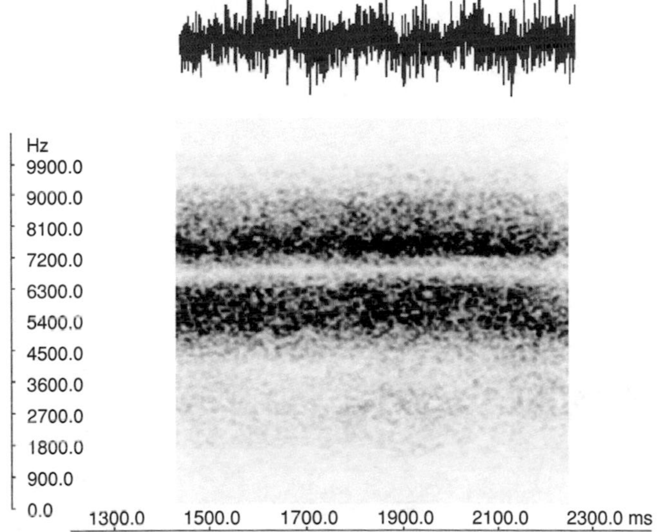

Figure 7.15 Waveform and spectrogram of [s]

Technical terms

acoustic phonetics
acoustics
amplitude
complex repetitive wave
cycle
decibel (dB)
Fourier analysis
formant
frequency
frication
fundamental (harmonic)
fundamental frequency
glottal wave
harmonic
Hertz (Hz)
intensity
F_0
loudness
millisecond
noise
oscillation
overtone
pitch
propagation
random noise pattern
resonance
resonance curve
sine wave
sinusoidal wave
spectrum
spectrogram
vibration
vocal tract

Exercises

Basic

1 Determine the frequency of the sine waves in Figure 7.16.

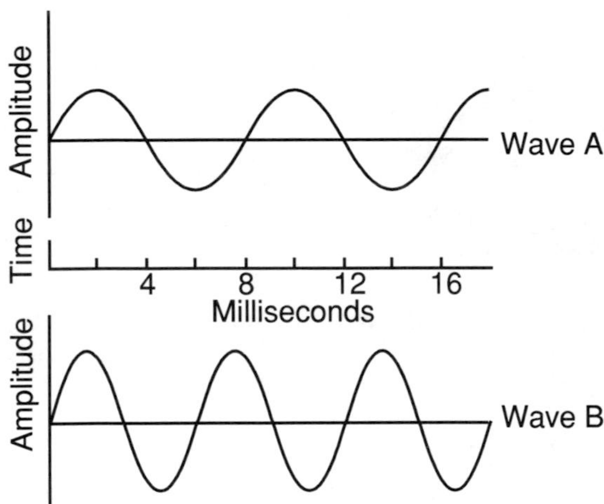

Figure 7.16

2 In Figure 7.17, what is the frequency of the wave (taken as a whole)? What is the amplitude at points a, b, and c of the wave in Figure 7.17? Use the amplitude scale 2 to –2 given at the left.

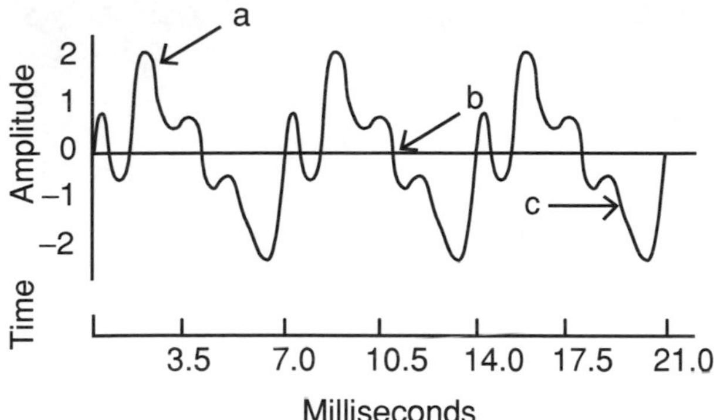

Figure 7.17

3 On the spectrogram in Figure 7.18,

a. Point out the 1st, 4th, and 10th harmonics.

b. Using the 10th harmonic, determine the fundamental frequency at the time indicated by the arrow.

c. What pitch changes would we hear during the course of the entire sound?

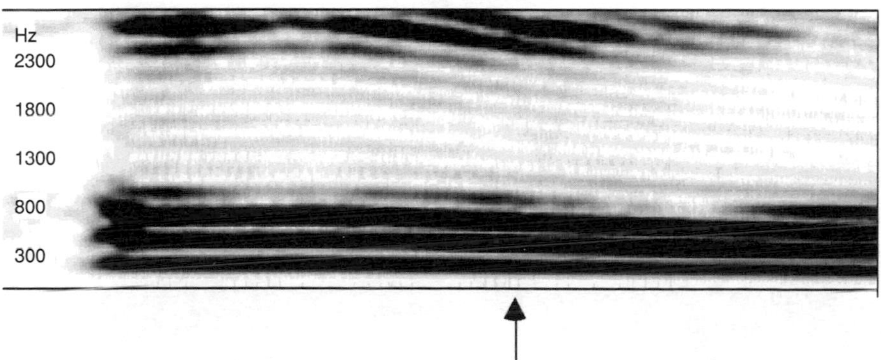

Figure 7.18

4 In Figure 7.19, two sine waves, B and C are given. You are to add them together to get the resulting complex wave A. To help you, waves B and C are shown together in dotted lines on the line where you are to draw wave A.

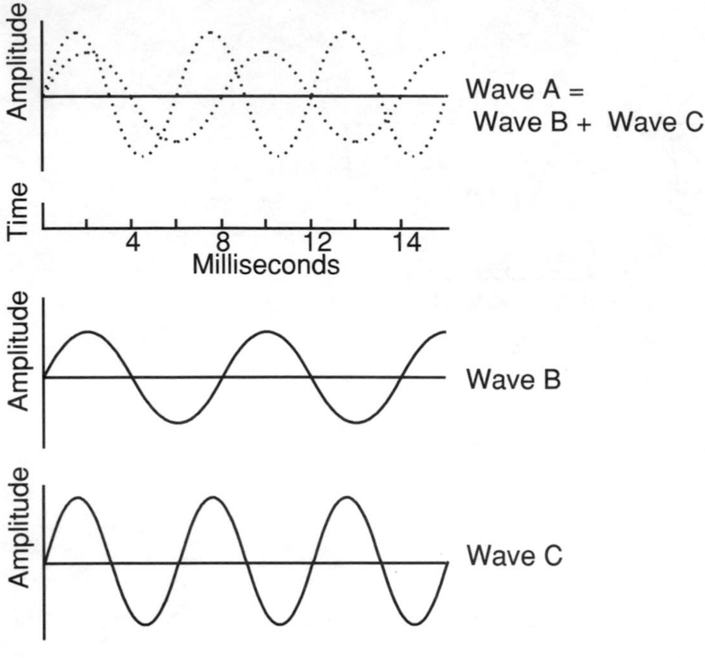

Figure 7.19

5 In the spectrum below (Figure 7.20), there are four formants. Label them F1, F2, F3, and F4 and determine the strongest frequency of each.

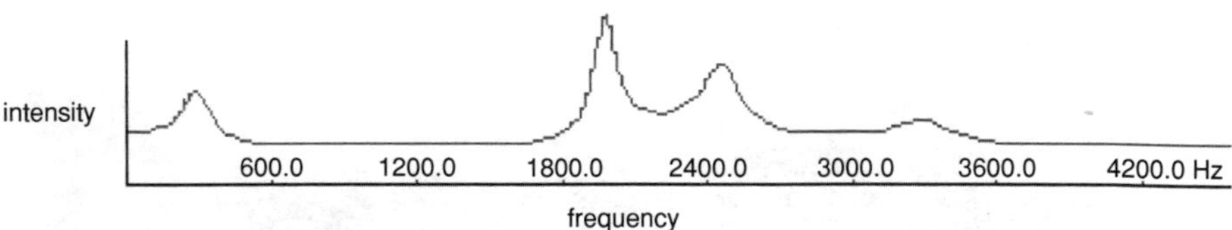

Figure 7.20

Advanced

6 The following selection is from *The Canterbury Tales* giving a reconstruction of how it would have been pronounced by Chaucer in the fourteenth century. If you are unfamiliar with any of the symbols, look ahead to find out how to pronounce them.

THE CANTERBURY TALES

General Prologue, 1–42

ʍan ðat ˈaˑpril wiθ iz ˈʃuˑrəz ˈsoˑtə
ðə druˑxt əv martʃ aθ peˑrsəd to θə ˈroˑtə
an ˈbaˑðəd ˈevri væjn in switʃ liˈkuˑr
əv ʍitʃ verˈtyˑ inˈdʒendrəd iz ðə fluˑr
ʍan ˈzefirus eˑk wiθ iz ˈsweˑtə brɛˑθ
inˈspiˑrəd haθ in ˈevri hɔlt and hɛˑθ
ðə ˈtendrə ˈkrɔpəz an θə ˈjuŋgə ˈsunə
haθ in ðə ram iz ˈhalvə kuˑrs iˈrunə
and ˈsmaˑlə ˈfuˑləz ˈmaˑkən ˌmeloˈdiˑə
ðat ˈsleˑpən ɑl ðə niˑçt wiθ ˈɔˑpən ˌiˑə
sɔˑ ˈprikəθ əm naˑˈtyˑr in ir kuˈraˑdʒəz
ðan ˈlɔŋgən fɔlk to gɔˑn ɔn ˌpilgriˈmaˑdʒəz
and ˈpalmərz fɔr to ˈseˑkən ˈstrɑwndʒə ˈstɹɔndəz
to ˈfernə ˈhalwəz kuˑð in ˈsundri ˈlɔˑndəz
an ˈspesjali frɔm ˈevri ˈʃiˑrəz ˈendə
əv ˈeŋgelɔnd to ˈkɑwntərbri ðæj ˈwendə
ðə ˈhɔˑli ˈblisful ˈmartir fɔr to ˈseˑkə
ðat hem haθ ˈhɔlpən ʍan ðat ðæj wɛˑr ˈseˑkə.

Whan that Aprill with his shoures soote
The droghte of March hath perced to the roote,
And bathed every veine in swich licour
Of which vertu engendred is the flour;
Whan Zephirus eek with his sweete breeth
Inspired hath in every holt and heeth
The tendre croppes, and the yonge sonne
Hath in the Ram his halve cours yronne,
And smale foweles maken melodie,
That slepen al the night with open ye
So priketh hem nature in hir corages;
Thanne longen folk to goon on pilgrimages,
And palmeres for to seken straunge strondes,
To ferne halwes, kowthe in sondry londes;
And specially from every shires ende
Of Engelond to Caunterbury they wende,
The hooly blisful martir for to seke,
That hem hath holpen whan that they were seeke.

Chapter 8

The acoustics of English sounds

Phoneticians have known for many years that it would be useful to analyse the spectra of various speech sounds. In the middle of the nineteenth century, Georg Ohm proposed the notion that our ear and brain act as though they perform a Fourier analysis on incoming sounds (Handel, 1989). Until the 1940s, the process of performing the necessary mathematical calculations, Fourier analysis, of a complex wave was so time-consuming that it was seldom attempted. World War II, however, saw the invention of the sound spectrograph which displayed the changing spectrum of a short segment of speech. During the 1950s and 1960s, a large amount of phonetic research was done using this machine. In recent years, computers have been used to analyse digitised speech. The spectrograms in this book were made on a Macintosh computer using the sound analysis program Signalyze (1994).

In this chapter you will learn about:

- spectrograms;
- formants;
- how English vowels and consonants are analysed acoustically.

Under the speaker's control, the vocal tract is capable of assuming a large number of different positions, filtering the source wave from the glottis and thus producing a corresponding number of different sounds. A basic task of the phonetician is to relate the variations in the output spectrum to the articulatory actions of the various sounds of language. In this chapter we will try to do this, first for the vowels of English and then for the consonants.

Spectrograms

Consider now the spectrograms in Figures 8.1 and 8.2. These are two different spectrograms of the exact same utterance 'a pony cart' [ə ˈpʰowni ˌkʰɑɹt], spoken with a GA accent. The first spectrogram (Figure 8.1) is called a **narrow-band spectrogram**; it is the kind that we saw in the previous chapter. The second spectrogram (Figure 8.2) is called a **wide-band spectrogram**. The two types of spectrogram are made by different settings of the analysis program. The technical details need not bother us. The narrow-band

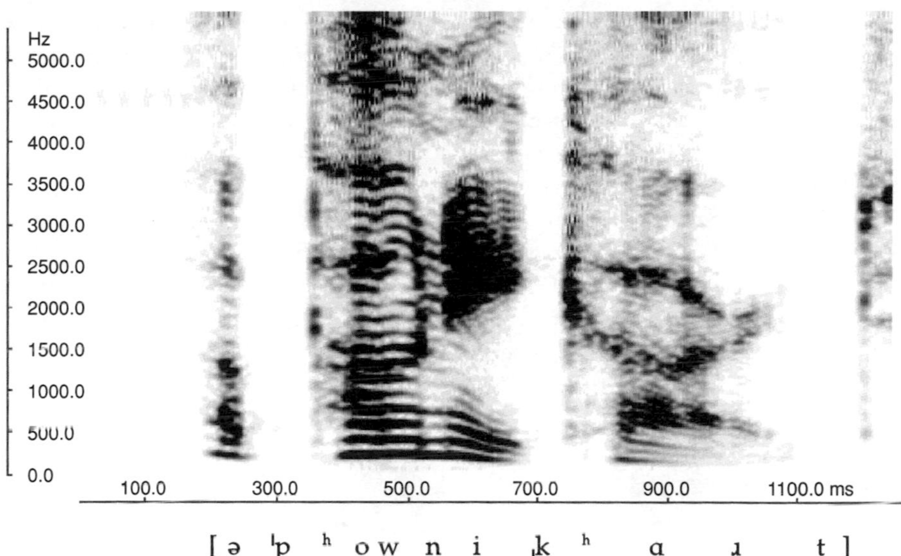

Figure 8.1 Narrow-band spectrogram of *a pony cart* (GA accent) (time in milliseconds)

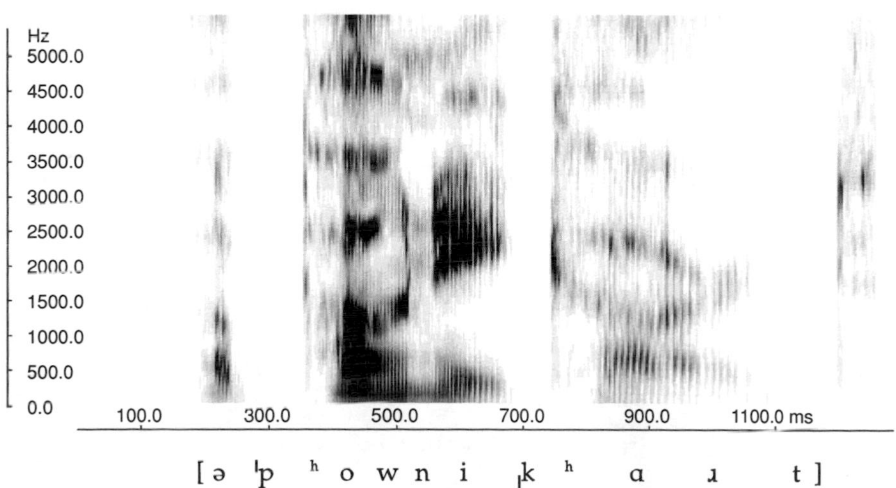

Figure 8.2 Wide-band spectrogram of *a pony cart* (GA accent) (time in milliseconds)

spectrogram gives good resolution for frequency, but blurs time somewhat; the wide-band spectrogram blurs frequency, but has good time resolution. Note that the individual harmonics are clear on the narrow-band spectrograms, but are blurred together on the wide-band spectrogram. On the wide-band spectrogram, we see thick, more-or-less horizontal, black lines, called **formants**. Formants indicate clusters of harmonics with high intensities, relative to their neighbours. Formants are particularly useful in distinguishing vowels. These are numbered from the one with the lowest frequency: F1, F2, F3, etc. In general, the wide-band spectrogram is more useful in phonetics than the narrow-band spectrogram.

Looking at the narrow-band spectrogram (Figure 8.1), we see the stops [p k t] as vertical gaps in the pattern; the vowels show up as harmonics. On the wide-band spectrogram (Figure 8.2), the stops are the same as before, but for the vowels we see formant patterns rather than harmonics. On both spectrograms, note that the stressed vowels [ow] and [ɑ] have greater intensity (shown as darkness) than the unstressed schwa.

English vowels

Vowel formants

Let's examine now the short vowels of English [ɪ ɛ æ ʊ]. The data we need are given in Figure 8.3 which shows the spectrograms for the words *pit, pet, pat,* and *put.*

In the vowel [ɪ], the first formant (F1) has its highest intensity at approximately 500 Hz; the second formant (F2) has an average frequency of about 2300 Hz. F3 is at 3000 Hz, and F4 at 4400 Hz. Table 8.1 shows the approximate frequency for each of the vowels.

The first three formants vary according to which vowel is being pronounced. Occasionally we see a fourth formant or higher. Formants F4 and higher vary among speakers, but not much for the same speaker. The higher

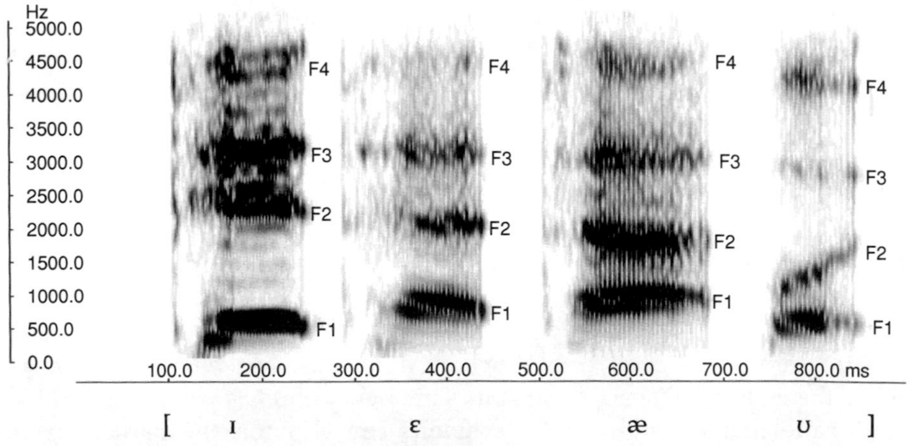

Figure 8.3 The vowels in *pit, pet, pat, put*

Table 8.1 Vowel formants of [ɪ ɛ æ ʊ]

	ɪ	ɛ	æ	ʊ
F1	500	700	800	500
F2	2300	2100	1800	1000–1500
F3	3000	3100	3000	3000
F4	4400	4500	4500	4300

formants are primarily determined by the shape and size of the individual's head, nasal cavity, sinus cavities, etc., physical characteristics which the individual cannot vary and thus are not relevant to phonetics.

Phoneticians focus on the first three formants for linguistic information. We see that F1 is low for [ɪ] and [ʊ], and higher for [æ] and [ɛ]. The distribution correlates fairly well, in reverse, to the articulatory height of the vowel; that is, if the tongue is high, the first formant is low, and if the tongue is low, the first formant is high.

Now consider F2. Going through these vowels in the order [ɪ ɛ æ ʊ], F2 starts high and becomes progressively lower. The height of F2 correlates roughly with the backness of the vowel, with [ɪ] being farthest to the front, and [ʊ] farthest to the back. Note that the changing quality of F2 for [ʊ] indicates that in this pronunciation, the shape of the vocal tract was changing.

Understanding why formants have the frequencies they do is too complex for us to investigate thoroughly, but we can understand a bit by looking at the front vowels. Think of the highest point of the tongue dividing the vocal tract into a front cavity and a back cavity. From the preceding chapter, we know that the resonating frequency is higher for a small cavity than for a large one. Moving from [ɪ] to [æ], the body of the tongue is pulled back, making the front cavity larger and the back cavity smaller. Thus, as we go from [ɪ] to [æ], the resonating frequency of the front cavity is lowered as it becomes larger, and the resonating frequency of the back cavity is raised as it becomes smaller. If we identify the back cavity with the first formant and the front cavity with the second formant, we can understand the relationship between the shape of the vocal tract and the frequencies of the formants.

Naturally, there is variation in formant frequencies, depending on the size of specific vocal tracts and their shape for specific vowels. However, measurements taken over large samples have produced averages such as those shown in Table 8.2. Note that the speaker in Table 8.1 has generally higher formants, suggesting possibly a slightly smaller vocal tract than

Table 8.2 English vowel formants for adult male speakers (RP from Gimson, 1980; GA from Peterson and Barney, 1952)

	RP			GA		
	F1	**F2**	**F3**	**F1**	**F2**	**F3**
i	280	2620	3380	270	2290	3010
ɪ	360	2220	2960	390	1990	2550
ɛ	600	2060	2840	530	1840	2480
æ	800	1760	2500	660	1720	2410
ɜ	560	1480	2520	—	—	—
ʌ	760	1320	2500	640	1190	2390
ɑ	740	1180	2640	730	1090	2440
ɒ	560	920	2560	—	—	—
ɔ	480	760	2620	570	840	2410
ʊ	380	940	2300	440	1020	2240
u	320	920	2200	300	870	2240

average. The differences between RP and GA are not great, particularly for F1 and F2. Humans seem to have the ability to adjust quickly to small differences between their own speech and that of other speakers, an ability which facilitates communication greatly.

Rather than trying to memorise these values, a useful way of remembering the formant frequencies relative to each other is to use the following rules of thumb illustrated in Figure 8.4:

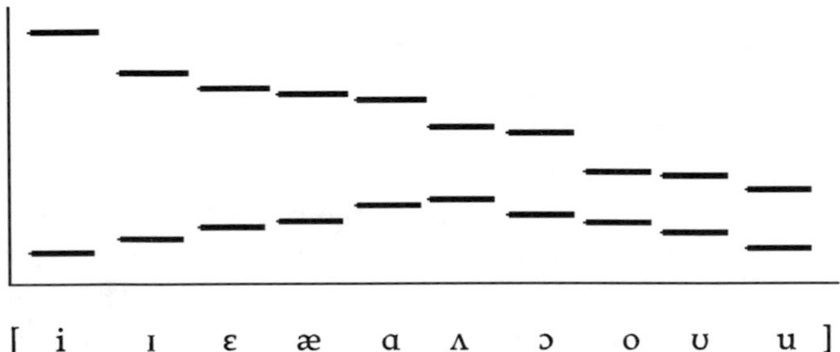

[i ɪ ɛ æ ɑ ʌ ɔ o ʊ u]

Figure 8.4 The pattern of the first two formants for the simple vowels of English

1 Line up the vowels progressively in the order:

high front → low front → low back → high back
i.e., [i ɪ e ɛ æ ɑ ʌ ɔ o ʊ u]

2 The following statements can then be applied to the vowels proceeding from left to right.

a F1 starts low and rises until the vowel [ɑ], then F1 falls.
b F2 starts high and falls.
c F3 is similar to F2, but higher.
d F2 for [ɔ] is a bit lower than we might expect.

Diphthongs

Diphthongs consist of a vowel and glide together. In Chapter 4 we described [aj] as moving from a low front to a high front position. From Figure 8.5 we can see that the first two formants for [aj] start off fairly close together, as we would expect for a low vowel. During the glide, they move apart, ending in the position for [i]. This makes sense since [j] is a glide with an end point roughly of [i]. In the spectrograms for [aw], the first two formants start off in the mid-range, similar to [a], and then both fall, moving closer together, as we would expect, moving to the position of the vowel [u]. Also, in Figure 8.5, we can see that in [ju], the glide with its moving formants precedes the vowel with its steadier formants. Can you explain the location and movement of the formants for [ɔj]?

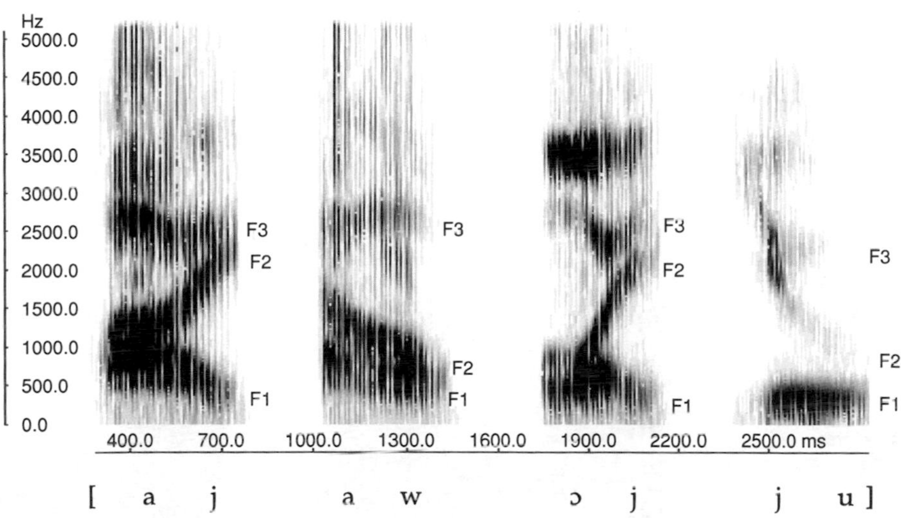

Figure 8.5 Spectrograms for the glides [aj aw ɔj ju]

In Figure 8.6 (overleaf), the formants in the GA diphthongs [ej] and [ow] move somewhat, showing the changing vowel quality of the diphthongs, but not so dramatically as with [aj] and [aw]. This is reasonable since the distance of going from [e] to [i] is less than that of [a] to [i]. In Figure 8.6, we also see that [i] and [u] have a slight diphthongal quality, as we noted in Chapter 4.

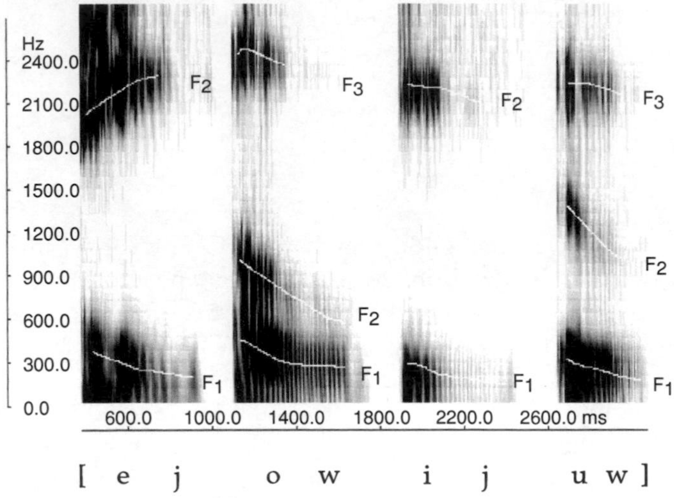

Figure 8.6 Spectrograms showing the glides [ej ow ij uw]

Vowel length

In Chapter 4, we discussed the allophonic lengthening of vowels in English. On a spectrogram, the length of a vowel can be measured quite accurately. Compare the spectrograms for *beat*, *bead*, and *bee* in Figure 8.7. You can easily see that the vowels are not of the same length. The vowel before a voiceless consonant is shorter; the vowel before a voiced consonant and in

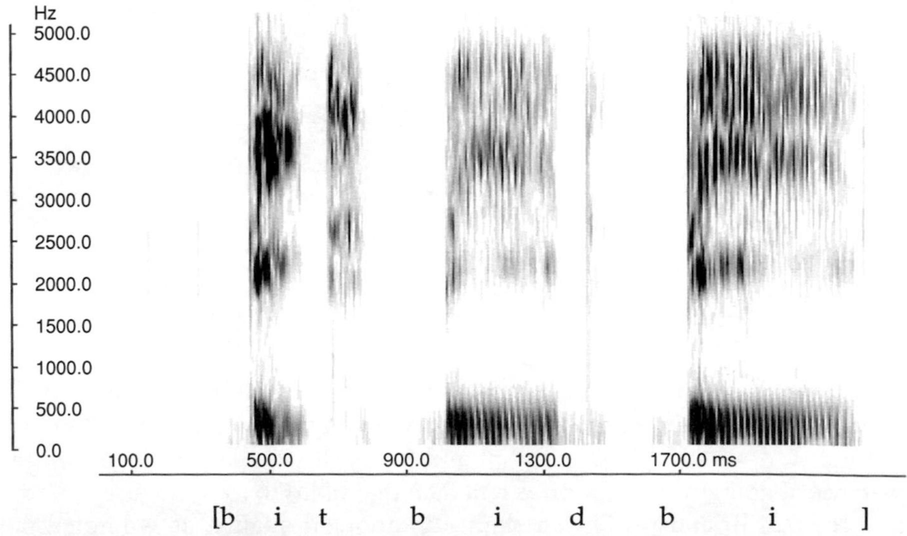

Figure 8.7 Spectrograms of *beat*, *bead*, *bee*

an open syllable is longer. This length is consistent with our statement of vowel length in Chapter 4.

Figure 8.8 shows the length of the diphthong /aj/ in the words *light, lied, lie.*

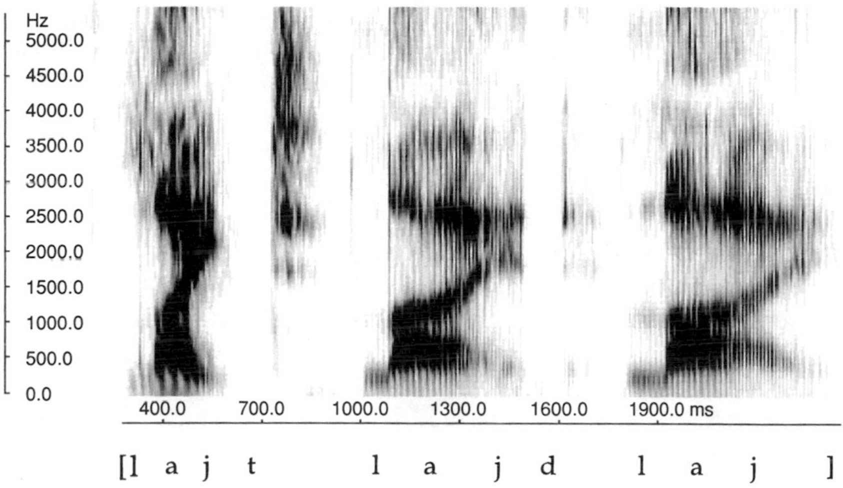

Figure 8.8 Allophonic length in [aj]: *light, lied, lie*

Stress

Consider the words *tendency* and *excessive,* shown in Figure 8.9. In the spectrograms for each word, you can see that the syllable with major stress

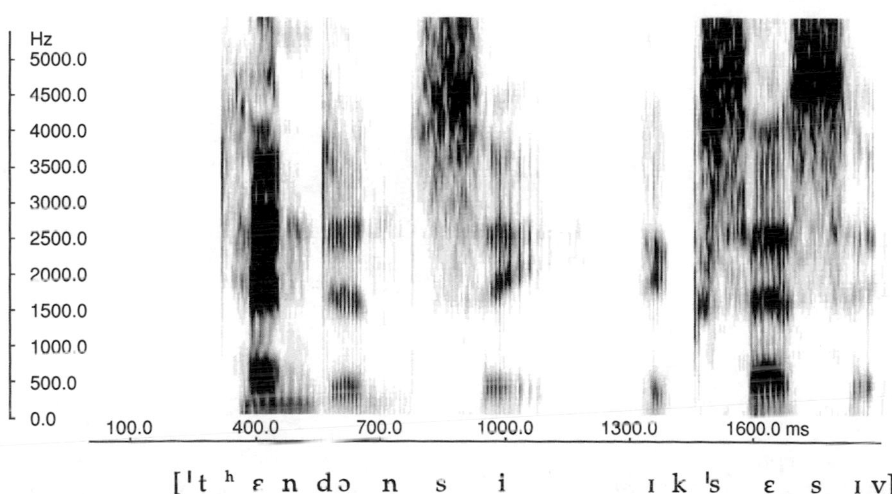

Figure 8.9 Stress appears as stronger intensity and longer vowels: *tendency, excessive*

has greater intensity and often lasts longer than those syllables which are unstressed. In *tendency*, the first syllable has stronger formants than do the other syllables. The first syllable in *excessive* is short and weaker, with less intensity; the middle syllable clearly has greater intensity than the other two syllables.

Figure 8.9 shows spectrograms for *tendency* and *excessive*. The stressed syllable in these words is easy to recognise. Note in both words as well that a final unstressed syllable tends to be longer than an unstressed syllable earlier in the word.

Voicing

In wide-band spectrograms of vowels, you frequently notice vertical lines. These **vertical striations** show voicing. Each of these striations corresponds to the opening and closing of the vocal folds. Striation is typical of voiced sounds generally. You can even tell the pitch of a sound by measuring the distance between two striations and calculating the frequency of the vibration at that time. With the better time resolution of the wide-band spectrogram, these striations show up clearly; on the narrow-band spectrogram with poorer time resolution, they are not visible.

The spectrogram in Figure 8.10 shows the rhyme of the word *there*, i.e. [ɛɹ] spoken with a GA accent. The word is said with a falling pitch. At the beginning of the vowel, the vertical striations are 6 ms apart, giving a frequency of 166 Hz. At the end, the striations are 12 ms apart, a frequency of 83 Hz. We hear the decrease in frequency as a decrease in pitch. The wider apart the striations, the lower the pitch. Voicing usually shows up stronger in the lower frequencies.

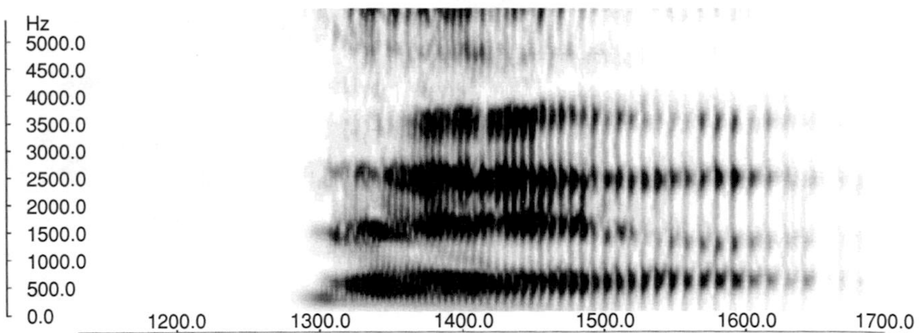

Figure 8.10 Spectrogram of the rhyme [ɛə] of *there* (RP accent). The vertical striations correspond to individual vibrations of the vocal folds

In Chapter 3, we discussed the voicing of consonants. Consonants in English are generally voiceless both at the very beginning and at the very end of a word. Compare the spectrograms in Figure 8.11 for *bit*, *pit*, *spit*. You can see that the [b] in *bit* is almost completely voiceless; with the

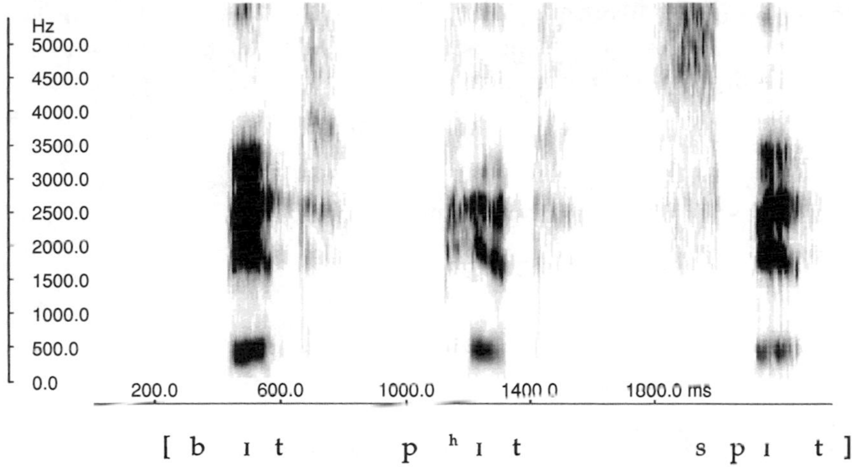

Figure 8.11 Spectrograms of *bit, pit, spit*

aspirated stop [pʰ] of *pit*, there is a period of voiceless aspiration which appears as a noise segment; in *spit*, the vowel is voiced immediately after the stop with no aspiration. We have already said that aspiration is realised as the delay in the onset of voicing.

English consonants

Consider the spectrogram in Figure 8.12 of *I can pass it*. Phonemically, the trancription is /ˌaj kən ˈpɑs ɪt/ in an RP accent. A narrow transcription

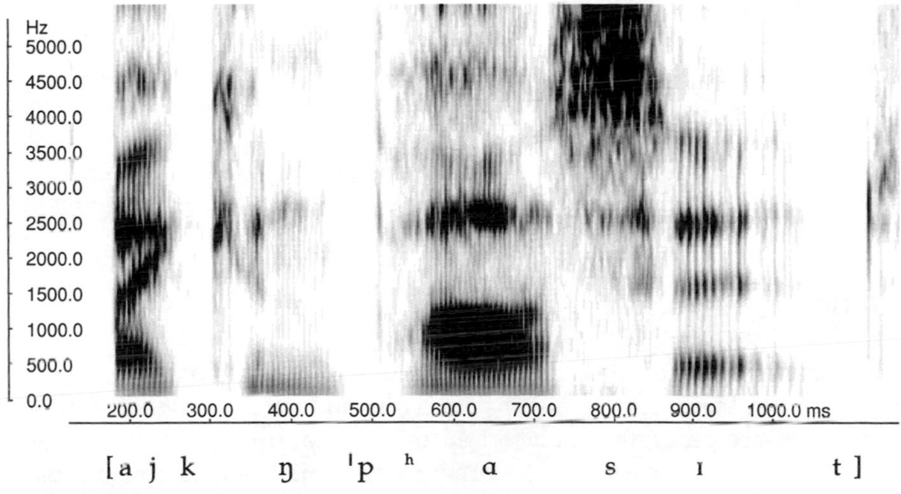

Figure 8.12 Spectrogram of *I can pass it* (RP accent)

would be something like [ˌaj kŋ̍ ˈpʰɑs ɪt]. The vowel portions show strong formant patterns. The stronger intensity in *pass* shows that it is the stressed syllable. The diphthong [aj] is at the beginning, the vowel [æ] is just past the middle, and the vowel [ɪ] is near the end. The stop consonants show up as gaps: first, [k] is fairly long, [pʰ] shows aspiration at its release as scattered bits of energy, and the [t] at the end is a gap. The fricative [s] shows up as a random noise pattern, without a formant pattern, and with energy particularly in the higher frequencies. The [s] of *pass* shows the random noise pattern.

Place of articulation

Place of articulation is not so readily determined from a spectrogram. Consider three voiceless stops [p t k]. During these three sounds, nothing is happening to make an acoustic impression: no air is exiting from the body, and the vocal folds are not vibrating. For each of these, the spectrogram shows a blank. How then can we distinguish three blanks, three gaps in the acoustic record? The answer is that we do not distinguish these sounds by themselves, but by the effect they have on their neighbouring sounds. Consider the sequences [pɛ tɛ kɛ]. The mouth, in moving from the [p] to the [ɛ], changes shape in a particular fashion. In moving from [t] to [ɛ], it changes shape in a different fashion, and from [k] to [ɛ], in a still different fashion. This means that the initial edge of the [ɛ] is slightly different for each of the three syllables [pɛ tɛ kɛ]. The edge of the vowel next to the consonant is called the **transition**, the time period when the mouth is changing shape between consonant and vowel.

The important spectrographic feature distinguishing the various consonant–vowel transitions is the second formant. If you examine the transitions in Figure 8.13, you will see that in [ɛbɛ], the edges of the second formant point down into the gap slightly; in [ɛdɛ], the transitions are fairly level; and in [ɛgɛ], the transitions point up into the gap. The preconsonantal velar transitions are further marked by a noticeable coming together of the second and third formants. You should not be surprised, however, if the place of articulation is not readily apparent in examining spectrograms.

Manner

The manner of articulation can often be determined from a spectrogram (Figure 8.14). During stops, no air passes out, and the spectrogram shows a gap. Stops are generally characterised by fairly abrupt onset and release. The release is often marked by a strong vertical **spike**. Aspirated stops have a bit of noise before the vowel formants begin. Fricatives, as we will see

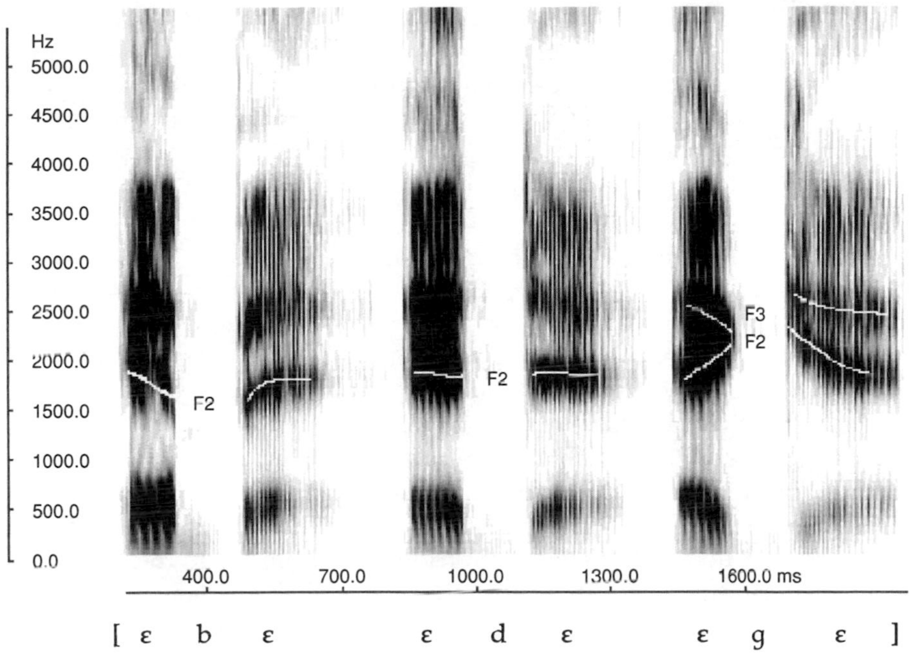

Figure 8.13 Spectrograms of [ɛbɛ ɛdɛ ɛgɛ] showing different places of articulation

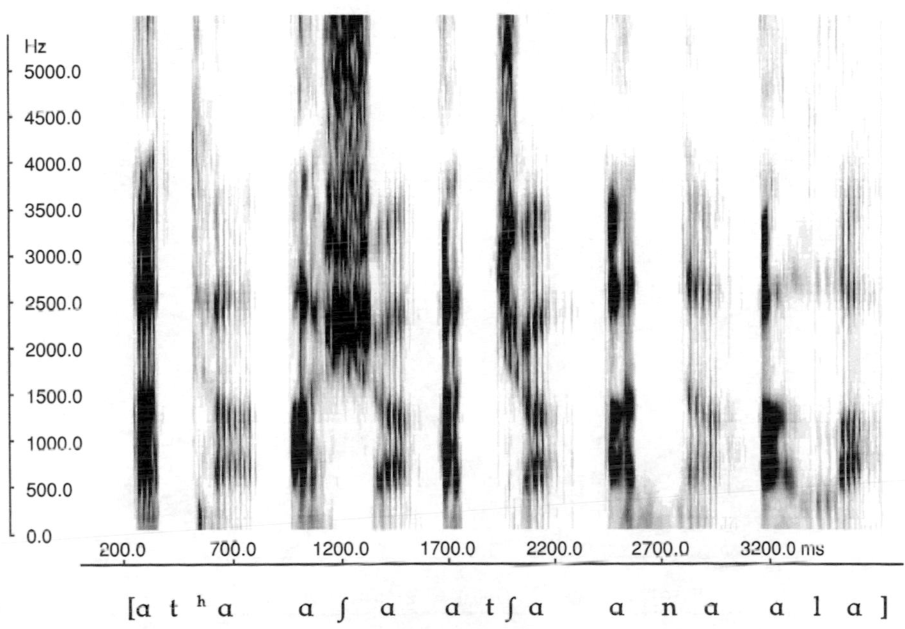

Figure 8.14 Spectrogram of [ɑtʰɑ ɑʃɑ ɑtʃɑ ɑnɑ ɑlɑ]

in the next section, are characterised by random noise. Affricates can be recognised by a gap for the stop portion followed by noise for the fricative portion. We have already seen that vowels show formant patterns with strong intensity. Laterals and nasals generally have formant patterns, but weaker than for vowels.

Fricatives

Fricatives are usually easy to distinguish from other sounds by the random noise pattern. They are not easy, however, to distinguish from each other. Figure 8.15 shows spectrograms of the English fricatives. Sometimes [f v θ ð] are so weak that they barely show up at all. The fricatives [s z ʃ ʒ] usually appear in spectrograms with energy in the higher frequencies. The alveolar fricatives [s z] have energy concentrated in the high frequencies, in the range 4000–8000 Hz (note the frequency scale at the left). The palato-alveolar fricatives [ʃ ʒ] are somewhat lower, in the range 2000–6000 Hz. The labiodentals [f] and [v] have their main noise around 6000–8000, but they are often quite faint. The voiced fricatives are similar to their voiceless counterparts; they often show vertical striations, and sometimes a **voice bar**, a formant-like band of energy at very low frequencies.

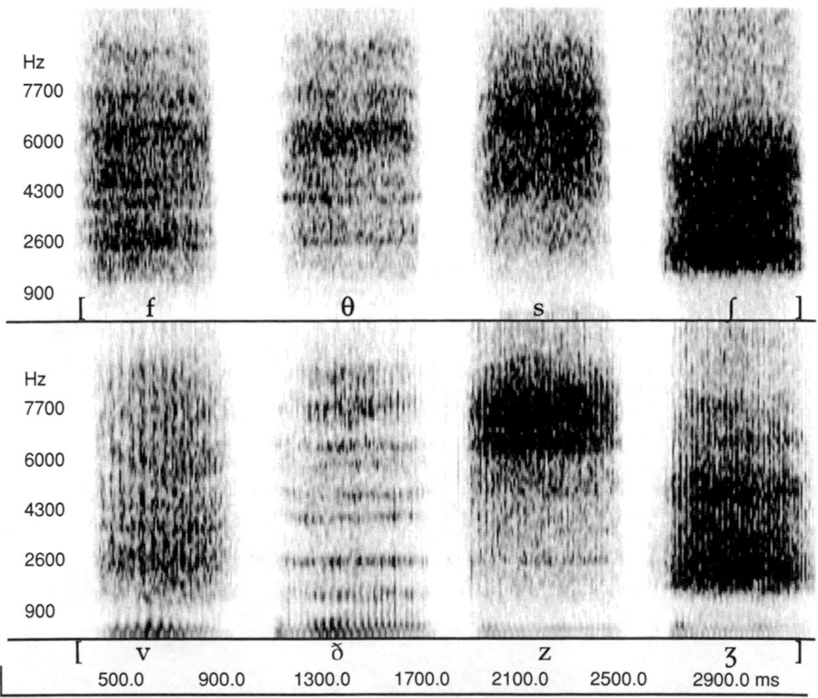

Figure 8.15 Spectrograms showing the noise pattern of fricatives

[h]

We have described [h] as a voiceless vowel. Accordingly, it shows up as a weak period of noise with energy at the frequency level of the formants of the following vowel, as in Figure 8.16.

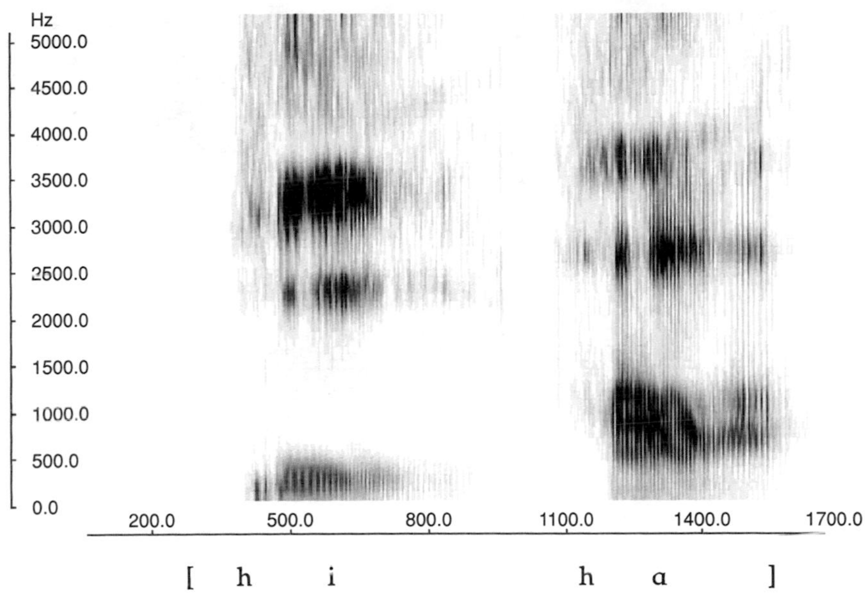

Figure 8.16 [h] before [i] and [ɑ]

Nasals

Nasals are voiced stops. The vocal folds are vibrating; there is a complete obstruction in the oral tract, and air is exiting only through the nose. As you can see from Figure 8.17, nasals have a weak formant-like pattern. They typically have energy at a low frequency around 500 Hz and again around 2500–3000 Hz. Note the abrupt loss of overall energy during the nasal. This sudden loss of intensity is due to special acoustic behaviour involved with opening the nasal passage. Also, the nasal cavity is less efficient than the oral cavity in transmitting energy to the outside. The place of articulation for the nasals shows up as for the oral stops: for example, for [m], the bilabial nasal, the second formant has a transition pointing down; for [n], the alveolar nasal, the second formant has a level transition; and the transition with a velar points up.

[ɹ]

The approximant [ɹ] lowers the third formant of the surrounding vowels. With postvocalic [ɹ] in rhotic accents, as in *her* [həɹ], the lowering may be present through most of the vowel. Figure 8.18 shows *head, hair, red, rare.* You can see [ɛ] with no rhotic element in *head*. Compare this with the initial [ɹ] in *red* and with the final [ɹ] in *hair*. *Rare* has an [ɹ] both initially and finally.

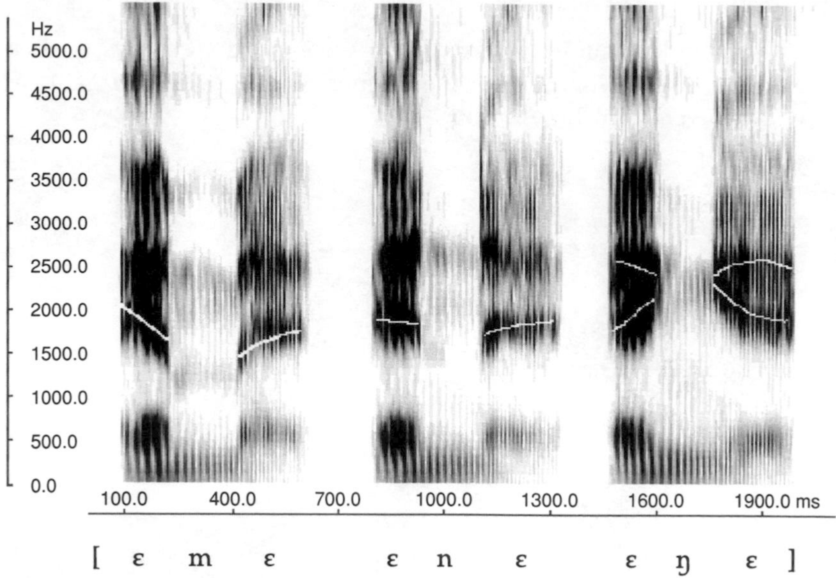

Figure 8.17 Spectrograms showing the nasals [m n ŋ]

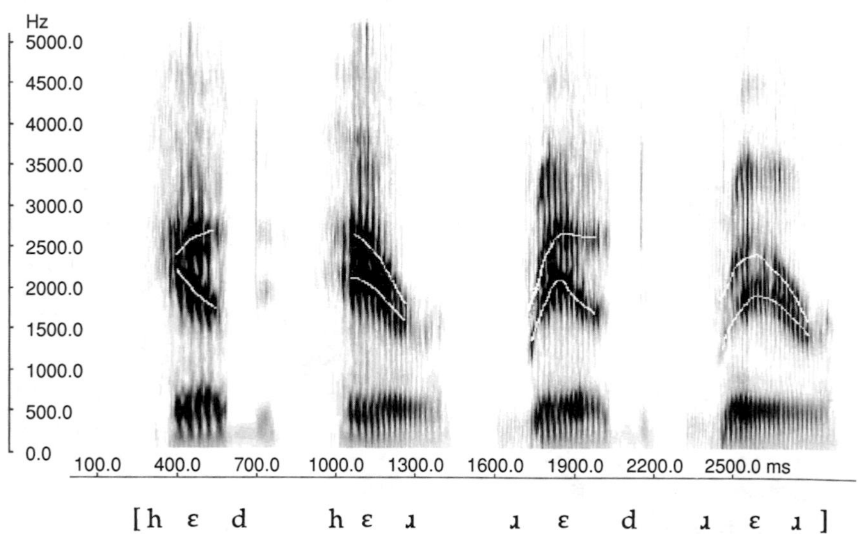

Figure 8.18 Spectrograms showing [ɛ] with and without [ɹ]: *head, hair, red, rare* (spoken with a GA accent)

Laterals

The English lateral, /l/ has a weak formant pattern. The difference between the clear [l] and dark [ɫ] may be seen in Figure 8.19. These have respectively the timbre of a high front vowel and of a high back vowel. With clear [l], F1

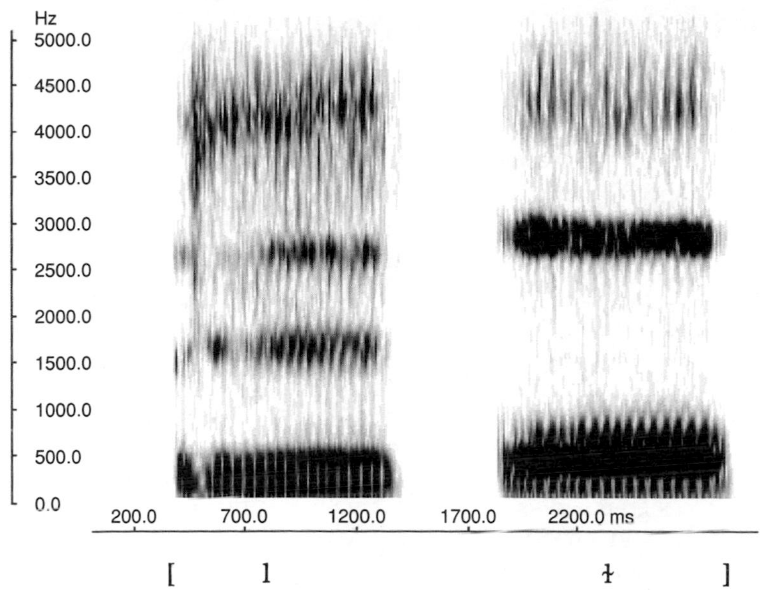

Figure 8.19 Clear and dark /l/

and F2 are quite far apart (around 300 and 1600 Hz). With dark [ɫ], F1 and F2 are both very close together (around 400 and 600 Hz). For both, F3 is around 2500 Hz.

Taps

Figure 8.20 shows *latter* and *ladder* in a GA accent. Note the much shorter gap for the tap [ɾ] than for the stop [d].

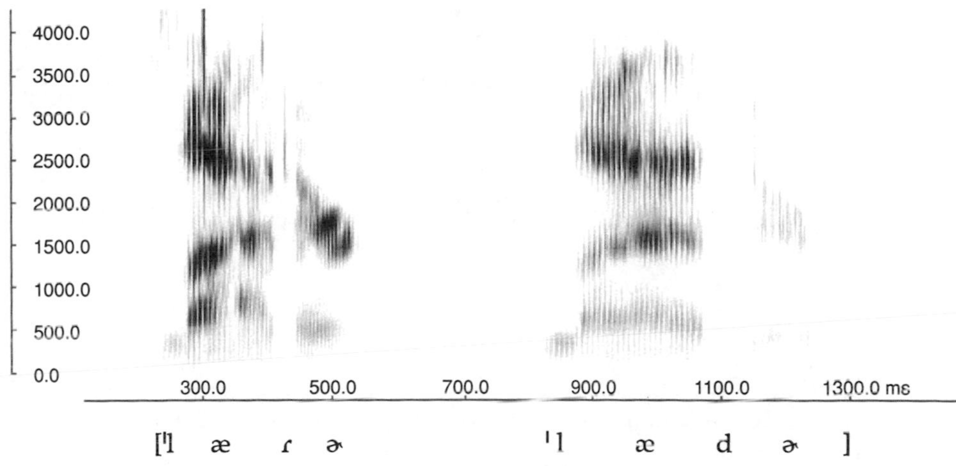

Figure 8.20 Spectrogram contrasting an alveolar tap and stop

Technical terms

formant	spike
spectrogram	transition
narrow-band spectrogram	vertical striation
wide-band spectrogram	voice bar

Exercises

Basic

'Reading' spectrograms requires patience and practice. Even experienced phoneticians cannot just sit down and see immediately what a spectrogram 'says'. In working with spectrograms, it is helpful to try to identify first the obvious features, and then to work on the more difficult parts. There is no need to start at the left and work steadily to the right; jumping around may be more helpful. Use your knowledge of the language to help you. Pay attention to the frequency and time scales.

1 Figure 8.21 shows a spectrogram of the vowels [ɪ ej ɑ ɔj]. Identify each vowel on the spectrogram with the correct symbol.

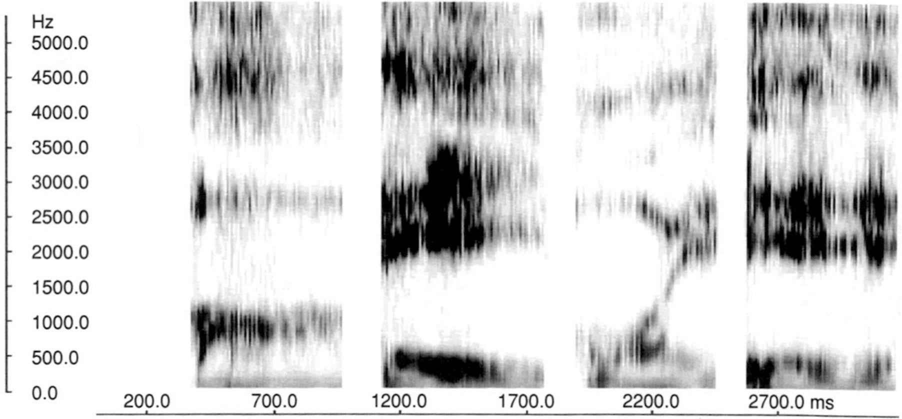

Figure 8.21

2 Figure 8.22 shows the words *kin, nick, latched, lashed.* Identify each word correctly and divide it into segments. Note that in most cases the release of the final stop is apparent.

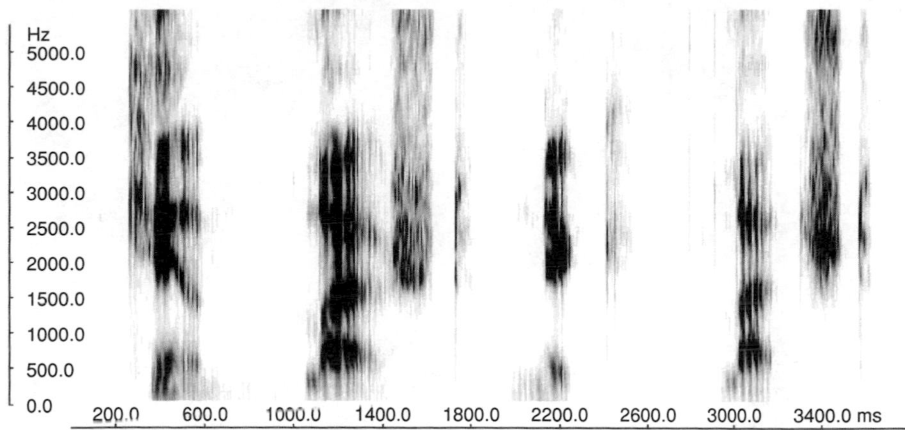

Figure 8.22

3 Figure 8.23 is a spectrogram of the sentence *Does Cathy play tennis?* Try to identify all the segments. Make a narrow transcription of the sentence, and place the appropriate symbol under each part of the spectrogram.

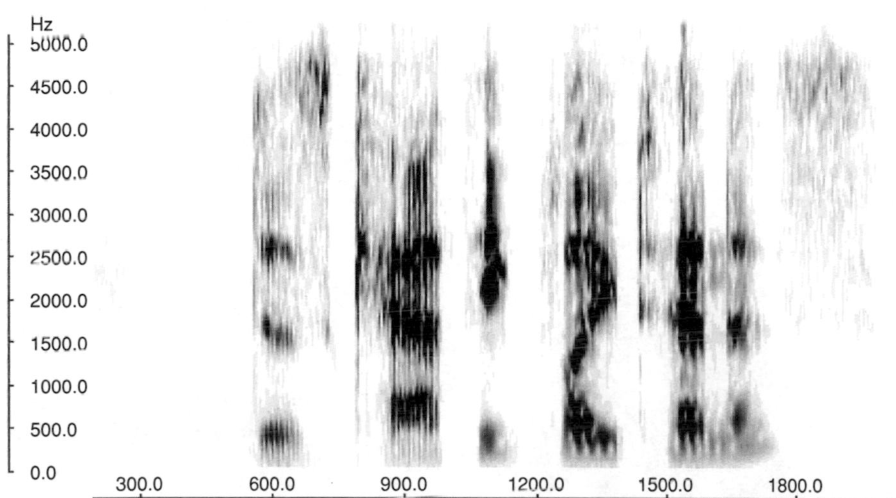

Figure 8.23

4 Figure 8.24 (overleaf) shows the sentence *I stayed in Glasgow* in an RP accent. Transcribe the sentence, and label the segments by placing the symbols below the appropriate portions of the spectrogram.

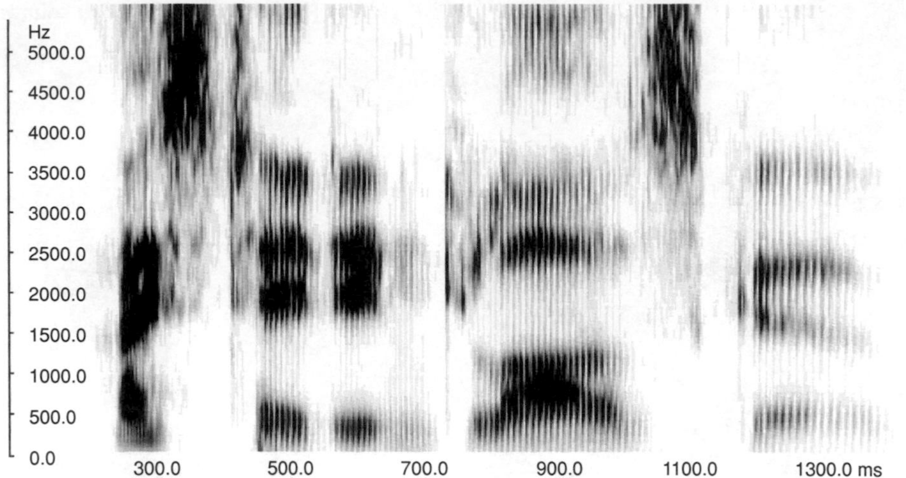

Figure 8.24

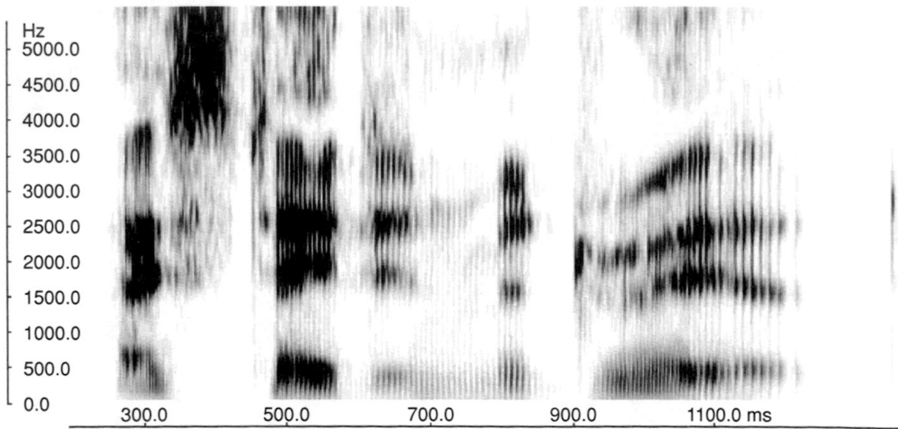

Figure 8.25

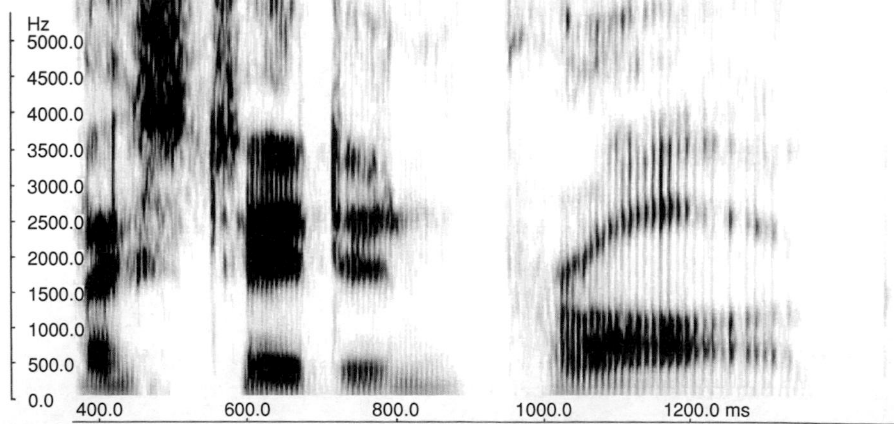

Figure 8.26

5 Figure 8.25 shows a spectrogram of the sentence *I stayed in* ——. The blank represents a capital city in Europe (RP accent). What is it?

6 Figures 8.26–28 are the same sentence with different European capitals all spoken with an RP accent. What are they?

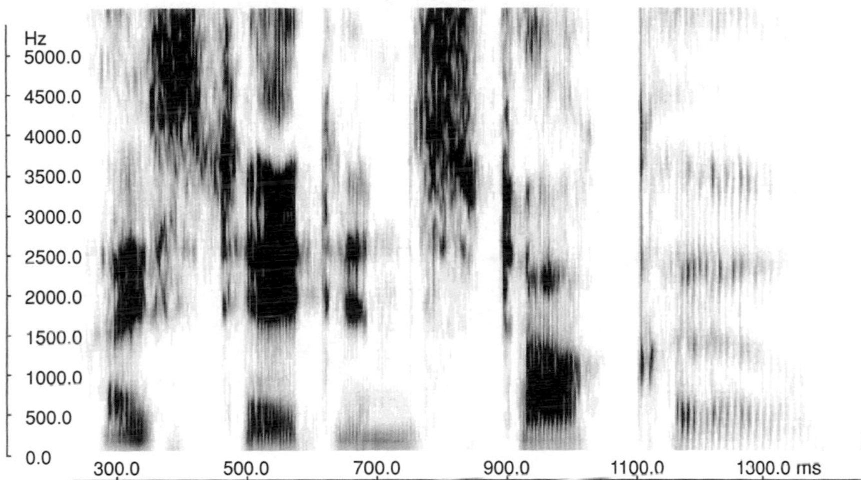

Figure 8.27

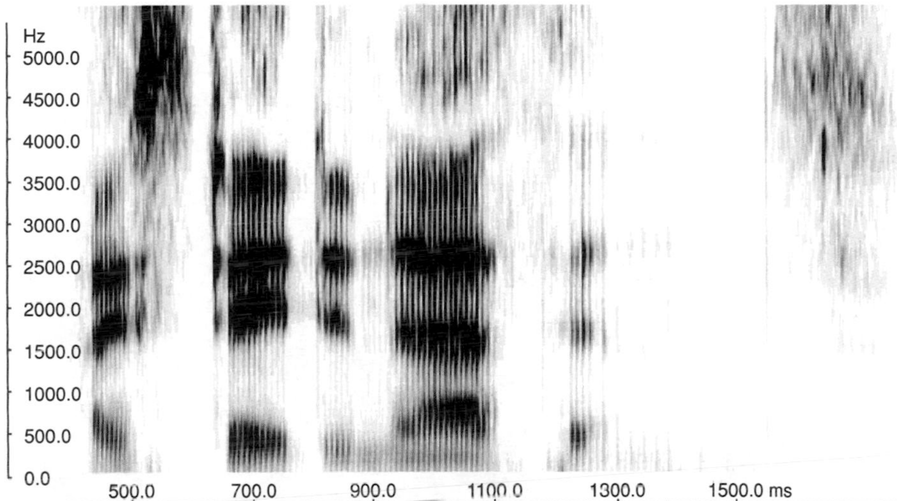

Figure 28

Advanced

7 In Figure 8.29, four of the following terms appear in the spectrograms, spoken with a GA accent: *anthropology, library science, linguistics, political science, sociology*. Identify which word goes with which spectrogram and which does not appear.

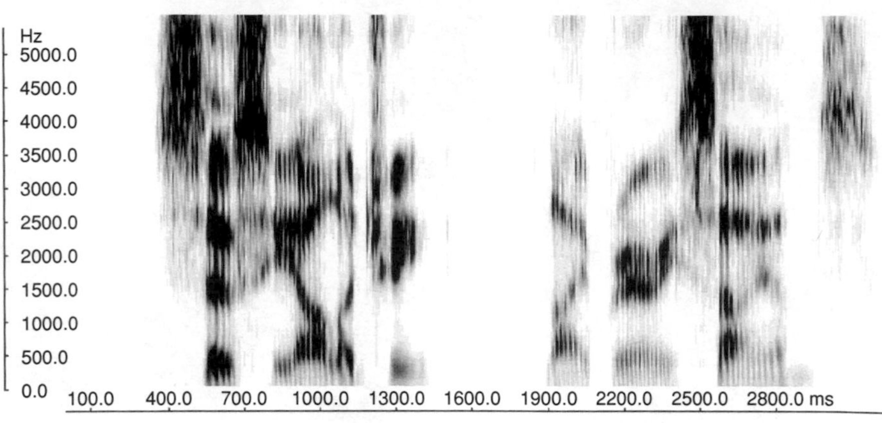

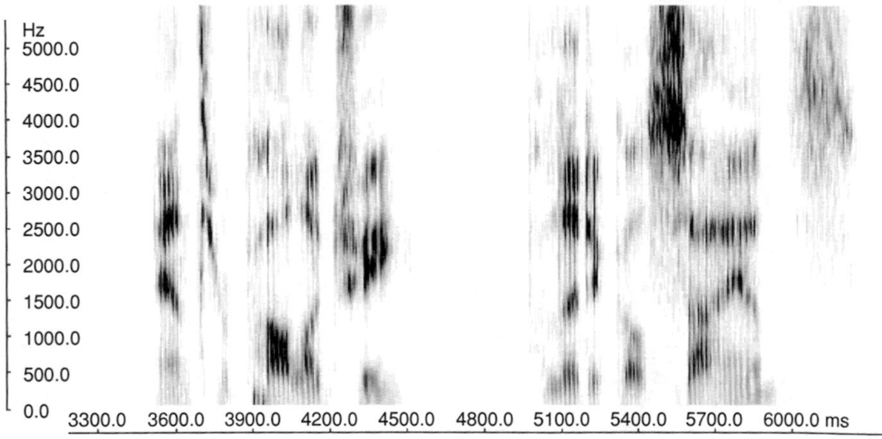

Figure 8.29

8 In Figure 8.30 are spectrograms of four common English girls' names spoken with an RP accent. Guess what they are. (Hint: All of these have been Queen.)

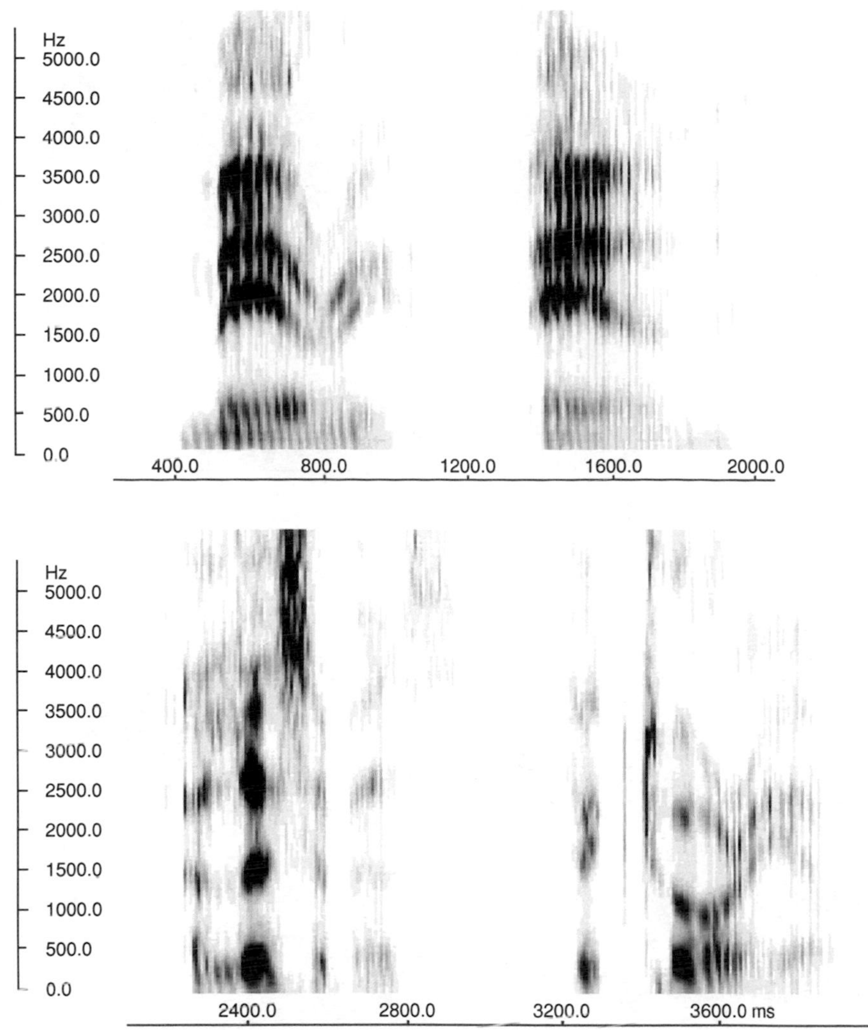

Figure 8.30

9 In Figure 8.31 are spectrograms of nicknames of the girls' names in question 9, spoken with a GA accent. Guess what they are.

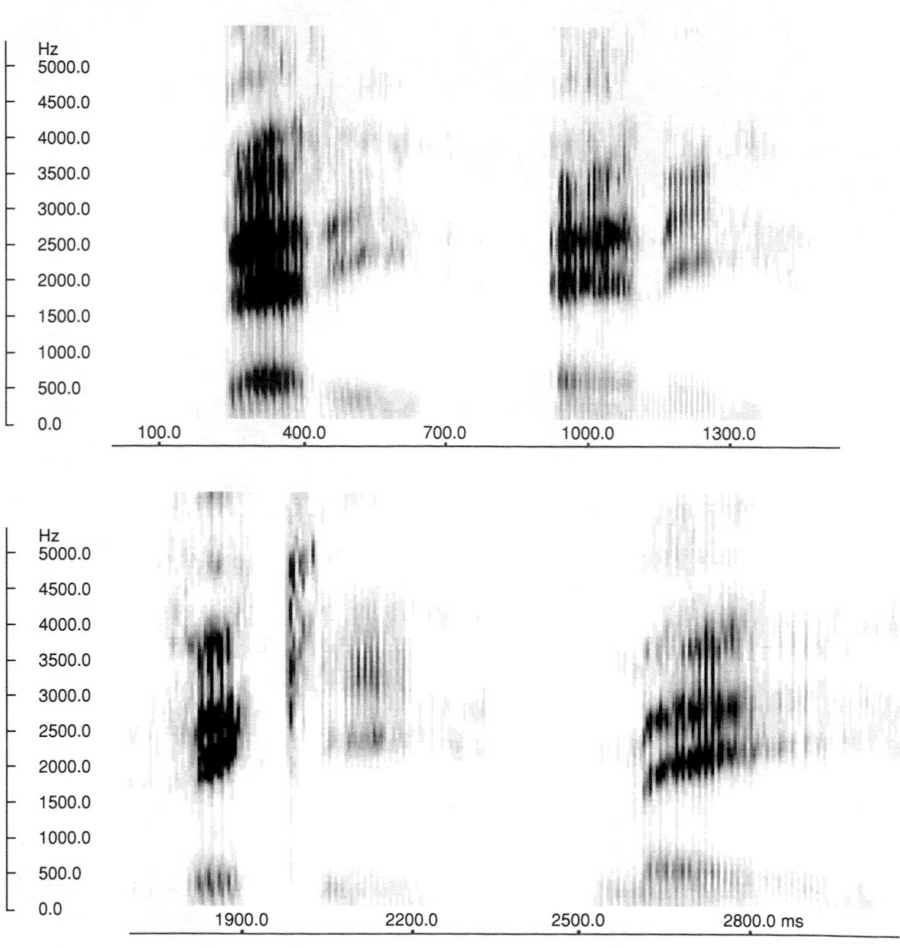

Figure 8.31

10 The following two spectrograms (Figures 8.32 and 8.33) are of titles of plays by Shakespeare. Guess what they are. One is spoken with a GA accent and one with an RP accent.

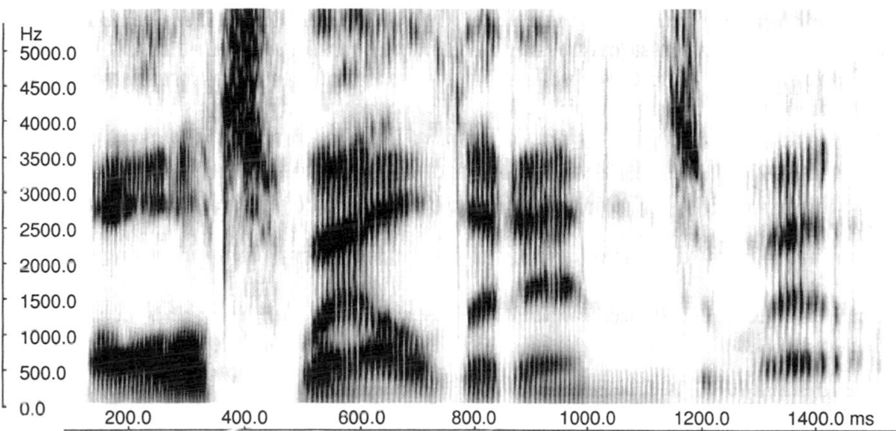

Figure 8.32

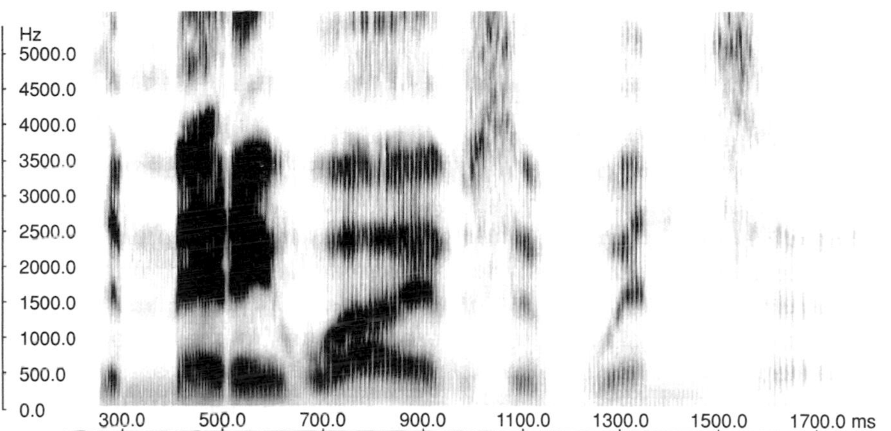

Figure 8.33

If you say [u ʊ o] while looking at your lips in a mirror, you will see that there is more rounding for the higher vowels and less as the vowels get lower. Languages differ as to the degree of rounding, but in any particular language, high vowels are generally more rounded than the lower ones.

Ordinarily, the lower jaw is lowered as we go from the higher to the lower vowels. You can, however, verify that jaw opening is not essential for producing different vowels. If you clench a pencil between your teeth, you will find that you are still able to produce a fairly good series of vowels – [i e ɛ a ɑ ɔ o u]. You can see that tongue and jaw movement are somewhat independent of each other. The tongue can compensate if the jaw is immobilised.

Languages often make the rounding slightly differently for front and back vowels (Figure 9.1). In back rounded vowels, for example [u o ɔ], the lips are typically extended and the sides drawn in to form a short tube. With front rounded vowels, for example [y ø œ], the lips are usually retracted slightly, leaving a narrow opening in the middle.

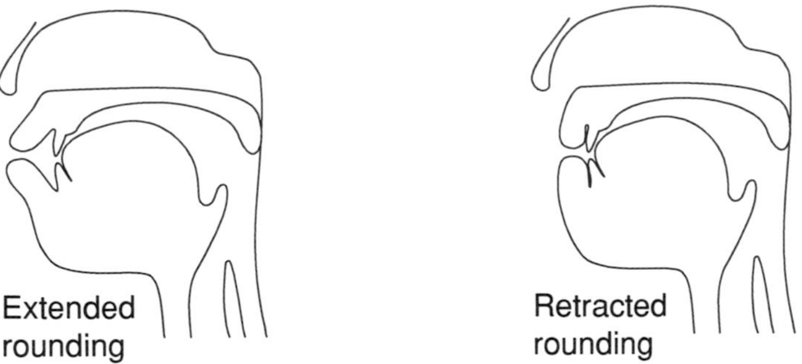

Figure 9.1 Lip rounding. Extended rounding is found with back vowels and retracted rounding with front vowels

Cardinal vowels

A very precise system used by phoneticians for describing vowels is the **cardinal vowel system**, elaborated by Daniel Jones and adopted by the **International Phonetic Association (IPA)**. This system picks certain vowels as basic or **cardinal** and describes all other vowels in terms of their relationship to these cardinal vowels.

On the chart in Figure 9.2, the enclosed figure defines the extreme limits of vowel production. The tongue position for [i] is shown by a solid line, and the tongue position for [ɑ] by a broken line. The black dots show the tongue position of the highest point of the tongue for cardinal vowel [i], the highest and farthest front vowel that you can make, and the highest point of the tongue for cardinal vowel [ɑ], the lowest and farthest back vowel that you can make. This figure is usually altered to the stylised quadrilateral

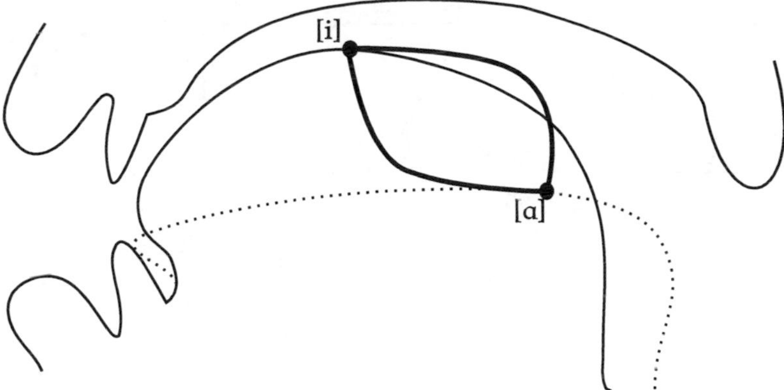

Figure 9.2 The extreme limits of vowel production

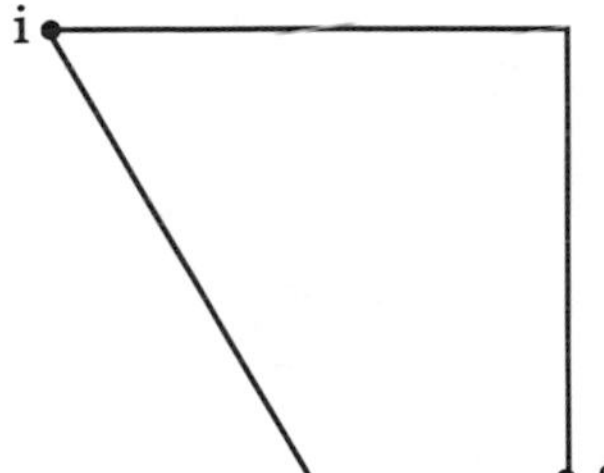

Figure 9.3 The cardinal vowel quadrilateral showing the cardinal vowels [i] and [ɑ]

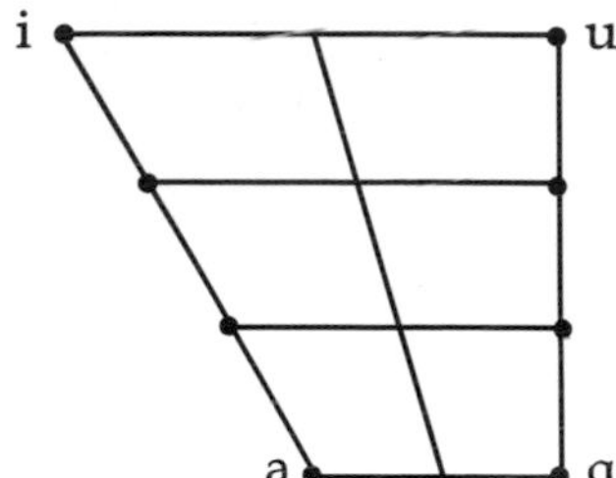

Figure 9.4 The vowel quadrilateral showing the extreme vowels and the internal divisions

shown in Figure 9.3. The black dots again show the positions of cardinal vowel [i] and cardinal vowel [ɑ].

Figure 9.4 shows the vowel quadrilateral divided equally from high to low. The dots in the corners correspond to the limits of the possible vowels that can be made: [i] and [u] are the highest vowels that can be made, [a] and [ɑ] the lowest, [i] and [a] the farthest front, and [u] and [ɑ] the farthest back. The vowel [a] is similar to English [æ] but at the low front extreme.

The quadrilateral has been divided into three equal parts from high to low. A diagonal line has been drawn showing the position of central vowels. The vowel quadrilateral represents the entire space where a vowel can be made. Any vowel can be described by showing its position inside this figure or on its edges.

Figure 9.5 (overleaf) shows the entire repertoire of cardinal vowels. Here, unrounded and rounded vowels are shown on different charts. It is common, however, for unrounded and rounded vowels to be shown on the same chart with the reader expected to know from the symbols whether a vowel is rounded or not.

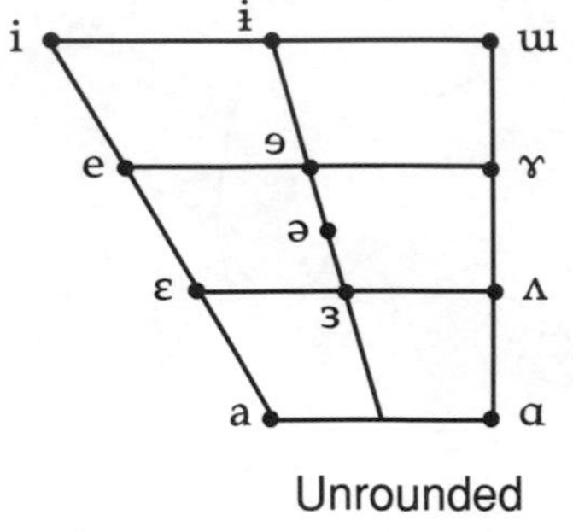

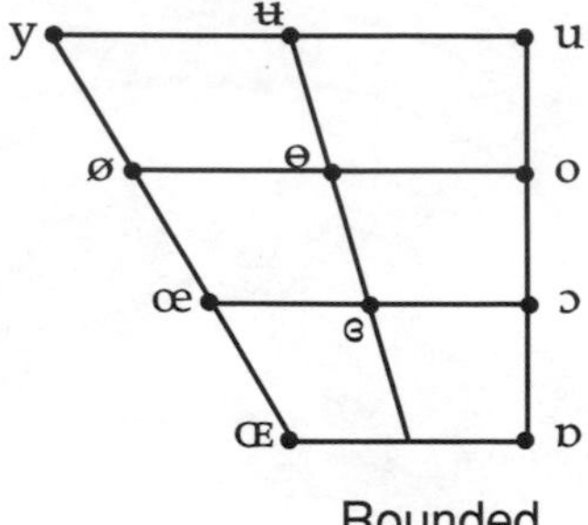

Figure 9.5 The cardinal vowels

We can use the cardinal vowel chart to locate any vowel. If we want to describe a particular vowel of a particular language, for example, the vowel of English *hat*, someone familiar with this system listens to the sound, and relates it to the fixed cardinal vowels. The process goes something like this: 'The vowel in English *hat* is a little higher than cardinal vowel [a], and a little farther back'. A dot for English [æ] can now be placed on the cardinal vowel chart as in Figure 9.6. The advantage of this system is that one person can learn and record a vowel on a chart, and another person, seeing this chart with no further information, can reproduce it quite accurately. Experiments have shown a high degree of accuracy in using this system (Ladefoged, 1967).

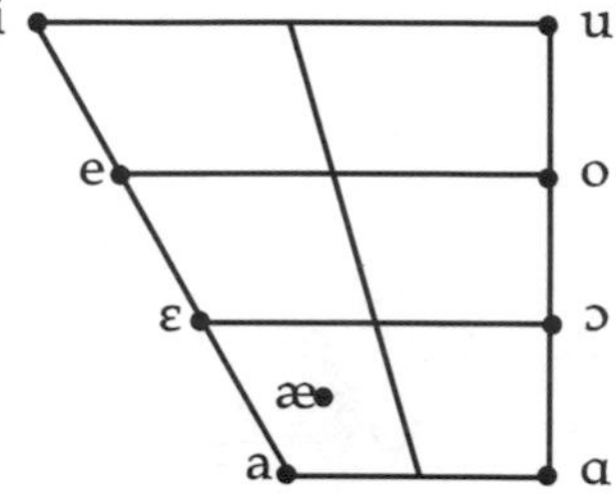

Figure 9.6 The vowel [æ]

Although the pronunciation of the cardinal vowels is best learned from someone already familiar with them, you can make a fairly close approximation by noting the following observations. Several of the French vowels are very close to cardinal vowel positions: in particular [i e ɛ a ɑ] (*vie, thé, mettre, patte, pâte*). RP speakers have a vowel close to cardinal [ɔ] in *law*. Cardinal [o u] are similar to the French vowels in *beau, tout*, but farther back.

Cardinal vowel symbols are used in two slightly different ways. They can be used to symbolise the cardinal vowels themselves. Other vowels can be located on the chart in relation to the cardinal vowels. Alternatively, the symbols can be used in a non-cardinal sense. Suppose that we plot dots for the vowels of some language on a cardinal vowel chart. We now want symbols for these vowels. We can attach the cardinal vowel symbols to the vowels of this language, choosing the symbol of the nearest cardinal vowel.

Not infrequently, a language has a transcription tradition which differs from the IPA principles. By the principles just advocated, the vowel in English *hat* should be transcribed [a], not [æ]. Some authors do this, but most follow the strongly established tradition of using [æ]. Note that this tradition of using [æ] instead of [a] only applies to English.

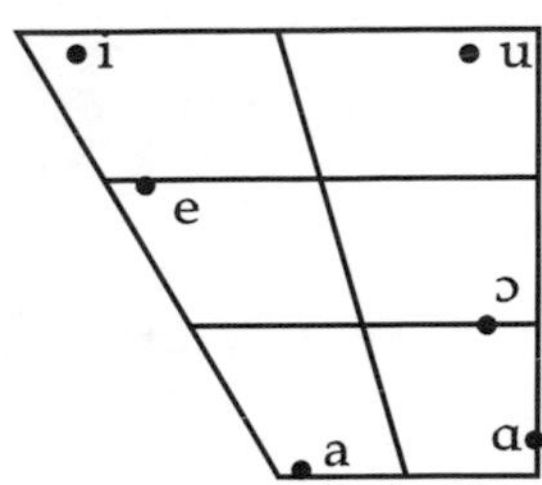

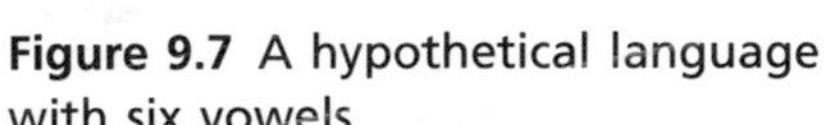
Figure 9.7 A hypothetical language with six vowels

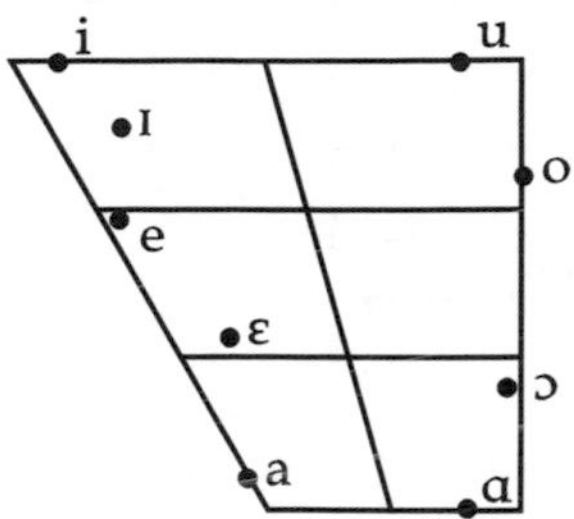

Figure 9.8 A hypothetical language with nine vowels

Consider now a language with nine vowels as shown in Figure 9.8. If we assign the closest cardinal symbols to these, as we did in Figure 9.7, we discover a problem. This language simply has more vowels than we have appropriate cardinal symbols. We have used [i] and also [e], but we need a symbol for a vowel between these. This situation is not uncommon in the languages of the world, and consequently, we sometimes have to resort to extra symbols, which the IPA has thoughtfully provided. Note that these extra symbols do not represent cardinal vowels; they are to be used in a general area of the vowel space, but they do not have a fixed definition as does a cardinal vowel. They are extra symbols to be used in addition to the cardinal symbols when describing a particular language. They are not to be used if an appropriate cardinal vowel symbol is available. We can now solve our problem in the language with nine vowels by symbolising the extra vowel as [ɪ].

Extra symbols with the areas where they are to be used (Figure 9.9, overleaf) are:

[ɪ]	lower high front unrounded, between [i] and [e]
[ʏ]	lower high front rounded, between [y] and [ø]
[æ]	higher low front unrounded, between [ɛ] and [a]
[ʊ]	lower high back rounded, between [u] and [o]
[ɐ]	higher low central unrounded, between [ɛ̞] and [ʌ̞]

If we have a six-vowel system as shown in Figure 9.7, we would use for these vowels the symbols shown there. The symbols must be used so as to suggest an approximately accurate sound to the reader. We pick [e] rather than [ɛ] as the symbol for the front mid vowel because the vowel in our hypothetical language is closer to cardinal vowel [e] than to cardinal vowel [ɛ]. Similarly, we pick [ɔ], not [o].

We tend to find the vowels [i e ɛ a ɑ ɔ o u] more often than [y ø œ ɶ ɒ ʌ ɤ ɯ]. The first group is sometimes called **primary** as opposed to **secondary** for the second group; they differ only in having reversed rounding. In

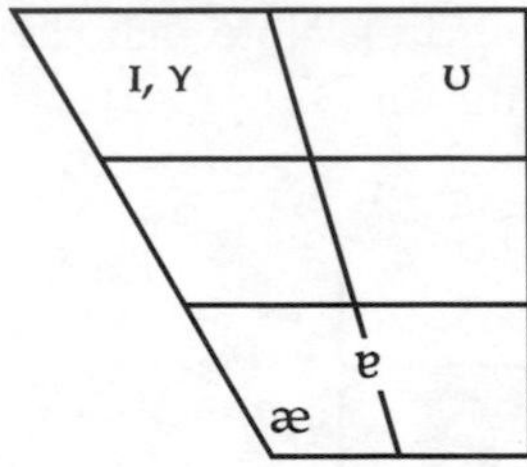

Figure 9.9 Extra symbols

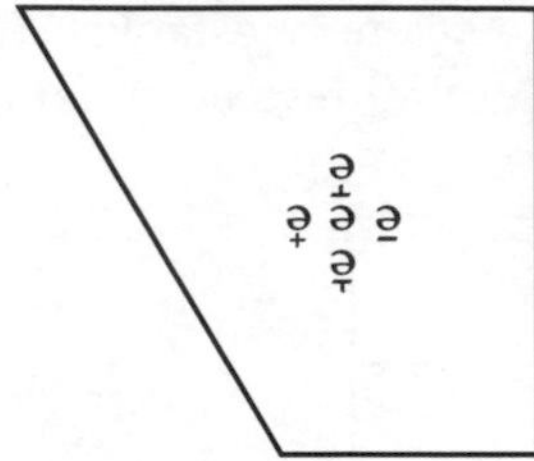

Figure 9.10 Use of vowel diacritics

discussing vowels, I will often use the primary vowels with the understanding that whatever is said could, in principle, be applied to the secondary vowels as well.

Most of the cardinal vowel symbols have a long-established tradition. However, some of the central vowels [ɘ ɵ ɜ ɞ], were given more specific definitions in the 1993 revision of the IPA. You may find slightly varied use of these symbols in earlier works.

Figure 9.10 shows how vowel diacritics can be used to indicate small differences. For example, starting with [ə] as a mid-central vowel, a vowel a bit to the front of this is shown with a subscript plus [ə̟]. Other diacritics are [ə̠ ə̞ ə̝] to indicate, respectively, vowels which are a bit farther back, lower, higher than the basic [ə]. These diacritics could of course be applied to any vowel.

Formant frequencies

Table 9.1 shows average frequencies of the first two formants for the cardinal vowels spoken by a male (Catford, 1988). By comparing the frequencies

Table 9.1 Formant frequencies of the cardinal vowels (Catford, 1988)

Unrounded			Rounded		
	F1	F2		F1	F2
i	240	2400	y	235	2100
e	390	2300	ø	370	1900
ɛ	610	1900	œ	585	1710
a	850	1610	ɶ	820	1530
ɑ	750	940	ɒ	700	760
ʌ	600	1170	ɔ	500	700
ɤ	460	1310	o	36	640
ɯ	300	1390	u	250	595

in Table 9.1 for unrounded and rounded vowels, you can see that rounding lowers the frequency of both formants, particularly the second. In general, the formant frequencies correspond to the pattern described in Chapter 8 for English, especially for the front vowels.

Additional vowel qualities

In addition to the main dimensions of height, backness, and rounding, vowels may have other qualities.

Nasalisation

Nasalised vowels are produced with a lowered velum, with air passing out through both the mouth and the nose. Nasalisation is shown by a **tilde** [˜]. Nasalised vowels are perhaps familiar from French. Traditional French has four nasalised vowels: [ɛ̃ œ̃ ɑ̃ ɔ̃]. The phrase *un bon vin blanc* 'a good white wine' illustrates all four: [œ̃ bɔ̃ vɛ̃ blɑ̃]. In modern French, [œ̃] is often pronounced as [ɛ̃]: [ɛ̃ bɔ̃ vɛ̃ blɑ̃].

Yoruba (Nigeria, West Africa) also has nasalised vowels and glides:

/fi/	*use*	/ijafĩ/	*wife*	/ĩj̃ɛ̃/	*that*
/ɔbɔ/	*monkey*	/ibɔ̃/	*gun*	/w̃ɔ̃/	*they*
/su/	*scatter seed*	/sũ/	*push*	/mɛr̃ĩ/	*four*

Yoruba

Chinantec /ˈtʃɪnɑnˌtɛk/, a language of Mexico, is reported as having three degrees of nasal vowels: oral, slightly nasal, and strongly nasal (Ladefoged, 1971; Merrifield, 1963).

/hɑ/	*so, such*	/hɑ̃/	*spreads open*	/hɑ̃̃/	*foam, froth*

Chinantec

Rhotacisation

Vowels can be rhotacised as in GA English. The **rhotacisation** is formed by curling the tip of the tongue to the back of the alveolar ridge or by retracting the tip into the body of the tongue and moving the front of the tongue forwards. In rhotacised vowels, there is often a hollowing of the body of the tongue which is not present with non-rhotacised vowels. Any vowel can be rhotacised although it is slightly more difficult to curl the tongue tip with high front vowels.

GA English /əɹ/ is a **rhotacised** or **rhotic** vowel. Phonetically, this is a single segment [ɚ], although we have analysed it phonemically as a sequence /əɹ/. One reason for analysing this sound as a single segment is because it can be sustained in its articulation: [ɚɚɚɚɚɚɚɚ]. It does not require a sequence [əəəəɹɹɹɹɹ]. Rhotacised vowels are symbolised with a diacritic [˞], e.g., [ɑ˞, o˞, u˞, ɚ].

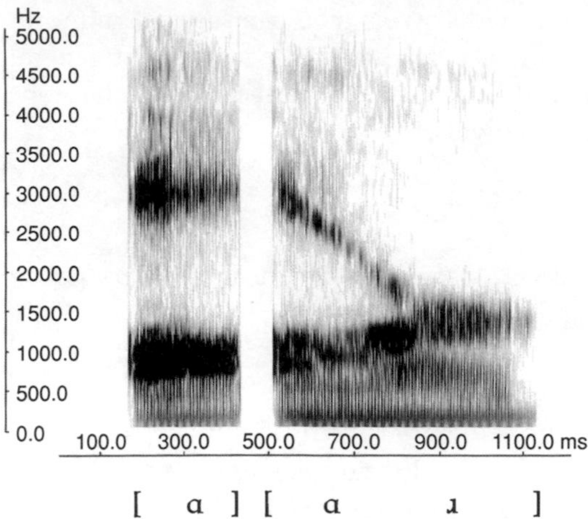

Figure 9.11 Plain and rhotacised /ɑ/

As shown in Figure 9.11, the presence of rhotacisation causes lowering of the third formant.

Expanded

In many languages of West Africa, the vowels are divided into two sets. In Akan (Ghana; Lindau, 1978), for example, Set A consists of [i̘ e̘ o̘ u̘], and Set B consists of [i̙ e̙ o̙ u̙]. Studies of Akan vowels (Ladefoged and Maddieson, 1996; Painter, 1973) show that the pharynx is expanded for the production of the vowels of Set B by moving the tongue root forward and by lowering the larynx (Figure 9.12 on p. 183). The IPA provides a diacritic [̙] for expanded (advanced tongue root) and [̘] for non-expanded (retracted tongue root). These vowel sets contrast: [fí̘] 'leave' and [fì̙] 'vomit'. Akan also shows vowel harmony in that any particular word will have only vowels of Set A or only vowels of Set B. Thus, we find [ò̘fí̘] 'he leaves', but [ò̙fɪ̙] 'he vomits', where the third singular prefix [ò̘ ~ ò̙] harmonises with the following vowel; similarly, [mì̘fí̘] 'I leave' and [mì̙fɪ̙] 'I vomit'. There is also a low vowel [a] which does not harmonise but occurs in words with both vowel sets.

Vowels of Set A are said to be **not-expanded**, and those of Set B **expanded**. The term 'advanced tongue root' has been suggested for 'expanded'. I prefer Lindau's (1978) term 'expanded' as it includes the lowering of the larynx (Figure 9.12). The larger pharyngeal cavity with expanded vowels gives a lowered first formant.

Length

Many languages have long and short varieties of the same vowel. **Length** is shown by [ː]; a single raised dot [ˑ] can be used to indicate an intermediate degree of length. The IPA dots are really small triangles.

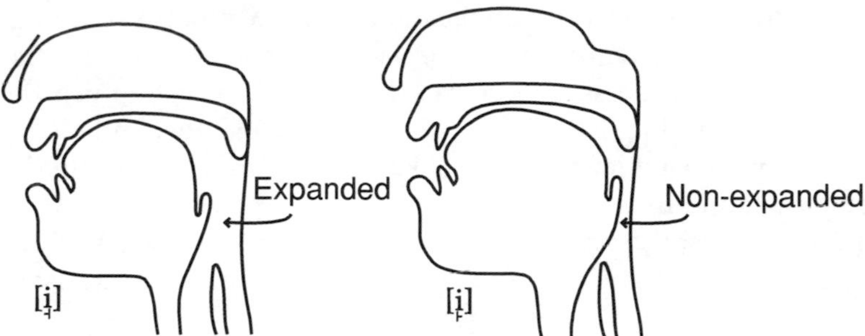

Figure 9.12 Non-expanded and expanded vowels in Akan. Note position of tongue root and of glottis

[ˈsapadʒ]	*sabaid*	‘fight’	[ˈsaːpadʒ]	*sàbaid*	‘Sabbath’
[ˈahið]	*athair*	‘father’	[ˈmaːhið]	*màthair*	‘mother’
[ənˈtul]	*an tuil*	‘the flood’	[ənˈtuːl]	*an t-sùil*	‘the eye’

Scots Gaelic

In languages with distinctive vowel length, long vowels are typically some 1.5 to 3 times longer than their short counterparts (Catford, 1977).

Tense–lax

The tense–lax distinction is controversial. Phonologists have frequently divided English vowels into tense–lax, as we did in Chapter 4. Phoneticians, however, have been unable to identify any articulatory or acoustic trait which consistently corresponds to this distinction. Generally, tense and lax have been used in two ways with vowels: of a pair of similar contrastive vowels, the higher and more peripheral one has been called tense, or, of a pair of vowels contrasting in length, the longer one has been called tense. You will recall that in Chapter 4 we justified the tense–lax distinction on distributional, not phonetic grounds. Catford (1977) has a useful discussion of this issue:

> For vowels, the existence of such a parameter [tense–lax] is dubious, and the use of tense/lax terminology in the phonetic description of vowels is seldom if ever necessary, and should be avoided. This does not mean that the tense/lax terminology is entirely useless in *phonological* description. Here, tense and lax may, perhaps, be usefully employed as labels to designate phonetically arbitrary classes of vowels that happen to be phonologically distinct. But it should then be made quite clear that the selection of terms may be phonetically vacuous. (Catford, 1977: 208)

Some authors (Halle and Stevens, 1969) have suggested that [expanded] be used for vowels to replace [tense] since no language requires both [tense] and [expanded] for vowels. Lindau's (1979) review of the research points out two differences between English and Akan. Unlike Akan, English speakers do not consistently lower the larynx for tense vowels, and further, only some speakers use tongue root movement to distinguish the two classes of vowels in English. I follow Lindau and use [expanded] for the distinction found in languages such as Akan and continue to use [tense] for the distinction found in English.

The term tense is clearly unsatisfactory. For some languages, such as English, it is, however, extremely useful. For the time being, it seems best to keep it, recognising its inadequacies.

Glides

A **glide**, or **semivowel**, is a moving vowel. Glides always occur next to a vowel. Thus [ɑj] in Figure 9.13 starts at the position of [ɑ] and moves to [i]. Similarly [jɑ] starts at [i] and moves to an [ɑ] position. The end of the glide in [ɑj] or the beginning of the glide in [jɑ] moves so quickly that we often cannot specify with certainty the exact point on a vowel chart.

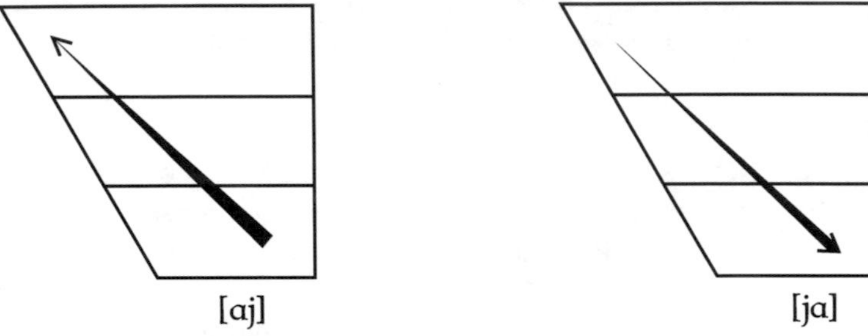

Figure 9.13 The diphthongs [ɑj] and [jɑ]

In principle, any vowel position can be used for a glide. A subscript cap [̯] is used to show lack of syllabicity, that is, to change a vowel symbol to that of a glide, as in [ə̯ ɛ̯ ʌ̯]. Four glides [i̯ u̯ y̯ ɯ̯] are so common that they have their own symbols: [j w ɥ ɰ]. The symbol [ʍ] is used for a voiceless [w].

Many authors write diphthongs as two vowels, as [ai] or [aɪ], rather than [aj]. Such transcriptions can obviously be converted to our system if we know whether [a] or [i] is the glide. Since [j] and [w] are common glides, but [a̯] is not, we rarely have difficulty with such transcriptions. A problem could arise, however, with a transcription such as [ui], since this could reasonably represent either [wi] or [uj]. See Appendix D for further discussion of the transcription of English.

Vowels always form the nucleus of a syllable and glides either precede or follow the vowel. Diphthongs with the sequence glide–vowel, as in [ja wɛ] are called **rising** diphthongs; those with the sequence vowel–glide, as in [aj ɛw], are called **falling** diphthongs. Note that falling and rising refer to prominence, not to vowel height. The glide is short and fleeting; by contrast, the vowel is longer and much more prominent.

Lindau, Norlin and Svantesson (1990) found that languages differ considerably in the time taken by the glide. English glides are rather slow; for example, in English [aw], the glide occupies about 80% of the total diphthong duration. In a similar diphthong in Chinese, however, the glide occupies only 40% of the total duration.

Technical terms

back
cardinal vowel
central
diphthong
expanded
falling diphthong
front
glide
high
International Phonetic Association
International Phonetic Alphabet (IPA)
length
low
mid
nasalised
primary vowel
rhotacised
rising diphthong
rounding
secondary vowel
tilde

Symbols

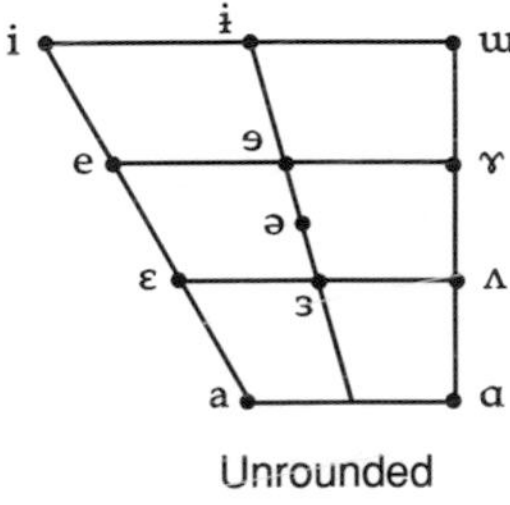

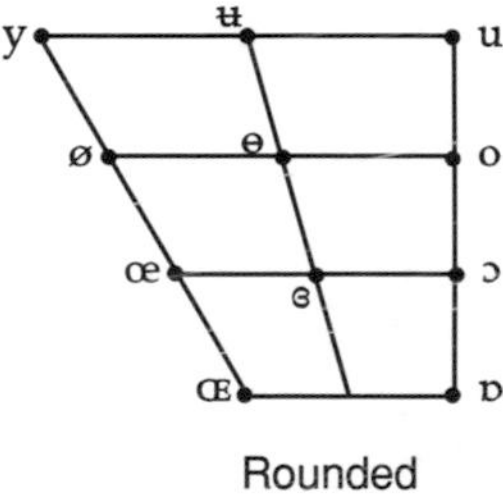

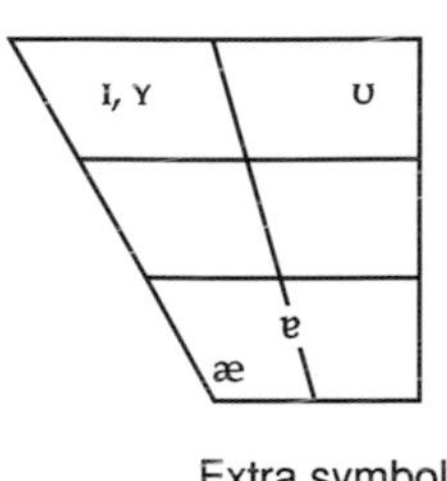

Figure 9.14

Exercises

Basic

1 Cardinal vowels are best learned from someone who knows them. However, you can approximate the primary vowels from the following descriptions:

[i] The highest completely front unrounded vowel which you can pronounce without making any audible friction.

[e] Something like the French vowel in *épée, fée.*
[ɛ] Something like the French vowel in *béte, faite.*
[a] The lowest completely front unrounded vowel that you can make.
[ɑ] The lowest completely back unrounded vowel that you can make. Think of saying [ɑ] for the doctor.
[ɔ] Something like the French vowel in *code, note.*
[o] Something like the French vowel in *faut, eau.*
[u] The highest completely back rounded vowel that you can make.

In all the following exercises in the rest of this book, the symbols have the value of cardinal vowels, unless otherwise specified, such as when a specific language is mentioned.

Try saying first just the front vowels: i e ɛ a.

Say them with a steady pitch and no glide. Ending the vowel with a sudden glottal stop can be useful in learning not to introduce a glide: [iiiiiʔ].

Now say them with the consonant [p]: pi pe pɛ pa.

Now say them with the following consonants: [f θ k n l b]:

e.g.: fi fe fɛ fa etc.

2 Now try the back vowels. Remember that they are rounded except for [ɑ].

u o ɔ ɑ

Try them now with the consonant [t]: tu to tɔ tɑ.

Try them with other consonants [z d m ð v ɣ]:

e.g.: zu zo zɔ zɑ

3 Now try all the primary vowels together. Be sure not to rush, saying each one clearly.

i e ɛ a ɑ ɔ o u

Try other orders:

i	ɛ	e	a	u	ɔ	o	ɑ
i	u	e	o	ɛ	ɔ	a	ɑ
ɑ	a	ɔ	ɛ	o	e	u	i
i	ɑ	e	ɑ	ɛ	ɑ	a	ɑ
u	ɑ	o	ɑ	ɔ	ɑ	i	ɑ
i	a	e	a	ɛ	a	ɑ	a
u	a	o	a	ɔ	a	ɑ	a

4 Now try the secondary vowels. These are made by reversing the rounding of the primary vowels. For example, to make [y], say [i] and round your lips. To make [ɯ], say [u], and unround your lips. Make sure that the position of your tongue does not move while you are changing the rounding.

Rounded	[i]	to get	[y]
	[e]		[ø]
	[ε]		[œ]
	[a]		[ɶ]
	[ɑ]		[ɒ]
Unrounded	[u]	to get	[ɯ]
	[o]		[ɤ]
	[ɔ]		[ʌ]

5 Practise these:

i	e	ε	a	ɑ	ɔ	o	u
y	ɔ	œ	ɶ	ɒ	ʌ	ɤ	ɯ
ɯ	ɤ	ʌ	ɒ	ɶ	œ	ø	y
i	e	ε	a	ɑ	ʌ	ɤ	ɯ
ɯ	ɤ	ʌ	ɑ	a	ε	e	i
u	o	ɔ	ɒ	ɶ	œ	ø	y
y	ø	œ	ɶ	ɒ	ɔ	o	u

Try the following exercises (Try them in both horizontal and vertical orders):

zi	zy	fi	fy	pi	py	li	ly
ne	nø	ʃe	ʃø	ðe	ðø	ke	kø
dε	dœ	fε	fœ	ŋε	ŋœ	jε	jœ
va	vɶ	la	lɶ	ha	hɶ	ʒa	ʒɶ
mɑ	mɒ	bɑ	bɒ	ðɑ	ðɒ	kɑ	kɒ
ɹɔ	ɹʌ	tʃɔ	tʃʌ	zɔ	zʌ	nɔ	nʌ
ŋo	ŋɤ	ʔo	ʔɤ	do	dɤ	ʃo	ʃɤ
ɹu	ɹɯ	θu	θɯ	ʒu	ʒɯ	lu	lɯ

7 Diphthongs. In the following chart, the first symbol is a vowel and the second is a glide; i.e., [ai] is the same as our usual [aj].

Make the following carefully, listening to the differences:

ai ae aε aɔ ao au

In practising the diphthongs in the following table, try doing them in different patterns: across, down, diagonal.

ei	εi	ai	ɑi	ɔi	oi	ui	yi	øi	œi	ɶi	ɒi	ʌi	ɤi	ɯi
ie	εe	ae	ɑe	ɔe	oe	ue	ye	øe	œe	ɶe	ɒe	ʌe	ɤe	ɯe
iε	eε	aε	ɑε	ɔε	oε	uε	yε	øε	œε	ɶε	ɒε	ʌε	ɤε	ɯε
ia	ea	εa	ɑa	ɔa	oa	ua	ya	øa	œa	ɶa	ɒa	ʌa	ɤa	ɯa
iɑ	eɑ	εɑ	aɑ	ɔɑ	oɑ	uɑ	yɑ	øɑ	œɑ	ɶɑ	ɒɑ	ʌɑ	ɤɑ	ɯɑ
iɔ	eɔ	εɔ	aɔ	ɑɔ	oɔ	uɔ	yɔ	øɔ	œɔ	ɶɔ	ɒɔ	ʌɔ	ɤɔ	ɯɔ
io	eo	εo	ao	ɑo	ɔo	uo	yo	øo	œo	ɶo	ɒo	ʌo	ɤo	ɯo
iu	eu	εu	au	ɑu	ɔu	ou	yu	øu	œu	ɶu	ɒu	ʌu	ɤu	ɯu
iy	ey	εy	ay	ɑy	ɔy	oy	uy	øy	œy	ɶy	ɒy	ʌy	ɤy	ɯy
iø	eø	εø	aø	ɑø	ɔø	oø	uø	yø	œø	ɶø	ɒø	ʌø	ɤø	ɯø

iœ eœ ɛœ aœ ɑœ ɔœ oœ uœ yœ øœ ɶœ ɒœ ʌœ ɤœ ɯœ
iɶ eɶ ɛɶ aɶ ɑɶ ɔɶ oɶ uɶ yɶ øɶ œɶ ɒɶ ʌɶ ɤɶ ɯɶ
iɒ eɒ ɛɒ aɒ ɑɒ ɔɒ oɒ uɒ yɒ øɒ œɒ ɶɒ ʌɒ ɤɒ ɯɒ
iʌ eʌ ɛʌ aʌ ɑʌ ɔʌ oʌ uʌ yʌ øʌ œʌ ɶʌ ɒʌ ɤʌ ɯʌ
iɤ eɤ ɛɤ aɤ ɑɤ ɔɤ oɤ uɤ yɤ øɤ œɤ ɶɤ ɒɤ ʌɤ ɯɤ
iɯ eɯ ɛɯ aɯ ɑɯ ɔɯ oɯ uɯ yɯ øɯ œɯ ɶɯ ɒɯ ʌɯ ɤɯ

Try the following:

iə̯ eə̯ ɛə̯ aə̯ ɑə̯ ɔə̯ oə̯ uə̯
yə̯ øə̯ œə̯ ɶə̯ ɒə̯ ʌə̯ ɤə̯ ɯə̯

8 Try saying a sequence of [ŋŋŋgɑɑŋŋŋgɑɑŋŋŋgɑɑ]. Each time you make the transition from [ŋ] to [g] or from [ɑ] to [ŋ], try to feel the velum going up or down.

Try this also with [nnndɑɑnnndɑɑnnndɑɑ] and [mmmbɑɑmmmbɑɑmmmbɑɑ].
Now try [dndndndn bmbmbmbm gŋgŋgŋgŋ].
Try saying a nasal vowel and then an oral one: [ɑ̃ɑ̃ɑ̃ɑ̃ɑ̃] [ɑɑɑɑɑ].
See if you can alternate them: [ɑ̃ ɑ ɑ̃ ɑ ɑ̃ ɑ ɑ̃ ɑ ɑ̃ ɑ].
Try this with other vowels: [i ĩ ɛ ɛ̃ u ũ], etc.
Practise:

bɑ bɑ̃ lɛ lɛ̃ dɔ dɔ̃
ka kã ɣi ɣĩ lo lõ

ɑsɑ̃ õfo uʒũ ɛ̃θɛ bɛlõ θɛ̃vɔ
ɹitɔ̃ gõzã sĩðа dũʒɑ pɛ̃θɑ fuʃẽ

9 Practise the nasal vowels in Gã (/gã/; Ghana). High tone is marked [´], and mid tone is unmarked.

/ʃi/	*to knock*	/ʃĩ/	*to leave*
/kɛ́/	*if*	/kɛ̃́/	*certainly*
/ka/	*to hammer*	/kã/	*to lie (on the ground)*
/kɔ/	*grass door*	/kɔ̃/	*to bite*
/fu/	*to moulder*	/fũ/	*a smell*

10 Practise nasal vowels in Ijo (Nigeria). Note the nasal glide [j̃].

/sãlo:/	*gills*	/afãfã/	*a type of tree*
/tũ/	*sing*	/ĩ:/	*yes*
/tɔ̃:mɔ̃/	*liken*	/bẽj̃/	*be full*
/ow̃ẽj̃/	*bite*	/sɔ̃ɾɔ̃/	*five*
/ũmba:/	*breath*	/ɔ̃j̃ãj̃ã/	*horse*

11 Practise the long vowels in Gã. High tone is marked [´], low tone is marked [`], and mid tone is unmarked.

/pì/	*welcome*	/pì:/	*many*
/ba/	*come*	/bà:/	*leaf*
/tɔ̀/	*bottle*	/tɔ:/	*to be replete*
/kò/	*certain*	/kò:/	*forest*
/bú/	*hole*	/bú:/	*mosquito net*

12 Practise the following long vowels and consonants from Icelandic. Remember that long sounds are held longer; they are not two separate articulations.

/lɛ:pjɑ/	*lick*	/bɛ:tʰrɔ/	*better*
/skrɔ:kʰvɑ/	*tell a lie*	/tʰvɪ:svɑr/	*twice*
/fɪn:ɔ/	*find*	/pʰɔb:ɪ/	*daddy*
/hɑʰt:ʏr/	*hat*	/fɪm:ɔ/	*five*

13 These are vowel sequences, not diphthongs, from Gã. Give the vowels equal weight.

/bíɛ/	*here*	/káò/	*sweet biscuit*	/àbéó/	*mishap*
/kùɛ̀/	*neck*	/àkúa/	*girl's name*	/wùò/	*fishing*
/ebiɔ/	*he asks*	/ehoɔ/	*he cooks*		

14 Practise the rounded glides in Gã. For [ɥ], try saying [j] with your lips rounded.

/wè/	*house*	/wɛ/	*to stop*	/wo/	*honey*
/ɥi/	*to avoid*	/ɥɛ/	*to cohabit*	/ɥere/	*to sit by the fire*

Advanced

15 Practise gliding from one vowel to another; go slowly enough to hear the intermediate vowels:

Start with [i] and gradually move through [e ɛ] to [a]: [i e ɛ a]
Do the same with [u] through [o ɔ] to [ɑ]: [u o ɔ ɒ]
Start with [y] and glide to [ɶ]: [y ø œ ɶ]
Start with [ɯ] and glide to [ɑ]: [ɯ ɤ ʌ ɑ]
Now go from [a] to [i]
From [ɒ] to [u]
From [ɶ] to [y]
From [ɑ] to [ɯ]

16 Practise sliding from [i] to [a] and back, and from [u] to [ɒ] and back. Now try going only from [i] to [e] and back. Do this several times, going slowly enough to hear the intermediate vowels. Try to keep the speed even.

Do the same thing for each of the following intervals:

[e – ɛ] [ɛ – a] [u – o] [o – ɔ] [ɔ – ɒ]

17 Practise again the interval [i – e]. Slide back and forth several times, and try to locate the vowel position which feels exactly half-way between [i] and [e]. Call it [i̞]. The diacritic [̞] is used to show a value slightly lower than the usual value. Now, say the sequence [i i̞ e i̞ i i̞ e]. Repeat this several times.

Repeat this procedure for the other intervals:

e e̞ ɛ e̞ e e̞ ɛ
ɛ ɛ̞ a ɛ̞ ɛ ɛ̞ a
u u̞ o u̞ u u̞ o
o ɔ̞ ɔ ɔ̞ o ɔ̞ ɔ
ɔ ɔ̞ ɒ ɔ̞ ɔ ɔ̞ ɒ

Repeat each of these several times.

Now try this:

i i̞ e e̞ ɛ ɛ̞ a
u u̞ o o̞ ɔ ɔ̞ ɒ
a ɛ̞ ɛ e̞ e i̞ i
ɒ ɔ̞ ɔ o̞ o u̞ u

Note that the IPA provides special symbols for some of these in-between vowels. The symbol [ɪ] can be used for any vowel lying anywhere between cardinal vowel [i] and [e]. Thus we could have replaced [i̞] with [ɪ]. Similarly, [æ] can be used for any vowel between [a] and [ɛ], and [ʊ] for any vowel between [o] and [u]. I have not included any secondary vowels here, but there is a symbol [ʏ] for any vowel between [y] and [ø].

We could alternatively symbolise the exercise as:

i ɪ e e̞ ɛ æ a
u ʊ o o̞ ɔ ɔ̞ ɒ

18 Many speakers of Canadian French have diphthongs instead of certain of the monophthongs of standard French. The following exercises illustrate both monophthongs and diphthongs.

mirer	/mi:re/	'look at'	*dealer*	/di:le/	'deal (v.)'
deal	/dɪjl/	'deal (n.)'	*fige*	/fɪjʒ/	'congeals'
mise	/mɪjz/	'wagers'			
juge	/ʒʏɥʒ/	'judges'	*abuse*	/abʏɥz/	'abuses'
pure	/pʏɥr/	'pure'			
bouge	/bʊwʒ/	'moves'	*ouvre*	/ʊwvr/	'work'
suit	/sʊwt/	'suit'	*rouge*	/rʊwʒ/	'red'
bréquer	/bre:ke/	'brake'	*féquer*	/fe:ke/	'fake'
péché	/pe:ʃe/	'sin'			
break	/brejk/	'break'	*fake*	/fejk/	'fakes'
steak	/stejk/	'steak'			
rosé	/ro:ze/	'pink'	*rose*	/rowz/	'rose'
saucer	/so:se/	'dunk'	*sauce*	/sows/	'sauce'
toaster	/to:ste/	'toast (v.)'	*toast*	/towst/	'toast (n.)'

19 Try saying this short selection from Sir Walter Scott's *Young Lochinvar* in a Scottish dialect (adapted from Grant, 1913):

YOUNG LOCHINAR

o ˈjʌŋ lɔxn̩ˈvɑˑr ɪz kʌm ˈʌwt əv
  ðə ˈwɛst
θrʉ ˈɔl ðə ˈwae̯d ˈbɔrdər hɪz ˈstid
  wəz ðə ˈbɛst
and ˈseˑv hɪz gʉd ˈbrɔdsɔrd hi
  ˈwɛpn̩z həd ˈnʌn
hi ˈrod ˈɔl ʌnˈɑrmd ənd hi ˈrod
  ˈɔl əˈlon
so ˈfeθfəl ɪn ˈlʌv ənd so ˈdɔntlɪs
  ɪn ˈwɔˑr
ðər ˈnɛvər wəz ˈnʌjt lʌjk ðə ˈjʌŋ
  lɔxn̩ˈvɑˑr
hi ˈsted nɔt fər ˈbrek ənd hi ˈstɔpt
  nɔt fər ˈston
hi ˈswam ðɪ ɛsk ˈrɪvər hwɛˑr ˈford
  ðər wəz ˈnʌn
bʌt, eˑr hi əˈlʌjtɪd ət ˈnɛðərbɪ ˈget
ðə ˈbrae̯d həd kənˈsɛntɪd ðə
  ˈgalənt ˈkem ˈlet
fɔr ə ˈlagərd ɪn ˈlʌv ənd ə ˈdastərd
  ɪn ˈwɔˑr
wəz tə wɛd ðə ˈfeˑr ˈɛlən
  əv ˈbreˑv lɔxn̩ˈvɑˑr

O, young Lochinvar is come out of
  the west,
Through all the wide Border his steed
  was the best,
And save his good broadsword he
  weapons had none;
He rode all unarmed, and he rode
  all alone.
So faithful in love, and so dauntless
  in war,
There never was knight like the
  young Lochinvar.
He stayed not for brake, and he stopped
  not for stone,
He swam the Eske river where ford there
  was none;
But, ere he alighted at Netherby gate,
The bride had consented, the gallant
  came late:
For a laggard in love, and a dastard
  in war,
Was to wed the fair Ellen
  of brave Lochinvar

Chapter 10

Place of articulation

Consonants are described in three ways: place, manner, and voicing. The **place of articulation**, or where they are made, is described in this chapter. The **manner of articulation**, or how they are made, is the topic of Chapter 11. In this chapter, we will limit ourselves primarily to three manners of articulation: stops, fricatives, and nasals. **Voicing** is described in Chapter 12.

In this chapter you will learn about:

- where consonant articulations are made;
- double articulations;
- secondary articulations.

Primary places of articulation

Consonants are formed by creating a constriction in the vocal tract; the place of articulation is defined as the parts of the vocal tract having the greatest constriction. The vocal tract consists of the organs above the larynx: the pharynx, the oral cavity, and the nasal cavity. We have already learned many places of articulation from an examination of English. This chapter will extend our knowledge to include all the places of articulation found in languages generally.

The major constriction, which may be a complete or partial closure, is made by the articulators coming together, generally by a lower articulator moving towards an upper articulator. The **lower articulators** are elements of the lower jaw – the lower lip, the lower teeth, and the tongue. The **upper articulators** are the upper lip, the upper teeth, the palate, the velum, the uvula and the rear wall of the pharynx. Places of articulation usually have a compound name giving the lower and upper articulators, with the name of the lower articulator first. Thus, apico-dental indicates that the lower articulator is the apex of the tongue, and the upper articulator is the upper teeth. Occasionally, when the lower articulator is obvious or unimportant, only the upper articulator is named: for example, *velar*, used alone, is interpreted as meaning *dorso-velar*. Table 10.1 illustrates a number of terms used to describe the articulators, with their Latin or Greek equivalents.

Table 10.1 Terminology

English	Latin or Greek		
	Noun	**Combining form**	**Adjective**
lip	labium	labio-	labial
tongue	lingua	linguo-	lingual
tip	apex	apico-	apical
blade	lamina	lamino-	laminal
front	—	—	—
back	dorsum	dorso-	dorsal
root	radix	radico-	radical
tooth	dens	denti-	dental
alveolar ridge	—	alveolo-	alveolar
(hard) palate	palatum	palato-	palatal
velum	velum	velo-	velar
mouth	os	oro-	oral
nose	nasus	naso-	nasal
throat	pharynx	pharyngo-	pharyngeal
voice box	larynx	laryngo-	laryngeal

Labial

Labial sounds are made with one or both lips and include bilabials, labiodentals, and linguo-labials.

Bilabial

The lower lip articulates with the upper lip to form a bilabial consonant (Figure 10.1). The term bilabial is used rather than labio-labial. The bilabial stops are voiceless [p] and voiced [b] as in English. The fricatives are voiceless [φ] phi, and voiced [β] beta. The nasal stop is [m] as in English. Bilabial stops and the nasal are extremely common in languages; indeed, a

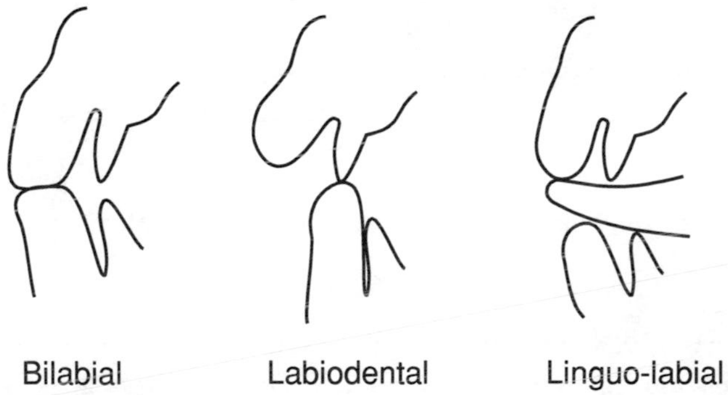

Bilabial Labiodental Linguo-labial

Figure 10.1 Labial articulations

language without them is noteworthy. Bilabial fricatives, however, are rather uncommon; languages tend to have bilabial stops and labio-dental fricatives.

Ewe (Ghana, West Africa) is unusual in having contrasting bilabial and labio-dental fricatives. High tone here is shown by [´] and low tone by [`].

/fà/	*puff adder*	/ɸà/	*yeast*
/fú/	*feather*	/ɸú/	*bone*
/vɔ̀/	*to finish*	/βɔ̀/	*python*
/vù/	*to tear apart*	/βù/	*blood*

Ewe

Labiodental

The lower lip articulates against the upper teeth to form labiodental consonants (Figure 10.1). Labiodental stops do not occur distinctively although they are quite easy to make if your teeth do not have gaps. The labiodental nasal [ɱ] is reported in Teke (Laver, 1994). It occurs allophonically in English words like *symphony* [ˈsɪɱfəni] where it is a homorganic nasal agreeing as to place of articulation with the following labiodental fricative [f] or [v]. As noted in the preceding section on bilabials, languages commonly have bilabial stops and labiodental fricatives.

The transition next to a labiodental consonant points down as with the bilabials (Figure 10.2). The fricatives have fairly faint noise.

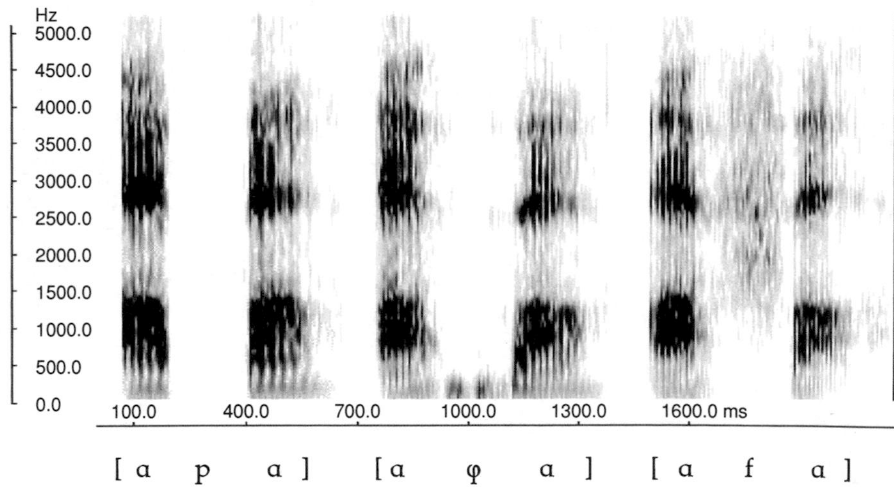

Figure 10.2 Spectrograms of bilabial and labiodental stops and fricatives

Linguo-labial

Maddieson (1989) reports a very rare **linguo-labial** sound with the tip or blade of the tongue articulating with the upper lip. The IPA uses a gull-shaped diacritic [̼] for this place of articulation.

/p̼atel/	*breadfruit*	/pətək/	*my head*	/tatel/	*father*
/nəm̼ək/	*my tongue*	/nəmək/	*my spirit*	/nani/	*goat*
/naβ̼at/	*stone*	/naβal/	*songfest*		

V'enen Taut (Austronesian, Vanuatu)

Coronal

Coronal sounds are made with the apex or lamina of the tongue. They include dentals, alveolars, alveolo-palatals, postalveolars, and retroflex sounds.

Dental

Dental sounds can be made with either the tip of the tongue, **apico-dental**, or with the blade, **laminodental**. The dental fricatives are voiceless [θ] **theta** and voiced [ð] **eth**. Other dental sounds are shown by using the alveolar symbol with the diacritic [̪], for example [t̪ d̪ n̪ l̪ r̪]. Because in a given language all the stops are usually all dental or all alveolar, you will find that in discussing a particular language, the diacritic is commonly omitted with the assumption that you will know whether [t d n] represent dentals or alveolars. Dental fricatives [s̪ z̪], with the blade of the tongue near the back of the upper teeth, can be made in addition to the dentals [θ ð]. **Interdentals** are made by thrusting the tongue slightly forward so that the tip protrudes between the teeth. Interdentals can be symbolised with [θ̟ ð̟].

Dental and alveolar stops rarely contrast with each other. Where they do, usually one place of articulation is apical and the other laminal. Temne and Sherbro, two West African languages of Sierra Leone illustrate the alternative ways of combining apical and laminal with dental and alveolar. The diacritics [̺ ̻] show apical and laminal articulations respectively.

Temne	t̺̪ɔk	*descend*	apico-dental
	t̻or	*farms*	laminoalveolar
Sherbro	t̻̪ɔk	*cloud*	laminodental
	t̺ɔk	*wash*	apico-alveolar

Malayalam (southern India) has a contrast between dentals and alveolars, both with apical articulation.

Bilabial	**Dental**	**Alveolar**	**Retroflex**	**Palatal**	**Velar**
təppi	pət̪t̪i	vətti	pəʈʈi		
searched	*hood*	*dried up*	*dog*		
	tʃət̪t̪u	tətte	tʃəʈʈəm		
	died	*parrot*	*rule*		
pəmmi	pən̪n̪i	tənnil	əɳɳi	kəɲɲi	məŋŋi
stealthily	*pig*	*in oneself*	*link*	*gruel*	*faded*
Bilabial	**Dental**	**Alveolar**	**Retroflex**	**Palatal**	**Velar**

nəmməɭ	kən̪n̪u	kənni	kəɳɳi	məɲɲəl	məŋŋəl
we	*calf*	*month*	*link*	*turmeric*	*dimness*

Malayalam

Dentals and alveolars both have a transition which points to the mid range (see Figure 10.3). If the vowel has a high F2, the transition will tend to point down; if the F2 is low, the transition will point up. With a vowel with an F2 in the mid ranges, the transition will tend to be level. The dental fricatives have a fairly faint noise pattern.

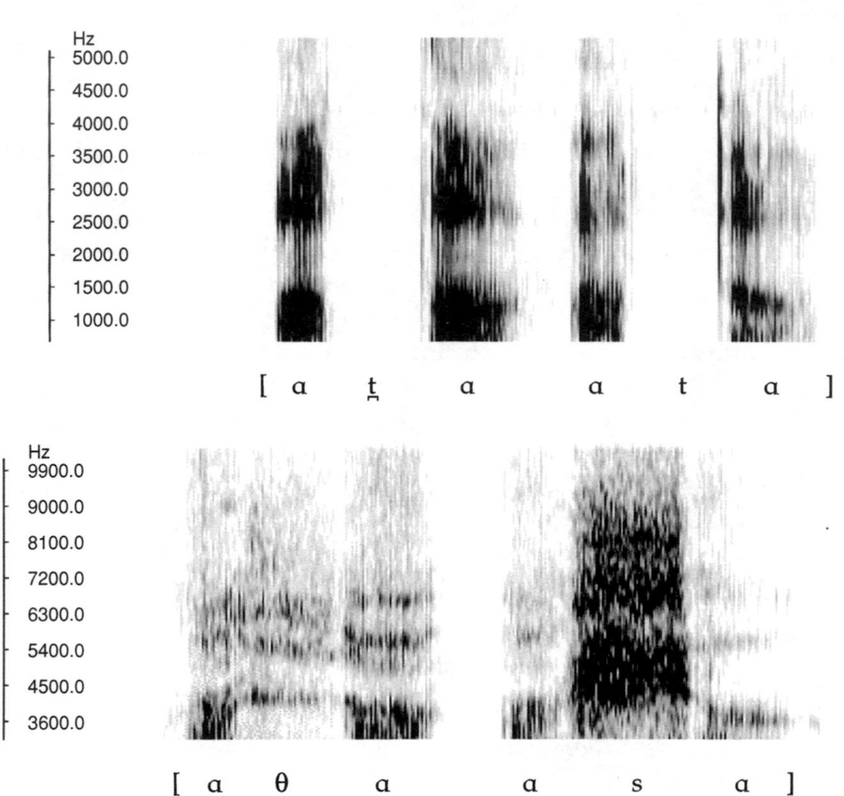

Figure 10.3 Spectrograms showing dental and alveolar stops and fricatives

Alveolar

As we saw under *dentals* above, **alveolar** sounds may be made with either the tip or blade of the tongue, known accordingly as **apico-alveolar** or **laminoalveolar**. The symbols are [t d n s z], familiar to us from English.

The transition for alveolar sounds is in the mid range, similar to the dentals, discussed above. The fricatives [s z] have quite strong noise in the higher frequencies (see [s] in Figure 10.3).

Alveolo-palatal

The IPA lists two fricatives as having an **alveolo-palatal** place of articulation, different from the postalveolars. They are produced with the tip of the tongue behind the upper teeth and with the blade quite close to the back of the alveolar ridge and to the forward part of the hard palate. Figure 10.4 shows the articulatory position of alveolo-palatals. The symbols are [ɕ] for the voiceless fricative and [ʑ] for the voiced fricative. In recent IPA charts, these sounds have been reduced to a secondary status. Ladefoged and Maddieson (1996) refer to [ɕ ʑ] as 'laminal palatalised postalveolars'. The distinction of postalveolar and alveolo-palatal, although useful for some languages, has not gained wide currency (Pullum and Ladusaw, 1996). Frequently you will find the terms used interchangeably to mean postalveolar (see the discussion below under postalveolar).

Polish has both alveolo-palatals and postalveolars.

/ʑarno/	*grain*	/ʒɑrno/	*handmill*
/koɕ/	*cut with scythe! (impv.)*	/koʒ/	*basket*
/bɨtɕ/	*to be*	/tɕma/	*moth*
/tɕɛnʲ/	*shadow*	/dʑɛnʲ/	*day*
/tʃɨstɨ/	*clean*	/dʒdʒɨstɨ/	*rainy*

Polish

Postalveolar

Postalveolar sounds are made with the blade of the tongue articulating with the area at the border of the alveolar ridge and the hard palate (Figure 10.4). The blade is lower than with the alveolo-palatals. Stops are fairly

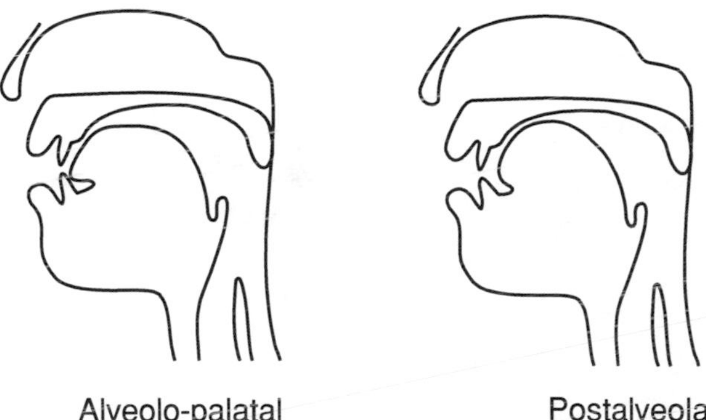

Figure 10.4 Alveolo-palatal and postalveolar places of articulation

rare in this region, although the fricatives [ʃ ʒ] and affricates [tʃ dʒ] are quite common in the languages of the world.

The alveolar fricatives [s z] and the postalveolar fricatives [ʃ ʒ] involve some difficulty in describing their point of articulation. X-rays show that both sounds are made with a variety of tongue shapes. The crucial thing seems to be to get the air stream to hit the teeth so as to produce the appropriate turbulence: with [s z], the air stream strikes the upper teeth, and with [ʃ ʒ], the air stream strikes the lower teeth. The terms alveolar and postalveolar are not wrong, but they must be interpreted with care. Figure 10.4 shows a typical position for postalveolars.

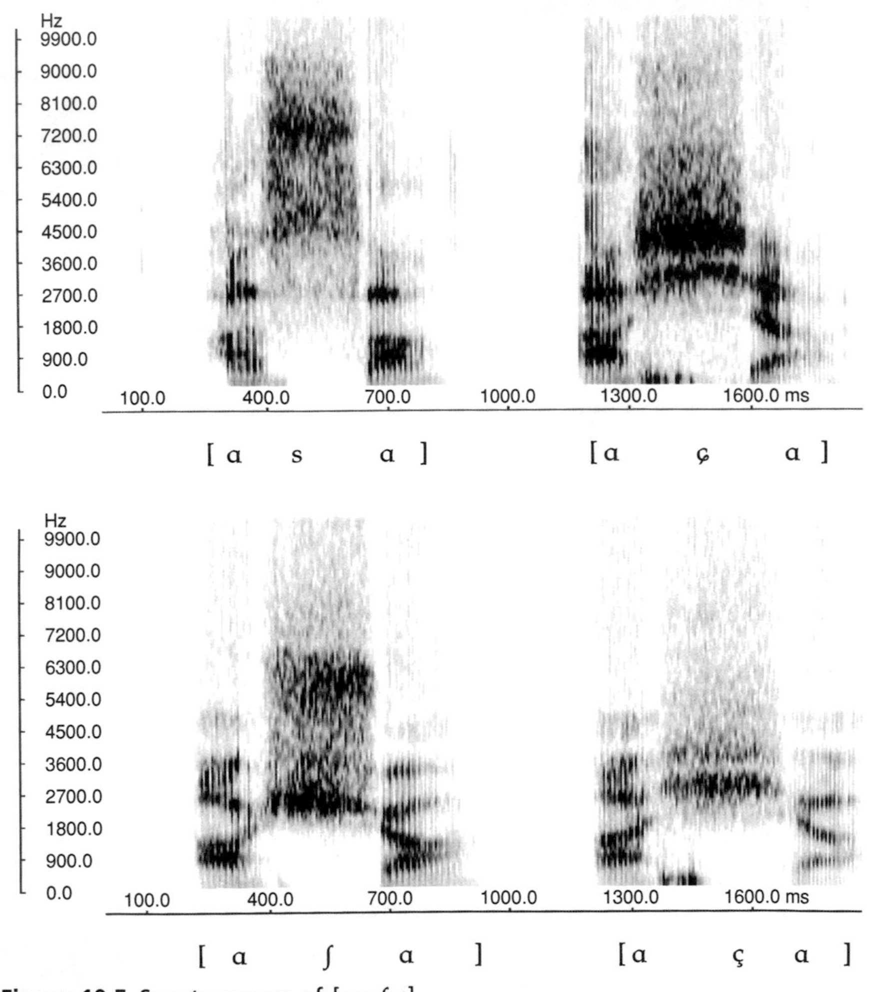

Figure 10.5 Spectrograms of [s ɕ ʃ ç]

Some authors refer to this point of articulation as palato-alveolar, alveolo-palatal, or alveopalatal. I recommend following the IPA usage, distinguishing **postalveolar** and **alveolo-palatal**, and not using palato-alveolar or alveo-palatal as technical terms.

The postalveolar fricatives have random noise in the higher frequencies, though generally not so high as the alveolars. See Figure 10.5.

Retroflex

Retroflex consonants can also be described as apico-postalveolar. The underside of the tip of the tongue articulates with the area at the border of the alveolar ridge and the hard palate, as in Figure 10.6. The body of the tongue is quite concave. The symbols for retroflex consonants are [ʈ ɖ ɳ ʂ ʐ ɭ] – the alveolar symbols modified by a lower hook. Auditorily, these sounds have a rhotic, or [ɹ]-like quality, which often extends to the adjacent vowels.

Figure 10.6 Retroflex

With retroflex consonants, the most general acoustic characteristic is that the third formant is lowered (see Figure 10.7).

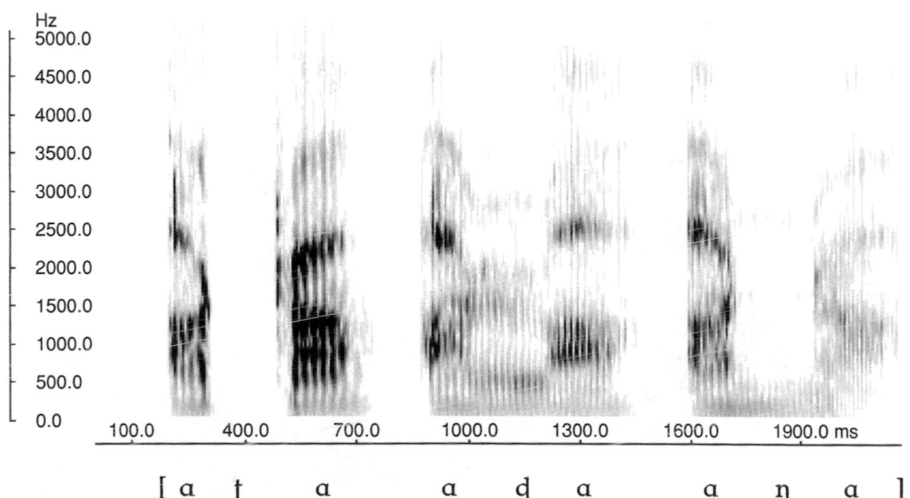

[a ʈ a a ɖ a a ɳ a]

Figure 10.7 Spectrogram of retroflex consonants

Dorsal

Dorsal sounds include those made with the front, back, or root of the tongue: palatal, velar, uvular, pharyngeal, and glottal.

Palatal

For **palatal** sounds, the front of the tongue articulates with the hard palate. Note that the tip of the tongue points down, often touching the lower teeth. The stops, voiceless [c] and voiced [ɟ], are considerably less common than alveolar or velar stops; the palatal nasal [ɲ], however, is quite common. The fricative symbols are [ç] for voiceless and [ʝ] for voiced.

Remember that the **front** of the tongue is located behind the tip and blade. Presumably, this usage derives from the fact that this part of the tongue is used in making front vowels.

Twi (Ghana, West Africa) contrasts alveolar, palatal, and velar stops.

/àtá/	*twin brother*	/càcà/	*straw mattress*	/ɔ́kà/	*he bites*
/ɔ́da/	*he lies*	/ɛ̀ɟá/	*father*	/àgóɹú/	*play*

Twi

German has a palatal fricative [ç] contrasting with a postalveolar [ʃ].

/vɪç/	*wich*	'yielded'	/vɪʃ/	*wisch*	'wipe (impv.)'
/fiçt/	*ficht*	'fences (vb)'	/fɪʃt/	*fischt*	'fishes (vb)'
/mɪç/	*mich*	'me'	/mɪʃ/	*misch*	'mix (impv.)'
/dɪç/	*dich*	'you'	/tɪʃ/	*Tisch*	'table'
/kɔjç/	*keuch*	'pant (impv.)'	/kɔjʃ/	*keusch*	'chaste'

German

Velar

The full term is **dorso-velar**, indicating that the back of the tongue articulates with the soft palate; however, the back of the tongue is the only articulator that is used to articulate with the velum, so the prefix dorso- is regularly omitted. Many people can make apico-velars, but they are not used in any language. (I have personally observed a linguist capable of placing the tip of the tongue behind the uvula!)

The stops are [k g] as in English, with the velar nasal [ŋ], **eng**. The voiceless fricative is [x], and the voiced fricative is [ɣ] **gamma**. Scots Gaelic distinguishes [k g x ɣ]. Try pronouncing the examples for a challenge.

/ə ˈku:/ *her dog*	/ə ˈxu:/ *his dog*	/ə ˈgoər/ *her goat*	/ə ˈɣoər/ *his goat*
/xaj/ *went*	/xa ˈxrədʒ/ *not believe*	/ɣaf/ *took*	/ˈhaxið/ *happened*
/ˈɣaxi/ *homewards*	/ˈahəraxəɣ/ *changing*	/gle: ˈɣu/ *very dark*	/ə ˈɣu:xəs/ *his birthplace*

Scots Gaelic

Often the position of a velar articulation is conditioned by the neighbouring vowel, as in English; [k̟ g̟] next to front vowels, and [k̠ g̠] next to back vowels.

The second and third formants in a vowel preceding a velar consonant come together just at the end of the vowel (Figure 10.8).

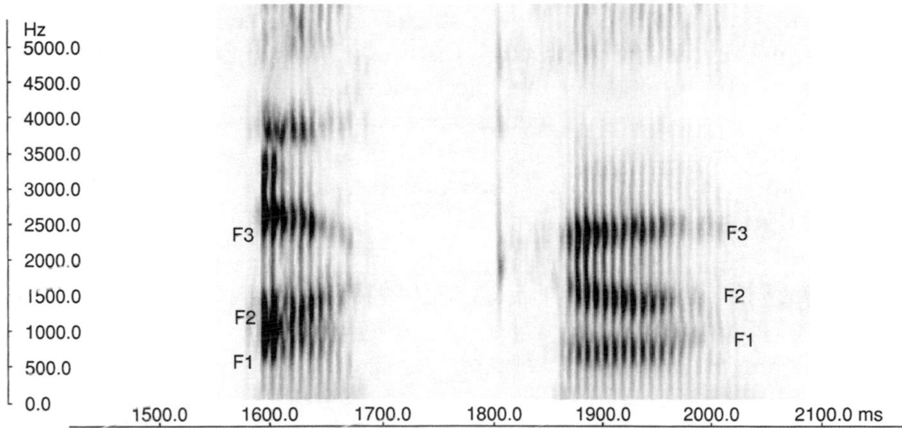

Figure 10.8 Spectrograms of velar stop pronounced between vowels. Note that the 2nd and 3rd formants appear to come together at about 2000 Hz during the stop

Uvular

For **uvular** consonants, the dorsum of the tongue articulates with the uvula (Figure 10.9). This feels like a velar sound made very far back in the mouth. The symbols are [q] for the voiceless stop, [ɢ] for the voiced stop, [ɴ] for the nasal, and [χ] the Greek letter **chi** /kaj/ for the voiceless fricative. The IPA uses the symbol [ʁ] for both the voiced fricative and the voiced approximant. I recommend the use of [ʁ] for the fricative and [ʁ̞] for the approximant. In handwriting [χ], make the one leg longer to distinguish it from [x].

Figure 10.9 Uvular

Quechua (South America) distinguishes palatal, velar, and uvular stops.

/caj/	*thee*	/kaj/	*to be*	/qan/	*you*
/cuŋka/	*ten*	/kusa/	*good*	/quj/	*give*
/cʰajna/	*like that*	/kʰuci/	*pig*	/qʰata/	*slope*

Quechua

Pharyngeal

Pharyngeal consonants are made by moving the root of the tongue back so that it is closer to the pharyngeal wall. The full term, though rarely used, is **radico-pharyngeal**. The **root** of the tongue is the vertical part, forming the forward wall of the pharyngeal cavity. Most people cannot make a complete pharyngeal closure, so only fricatives are found. A pharyngeal nasal stop is an impossibility; if the air stream is completely blocked at the pharynx, no air can escape through the nose. The symbols are [ħ] for the voiceless fricative and [ʕ] for the voiced fricative.

Arabic has a glottal stop as well as voiced and voiceless pharyngeal fricatives. Butcher and Ahmad (1987) note that in Arabic /ʕ/ is often a voiced approximant with no fricative noise and often with a creaky voice (see Chapter 12).

/ħa:l/	*condition*	/ʕa:l/	*fine*
/ħadi:d/	*iron*	/wadi:ʕ/	*he is weak*
/biˀr/	*a well*	/suˀl/	*wish*
/qurˀa:n/	*Koran*	/faˀs/	*axe*

Arabic

Epiglottal

Traditionally, the epiglottis has not been regarded as playing a part in phonetics. Laufer and Condax (1979), however, have shown that in producing the voiceless pharyngeal [ħ] of Arabic and oriental Hebrew, the epiglottis is folded back. You can feel the movement of the epiglottis moving back if you swallow slowly and feel the moment of complete closure. For further details, see Catford (1988) who also mentions epiglottal stops in languages of the Caucasus.

Glottal

Glottal is a curious category. It comprises three sounds: **glottal stop** [ˀ] and the fricatives [h] and [ɦ]. These sounds function as consonants and can be said to have a **glottal** or **laryngeal** point of articulation. On the other hand, from a purely phonetic point of view, [ˀ] is a state of the glottis involving complete closure of the vocal folds, [h] is a voiceless vowel, and [ɦ] is a breathy voiced vowel (see Chapter 14).

Tagalog (/təˈgɑləg/; Philippines) has a contrastive glottal stop and also a final [h].

/ˀa·naj/	*termite*	/ha·naj/	*row*
/kaˀo·n/	*fetch*	/kaho·n/	*box*
/ba·taˀ/	*child*	/ba·tah/	*bathrobe*
/magˀalis/	*remove*	/magalis/	*full of sores*

Tagalog

Double articulation

It is possible to make two stops at the same time, for example, a [k] and a [p] (see Figure 10.10). Both closures are made and released simultaneously, or almost so. We say that such a sound has a **double articulation**, and call it a **labial-velar**. It is symbolised as [k͡p], with the tie-bar showing that the [k] and the [p] are simultaneous. The labial-velars [k͡p, g͡b, ŋ͡m] are quite common in many languages of West Africa. Occasionally we find labial-alveolars [p͡t, b͡d, m͡n]; other combinations are possible, but rarely found. Maddieson (1984) has claimed that these are all sequences of two stops at the phonemic level.

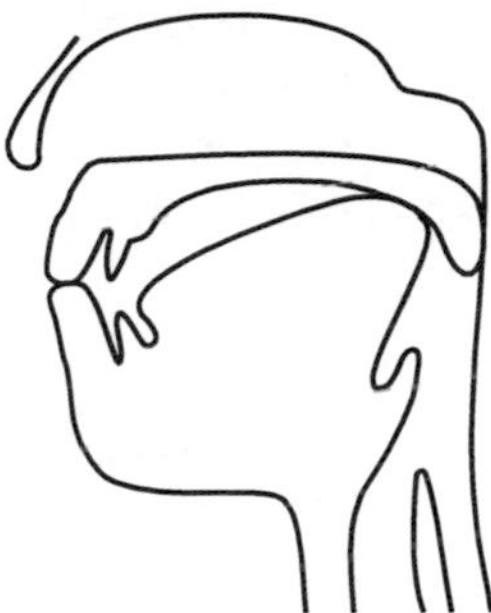

Figure 10.10 Labial-velar

The term *labiovelar* is sometimes seen instead of *labial-velar*. Given the system of terms used here, *labiovelar* would mean that the lower lip articulates with the velum. This seems to be stretching things a bit. For the double articulation, I will use labial-velar.

The essential element of a double articulation is that it must have two different simultaneous points of articulation, each with the same degree of stricture. Thus, doubly articulated fricatives are possible, although rare: [v͡z, θ͡x]. The glide [w] has a double articulation of a labial-velar approximant.

Sherbro contrasts [b] and [g͡b].

/bi/	*have*	/g͡bí/	*all*	/bàŋ/	*evil*	/g͡bàŋ/	*hat*

Sherbro (West Africa, Sierra Leone)

Bura (Nigeria; Ladefoged, 1964) has the doubly articulated stop [p͡t] and also the doubly articulated affricates [p͡ts] and [p͡tʃ].

/p͡tá/	*hare*	/p͡tsa/	*roast*	/p͡tʃi/	*sun*

Bura (Nigeria)

Some accents of Swedish have a simultaneous [ʃ͡x], also symbolised as [ɧ], a voiceless postalveolar-velar fricative.

själ	/ɧɛl/	'soul'	*tjugo*	/ɧʉgu/	'twenty'
skjorta	/ɧorʈɑ/	'shirt'	*sköld*	/ɧœld/	'shield'

Swedish

Secondary articulations

Secondary articulations are the addition of a secondary, lesser constriction to the greater, **primary articulation** of a consonant. Thus, if we add lip rounding to a [k], we get a labialised [kʷ]. The primary articulation is the velar stop; the secondary articulation is lip rounding. A useful way of understanding secondary articulations is to think of them as adding a vowel quality to a consonant. In the case above, the vowel quality of [u] has been added to the [k]. The common secondary articulations, applied to an alveolar stop, are shown in Figure 10.11.

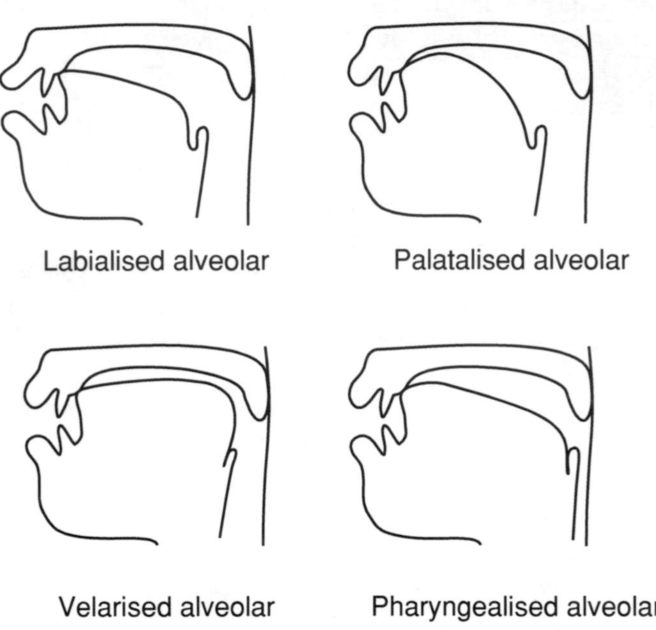

Secondary articulation	Vowel quality	Symbol	Examples
Labialisation	[u]	[ʷ]	[tʷ pʷ sʷ]
Palatalisation	[i]	[ʲ]	[tʲ pʲ sʲ]
Velarisation	[ɤ]	[~]	[ɫ t̴ n̴ s̴] or [lˠ tˠ nˠ sˠ]
Pharyngealisation	[ɑ]	[~]	[ɫ t̴ n̴ s̴] or [lˤ tˤ nˤ sˤ]

Figure 10.11 Secondary articulations

Secondary articulations may be conditioned or inherent. Consonants regularly become labialised next to rounded vowels or palatalised next to front vowels; these secondary articulations are thus conditioned by the neighbouring environment. On the other hand, they may have inherent secondary articulations. In English, for example, [ʃ] and [ɹ] are rounded no matter what vowels they are next to: e.g., *sheep* [ʃʷip], *reap* [ɹʷip].

Labialisation

Labialised sounds involve lip rounding, that is a rounded vowel quality, usually high and back. Labialised consonants are quite common. Labialised consonants can be specified [round].

Twi contrasts plain and labialised palatals.

/càcà/	*straw mattress*	/òcʷáʔ/	*he cuts*
/òɟá/	*he leads*	/òɟʷa/	*he carves*
/òɲá/	*he finds*	/ɲʷá/	*snail*
/ɔ̀ʃɛ́/	*he puts on*	/ɔ̀ʃʷɛ́/	*he looks at*

Twi (West Africa)

Palatalisation

Palatalised consonants have the front of the tongue more towards the palatal region than normal, that is having a high front unrounded vocalic position. In many of the Slavic and Celtic languages, the consonants may be divided into plain (i.e., non-palatalised) and palatalised.

The term **palatalisation** is used in two quite different ways. One, as here, describes a secondary articulation. The other way describes a process which may or may not involve a secondary articulation. We may say that a certain language has a process of palatalisation. This means that under certain conditions certain sounds move towards a more palatal position. This could mean the addition of a secondary articulation: [t] → [tʲ]. Alternatively, palatalisation is commonly used to mean other changes such as [t] or [k] → [c] or [k]. In these cases, the sounds [c] and [tʃ] are more palatal than [t] or [k], but neither has a secondary articulation.

Ukrainian contrasts plain and palatalised consonants.

/lak/	*varnish*	/lʲak/	*fright*
/ʃal/	*rage*	/ʃalʲ/	*shawl*
/ɦrɪwna/	*penalty*	/ɦrɪwnʲa/	*3-kopek coin*
/kin/	*public place*	/kinʲ/	*horse*
/rasa/	*race*	/rʲasa/	*cassock*
/kruk/	*raven*	/krʲuk/	*hook*

Ukrainian

Velarisation

Velarised consonants involve raising the tongue more towards a velar position than usual, that is a high back unrounded vocalic position. Velarised [ɫ], known as 'dark-l' is quite common. In [ɫ], the tip of the tongue is at the alveolar ridge (or teeth), and the sides of the tongue are down as usual. However, the back of the tongue, rather than being fairly flat, is raised towards the velum in the position of an approximant.

Scots Gaelic contrasts three types of laterals and nasals: plain, velarised, and palatalised. The plain sounds are alveolar; the velarised and palatalised ones are dental.

Plain		**Velarised**		**Palatalised**	
/ˈbalə/	*town*	/ˈbaɫ̪ə/	*ball, wall*	/ˈkal̪ʲɔx/	*old woman*
/ə ˈlɔər/	*his book*	/ə ˈɫ̪ɔx/	*his, her lake*	/ə ˈl̪ʲɔər/	*her book*
/ian/	*bird*	/ˈbliən̴̪ə/	*year*	/ian̪ʲ/	*John*
/ə ˈniən/	*his daughter*	/ə n̴̪abi/	*his, her neighbour*	/ə ˈn̪ʲiən/	*her daughter*

Scots Gaelic

The IPA allows using the same symbols for velarisation and pharyngealisation. This works because languages are not known to use both. If we need to distinguish them, we can use a diacritic [ˠ] (a small superscript gamma) for velarised consonants, and a diacritic [ˤ] (a small superscript [ʕ]) for pharyngealised ones: [tˠ tˤ].

Pharyngealisation

Pharyngealised sounds involve a lowering of the back of the tongue and a retraction of the root, thus effecting a narrowing of the pharynx. They are also transcribed with [~]. Pharyngealised sounds are not very common, although they are found in Arabic.

/mas:/	*to touch*	/ma̴s̴:/	*to suck*	/ba:z/	*falcon*	/ba:z̴/	*to be spoiled*

Arabic

Technical terms

- advanced
- alveolar
- alveolo-palatal
- apico-alveolar
- apico-dental
- bilabial
- coronal
- dental
  - interdental
- dorsal
- dorso-velar
- double articulation
- epiglottal
- front
- glottal
  - glottal stop
- labial
  - labialisation
  - labialised
- labial-velar
- laminoalveolar
- laminodental
- laryngeal
- linguo-labial
- lower articulators
- manner of articulation
- palatal
  - palatalisation
  - palatalised
- pharyngeal
  - pharyngealisation
  - pharyngealised
- place of articulation
- postalveolar
- primary articulation
- radico-pharyngeal
- retracted
- retroflex
- root
- secondary articulation
- upper articulators
- uvular
- velar
  - velarisation
  - velarised
- vocal tract

Symbols

Table 10.2 Symbols for stops, fricatives and nasals

	bilabial	labiodental	dental	alveolar	alveolo-palatal	postalveolar
stops	p b		t̪ d̪	t d		
fricatives	ɸ β	f v	θ ð	s z	ɕ ʑ	ʃ ʒ
nasals	m	ɱ	n̪	n		

	retroflex	palatal	velar	uvular	pharyngeal	glottal
stops	ʈ ɖ	c ɟ	k ɡ	q ɢ		ʔ
fricatives	ʂ ʐ	ç ʝ	x ɣ	χ ʁ	ħ ʕ	h
nasals	ɳ	ɲ	ŋ	ɴ		

[ɧ] is a voiceless postalveolar-velar fricative = [ʃ͡x].

Symbols with special names

β *beta*
ɸ *phi*
θ *theta*
ð *eth*

ʃ *esh*
ʒ *ezh*
ç *c-cedilla*
ɣ *gamma*

ŋ *eng*
χ *chi*
ʔ *glottal stop*

Diacritics

◌̪ dental
◌̺ apical
◌̻ laminal
◌͡◌ simultaneous articulation

◌̝ raised
◌̞ lowered
◌̟ fronted
◌̠ backed

Exercises

Basic

1 Bilabial fricatives: [ɸ] and [β]. Note that /ɸ β/ are bilabial and that /f v/ are labiodental. To make /ɸ/ form your lips so as to make a /p/, hold the lips together in a relaxed fashion and blow through them. Try saying:

ɸi ɸaj ɸəw ɸʌm

Now try with beta:

βi	βɪ	βej	βɛ	βæ
φɑ	βɔ	φ ɪ	βu	φɔj
βow	φʊ	βug	φ jm	βʌl

Some people have trouble making these sounds without a following /w/: /φwɑ/ rather than /φ ɑ/. If this is the case for you, try extending the /φ/: /φφφφφ/. Practise this a couple of times, and then try opening the lips suddenly to /ɑ/ – sneak up on the /ɑ/. Now try the corresponding trick with /βββββ/.

If you still have trouble with /φ β/, try smiling; pretend to blow out a candle while still smiling.

Some people use [φjuuuuuuu] *phew!* when they are relieved or tired.

Be sure to keep /φ β/ separate from /f v/. If you find /φ/ turning into an /f/, extend your lower lip a bit. Ultimately the /φ β/ should have about the same lip position as /p b/, except slightly open. Practise the following pairs:

pɑ	fɑ	fɑ	pɑ
pɑ	φɑ	fɑ	φɑ
φɑ	pɑ	φɑ	fɑ
bɑ	βa	vɑ	βɑ
βɑ	vɑ	βɑ	bɑ

2 Ewe (Ghana, West Africa)

ɛβɛ	*the Ewe language*	ɛvɛ	*two*
eφa	*he polished*	efa	*he was cold*
eβlo	*mushroom*	evlo	*he is evil*
eφle	*he bought*	efle	*he split off*

3 Try these nonsense words:

pɑfɑ	φufu	vɛbɛ	pɛφɛ	baβɑ	βʌvʌ
fiφi	βɔvɔ	φiβi	pifɑ	φuβʌ	βaβu
bɔφɪ	βɔvɛ	fɛvɔ	fɛφɑ	φʊbu	vɒφu
vʌfæ	φɪvɔ	bʌvæ			

4 Read the following poem aloud:

Peter Piper picked a peck of pickled peppers;
A peck of pickled peppers Peter Piper picked.
If Peter Piper picked a peck of pickled peppers,
Where's the peck of pickled peppers that Peter Piper picked?

a. Now try reading it, substituting [φ] for [p].
b. Now try it with [β].
c. Try it with unaspirated [p].

5 Place the tip of your tongue against the upper teeth and produce the apico-dental stop [t̪ d̪]. Draw the tip back to the alveolar ridge to produce apico-alveolar stops [t d]. Now pull the tip behind the alveolar ridge to produce a retroflex stop [ʈ ɖ]. In making a retroflex stop the tongue should be curled back sufficiently so that the underside of the tongue comes into contact with the upper surface. Try the following:

ɑd̪ɑ	ɑdɑ	ɑɖɑ
id̪i	idi	iɖi
od̪o	odo	oɖo

In like manner, place the blade of the tongue against the teeth to produce a laminodental stop. Then pull the blade back to the alveolar ridge and produce a laminoalveolar stop.

ɑd̪ɑ   ɑdɑ   ed̪e   ede   ud̪u   udu

Try the following dentals, first make them apico-dental and then lamino-dental:

ɛt̪i	ɔn̪ɪ	ɒl̪ɛ	æd̪ʌ	ɒl̪ɛ
un̪ʊ	ʊtɑ	ɑdɔ	ʊt̪ɪ	dod̪i

6 If you start producing an [i], and then move the tongue higher, you will produce an approximant [j]. If you move the tongue higher until friction-like noise is present, you will produce a voiced fricative [ʝ]. Now, making sure that the tip of the tongue is near your lower teeth, move the tongue higher so as to make a complete closure and you will produce a palatal stop [ɟ].

Try pronouncing the palatals [c ɟ ç ʝ ɲ ʎ] with all eight cardinal vowels:

e.g.: [ci ce cɛ ca cɑ cɔ co cu]

Now try:

cice	ɟaɟɛ	ɲuɲɔ	ʎɛʎæ
ɟacɔ	ʎɛɲa	ɲiço	cuʎe
teʝi	çeɟæ	nɛʝu	nɔɲo
ɲoŋe	ɟɔti	ʝɛʎi	leʎa

Try these build-up patterns:

ˈtɑ ɟɛ ˈçe zu ˈcɛ ɲɔ θo ˈdi cɔ ˌʎi ʝe ˈd̪a

Now, start with an [i], and move the tongue forwards. You should produce a [ʑ]. Practise these:

ʑi	ɕi	siɕi	ʑiʑi	ɕiçi	ʑiʝi	ziʑi	ɕaʑa
ɕa	ʑa	ça	ʝa	saʃa	çaʑa	aʝa	ʃɑɕa

7 Try these nonsense words:

fɛço	çesa	ʝivɑ	ʝaʒo	çuxɔ	xɛçi
ʃaçe	zɛʝu	ɣɔʝe	ʝɑɣi	ɸoçaʎ	çɔʎaʝ
ʝuʝɛç	çediʝ	ɟiʝɛc	ʝaciç		

8 German:

/ziˑk/	*Sieg*	'victory'	/ziˑç/	*siech*	'sickly'
/rɛkt/	*reckt*	'stretches'	/reçt/	*recht*	'right'
/nɪkt/	*nickt*	'nods'	/niçt/	*nicht*	'not'
/ʃtrajk/	*Streik*	'strike'	/ʃtrajçt/	*streicht*	'strokes'
/kiˑnoˑ/	*Kino*	'movie'	/çeˈmi/	*Chemie*	'chemistry'

9 Bengali (/ˌbɛŋˈgɑli/; India). Try the following, paying attention to the aspiration:

/pʰɔl/	*fruit*	/tɔpʰat/	*distance*
/bɔropʰ/	*ice*	/pʰeni/	*candy floss*
/tʰoli/	*bag*	/gatʰa/	*poem*
/pɔtʰ/	*road*	/tʰana/	*police station*
/kʰil/	*bolt*	/ɔkʰil/	*entire*
/nokʰ/	*nail*	/akʰroʈ/	*walnut*
/ʈʰunko/	*fragile*	/aʈʰa/	*glue*
/kaʈʰ/	*wood*	/aʈʰaro/	*eighteen*
/tʃʰobi/	*picture*	/atʃʰar/	*to thrash*
/matʃʰ/	*fish*	/tʃʰoʈo/	*small*

10 The sounds [x] and [g] are two new consonants. The sound [x] is a voiceless velar fricative; [ɣ] is a voiced velar fricative. The symbol [ɣ] is the Greek letter gamma [ˈgæmə].

Hints:

a. The sound [x] is in Scottish *loch* [lɒx], and in German *ach* [ɑx] or *Bach* [bɑx].
b. Many people have this sound in an expression of disgust *yeccchhh* [jɛxxx].
c. Try saying [kɑ], then say it again but release the [k] very slowly – [kxxɑ].
d. Children sometimes use [kxxxxx] to imitate the sound of a gun.
e. Say [k], but make it very weak.

Once you have some success with [x], try these combinations.

xɑ	xu	xɔ	xu	xɒ	xʊ
xɔxɑ	xɑxu	xuxʌ	xɑxæ	xɒxɔ	xæxʊ

Try the following, making sure that the back of your tongue stays back and does not slip forwards.

xɑxɛ	xɔxæ	xʊxi	xɑxi	xuxʊ
xɔxʊ	xɒxɛ	xixɛ	xæxɛ	xoxɑ

11 Try the following words in German with [x].

/bɑx/	*Bach*	'stream'	/bux/	*Buch*	'book'
/tawxt/	*Taucht*	'dips'	/nɑx/	*nach*	'towards'
/bawx/	*Bauch*	'bell'	/vɑxən/	*wachen*	'wake'
/dɔx/	*doch*	'but'	/vɑxt/	*wacht*	'wakes'
/vɔxən/	*Wochen*	'weeks'	/hox/	*hoch*	'high'
/kɔxt/	*kocht*	'cooks'	/zuxən/	*suchen*	'seek'
/brux/	*Bruch*	'breach'	/buxt/	*Bucht*	'inlet'

12 The sound [ɣ] is like [x], but voiced.

Hints:

a. Say [x] with voicing. Try [ssssszzzzz] and then [xxxxxɣɣɣɣɣ].
b. Say [ga] and release the [g] very slowly to produce [ɣɣɣɣɑ].
c. Start with [ɑ], raise the back of your tongue slowly so as to make a [ɣ]. Just before you get to [g], you should be making a [ɣ].
d. Try making the following:

ɣɑ	ɣu	ɣɔ	ɣu	ɣɒ	ɣʊ
ɣɔɣɑ	ɣɑɣu	ɣuɣʌ	ɣɑɣæ	ɣɒɣɔ	ɣæɣʊ

Try the following again making sure that the back of your tongue stays back and does not slip forwards.

ɣɑɣɛ	ɣɔɣæ	ɣʊɣi	ɣɑɣi	ɣuɣʊ
ɣɔɣʊ	ɣɒɣɛ	ɣiɣɛ	ɣæɣɛ	

13 Try the following sentences, replacing the velar stops with the corresponding fricative:

Queen Catherine kissed her crotchety cousin and complimented her colleague King Carl the Cantankerous.

Gertie's granny goes gaga over great gooey green gumdrops from Guernsey.

14 The following are names of Georgian (former USSR) towns; pay particular attention to the consonant clusters:

tbilisi	bɑtumi	tsxinvɑli	mtsxetɑ
kutɑisi	bolnisis	soxumi	mɑxɑrɑdze
gori	rustɑvi	ɑxɑltsixe	poti
gɑgrɑ	duʃeti	telɑvi	sɑtʃxere

15 Now try the following nonsense words:

xɑxʌ	xɪkʌ	ɣuɣɒ	xʊgɪ	kʊxɔ
kuɣɛ	guɣɑ	xægɔ	ɣɛxæ	ɣɛɣɑ

These are a little harder.

ˈpivʊs	ˈdiɣæʃ	mɛˈtuʒ	βɛˈðug	zæxˈɪφ
ŋæˈθɔk	hɛˈxuɣ	ˈwæmfɔɣ	ˈʒeθxɛl	ˈŋɒφθʊd
xʌnˈsɪʃˈ	βuŋvæɣ	ˈhɔxsæɣ	hɪˈlʌʒ	gɑsˈðim

16 Tagalog (/təˈgɑləg/; Phillipines). Practise glottal stops and initial [ŋ] in the following:

/ŋaˈjon/	*now*	/ŋiˈti/	*smile*	/ˈŋaŋaʔ/	*betel nut mixture*
/ŋaˈwaʔ/	*to cry*	/ˈŋipin/	*tooth*	/ŋitˈŋit/	*irritation*
/ˈnanaʔ/	*pus*	/naˈwaʔ/	*may it be so*		

17 Georgian:

/bgerɑ/	*sound*	/dgɑs/	*stands*	/dʒgupi/	*group*
/dɣe/	*day*	/midzɣvnɑ/	*dedication*	/pxizeli/	*sober*
/pkvili/	*flour*	/txovnɑ/	*request*	/tkven/	*you (pl)*
/tkvɑ/	*he said*	/tsxovrebɑ/	*life*	/tskerɑ/	*looking*
/tsxɑdi/	*clear*	/tsxviri/	*nose*	/tʃkɑri/	*fast*

18 Ewe contrasts a velar and a pharyngeal fricative: [x] and [ħ].

xá	*broom*	ħà	*song*
xɔ̀	*house*	àħò	*widow*
xexí	*umbrella*		

19 Labialisation involves lip rounding. It may occur alone or in combination with the other secondary articulations.

tʷɑ	dʷɑ	sʷɑ	zʷɑ	nʷɑ	lʷɑ
kʷɛgi	lʷɑɲu	kodʷɛ	ŋʷaɹi	xeθʷɑ	xʷɑnɔ

20 Gã has labialised fricatives and affricates.

/tʃa/	*to dig*	/tʃʷa/	*to strike*
/dza/	*to divide*	/dzʷa/	*to break*
/dzɛ́i/	*there*	/dzʷɛ́i/	*rubbish*
/ʃɛ/	*to reach*	/ʃʷɛ/	*to remain*
/ʃanɛ/	*to slip*	/ʃʷane/	*afternoon*

21 Practise the following palatalised consonants:

bʲo fʲɛ φʲa βʲɛ pʲi

With palatalisation, the tongue assumes a position more like a palatal articulation, that is, the front of the tongue moves towards the palate more than usual. Try these:

tʲɑ	kʲɑ	dʲe	gʲɛ	sʲɑ	xʲe
d̪ʲeɣg	tʲy	tʲɔ	nʲøkje	lalʲʌ	n̪ʲɛʃu

In [sʲ], the palatalisation is simultaneous with the [s]; in [sj] there is a sequence with one sound following the other.

sʲɑ   sjɑ   sʷi   swi   fʲe   fje   θʷɛ   θwɛ

Practise these plain and palatalised dentals:

ˈt̪ɑt̪ʲɑ   ˈn̪ʲɔn̪ɔ   ˈl̪ʌl̪ʲʌ   ˈd̪ʲod̪e
ˈt̪ʲit̪eˈt̪ʲɛ   t̪ɑt̪ʲɑˈt̪ɔ   ˈt̪ʲɑt̪ɔt̪ʲu   ˈt̪et̪ʲut̪ɛ

Remember to keep the [tʲ] one segment, and not a sequence of [tj].
Don't let palatalised sounds become affricates such as [ts – tʃ – tθ].
If labialisation occurs simultaneously with palatalisation, the resulting secondary articulation can be transcribed as [ᶣ].

tᶣɑ   dᶣɛ   lᶣɔ   kᶣo   tᶣɛɣɒ   danᶣu   kᶣɑlɔ   sᶣinu

22 Velarised consonants involve a secondary velar or high back unrounded vocalic position. Practise saying:

li   le   lɛ   lɑ   lʌ   lɤ   lɯ

Velarised [ɫ] is like the [l] of [lɯ]. Practise:

ɛɫɛ   ᵰana   ᵴɑsɑ   zʌᵴʌ   ɤɫ̥ɤ
ᵰɛnɛ   ᵵete   ᵭidi   iᵰɛ   tade
ᵴɑᵶi   ɸoᵰi   ɛlɑ   bɛɫɑ   bɛlʲɑ
lʲeɫɑ   ɑɸu   njɑɸu   nɑɸu   nʲɑɸu

23 Greek

/skandzóxiros/	*porcupine*	/míɣðalo/	*almond*	/vðela/	*leech*
/ksíroś/	*dry*	/exθrós/	*enemy*	/ɣáj ðaros/	*donkey*
/fθáno/	*I arrive*	/ɣlistró/	*I slip*	/sinɣnómi/	*forgiveness*
/ftjáno/	*I make*	/avɣó/	*egg*	/ɣambrós/	*bridegroom*

24 To make double articulations, close the lips to make a [p]. Keeping them closed, make a [k]. Now, release the [k͡p]. Make sure that the two closures are released simultaneously. Try the same process with [p͡t].

k͡pɑ   p͡tɑ   g͡bɑ   ek͡pe   ep͡te   eg͡be

The tie bar [͡] indicates that the sounds are made simultaneously. Although the order given above is traditional and should be used ordinarily, practise saying them from transcriptions using the reverse order. This may correct any problem that you may have with not making the release of the stops simultaneously.

k͡pɑ   p͡kɑ   p͡tɑ   t͡pɑ   g͡be   b͡ge   b͡de   d͡be

Also try:

f͡sɑ   f͡xe   s͡xɛ   v͡zo   z͡ɣu   v͡ɣɑ

25 Try the following labial-velar articulations in Gã; [´] indicates high tone, [`] indicates low tone, and mid tone is unmarked.

/k͡pàí/	*cheeks*	/k͡pàk͡pó/	*billy goat*	/g͡bɛ̀/	*road*
/àk͡pákí/	*calabash*	/g͡bòg͡bò/	*wall*	/g͡békɛ̃/	*child*
/àg͡bà/	*bivouac*	/ŋ͡mé/	*bell*	/éŋ͡mɔ̃mi/	*ocru*

Advanced

26 Practise pronouncing the following:

ɲæmy	nyŋ̊œ	mumo	sɯsɤ	fofʌ	ŋ̊ɒn̪ɤ
mɶŋ̊y	nɤɲ̊ɯ	lœði	ɸypʌ	jɶge	jeʃɶ
ɹɛvɶ	ɣɒça	tœʒʌ	fɑzɒ	xɤsɔ	hyβɯ

27 [s̪ z̪]. Try making dental varieties of [s] and [z] by starting with an alveolar [s] and moving the tongue forward until it is behind the upper teeth.

sɑ s̪ɑ zɑ z̪ɑ
ˈsos̪oθo seθeˈz̪efe ziˈvɛz̪ɔ ʃaˌnus̪o ˈzeˈθɛzɛ ðɛs̪ɛˌʃɛz̪ɛ

28 Retroflex consonants. Try the following:

tɑ	ʈɑ	dɑ	ɖɑ	nɑ	ɳɑ
lɑ	ɭɑ	sɑ	ʂɑ	zɑ	ʐɑ
ɑʈɑ	aɖa	uɳu	oɭo	ɔʂɔ	eʐe
ɑɭɑ	ʈɔtɛ	diɖo	ɳune	ˀɔɖa	ɭila
ɖɛdɑ	ʂesa	zɔʐɑ	taʈ̪iʈu	ɖiɖ̪anɛ	loɖɛnɑ
ɳɛluzɔ	soʂiɖɛ	ʐesɔli	taɭeʂu	ʈenɔɖa	ʐɑziʐɛ

29 Hungarian. Try the following words with postalveolar affricates and palatal stops. Remember to keep the tip of your tongue pointed down for the palatals.

/tʃɒlaːd/	*family*	/hɒrtʃɒ/	*catfish*	/ɑːtʃ/	*carpenter*
/laːndʐɒ/	*lance*	/dʐɛm/	*jam*	/cuːk/	*hen*
/kaːrcɒ/	*playing card*	/korc/	*gulp*	/ɟønɟ/	*pearl*
/hɒɲɟɒ/	*ant*	/kor/	*age*	/ɒkɒrok/	*I want*
/jeːɡ/	*ice*	/ɛɡeːr/	*mouse*	/haŋɡ/	*voice*

30 For each vowel [y ø œ ɶ ɑ ʌ ɤ ɯ], pronounce them after each of the following consonants: z ʒ ʐ θ ʃ ç ʝ s̪ ð

e.g.: zy zø zœ zɶ zɑ zʌ zɤ zɯ

Now try the following vowels in the same fashion after the consonants below:

ɯ y ɤ ø œ ʌ œ ɒ ɶ
l ɭ̊ j ˀ ʍ l̥ ʈ j̥

31 Twi (West Africa) shows labialised palatals:

/caca/	*mattress*	/ocʷa/	*he cuts*
/oɟa/	*he leads*	/oɟʷa/	*he carves*
/ɔɲa/	*he finds*	/ɲʷa/	*snail*
/ɔʃɛ/	*he puts on*	/ɔʃʷɛ/	*he looks at*

32 Pharyngealisation involves a lowering of the back of the tongue and a retraction of the root, thus effecting a narrowing of the pharynx.

a. Try saying a low, back [ɑ], and then making it even lower and farther back.

b. With your thumb and finger, push gently in and down just above your adam's apple while saying [ɑ].

c. Say [lɑ] while doing a. and b. above. This should give you a pharyngealised [ɫɑ].

d. Some people find the following method quite succesful: think of the pharyngeal action as weak gagging. If you touch your velum with your finger, you will usually trigger the gag reflex. What you are looking for is a very weak version of this gag reflex. Remember: nausea = success.

ɫ ɫ ɫ ɫ ɫ	z̴ɑ	s̴ɑ	n̴ɑ	b̴ɑ
	ɡ̴ɑ	d̴ɑ		

33 Try these examples from Arabic.

/ti:n/	*figs*	/t̴i:n/	*mud*
/darb/	*lane*	/d̴arb/	*striking*
/se:f/	*sword*	/s̴e:f/	*summer*
/zuhu:r/	*flowers*	/z̴uhu:r/	*appearance*
/ʔis̴a:s̴/	*punishment*	/ʔis̴as̴ha/	*her stories*
/taxs̴i:s̴]/	*specialisation*	/ʔas̴is̴ha/	*he punished her*
/maxs̴u:s̴/	*special*	/ʕus̴us̴he/	*her coccyx*

Chapter 11

Manner of articulation

In Chapter 10 we classified consonants according to their place of articulation. In this chapter, we examine the other major aspect of consonants – **manner of articulation**. A primary aspect of manner is the degree of **stricture**; that is, does the air have a free passage through the mouth or is there an obstruction? By varying the degree of obstruction, we can make different sounds. **Nasality** is another way of varying sounds, by allowing air to pass out of the nose or not. As well, some sounds are **lateral** with the air passing out through the sides of the vocal tract, but not through the middle.

In this chapter you will learn about:

- how different consonants are made at the same place of articulation;
- lateral and nasal consonants;
- taps, flaps, and trills.

Degree of stricture

Say the vowel [ɑ]; notice that air passes freely out of the mouth. In saying this vowel we have the tongue low, creating as little obstruction as possible. To see your throat, doctors ask you to say [ɑ] to get the oral cavity as open as possible. Now say a long [llllllll]. Here, air obviously passes out of the mouth, but not so freely as with [ɑ]; the articulators are positioned so as to form a partial obstruction in the vocal tract. If you try a long [ffffffff], the closure is even tighter, causing a certain amount of **frication**, or friction-like noise. If you try to make a long [pppppppp], your cheeks may puff out a bit, but no air escapes as there is a complete closure.

We distinguish four degrees of **stricture**. Sounds made with the least stricture are vowels; the others are consonants. Table 11.1 shows the four categories with their degree of stricture.

Table 11.1 Degree of stricture

Category of sound		Degree of stricture
Consonant	Stop	no air passes out through the mouth
	Fricatives	partial obstruction; noticeable frication
	Approximants	little obstruction; no frication
Vowels		stricture no greater than for [i]

Obstruents

Oral stops, fricatives, and affricates together form the class of **obstruents**. Non-obstruent sounds are called **sonorants**, comprising nasals, approximants, and vowels; the sonorant consonants are discussed below.

Stops are defined as having no air passing out through the mouth; **oral** sounds have no air passing out through the nasal passage. **Oral stops**, thus, involve closure of both the oral and nasal passages. **Nasal stops** have air passing out through the nasal passage, but not through the mouth. Nasal stops are usually voiced. Oral stops may be voiced or voiceless. Nasal sounds are discussed at the end of this chapter. With voiceless stops, no sound is heard from the onset of the stop to its release. With voiced stops, the sound of the vibrating vocal folds is heard; however, the loudness of the voicing is muted as the vibration has to pass through the soft tissues of the neck and cheeks. Three points about stops will be explained in Chapter 12: voicing, aspiration, and glottal stops.

With **fricatives**, the constriction in the oral cavity allows air to pass out of the mouth, but it is close enough to cause turbulence in the air stream producing frication. Fricatives occur at all places of articulation. The sound [h] is often called a glottal fricative. Phonologically, [h] behaves like a consonant; phonetically, however, it is a voiceless vowel with the same tongue position as the following vowel. The fricatives [s z ʃ ʒ] are called **sibilants**. Fricatives are also known as **spirants**.

Affricates consist of a stop immediately followed by a homorganic fricative. **Homorganic** means 'having the same place of articulation'; this is interpreted somewhat loosely to mean that the stop and fricative are both labial, both coronal, or both dorsal: thus, [pɸ pf tθ ts tʃ] are all affricates, but [px kf tf qθ] are not.

Figure 11.1 (overleaf) shows a spectrogram of 'Peggy's speech was good'. From Chapter 8, we expect that the stops will show a gap in the acoustic pattern; we find gaps for the [p] in *Peggy's* and *speech* and for the [g] and [d] in *good*. The gap is typical of stops. The **spike** at the end of the [pʰ] is typical

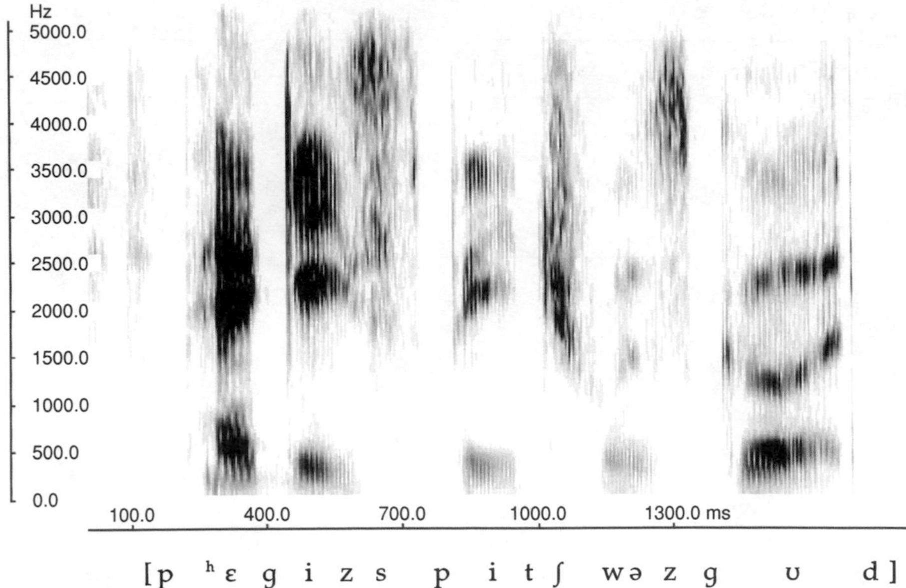

Figure 11.1 'Peggy's speech was good'

of the release of stops. The aspiration of the [pʰ] of *Peggy's* can be seen just at the end of the gap as a bit of random noise before the vowel. Fricatives show random noise as in the [z] of *Peggy's* and *was*, and in the [s] of *speech*. Affricates, such as the [tʃ] of *speech*, consist of a stop, appearing as a gap, followed by a fricative, appearing as random noise.

Approximants

Approximants have an articulatory constriction closer than the vowel [i], yet without the frication of fricatives. Any fricative can be turned into an approximant by widening the constriction until the frication ceases. Try making a [v]; gradually increase the opening until the friction ceases. The sound you are now making is a voiced labiodental approximant [ʋ]. Semi-vowels are classified as approximants. Approximants are usually voiced. Quite a number of approximants are laterals which are discussed separately below. Although we can make approximants at any place of articulation, only certain ones are common; the symbols for fricatives and approximants are shown in Table 11.2.

The symbols [ɹ] and [ɻ] can be used to distinguish two types of rhotic sound: [ɹ], typical of English, for a more advanced approximant, and [ɻ] for a more retracted, retroflexed sound. The symbol [ʍ] represents a voiceless [w].

Table 11.2 Approximants and fricatives

	bilabial	labiodental	dental	alveolar	alveolo-palatal	postalveolar
fricative	ɸ β	f v	θ ð	s z	ɕ ʑ	ʃ ʒ
approximant		ʋ		ɹ		

	retroflex	palatal	velar	uvular	pharyngeal	labial-palatal	labial-velar
fricative	ʂ ʐ	ç ʝ	x ɣ	χ ʁ	ħ ʕ	ɥ̊˔ ɥ˔	ʍ˔ w˔
approximant	ɻ	j	ɰ	ʁ̞		ɥ̊ ɥ	ʍ w

Liquids include lateral and rhotic sounds. **Rhotic** sounds are ones with an r-like quality. They include [ɹ], [ɻ], and [ʁ̞], as well as the taps and trills discussed below. As we pointed out in Chapter 3, the English /ɹ/ can be made either with the tongue tip up or with it down. The **laterals** are discussed below.

The semivowels [j ɥ w ɰ] are considered to be approximants, having respectively palatal, labial-palatal, labial-velar, and velar places of articulation. Note that [w ɥ] are IPA approximant symbols; the corresponding fricatives can be transcribed as [w˔ ɥ˔]. The uvular approximant can be shown as [ʁ̞].

The approximants are very similar to the vowels and thus have acoustic characteristics resembling those of vowels (Figure 11.2 overleaf). In particular, the glides have formant structures like the corresponding vowels.

Trills, taps, and flaps

Trills

Two types of **trill** are commonly found: one with the tip of the tongue at the alveolar [r] or dental [r̪] region; in these, the tongue tip strikes the upper articulator several times very quickly. The other trill is uvular [ʀ]; with it, the uvula strikes against the dorsum of the tongue.

Trills are not made by consciously controlling the motion of the tongue; rather, the tongue is placed in the appropriate position and tension, air is blown through the gap, and aerodynamic forces cause the tongue to vibrate rapidly against the upper articulator. The Bernoulli effect, which is explained

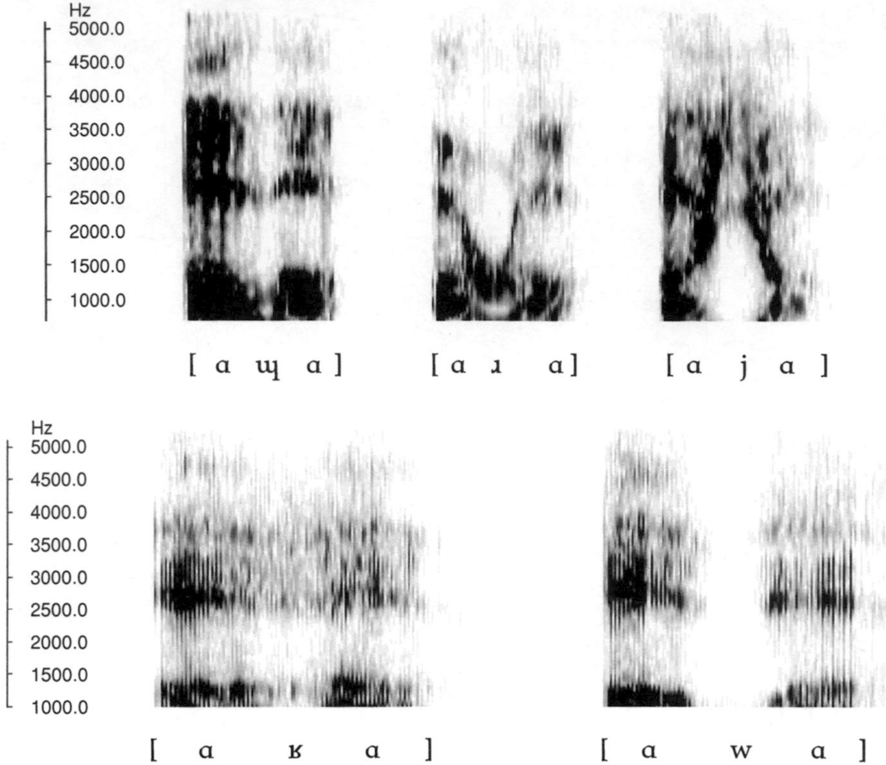

Figure 11.2 Spectrograms of approximants

in Chapter 12, pulls the articulators together, and the air stream from the lungs pushes them apart again. This sequence of events happens several times rapidly, causing the trill.

The uvular trill is made by raising the back of the tongue so that the air stream causes the uvula to vibrate against it. Snoring often involves a uvular trill made while breathing in. Figure 11.3 shows an alveolar and a uvular trill.

An alveolar fricative trill [r̝] occurs in Czech, as in the name of the composer Dvořák [dvor̝ak]. Here the body of the tongue is raised towards the postalveolar region, high enough to produce frication.

A bilabial trill is reported as occurring very rarely as a consonant; it is reported more often as occurring in impolite society. If needed, it can be written with a [ʙ]. The contrast between a bilabial trill and a bilabial stop is shown in the following examples from Ngwe (Cameroun; Ladefoged, 1971).

/mʙɤ/	*tadpoles*	/mbɛm/	*seed*

Ngwe

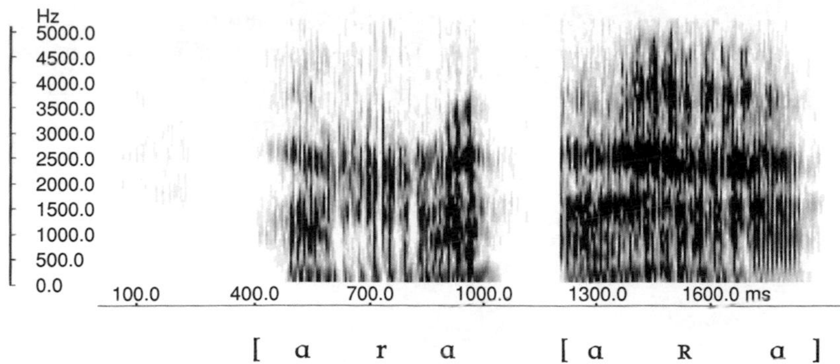

[ɑ r ɑ [ɑ ʀ ɑ]

Figure 11.3 Spectrogram of an alveolar and a uvular trill

Taps

In Chapter 3, we learned that the typical North American English intervocalic allophone of /t/ is usually a voiced tap [ɾ]. **Taps** are often described as a trill of one vibration. The sensation is that the tongue is flicked against the upper articulator like a ballistic missile in that the speaker does not exercise control over its movement once the action begins. A stop, in contrast, is like a guided missile in which the action is under the control of the speaker for the duration of the sound.

Spanish contrasts a dental tap with a dental trill.

caro	/kaɾ̪o/	'dear'	*carro*	/kar̪o/	'cart'
pero	/peɾ̪o/	'but'	*perro*	/per̪o/	'dog'
fiero	/fjeɾ̪o/	'fierce'	*fierro*	/fjer̪o/	'horse-shoe'
yero	/jeɾ̪o/	'lentil'	*hierro*	/jer̪o/	'iron'

Spanish

Flaps

With a **tap**, the active articulator returns to its point of origin. With a **flap** the active articulator starts in one position, strikes the place of articulation in passing, and ends the movement in a position different from where it began. Apical and labiodental flaps have been described. With the apical flap, the tip of the tongue is curled back in the oral cavity; then, it moves forward striking the alveolar ridge, and ends with the tip forward in the mouth. The place of articulation is usually retroflex: [ɽ]. Hausa (Nigeria, West Africa) contrasts a flap and a tap:

/báɽa/ servant /báɾà/ begging

Hausa

A labiodental flap, although rare, occurs in Shona (Ladefoged, 1971). The lower lip is curled back and strikes the upper teeth in passing as it moves forward. The labiodental flap in Shona (/ˈʃonə/; Southern Africa) is shown here as [vᵇ].

kovᵇó *blackness* wóvᵇo *movement*

Shona

Laterals

Laterals are made with the sides of the constriction open, allowing air to escape. We have discussed the English alveolar lateral [l] in Chapter 3. Other laterals are shown below:

	dental	alveolar	retroflex	palatal	velar
laterals	l̪	l	ɭ	ʎ	ʟ

The dental, alveolar, and retroflex laterals are made by placing the tip of the tongue at each place of articulation and allowing air to escape at the sides. The palatal lateral is formed by raising the medial portion of the front of the tongue to the palate and allowing air to escape at the sides. A similar movement with the medial portion of the back of the tongue against the velum produces the velar lateral.

The dental and alveolar laterals can take on the colour of any vowel, for example [lⁱ lʸ lᵉ lᵃ lᵒ lᵘ lᵚ] where the raised vowel indicates the vowel quality. The tip of the tongue is at the teeth or alveolar ridge, and the body of the tongue assumes the various vowel shapes. In fact, it is sufficient to distinguish only two vowel qualities: front unrounded [lⁱ] and back unrounded [lᵚ]. These are known respectively as **clear-l** and **dark-l**. The back unrounded quality of dark-l can be thought of as velarisation. Normally, clear-l is transcribed as [l], and dark-l as [ɫ], using [~], the diacritic for velarisation.

Laterals are not necessarily approximants (Maddieson and Emmorey, 1984). For each lateral sonorant, there is a corresponding fricative. The alveolar lateral fricatives have special symbols: [ɬ] for voiceless and [ɮ] for voiced. Approximant laterals can be syllabic: [l̩].

Bilabial laterals are easily made but are not found in languages of the world. Velar laterals are extremely rare, but they are found in Melpa, a language of Papua New Guinea (Ladefoged, Cochrane and Disner, 1977).

		dental	alveolar	retroflex	palatal
fricatives	**voiced**	ɮ̪	ɮ	ɭ˔	ʎ
	voiceless	ɬ̪	ɬ	ɭ̊˔	ʎ̝̊
approximants	**voiced**	l̪	l	ɭ	ʎ
	voiceless	l̪̊	l̥	ɭ̊	ʎ̥

The voiceless lateral [ɬ] in Welsh, spelled *ll*, is frequently **unilateral**, or open only at one side.

/ɬɑn/	*church*	/araɬ/	*other*
/ɬin/	*ship*	/ɬond/	*full*

Welsh

Laterals generally have weak formants at frequencies around 250, 1200, and 2400 Hz (Figure 11.4).

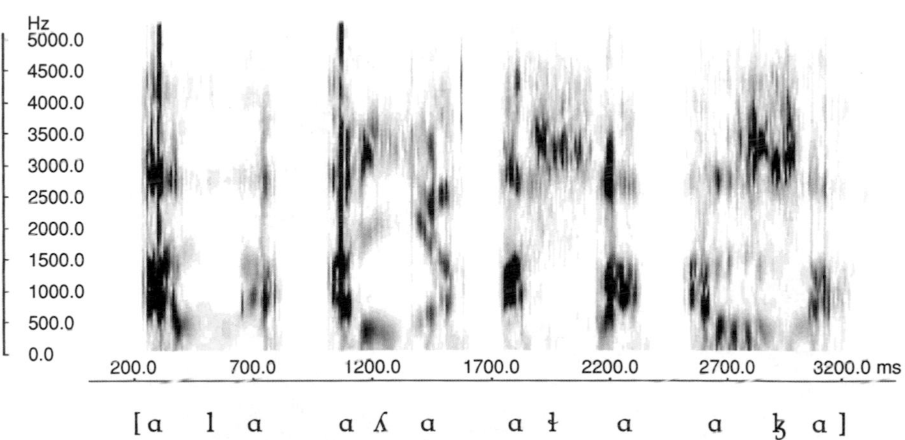

Figure 11.4 Spectrograms of laterals

Nasals

Nasals are made with a velic opening with air going out through the nasal passage. The term **nasal**, used alone, means *nasal stop*. Otherwise the type of sound must be specified, as in *nasal fricative, nasal lateral*, etc. Nasal fricatives and approximants occur, but usually as the result of being next to a nasal vowel. Nasal stops are ordinarily voiced. Nasals can be syllabic. The symbols are:

	bilabial	labiodental	dental	alveolar	retroflex	palatal	velar	uvular
nasal	m	ɱ	n̪	n	ɳ	ɲ	ŋ	ɴ

Nasals show weak formant-like patterns, with one formant typically around 250 Hz and another at about 2200 Hz.

Prenasalised stops

Many languages have **prenasalised** stops. In these sounds, a short homorganic nasal precedes a stop; the nasal is not syllabic.

/ḿbàŋk/	*ropes*	/ŋ́wú/	*die!*	/ǹdʒɛ̀ː/	*food*
/ńsákà/	*Good morning*	/ḿmɛ́n/	*water*	/ŋ͡m̀g͡bì/	*fog*

Sherbro

Technical terms

affricate
approximant
clear-l
dark-l
flap
fricative
homorganic
lateral
liquid
manner of articulation
nasal
  nasality
obstruents
oral
prenasalised
rhotic
sibilant
sonorant
spike
spirant
stop
  nasal stop
  oral stop
stricture
tap
trill
unilateral

Symbols

Table 11.3 Symbols for stops, fricatives, and nasals

	bilabial	labiodental	dental	alveolar	alveolo-palatal	postalveolar
stops	p b		t̪ d̪	t d		
fricatives	ɸ β	f v	θ ð	s z	ɕ ʑ	ʃ ʒ
nasals	m	ɱ	n̪	n		

Table 11.3 (Cont'd)

	retroflex	palatal	velar	uvular	pharyngeal	glottal
stops	ʈ ɖ	c ɟ	k ɡ	q ɢ		ʔ
fricatives	ʂ ʐ	ç ʝ	x ɣ	χ ʁ	ħ ʕ	h
nasals	ɳ	ɲ	ŋ	ɴ		

[ɧ] is a voiceless postalveolar-velar fricative = [ʃ͡x].

Table 11.4 Double articulations

	labial-alveolar	labial-palatal	labial-velar
stop	p͡t b͡d	p͡c b͡ɟ	k͡p ɡ͡b
fricative		ɥ̊˔ ɥ˔	ʍ˔ w˔
approximant		ɥ̊ ɥ	ʍ w
nasal	m͡n	m͡ɲ	ŋ͡m

Table 11.5 Laterals

		dental	alveolar	retroflex	palatal
fricatives	**voiced**	ɮ̪	ɮ	ɭ˔	ʎ˔
	voiceless	ɬ̪	ɬ	ɭ̊˔	ʎ̊˔
approximants	**voiced**	l̪	l	ɭ	ʎ
	voiceless	l̪̊	l̥	ɭ̊	ʎ̥

Table 11.6 Rhotic consonants

dental trill	r̪
alveolar trill	r
alveolar fricative trill	r̝
uvular trill	ʀ
bilabial trill	ʙ
alveolar tap	ɾ
labiodental flap	v[b]
retroflex flap	ɽ
lateral flap	ɺ

Exercises

Basic

1 Review:

ɸiˀɑ	xɔɣɑ	ˀæβɑ	βɛxɔ	ɣɒβɑ	ɸʌɣɒ
xɑˀɒ	ɣɑɸɔ	ˀɔɸʌ	ɸɒxɔ	βɒɸæ	βɔˀɒ

2 German:

/tawkt/	*is of use*	/tawxt/	*dips*
/dɔk/	*dock*	/dɔx/	*but*
/ʃta:kən/	*stuck (pl)*	/ʃta:xən/	*pricked (pl)*
/nakt/	*naked*	/naxt/	*night*
/pɔkən/	*pockmarks*	/pɔxən/	*beat*
/lɔkt/	*entices*	/lɔxt/	*perforates*
/bu:k/	*baked*	/bu:x/	*book*
/pawkən/	*practise*	/hawxən/	*breathe*

3 Build-up. Start with [gɑ], then try, [ˈgɑ lu], then [ˈgɑ lu ŋɔ], etc.

ˈgɑ lu ˈŋɔ ɹɪ ˈθæ sɒ
ˈxo n̪i hʊ ˈtʃeɪ vu ˈβʌ
dʊ ˌɣɒ ɾɛ ɸow ˈvɪ ˀe

Try the build-up starting at both the left and at the right sides.

4 Affricates. Pronounce:

tʃɑ dʒu tsɑ dzu pfɑ pɸɑ bβu
t̪θɑ d̪ðu cçɑ kxɑ gɣu bvu ɟʝɑ

Build-up exercises:

ˈpfɑ gɣe ˈpɸo dzɛ ˈcçɔ t̪θi
kxi ˈd̪ðɔ tse ˈɟʝo tʃa ˌbβɛ

Remember to try starting the build-up from both ends. Now try these:

ˈpfɛkɑdʒ ˈbβeɹits ˈd̪ðeɱɔcç ˈɟʝulidʒ ˈt̪θonagɣ ˈbvoʒɛtʃ

And these reversed affricates:

eɸp ɛvb ɛθt̪ ɛzd ɛʃt ɛʝɟ ɛxk
oçc oʒd ost oðd̪ ofp oβb oɣg

5 Try these Ewe words:

/tsì/	*water*	/dzì/	*heart*
/tsé/	*to bear fruit*	/dzè/	*salt*
/tsà/	*to wander*	/dzà/	*to fall (rain)*
/tsò/	*to cut*	/dzò/	*fire*
/tsù/	*madness*	/dzù/	*to insult*

6 Try the affricates in these German words:

/ˈpfʊnt/	*pound*	/ˈpsɑlm/	*psalm*
/ˈpflawmə/	*plum*	/ˈtsɑːl/	*number*
/ˈtʃɛçə/	*Czech*	/ˈtsyndən/	*ignite*
/ˈtsvɛtʃgərn/	*damsons*	/ˌpsyçoloˈgi/	*psychology*

7 Pig Latin is good dexterity practice. One variety moves an initial consonant (cluster) to the end of the word, and then the suffix [ej] is added:

key	/ike/	*book*	/ʊkbe/	*damage*	/æmɪdʒde/
stop	/ɑpste/	*thwart*	/ɑɹtθwe/	*watch*	/ɑtʃwe/

Read the following passage of Pig Latin aloud (GA accent):

/ənɛsəzvej ɪʒənvej əvej æpɪnɪshej əzwej owsklej ʊtej iŋbej aɹdmej ajbej ɪnstənzwej ʌnfɔɹtʃənətej ɛfərənspɹej əɹfej ændkej ɔgdej udfej æθəɹɹej ænðej əɹfej əɹhej itmej owfle, əðej ɛsɪpiɹej əvej ɪtʃwej iʃej ədhej ɪvənstɹej owsej ɑŋlej ətej əɹfɛktpe, ɔlðowej ɪtej ʊdʃej ibej tɪdnej ətðej ihej ɪddej owgej ɪnej əɹfej əðej ɛɾəɹbej ændzbɹej əndej ɑtnej ætðej iptʃej ʌfstej./

8 Practise these nonsense forms. Be sure not to rush – aim for accuracy, not speed.

ˈpɯçyŋɑ ˈtɤʒamɤ ˈɖiɣɒŋɶ ˈkɒβɛɳœ ˌgeçaˈdy ˌløxiˈn̪ɔ
ˌbʌʔɤˈmɯ ˌtøʌʐeθu ʔʌˈs̪ɑɸɯ ˈʒɶɣɔl̥ɒ tœˌpoˈfe ˈmʌˈcyxɛ

And these:

ˈlɑdʒiˌpʰɛ   ˈpfeʂɑˌcʰu   ˈɓβɛʈiˌʄɔ   kɔˈɲɛce
ŋeˈdlɛtɔ   ʐeˈlokxa   ˌɭiɟʄaˈɹ̰u   ˌcçaɖɛˈɟɑ

9 Uvular stops are made with the back of the tongue against the uvula. To make these, start with [ki ke kɛkɑ]; feel the place of articulation moving steadily back. Now starting with [kɑ], try to move the stop back as far as it will go. You should be producing a uvular [qɑ]. Practise:

qɑ   qɑ   qɑ   qɔ   qo   qu

Try these, being very careful not to move the tongue forward:

qɑ   qa   qɛ   qe   qi

Now try the voiced stop:

ɢɑ   ɢɔ   ɢo   ɢu
ɢa   ɢɛ   ɢe   ɢi

10 The uvular fricatives are made by opening the closure slightly. Try starting with a velar [xɑ] and moving it back to [χɑ]. Then, do the same going from [ɣɑ] to [ʁɑ].

χɑ   χɔ   χo   χa   χu   χɒ   χi   χɛ
ʁɑ   ʁo   ʁɔ   ʁa   ʁu   ʁɒ   ʁi   ʁɛ

11 The uvular approximant [ʁ̞] is made like a weak version of [ʁ]. Start with [ʁ] and lessen the constriction until the friction is removed. To make the nasal [ɴ], start with [ɢ], and lower the velum to allow air to pass through the nose.

ʁi   ʁ̞y   ʁ̞ɛ   ʁ̞ɑ
ʁo   ʁ̞o   ʁu   ʁ̞u

Practise the uvular fricative in French; note that sometimes it is voiceless.

rose	/ʁoz/	'rose'	*tour*	/tuʁ/	'turn'
rat	/ʁa/	'rat'	*part*	/paʁ/	'leaves'
arbre	/aʁbʁ/	'tree'	*poutre*	/putʁ̥/	'girder'
trente	/tʁɑ̃t/	'thirty'	*Paris*	/paʁi/	'Paris'

Practise:

qɑ   qi   ɢoɣe   χoχɛ   ʁɑʁɛ   ɴɑɴe
qaɢi   ɢoɴa   ɴeχa   xɔχe   ʁɔqɛ   qaʁi
χuʁi   ɴeʁi   qoɢɛ   qɔɢu   ŋɔɴu   χexɑ
ɣaʁɛ   ɣeʁi   qaqi   ɴwɲa   ʁɔɣɑ   xoʁɛ

12 The trills are not so much the result of conscious movement as of arranging the tongue appropriately and then blowing air out. To make the alveolar trill [r], try these suggestions:

a. Place the tip of your tongue at the back of the alveolar ridge. Blow fairly hard out your mouth. Try to relax your tongue.

b. Many children make this sound to imitate airplanes, engines, machine guns, etc.

c. Some people find trills easier after [p]: [pr pr].

prɑ ɹɑ trɑ krɑ ri re rɛ ra
rɑ rɔ ro ru ɑrɑ ɑɾɑ ɑɹɑ ɑrɑ
eru ori iɾɔ eɾo ɑrɛ ɛɾɔ eɹa aro

13 The uvular trill is made with the back of the tongue close to the uvula. The symbol is [ʀ]. Most people make a uvular trill when gargling. Try gargling with some water to get the feel of the uvular trill; then, try gargling only with saliva. This should produce a uvular trill.

Some people have luck starting from snoring. First try snoring while breathing in, and then try snoring while breathing out. Try the following steps:

a. Hold your fingers over your nostrils. Snore. Breathe out without changing anything else. Keep the back of your mouth very relaxed.

b. Try the uvula trill after [g]: [gʀ gʀ].

c. Try a voiced uvular fricative [ʁ]; then relax the tongue.

d. Sitting in a chair with a fairly high back, lean your head back until it is supported by the chair-back. It is important to be relaxed. Now try [ʀ].

e. Be patient. Rome was not trilled in a day. Practise:

gʀɑ kʀɑ bʀɑ dʀɑ tʀɑ ɑʀɑ eʀe oʀo
uʀɔ eʀɑ eʀc ere eʀe eɹe eʀe ʀɑʀo
rɑʀo ʀɑʀo ʀɑro ɹɑʀo

14 The bilabial trill is rare, but fun; it can be transcribed as [ʙ].

ʙ ʙ ʙ ʙ ʙ r r r r r ʀ ʀ ʀ ʀ ʀ

To entertain and amuse your friends, try a uvular trill; keep it going and add an alveolar trill; keep both going and add a bilabial trill [ʙ͡rʀ]. This sounds something like a motorboat starting or a ruffed grouse in heat. Practise at home before attempting this at cocktail parties. You're sure to get compliments on your progress in phonetics.

Advanced

15 Spanish has both [β̞] and [ɰ]. To make [β̞], start with [β] and gradually open the lips just until the fricative noise disappears. For [ɰ], do the same thing starting from [ɣ].

haba	/ˈaβ̞a/	'bean'
avance	/aˈβ̞anse/	'advance'
aguzar	/aɰuˈsar/	'sharpen'
vega	/ˈbeɰa/	'plain, meadow'
nabas	/ˈnaβ̞as/	'turnips'
abusar	/aβuˈsar/	'abuse'
la gula	/laˈɰula/	'the gluttony'
mucho gusto	/ˈmutʃoˈɰusto/	'great pleasure'

16 Be sure to keep these distinct [ø œ ə]:

œ ø ə œ ə ø œ œ ə ə ø œ
møbə sœlə fœɲə sədœ
nəkø ʒøpə ŋœlø ɹəfø

17 Central vowels lie between front and back vowels. Practise sliding front to back and from back to front.

i – ɯ e – ɤ ɛ – ʌ a – ɑ y – u ø – o œ – ɔ ɶ – ɒ
ɯ – i ɤ – e ʌ – e ɑ – a u – y o – ø ɔ – œ ɒ – ɶ

18 Practise

i ɨ ɯ ɯ ɨ i y ʉ u u ʉ y i y i ɨ ʉ ɨ ɯ ʉ ɨ ɨ i ɯ a ɐ ɑ ɑ ɐ a
ø o ø o ɤ ø ʉ ø o ø ɤ u e ə ɤ ɤ ə e o ə œ ø ə ɛ ɨ ə a ɐ a ɨ
miʃɨ ɸuzʉ bosə ɸeˀo kʉfɨ cɐɹə jəxɐ ɲɑdʒɐ
lavʌ piðʉ nɯŋɨ weɟə sotʃə xɒdzɑ ʒɨɣɐ θugʉ

19 Two pharyngeal fricatives are possible: voiceless [ħ] and voiced [ʕ]. Production hints:

a. Say [ɑ], making it as low and far back as possible; your pharynx should feel tense.

b. With your thumb and forefinger, press gently down and back on your adam's apple.

c. Try the voiceless [ħ] first, and then the voiced [ʕ].

ħɑ ħɑħɑ ħo ħoħo ʕɑ ʕɑʕɑ
ʕɛ ʕɛʕɛ ɑhɑ ɑħɑ ɑʕɑ ɑʁɑ
ɑˀɑ ɑħɑ ɑχɑ ɑxɑ ɑʕɑ ɑħɑ
ɑħɔ ɛʕɒ ɑʕe oħɑ ɛʕɑ hɛħɛ

20 Try the labiodental flap [vᵇ] found in Gbeya (/ˈɡ͡bejɑ/; Central African Republic):

/guvᵇuuŋ/	*deep place in river*	/hɔvᵇɔk/	*passing out of sight*
/vᵇɔŋ/	*hitting something*	/hɔvᵇɔvᵇɔ/	*shout of victory*

21 Inuktitut (Northwest Territories, Canada) is known for its uvulars and long words. Be sure not to rush.

uqsuaɴnigaa	*The sea is calm and flat.*
qaumaakkirnigaa	*It is dawning.*
punniliurutiniaripkin	*I will make bread for you.*
uqallautiniaripkin	*I will tell you.*
anurauvallaarniqtuaq	*It is too windy.*
tigusunngitaa	*He does not want to take it.*
jaraiqsiqaaqtuaq	*He is going to get ice.*
siniktiɹiiqpauŋ	*Is he keeping him from sleeping?*
tuktulaigaqsijuami	*I am going to hunt caribou.*
aŋaatdʒliaqtuaq	*He went to church.*
uqaqsuqtuaq	*She used an interpreter.*
qamrulgujuq	*He snores a lot.*

Chapter 12

Phonation

In the three preceding chapters, we have examined how the vocal tract is shaped to produce the various sounds of language. We now turn our attention to the activities of the vocal folds which are collectively known as **phonation**.

In this chapter you will learn about:

- the anatomy of the larynx;
- the various adjustments of the vocal folds;
- voice onset time.

Anatomy

The **larynx** (Figures 12.1–12.2) is a complex structure, cylindrical in shape, composed of cartilages held together by ligaments, and supporting several muscles. Crucial to sound production are the **vocal folds**. These are two horizontal shelves of muscle and ligament lying just behind the adam's apple. They assume a variety of positions so as to affect the air stream coming from the lungs. We are already familiar with the voiced and voiceless states of the vocal folds, phonetically their most important adjustments. The vocal folds are often called vocal cords; keep in mind, however, that they are solid structures and not cord-shaped.

Apart from aiding speech, the vocal folds prevent foreign objects from entering the lungs. Also, when closed, they stabilise the rib cage when the lungs are inflated. This is useful in lifting heavy objects, in defecation, and in child-birth.

The larynx (Figure 12.1) sits atop the **trachea**, a tube made up of a series of cartilagenous rings and resembling a vacuum-sweeper hose coming up from the lungs. Immediately above the trachea is the **cricoid cartilage**, shaped like a signet ring with the shield at the back. You can feel the top of the trachea by placing a finger at the top of your chest in the notch at the centre of the collarbone. If you press gently, holding your head back, the cricoid cartilage is the larger ring protruding slightly forward. Just above the cricoid cartilage is a plough-shaped cartilage called the **thyroid cartilage**. The forward point of the thyroid cartilage is easily identified as the adam's apple.

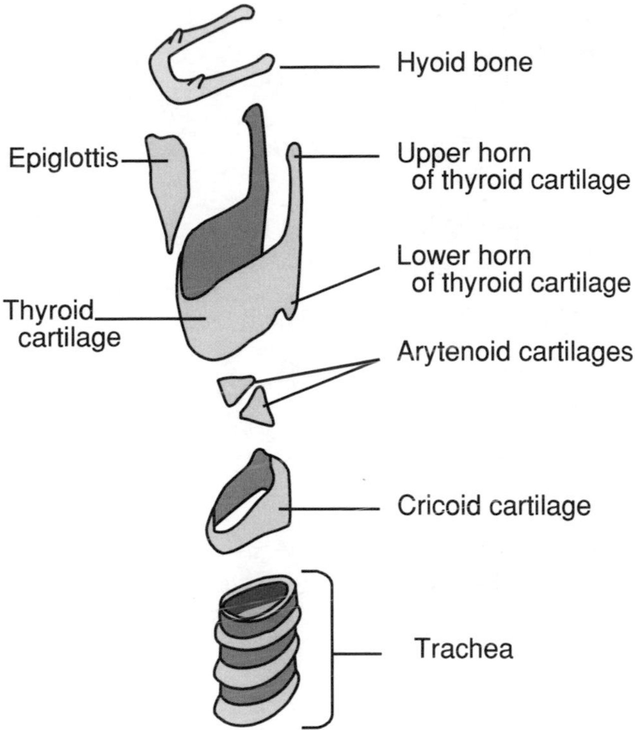

Figure 12.1 The parts of the larynx with the hyoid bone and trachea

At its rear, the thyroid cartilage has two horns pointing down and two pointing up. The two lower horns attach to the outer edges of the cricoid cartilage in such a way that the thyroid cartilage can pivot forwards and backwards on the cricoid cartilage. The thyroid cartilage provides a shield for the vocal folds, which are attached at the rear of the point forming the adam's apple. The **arytenoid cartilages** are small and pyramid-shaped. They sit atop the rear of the cricoid cartilage on either side.

A leaf-shaped object in the pharynx, the **epiglottis**, forms something of a hood over the main part of the larynx. Its function in the human body is uncertain, and its presence is a hindrance to observation of the larynx. Behind the chin is the **hyoid bone**, shaped like a horseshoe. The hyoid bone provides support for the muscles of the tongue sitting above it, and it is connected by muscles to the larynx below. The hyoid bone has the small distinction of being the only bone in the body not immediately attached to another bone.

Figure 12.1 shows the parts of the larynx separated from each other. Figure 12.2 provides a side view of the larynx. The front of the larynx is to the left. Notice that the lower horns of the thyroid cartilage are fastened to

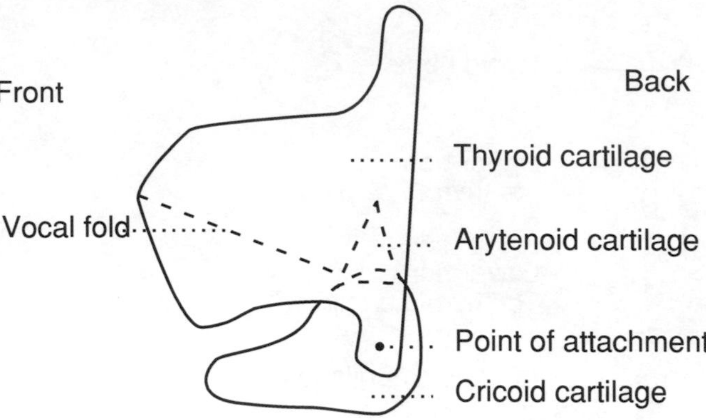

Figure 12.2 Side view of the larynx

the outer rim of the cricoid cartilage. This attachment allows the thyroid cartilage to rock back and forth. The vocal folds and arytenoid cartilages are shown by broken lines as they are hidden from view by the wall of the thyroid cartilage.

Glottis

The **vocal folds** (Figures 12.3–12.4) are two horizontal shelves of ligament and muscle joined together at the front to the thyroid cartilage and at the rear to each of the arytenoid cartilages. Together with the arytenoid cartilages, they form a triangular space known as the **glottis**, through which air passes as it comes up from the lungs. The part of the glottis between the vocal folds is called the **ligamental glottis**, and the part lying between the arytenoid cartilages is called the **cartilagenous glottis**. The shape of the glottis is controlled by a number of muscles. The arytenoid cartilages can rotate on their base, and they can move forwards and backwards slightly. These movements give the glottis a variety of shapes which produce various sounds as we shall see later in this chapter.

Figure 12.4 shows a vertical view of the larynx. You can see the vocal folds as shelves of tissue. Above them are overhanging folds known as the **false vocal folds**. Between the vocal folds and the false vocal folds is a cavity known as the **Ventricle of Morgagni**.

The false vocal folds are generally not used distinctively in speech. Catford (1977) reports them used in the type of singing known as 'scat' singing which was used by a 1930's jazz singer Cab Calloway, and also in the singing of certain Tibetan monks. He also reports Chechen, a Caucasian language, as having the interesting contrast [daˀa] 'eat', with a plain glottal

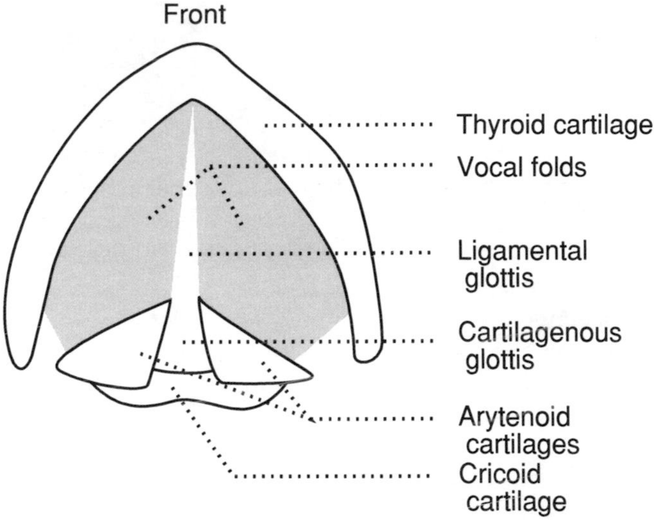

Figure 12.3 View looking down at the larynx. The vocal folds are nearly closed with only a small triangular gap between the arytenoid cartilages

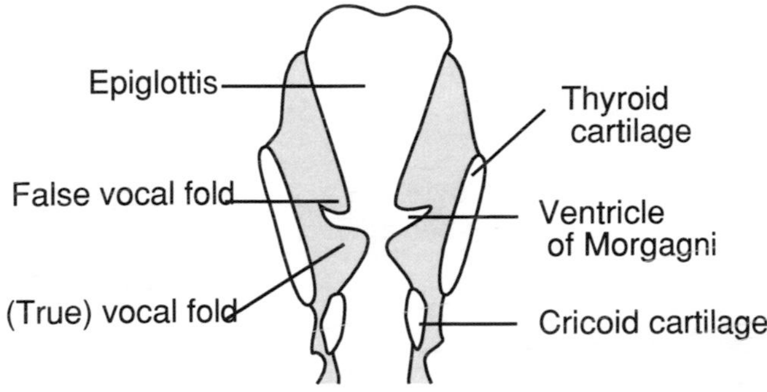

Figure 12.4 Cross-sectional view of the larynx from behind

stop and [daˤʔa] 'castrate', where [ˤʔ] indicates a simultaneous closure of the vocal folds and the false vocal folds.

States of the glottis

The glottis can be shaped in a variety of ways, some used in language and some not (Laver, 1980, 1994). The basic states of the glottis for us are glottal stop, voiceless and voiced. We will examine these first and then look at the other states.

Basic states

Glottal stop

The entire glottis is closed for the **glottal stop** [ʔ]. Glottal stops are easy to make; just hold your breath with your mouth open. They are, however, harder for English speakers to control and to hear. Many speakers of English have special forms to indicate 'no' [ˈʔʌ̃ʔʌ̃] or [ˈʔm̩ʔm̩]. In either case, both syllables begin with a glottal stop. Try saying these forms deliberately to get a better feel for glottal stops.

Figure 12.5 shows a schematic glottis, positioned for a glottal stop. The vocal folds are together and thus shown as a single line; the arytenoid cartilages are shown as two triangles. The entire glottis is closed and no air can pass through.

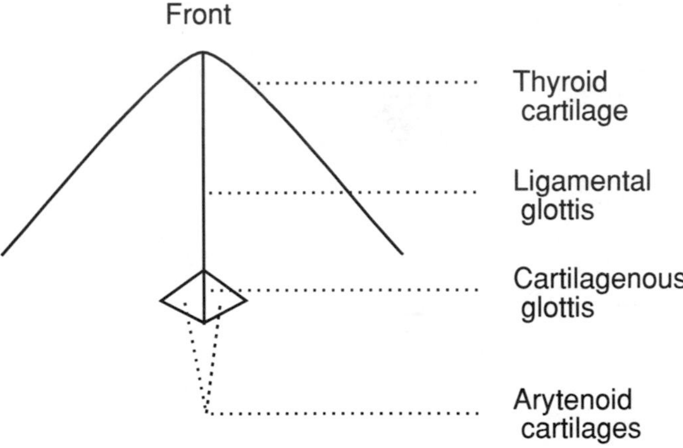

Figure 12.5 Glottal stop

Glottal stops are marked by a complete absence of energy, with no strong transitional distinctions in the neighbouring sounds.

Voiceless

For **voiceless** sounds, the vocal folds are partially open, although not completely open. Say a long [hhhhh] with the vowel quality of [ɑ]; this is simply a voiceless vowel [ɑ̥]. You can hear the soft frication noise of voicelessness. Voiceless sounds involve considerably greater air-flow than voiced sounds (Lieberman and Blumstein, 1988). Figure 12.6 shows the vocal folds positioned for a voiceless sound. The ligamental glottis is slightly open as is the cartilagenous glottis. Air can pass through, creating the kind of noise heard in a very soft [h]. Note that voiceless is a specific adjustment of the glottis and not just the absence of voicing. **Nil phonation** is the absence of voicing and can be achieved by a glottal stop, voicelessness, or an insufficient air-flow.

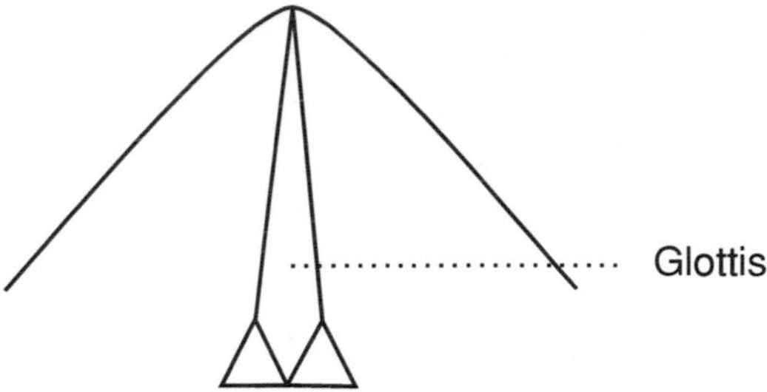

Figure 12.6 Voiceless

Obstruents often occur both voiceless and voiced. Sonorants are rarely voiceless although Burmese contrasts voiced and voiceless sounds.

/lɑʔ/	*be bare*	/l̥ɑʔ/	*uncover*
/lu/	*almost*	/l̥u/	*set free*
/mɑʔ/	*be steep*	/m̥ɑ̃/	*estimate*
/mi/	*inadvertently*	/m̥owʔ/	*blow*
/naʔ/	*be fully cooked*	/n̥a/	*nose*
/now/	*be awake*	/n̥owʔ/	*month*

Burmese

Vowels are normally voiced; high vowels are voiceless in Japanese when surrounded by voiceless consonants.

[çi̥to]	*person*	[aɹimaçi̥ta]	*it was there*
[ɸɯ̥kai]	*deep*	[aki̥kaze]	*autumn wind*
[kɯ̥sɯɹi]	*medicine*	[ki̥tsɯ̥tsɯ̥ki]	*woodpecker*

Japanese

Voiceless sounds are characterised by low energy, usually without a formant pattern.

Voiced

Figure 12.7 (overleaf) shows the glottis during voicing. The cartilagenous glottis is shut, and the wavy line indicates that the vocal folds are vibrating. To produce the vibration, the vocal folds come together and then open, allowing the air to escape in short bursts.

The mechanism of voicing is fairly complex. To understand it, we need to learn about the **Bernoulli principle** first. According to this principle, a moving stream of gas or liquid will tend to pull objects from the sides of the stream to the middle. The faster the stream flows, the stronger the pull. You have probably experienced the phenomenon of a classroom door that opens into the room suddenly blowing shut when a breeze blows down the

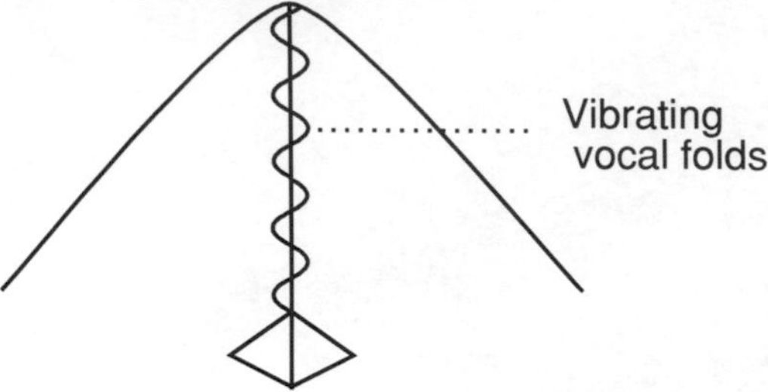

Figure 12.7 Voicing

corridor pulling the door towards the stream of air. Similarly, when you turn on a bathroom shower and create a stream of water, a shower curtain will swing inwards.

In voicing, the vocal folds are held fairly closely together. When a stream of air from the lungs passes between them, the Bernoulli effect pulls them together. As soon as they are together, the Bernoulli effect ceases and the force of the air stream from below pushes them apart again. As soon as they are apart, the Bernoulli effect comes into play again and pulls them together, and the process continues. The vocal folds also have an elastic tension which tends to bring them together.

Thus, to produce voicing, the speaker positions the vocal folds appropriately with a suitable tension and then pushes air out of the lungs through them. The result of the actions of the vocal folds is to impose a wave-like pattern of alternating pressures on the air stream as it enters the upper vocal tract which acts as a resonator on the air stream (Figure 12.8).

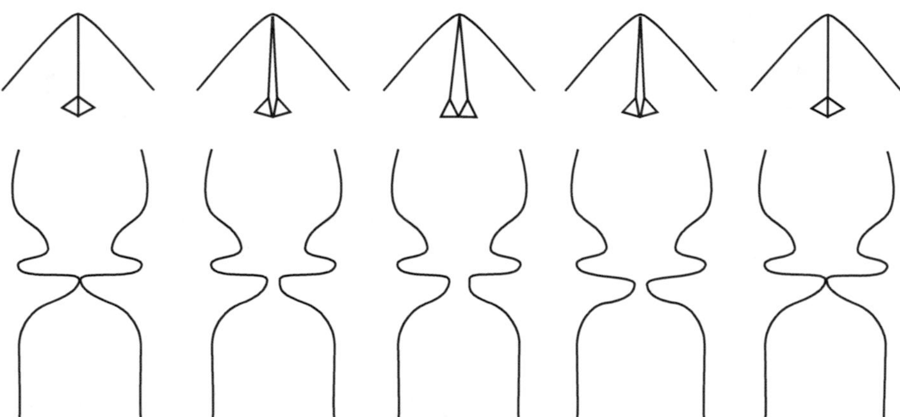

Figure 12.8 Vocal fold activity during one cycle of voicing. The upper drawing shows the glottis from above. The lower drawing shows the larynx from behind. Time goes from left to right

The rate of these pressure alternations is known as the **vibration rate** of the vocal folds. The vibration rate of the vocal folds controls the fundamental frequency of a sound and thus its perceived pitch. From physics we know that the vibrating frequency of a string depends on two properties: length and tension. A longer string vibrates at a lower frequency than a shorter one; a lax string vibrates at a lower frequency than a taut one. Both the length and the tension of the vocal folds can be varied, but varying the tension of the vocal folds is the primary means of changing the vibration rate. The length and tension of the vocal folds can be altered in three ways: (1) the thyroid cartilage can be tilted forward, stretching the vocal folds; (2) the position of the arytenoid cartilages can be moved, changing the length and tension of the vocal folds; and (3) the vocal folds themselves consist partially of muscles which can be tensed.

The angle of the thyroid cartilage changes for boys at puberty, lengthening the vocal folds. Boys often experience the so-called 'breaking' in their voice, a sign that they have not yet become used to the new length of their vocal folds. In adults, men have longer vocal folds than women, and thus lower-pitched voices; children have shorter vocal folds than women and thus higher-pitched voices. As a result of the change in angle of the thyroid cartilage, the adam's apple is more prominent with men than with women.

Obstruents regularly occur in both voiced and voiceless forms. Sonorants and vowels are usually voiced.

Voicing involves a series of bursts of energy, organised in formant patterns. On a wide-band spectrogram, voicing is identifiable as vertical striations during the voiced portions. Figure 12.9 shows a pronunciation of the syllable [hɑ]. During the [h], we see the random noise pattern caused by the voicelessness. During the [ɑ], we see the striations typical of voicing. Since the striations correspond to bursts of air coming through the glottis as it vibrates, we can calculate the frequency of the vocal fold vibrations by measuring the time elapsed between striations at that time.

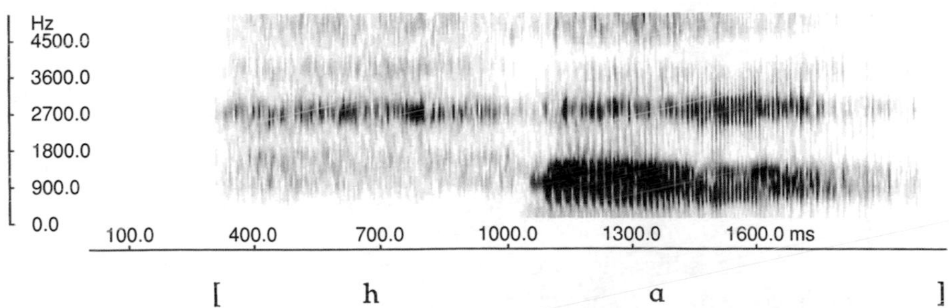

Figure 12.9 The syllable [hɑ]. If the distance between two adjacent vertical striations during the [ɑ] is measured, the fundamental frequency can be calculated

Other adjustments of the glottis

Deep breathing

For deep breathing, the glottis is opened as far as possible, allowing air to pass freely in and out. Frication may be heard if the air passes the edge of the vocal folds at a high velocity, causing turbulence. Figure 12.10 shows the glottis wide open for deep breathing.

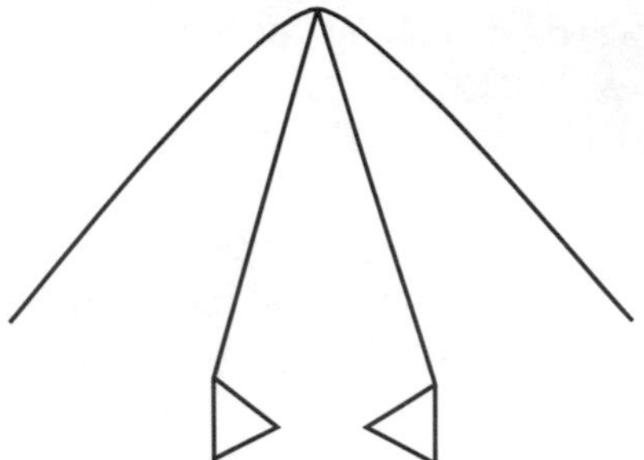

Figure 12.10 Deep breathing

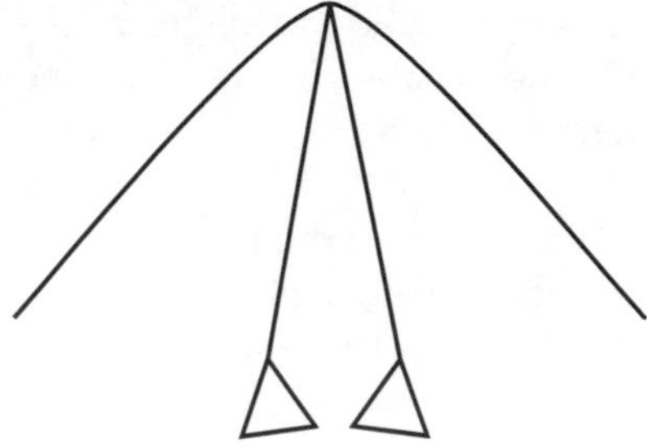

Figure 12.11 Quiet breathing

Quiet breathing

In quiet breathing, the glottis is more open than for voiceless, yet more closed than for deep breathing. The pressure is not strong enough to cause frication. Figure 12.11 shows the glottis for quiet breathing.

Breathy voice

Breathy voice is sometimes described as 'murmur'; there is vibration as in voicing, but there is a breathy quality as well. Intervocalic /h/ in English is a breathy voiced [ɦ], as in *ahead, ahoy*. Place your hands over your ears, and say *ahead* /aˈhɛd/. You will feel vibration throughout the /h/. The /h/ cannot simply be voiced, because it would then be undistinguishable from the /ɛ/. It is not voiced, but breathy voiced [ɦ].

Two types of mechanism for producing breathy voice occur. In one, the vocal folds are vibrating, but are positioned far enough apart that they do not close completely, allowing air to escape giving the breathy quality. The other type of breathy voice is produced by having the vocal folds vibrate, but with an open cartilagenous glottis allowing the air to escape. The two mechanisms for breathy voice are shown in Figure 12.12. A spectrogram of a breathy voiced vowel is shown in Figure 12.13.

Breathy voice is not used linguistically for extended stretches of speech, but languages sometimes have individual breathy voiced sounds. Many people have some breathy voice as a personal characteristic of their speech

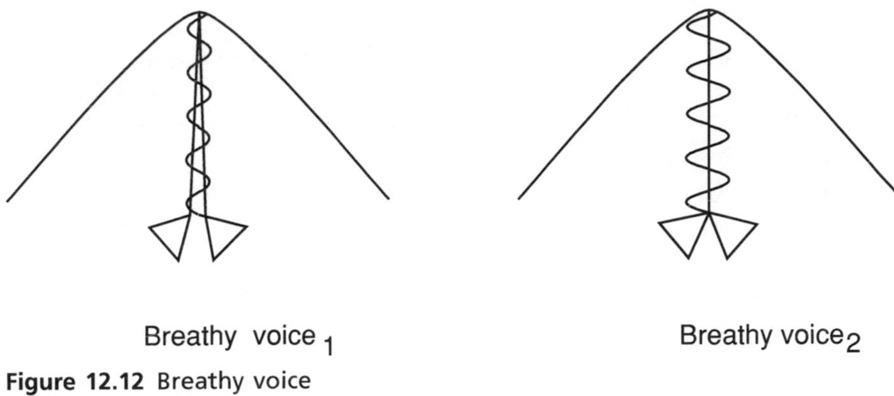

Figure 12.12 Breathy voice

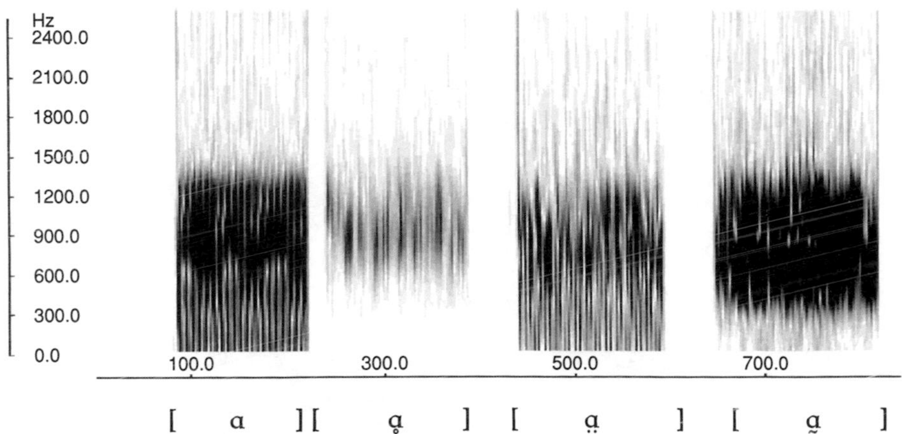

Figure 12.13 Spectrograms of various glottal adjustments

if the vocal folds do not close completely or smoothly. The diacritic for breathy voice is two subscript dots [̤] with a voiced symbol.

Breathy voiced sounds are well known in languages of the Indian subcontinent. The following examples from Hindi (India) show contrastive voiced and breathy voiced stops and affricates. Breathy voiced stops are discussed further below.

/bal/	*hair*	/b̤al/	*forehead*
/d̪an/	*charity*	/d̪̤an/	*paddy*
/ɖal/	*branch*	/ɖ̤an/	*shield*
/dʒəl/	*water*	/d̤ʒ̤əl/	*glimmer*
/ɡan/	*song*	/ɡ̤an/	*kind of bundle*

Hindi

Creaky voice

With **creaky voice** (also known as 'vocal fry' or 'glottal fry'), the arytenoids are tightly closed, allowing only a portion of the vocal folds to vibrate (Figure 12.13). The result is a very low pitched vibration. The sound of creaky voice is often described as similar to the noise a stick makes when run along a picket fence. Creaky voice is not ordinarily used for extended speech, but in some languages, individual sounds are made with creaky voice. Some RP speakers trail off sentences with creaky voice, a social effect sometime associated with snobbery. The diacritic for creaky voice is a subscript tilde [̰].

Margi (Nigeria; Hoffman, 1963) has various sounds with creaky voice.

/bəlam/	*baboon*	/b̰əb̰u/	*walk*
/dəgəl/	*bed*	/d̰əfɯ/	*mush*
/wa/	*who?*	/w̰al/	*great*
/jɯ/	*love*	/j̰ɯ/	*do*

Margi

In Danish, a phenomenon known as **stød** is used in certain syllables. It involves a creaky voice and a decrease in intensity and pitch. In emphatic speech, a glottal stop may occur.

[vɛn]	*friend*	[ven̰]	*turn!* (impv.)
[vɛl]	*well*	[vɛl̰]	*spring!* (impv.)
[du]	*you*	[dṵ]	*tablecloth*
[bœn]	*beans*	[bœn̰]	*peasants*

Danish

Falsetto

In **falsetto**, the vocal folds are held very tightly, allowing vibration only at the edges (Catford, 1977). Falsetto appears not to be used distinctively in speech although it is reported in honorific greetings in Tzeltal (Mexico). Singers, particularly men, often use falsetto to sing notes higher than their normal range. Yodelling involves a singing alternation between regular voice and falsetto.

Whisper

I will distinguish **whisper**, a state of the glottis, from **whispering**, a way of speaking quietly. Whisper involves an open cartilagenous glottis with no ligamental vibration. When you are whispering, you can feel your adam's apple to verify that your vocal folds do not vibrate and that thus there are no voiced sounds in whispering. Nevertheless, you can easily verify that in whispering the English words *seal* and *zeal* are distinct. If nothing is voiced, how then is a [z] distinct from an [s]? The answer is that in whispering, voicing is replaced by another adjustment of the vocal folds – whisper. There is no IPA diacritic for whisper; I use three subscript dots [...]. Whisper is not used in ordinary speech, although whispering is a human universal.

	Ordinary speech	Whispering
/s/	[s] voiceless	[s] voiceless
/z/	[z] voiced	[z̤] whisper

Voice onset time

Most languages have two contrastive sets of stops – voiced and voiceless. It is not always simply the case that one set uses the voiced glottal adjustment and the other uses voiceless. French, English and Scots Gaelic all have two contrast phonemes /t/ and /d/ in word initial position, but this phonemic difference is manifested in different ways. In French, the two sounds are simply voiced and voiceless. In English, /d/ is partially voiceless, and [t] is completely voiceless. In Scots Gaelic, both /d/ and /t/ are completely voiceless. The languages differ in the timing of the onset of voicing. Some authors use the terms **fortis** and **lenis** for the phonological difference, reserving **voiceless** and **voiced** for the phonetic activity of the vocal folds. Thus French fortis /t/ and Scots Gaelic lenis /d/ are both unaspirated voiceless stops. Other authors have used **tense** and **lax** for the phonological distinction.

Figure 12.14 is a line diagram showing **voice onset time (VOT)** in French, English, and Scots Gaelic. Pay particular attention to the relative timing of events. Voice onset time refers to the time at which voicing occurs in relation to the release of the stop. It is useful in characterising the phonetic facts clearly. Looking first at the onset of voicing for /d/ in Figure 12.14, we see that in French, voicing starts immediately at the beginning of the stop,

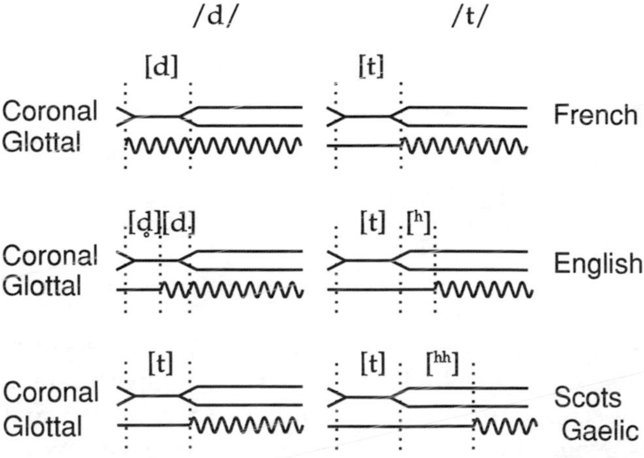

Figure 12.14 VOT of /t/ and /d/ in French, English and Scots Gaelic

phonetically a straightforward [d]. In English, voicing starts mid-way through the stop; we can represent this as [d̥d] showing the voiceless onset. (Recall that [d̥] = [t].) In Scots Gaelic, voicing starts at the release of the stop, producing a phonetic [t]. If we now look at the onset of voicing for /t/, we see that in French voicing starts immediately at the release of the stop, producing a straightforward [t]. In English, the voiceless period persists into the vowel, giving an aspirated [tʰ]. In Scots Gaelic, the delay of VOT is even greater than for English, with a strongly aspirated stop, which we can symbolise as [tʰʰ].

We see that French /t/ and Scots Gaelic /d/ are identical in their glottal behaviour although one is called 'voiced' and the other 'voiceless'. The terms *voiced* and *voiceless* when used with consonants often represent a difference in VOT, rather than a phonetic description of vocal fold activity. Voiced sounds have an earlier VOT than voiceless sounds.

Sounds like the English or Scots Gaelic /t/ with the stop voiceless and the voicelessness carrying on into the following segment are called **aspirated**. Note that the following segment may be a vowel, *pay* [pe̥e], or a sonorant, *play* [pl̥e]. English has light aspiration, whereas Scots Gaelic has heavy aspiration. In an English word like *stop*, with an unaspirated [t], the VOT is at the release of the stop and thus similar to that of a French /t/ or Scots Gaelic /d/.

Table 12.1 gives the voice onset times for a number of languages. Dutch, Cantonese, and English have a two-way contrast in VOT. Thai and Hindi have a three-way contrast. No language is known to have a four-way contrast of voice onset time. A positive value for VOT means that voicing onset occurs after the release of the stop; a negative value means that voicing onset precedes the release of the stop. Some speakers of English have a slightly different pattern with a VOT of about 30 ms for /b d g/.

Voice onset time is not the only attribute of aspiration. Aspiration also may involve greater subglottal force. This force holds the vocal folds apart longer, thus preventing voicing.

Scots Gaelic also has preaspiration before medial and final voiceless stops: [ʰp ʰt]. Before [k], the aspiration is usually realised as a velar fricative [xk].

/kɔʰp/	*foam*	/ˈʃnʲɛːʰpən/	*turnips*
/kaʰt/	*cat*	/ˈkrɔʰtəɫ/	*lichen*
/maxk/	*son*	/ˈfaxkəɫ/	*word*

Scots Gaelic

Voice onset time is fairly easily measured from a waveform or a spectrogram. Aspiration appears as a fairly faint burst of energy on a spectrogram. Figure 12.15 shows a spectrogram of voiced, voiceless, unaspirated and aspirated bilabial stops. Notice the noise after the release of the aspirated stop which is absent in the release of the plain stop.

Table 12.1 VOT for several languages times in milliseconds (Lisker and Abramson 1964)

Dutch	b	d		g	p	t		k				
	−85	−80		25	10	15		25				
Cantonese					p	t		k	p^h	t^h		k^h
					9	14		34	77	75		87
English	b	d		g					p^h	t^h		k^h
	−101	−102		−88					58	70		80
Thai	b	d			p	t		k	p^h	t^h		k^h
	−96	−102			3	15		30	78	59		98
Hindi	b	d	ɖ	g	p	t	ʈ	k	p^h	t^h	$ʈ^h$	k^h
	−85	−87	−76	−63	13	15	9	18	70	67	60	92

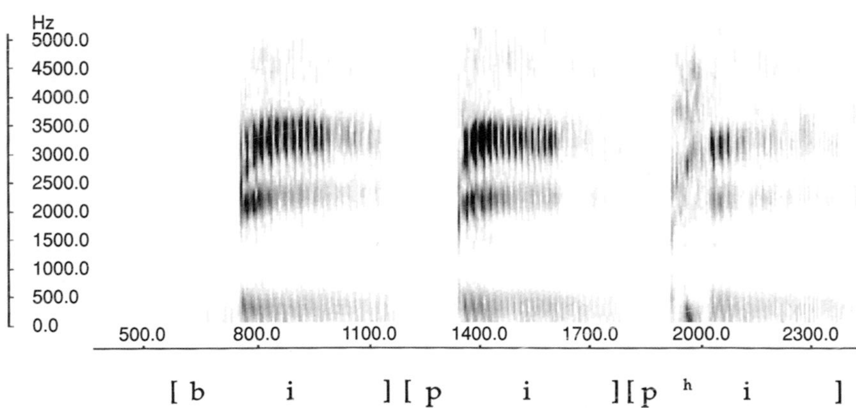

Figure 12.15 A three-way distinction in VOT

Korean has an unusual three-way series of stops. According to Kim (1965, 1970), the set [p t k] are lax. The other stops are tense: [p* t* k*] are unaspirated, and [p^h t^h k^h] are aspirated. Tenseness here is manifested as greater length and greater air pressure.

/pam/	*night*	/p*ul/	*horn*	/p^har/	*arm*
/pəːl/	*bee*	/p*alɯda/	*be quick*	/p^hi/	*blood*
/tal/	*moon*	/t*al/	*daughter*	/t^haːl/	*mask*
/toːl/	*stone*	/t*am/	*a crack*	/t^hək/	*chin*
/kat/	*hat*	/k*ul/	*honey*	/k^ho/	*nose*
/kot/	*place*	/t^hok*i/	*rabbit*	/k^hoŋ/	*bean*

Korean

Breathy voiced stops

We discussed breathy voice earlier in this chapter. This adjustment of the glottis is used in many of the languages of India which typically have four kinds of contrastive stops. Three kinds are familiar to us. The stops [p b pʰ] are voiceless, voiced and voiceless aspirated. The fourth kind is breathy voiced. It has often been referred to as a voiced aspirate. In our terms, aspiration is manifested as voiceless, so a voiced aspirated stop is a contradiction in terms. Ladefoged (1993) has argued that the stop portion of these sounds is voiced, but there is a following portion (occupying the same time portion as aspiration with the aspirated stops) in which the vocal folds assume a breathy voiced position. Figure 12.16 shows the timing of the events for a breathy voiced bilabial stop.

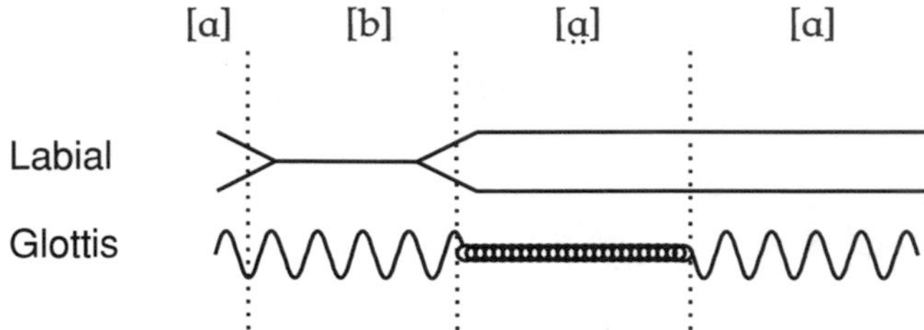

Figure 12.16 Breathy voiced stop

Technical terms

arytenoid cartilages
aspiration
  aspirated
Bernoulli principle
breathy voice
cartilagenous glottis
creaky voice
cricoid cartilage
epiglottis
false vocal folds
falsetto
fortis
glottal stop
glottis
hyoid bone
larynx
lax
lenis
ligamental glottis
phonation
  nil phonation
tense
thyroid cartilage
trachea
Ventricle of Morgagni
ventricular
vibration rate
vocal folds
voiceless
voice onset time (VOT)
whisper
  whispering

Symbols

[ɦ] breathy voiced vowel

Diacritics

[̰] creaky
[̤] breathy voice
[ɰ] whisper

Exercises

Basic

1 Practise the following:

ffffffff vvvvvvvvv fffffffff   ssssssssss zzzzzzzz sssssssss
ðððððððð θθθθθθθ ðððððððð   ʒʒʒʒʒʒʒʒʒʒ ʃʃʃʃʃʃʃʃʃʃʃ ʒʒʒʒʒʒʒʒʒ

Now try:

f v f v f v   s z s z s z   ʃ ʒ ʃ ʒ ʃ ʒ ʃ ʒ   θ ð θ ð θ ð

2 Practise changing the voicing with sonorants:

l l̥ l l̥ l l̥ l l̥ l   m m̥ m m̥ m m̥ m m̥ m   ɹ ɹ̥ ɹ ɹ̥ ɹ ɹ̥ ɹ ɹ̥ ɹ   n n̥ n n̥ n n̥ n n̥ n
n̥ɛn̥   lɪl̥   nun̥   m̥em
mɑm̥   lul̥   ɹɔɹ̥   nin̥

3 Practise:

dɛlθz   masl̥f   slvɑn   sl̥ifp
fm̥og   kɹ̥ɛn̥   hɪ̥fts   vtɔkn̥ul

4 Gradual changes. Start at the top of each column and work down:

ˈpɪðukælm̥ɔ   ˈʔisuɹdɛnoˈɣu
ˈpɪðukælm̥ɒ   ˈʔisuɹtɛnoˈɣu
ˈpɪðukɛlm̥ɒ   ˈʔizuɹtɛn̪oˈɣu
ˈpɪðukelm̥ɒ   ˈʔizultɛn̪ɔˈɣu
ˈbɪðukelm̥ɒ   ˈʔɪzultæn̪ɔˈɣu
ˈbɪðugelmɒ   ˈʔɪzuɹtæn̪ɔˈɣʊ

5 Voiced and voiceless laterals. Start with a voiced approximant [l], then make it voiceless [l̥]; you should not have any more friction than you would have with [h]. Practise the following:

l l l l l l̥ l̥ l̥ l̥ l̥
ɑlɑ   ɛlɛ   il̥i   ol̥o   lɑl̥o   l̥ul̥ɛ   lil̥e   lɔl̥ɑ

Start with [l l l l l]; gradually raise the body of the tongue (not the tip) to produce a strong fricative [ɮ ɮ ɮ ɮ ɮ]. Make sure that the tip of the tongue remains against the alveolar ridge.

ɮo   ɮi   ɮɑ   loɮi   ɮeʒa   ɮɛli   luɮa   ɮelɔ

Now say [l]; devoice it to [l̥]; raise the body of the tongue to get a strong fricative [ɬ]; then voice it to [ɮ]. Alternatively, start with [l]; raise the tongue to get [ɮ]; now devoice it to [ɬ].

l l l l l	l̥ l̥ l̥ l̥ l̥	ɬ ɬ ɬ ɬ ɬ	ɮ ɮ ɮ ɮ ɮ	l l l l l	ɮ ɮ ɮ ɮ ɮ	ɬ ɬ ɬ ɬ ɬ	l̥ l̥ l̥ l̥ l̥
ɬɛ	ɬu	ɬɔ	ɬo	lʒe	l̥i	lɑ	l̥ɛ
luɬɑ	ɮoɬe	laɮe	lɛl̥i	lɛɬi	lɛɬa	ɬale	ɬɔɮa

6 Breathy voice. In Engish, /h/ between vowels is usually breathy voiced [ɦ]. Try saying *aha, ahead, ahoy.* Now try to prolong the [ɦ]: [ɑˈɦɑ – ɑˈɦɦɦɦɦɑ]. Now try to eliminate first the initial vowel and then the final one, ending up with just [ɦɦɦɦɦ]. Breathy voice with other consonants is written with [̤] underneath. Try:

ɦɑ	ɦɛ	ɦi	ɦo	ɦu	ɦe
b̤ɑ	d̤ɑ	g̤ɑ	b̤o	d̤o	g̤o
b̤ed̤i	g̤ub̤ɔ	d̤ag̤ɛ	ɦeb̤ɛ	d̤ɛɦṳ	b̤od̤i

7 Gujarati (/ˌgudʒˈrɑti/; India) distinguishes breathy voiced stops and vowels:

/baɾ/	*twelve*	/pɔɾ/	*last year*
/ba̤ɾ/	*outside*	/pɔ̤ɾ/	*early morning*
/b̤aɾ/	*burden*	/pʰɔdz/	*army*
/a̤r/	*obstruction*	/aɻ/	*bones*

8 Bhojpuri (/ˌbʱodʒˌpuri/; India) has breathy voiced nasals. Practise these:

/sɑmɑr/	*battle*	/sɑm̤ɑr/	*be careful*
/ɑnɑːr/	*pomegranate*	/ɑn̤ɑːr/	*darkness*
/bɑːnɑr/	*monkey*	/ɑːn̤ɑr/	*blind*
/kɑːn/	*ear*	/kɑːn̤/	*shoulder*

9 Bengali (/bɛŋˈgɑli/; India) has breathy voiced stops:

/b̤ag/	*part*	/gob̤ir/	*deep*
/lob̤/	*greed*	/b̤ubon/	*earth*
/d̤onuk/	*bow*	/did̤a/	*doubt*
/kãd̤/	*shoulder*	/d̤up/	*incense*
/g̤ɔr/	*room*	/ag̤at/	*blow*
/bag̤/	*tiger*	/g̤ug̤u/	*dove*

10 Creaky voice [̰] sounds like a stick on a picket fence. Open the mouth wide, and say [ɑː]. Start at a low pitch, and try to go as low as you can; now try to go even lower. This often results in creaky voice.

a̰ ḭ o̰ ḛ ṵ ɛ̰ ɑ̰ ɔ̰

11 Lango (Sudan) has both creaky vowels and creaky consonants:

/lee/	*animal*	/lḛḛ/	*axe*
/man/	*this*	/ma̰n̰/	*testicles*
/kor/	*chest*	/ko̰r̰/	*hen's nest*
/tur/	*break*	/tṵr̰/	*high ground*

Advanced

12 Whisper. We will symbolise this with [...]. Try whispering the sentence below (GA). Listen to the shifts between voiceless and whisper:

Where	can	he	find	it?
[w ɛ ɹ	k ə n	h i	f a j n d	ɪt]

Try whispering these pairs, concentrating on the sounds with whisper.

seal	zeal	ether	either
fat	vat	pressure	pleasure

13 Try the following Bengali retroflex and palato-alveolar sounds. Note especially the aspirated and breathy voiced stops.

/ʈʰunko/	*fragile*	/aʈʰa/	*glue*	/kaʈʰ/	*wood*	/aʈʰaro/	*eighteen*
/ɖ̤ak/	*drum*	/ɖ̤al/	*shield*	/ɔɖ̤el/	*sufficient*	/ɖ̤ima/	*slow*
/tʃʰobi/	*picture*	/atʃʰar/	*to thrash*	/matʃʰ/	*fish*	/tʃʰoʈo/	*small*
/d̤ʒ̤op/	*bush*	/nird̤ʒ̤ɔr/	*spring*	/mad̤ʒ̤/	*middle*	/d̤ʒ̤inuk/	*oyster*

14 Try the following alveolo-palatals from Japanese:

/tɕi/	*blood*	/kɯ̥tɕi/	*mouth*	/tɕi̥sei/	*topography*
/ɕima/	*island*	/ɕaɕin/	*photograph*	/ɕi̥sei/	*municipal government*

15 Abi Dabi /ˈɑbiˌdɑbi/ is considered by many to be a gourmet Pig Latin. The rule is that the sequence [əb] is inserted before each vowel or diphthong. An RP accent is used here.

cat	/kəbæt/	*dog*	/dəbɑg/	*try*	/tɹəbaj/
at	/əbæt/	*strip*	/stɹəbɪp/	*flat*	/fləbæt/
lousy	/ləbawzəbi/	*carcinogenic*	/kəbɑsəbɪnəbəwdʒəbɛnəbɪk/		

Pronounce and decode the following Abi Dabi utterances:

SIGNS FOUND IN PUBLIC PLACES

/ðəbə ləbɪft əbɪz bəbiəbɪŋ fəbɪkst fəbə ðəbə nəbɛkst fjəbu dəbejz. djəbʊəɹəbɪŋ ðəbæt təbajm wəbi ɹəbɪgɹəbɛt ðəbət jəbu wəbɪl bəbi əbʌnbəbɛəɹəbəbəl/

/ðəbə pəbəɹəbejd təbəməbɒɹəbəw wəbɪl təbejk pləbels əbɪn ðəbə məbɔnəbɪŋ əbɪf əbɪt ɹəbejnz əbɪn ðəbə əbɑftəbənəbun/

/nəbəw tʃəbɪldɹəbən əbələbawd əbɪn ðəbə məbətəbəɹnəbɪtəbi wəbɔdz/

/əbæz fəbə ðəbə tɹəbawt səbɜvd jəbu əbæt ðəbə həbəwtəbɛl məbɒnəbəpəbəwl, jəbu wəbɪl bəbi səbɪŋəbɪŋ əbɪts pɹəbejzəbɪz təbə jəbʊ gɹəbændtʃəbɪldɹəbən əbæz jəbu ləbaj əbɔn jəbə dəbɛθbəbɛd/

Chapter 13

Air stream mechanisms

In our discussion of sounds so far, we have simply assumed that the lungs produce an air stream which is modified by the larynx and vocal tract. This is, indeed, the way the vast majority of phonetic sounds are produced. In this chapter, we will discuss other ways which are used to move air in and out of the body to produce sounds.

For phonetic sounds to occur, air must move past the articulators. This moving air is called the **air stream**; it is set in motion by the **air stream mechanism**. The anatomical organ whose action sets the air stream in motion is called the **initiator**. The air stream may be **egressive**, flowing out of the body, or **ingressive**, flowing into the body.

In this chapter you will learn about:

- the various ways languages move air in and out of the body;
- the kinds of sounds made by different air stream mechanisms.

Air pressure

All air stream mechanisms work by changing the air pressure in the vocal tract. A basic principle of physics, **Boyle's Law**, says that the pressure of a gas varies inversely with its volume. A second principle is that, if possible, gas will move so as to equalise different pressures.

Consider Figure 13.1, which shows an experiment with a container having a movable top and a door on the side. At the beginning of the experiment (Figure 13.1a) the door is open, and the air pressure is the same both inside the container and outside (arbitrarily shown as 0). In Figure 13.1b the door is closed; then in Figure 13.1c the top of the container is lowered to make the container smaller. According to Boyle's Law, if the volume is thus decreased, the air pressure is increased. The resulting air pressures are shown in Figure 13.1c. The outside air pressure remains at [0]; however, the inside pressure is now greater, shown as [+]. If the door is now opened (Figure 13.1d), the air will rush out to equalise the pressure inside the container with that outside.

In a second experiment shown in Figure 13.2, the door is again open (Figure 13.2a), and the air pressure both inside and outside the container is

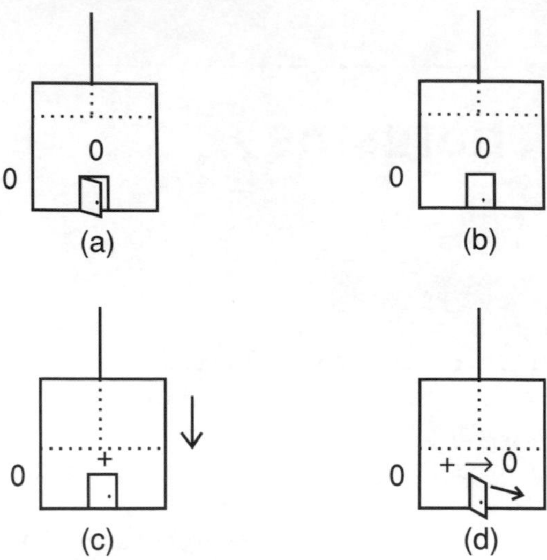

Figure 13.1 A reduction in the size of the container causes an increase in the pressure within the container. On opening the door, air rushes out

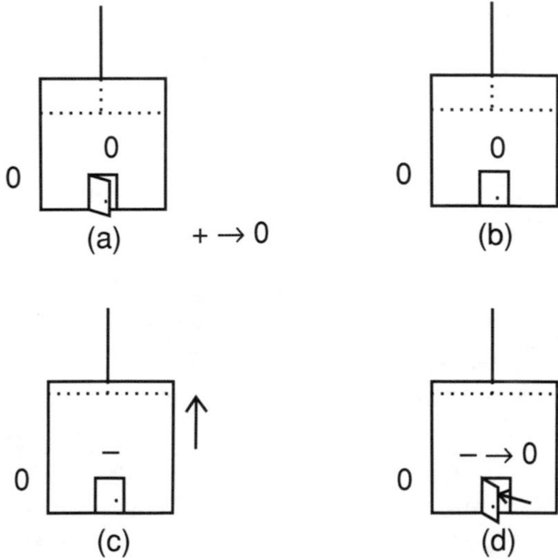

Figure 13.2 An increase in the size of the container causes a decrease in the pressure within the container. On opening the door, air rushes in

[0]. In Figure 13.2b, the door is shut, and in Figure 13.2c, the top of the container is raised thus increasing the volume of the container. Boyle's Law says that if the volume is increased, the pressure is decreased, here shown as [–]. In Figure 13.2d, the door is opened and air rushes in to equalise air pressures inside and outside the container.

In speech production, our body is the container, and the door is our mouth and nose, opening to the outside world. By changing the volume of our lungs, we can change the air pressure; if our oral or nasal passage is open, air moves in or out of our body. If we expand our chest cavity, pressure inside is lowered, and air flows in. If we contract our chest cavity, pressure inside is raised, and air flows out.

Air stream mechanisms

Three air stream mechanisms occur in language. The mechanisms are known as **pulmonic**, **glottalic**, and **velaric**. The initiators for these mechanisms are, respectively, the lungs, the glottis, and the velum. Each of these mechanisms can occur with an egressive or ingressive air stream.

Pulmonic air stream mechanism

The primary air stream mechanism for speech is **pulmonic** with the lungs as initiator. All sounds of English are pulmonic. In fact, most languages in the world use only pulmonic egressive sounds, and of those languages that use other kinds of air stream mechanisms, the great majority of their sounds are still pulmonic egressive.

The primary function of the lungs is, of course, for breathing; speech is a secondary phenomenon and accompanies breathing. When the lungs are contracted, the air pressure is increased, and air flows out. When the lungs are expanded, the air pressure is decreased and air flows in.

The two lungs sit inside the rib cage (Figure 13.3). They consist of soft, non-muscular tissue and have an elastic property, like a sponge, allowing

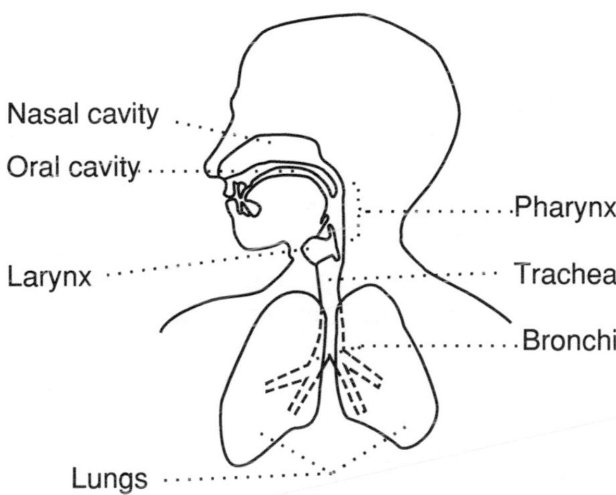

Figure 13.3 A view of the lungs and vocal tract

them to be expanded and contracted. As with a sponge, if the size of the lungs is altered, the elastic property exerts a force to return the lungs to their resting size. The two lungs are independent, so if one is injured, we can still breathe with the other one. The right lung is slightly larger than the left one.

The tiny tubes within the lungs are supplied with air by a pair of tubes, one for each lung, called a **bronchus**. The two **bronchi** join to form the **trachea**, which is formed of rings of **cartilages**. The cartilagenous rings are not complete, but are closed at the rear by membrane. Just behind the trachea is a tube called the **œsophagus**, which carries food from the mouth to the stomach. Having the trachea formed of rings rather than being a solid tube is useful in allowing us to bend our neck more easily.

Several muscles control the rib cage. The **external intercostals** lift the rib cage and hold it up, inflating the lungs. These can be termed the ingressive muscles. Other muscles, the **internal intercostals**, pull the rib cage down and deflate the lungs. The **abdominal muscles** also help deflate the lungs. The internal intercostals and the abdominals can be termed the egressive muscles. As explained above, the lungs are elastic and will resist expansion and contraction, attempting to return to their resting size.

Singing teachers often claim that the **diaphragm**, a large dome-shaped muscle lying just below the lungs, is very important in sound production. However, Bouhuys (1974) suggests that it does not play a significant role in either speech or singing.

The maximum capacity of the lungs is about seven litres (Hixon, 1987). If you breathe out as much as you can, some two litres of air still remain in the lungs. Thus, at a maximum, you have the use of five litres of air for speech. At rest, we breathe slowly both in and out. In speaking, however, we breathe in quickly and then breathe out over a prolonged period, using the egressive air for speech.

Draper, Ladefoged and Whitteridge (1960) found that we use the ingressive muscles to inflate the lungs and then we continue using them in breathing out to slow down the contraction of the lungs which results from their inherent elastic property. In exhaling, after the lungs pass their point of rest, we bring the egressive muscles increasingly into play to push the air out and to overcome the increasing elastic force which resists compression.

Figure 13.4 presents a stylised chart which we will use to show the various types of air stream mechanism. The outside air pressure is arbitrarily set at [0]. Air pressure is marked in the lungs, pharynx, and mouth; [+] indicates a pressure higher than the outside air pressure, and [–] indicates a pressure lower than the outside air pressure. Pressure in the lungs is known as **subglottal pressure**.

Look at Figures 13.4a and 13.4b to understand how this diagram represents the vocal tract. Figure 13.4a shows a bilabial stop with closure at the

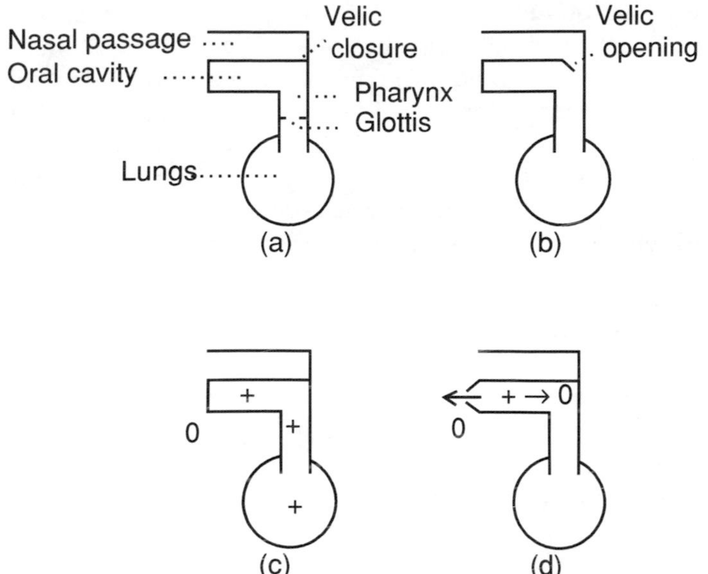

Figure 13.4 Air pressures in the vocal tract

end of the oral cavity. Figure 13.4b shows a bilabial nasal with velic opening allowing air to pass out through the nasal cavity.

Figure 13.4c shows a **plosive**, that is, an egressive pulmonic stop, before its release. The chest cavity has been contracted with the result that the subglottal pressure is greater than the outside air pressure. Since there are no obstructions, this increased air pressure has spread to the pharynx and oral cavity as well. The nasal passage is shut off. Figure 13.4d shows the plosive at the moment of release. When the lips open, the greater air pressure inside the vocal tract causes air to flow outwards until the air pressure inside the vocal tract equals that of the outside.

Pulmonic ingressive sounds are quite easy to make. Speakers occasionally use that air stream mechanism for short utterances so as to continue talking while breathing in, as in counting. The vocal folds do not vibrate well with ingressive air, so voiced sounds are a bit odd. Boys in Switzerland are reported using ingressive air while courting girls outside their bedroom window; their intent is to avoid identification by the girls' parents (Dieth, 1950).

Figure 13.5 shows the production of a pulmonic ingressive stop. While a stop is being produced, the chest cavity has been enlarged, lowering the air pressure inside. When the stop is released, air flows into the body until the inside and outside air pressures are equalised.

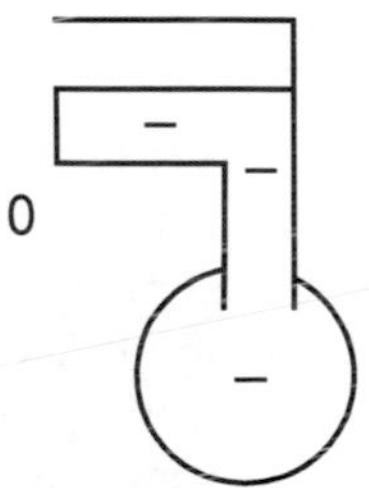

Figure 13.5 Pulmonic ingressive

Languages rarely use pulmonic ingressive sounds as regular speech sounds; however, Danin, a ritual language of the Lardil in Australia, according to Hale (Catford, 1977), has a pulmonic ingressive [l]. Pulmonic ingressive fricatives have been reported in Tsou (Austronesian, Taiwan) as variants of the egressive fricatives (Fuller, 1990). Speakers in Newfoundland sometimes pronounce *yeah* in the sense of 'yes' with an ingressive pulmonic air stream; the same thing happens in Swedish, where /jɑ/ 'yes' is frequently heard with an ingressive pulmonic air stream.

Glottalic air stream mechanism

The larynx can move up and down in the neck. You can feel this movement if you put your fingers lightly on your adam's apple and swallow. Figure 13.6 shows that if the vocal folds are closed in a glottal stop and the larynx then raised, the air pressure of the pharynx and mouth is raised. (We are not concerned here with the subglottal pressure.) This forms our second air stream mechanism, **glottalic**, in which the glottis is the initiator, moving up and down like a piston. Because of the small size of the supralaryngeal vocal tract, the glottalic air stream mechanism cannot be continued very long, but it can create quite high pressures.

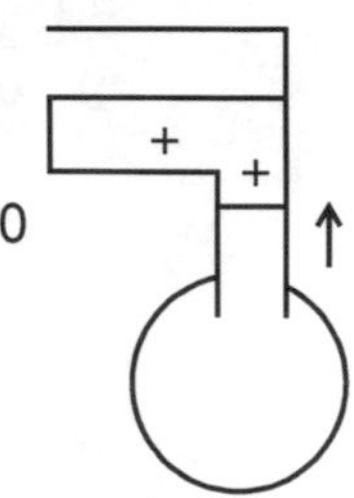

Figure 13.6 Ejective. Glottalic egressive

Glottalic egressive stops are called **ejectives**. They are transcribed with the symbol for a voiceless stop, with the diacritic [ʼ]: [pʼ tʼ cʼ kʼ qʼ]. Glottalic egressive fricatives and affricates are also possible: [fʼ sʼ ʃʼ tθʼ tsʼ tʃʼ].

/tʼanta/	*bread*	/tʼaqa/	*group*
/cʼakij/	*to be thirsty*	/cʼuʎu/	*cap*
/kʼucu/	*corner*	/hajkʼa/	*how many*
/wisqʼaj/	*to close*	/qʼupi/	*warm*

Quechua (South America)

Glottalic ingressive sounds, Figure 13.7, can be made without a great deal of difficulty. The glottis is closed, and then the larynx is lowered prior to release. In fact, however, these sounds are very rare in languages although they have been reported in two languages of Central America: Tojolabal (Pike, 1963) and Cakchiquel (Campbell, 1973).

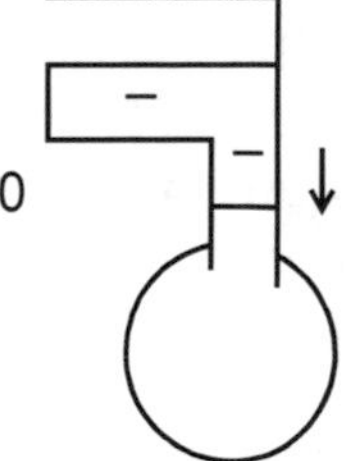

Figure 13.7 Glottalic ingressive

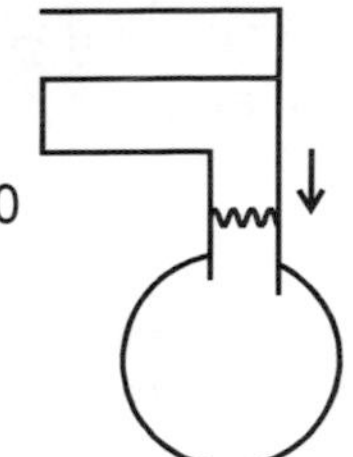

Figure 13.8 Implosive

Although pure glottalic ingressives are rare, a somewhat related mechanism producing sounds called implosives is occasionally found. **Implosives** involve a downward-moving larynx. Normally, voicing occurs when air is pushed upwards through the glottis. With implosives, the vocal folds vibrate as the larynx is pushed downwards through the air. Figure 13.8 illustrates this with a wavy line showing the vibrating vocal folds. Implosives are transcribed with modified forms of the voiced stops: [ɓ ɗ ɠ]. Laver (1994) argues that some pulmonic egressive air-flow is also involved.

Gbeya (Central African Republic) has bilabial and apico-postdental implosives. The term *apico-postdental* means that the tip of the tongue is at the boundary of the teeth and alveolar ridge.

/ba/	*to take*	/ɓa/	*to disavow*
/bi/	*to extinguish*	/ɓi/	*to pick fruit*
/dik/	*to thunder*	/ɗik/	*to sift*
/dɔk/	*to be muck*	/ɗɔk/	*to be weak*
/gede/	*certain tree*	/ɠeɗe/	*buttock*

Gbeya

Velaric air stream mechanism

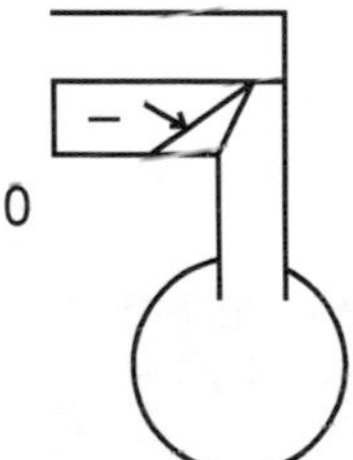

Figure 13.9 Click. The body of the tongue is drawn back, enlarging the oral cavity

The third air stream mechanism we encounter is **velaric**. Velaric ingressive stops are known as **clicks**. The back of the tongue and the velum act as the initiator as shown in Figure 13.9; the diagonal lines show the tongue making a dorso-velar closure; this closure is always present in velaric sounds. Simultaneously, a closure is made farther forward, for example, the lips, to seal the oral cavity. Then the tongue is pulled down and back, enlarging the cavity and thus lowering the air pressure inside the oral cavity. When the lips are opened, air flows in. The resulting sound is called a bilabial click, or more commonly, a kiss.

As ordinary consonants, clicks are found only in the languages of Southern Africa. In many other cultures, however, they are used as special sounds. In English, a dental click [|], often written *tsk-tsk*, is used to indicate displeasure or concern. An alveolar lateral click [||] is used to urge on horses.

In the release of this click, only one side of the tongue is lowered on release. A palato-alveolar click is symbolised [ǂ]. For an alveolar or postalveolar click the symbol [!] is used. The bilabial click is transcribed [ʘ].

	Voiceless unaspirated	Voiceless aspirated	Delayed aspiration	Voiced nasal	Glottal closure
Dental	|goa *put into*	|kho *play an instrument*	|ho *push into*	|no *measure*	|o *sound*
Palatal	ǂgais *calling*	ǂkharis *small one*	ǂhais *baboon's arse*	ǂnais *turtledove*	ǂais *gold*
Alveolar	!goas *hollow*	!khoas *belt*	!hoas *narrating*	!noras *pluck maize seeds*	!oas *meeting*
Lateral	||garos *writing*	||khaos *strike*	||haos *special cooking place*	||naes *pointing*	||aos *reject a present*

Nama

Languages with clicks often have an large number of them. Nama is a language of Southern Africa having 20 clicks. A voiced click, for example, involves a pulmonic [g] so that the vocal folds are vibrating simultaneously with the click. In nasal clicks, a pulmonic /ŋ/ is made simultaneously with the click. In an aspirated click, the onset of voicing is delayed. Here [!] is used to represent an alveolar click.

Velaric egressive sounds (Figure 13.10) are not found as speech sounds. Many people, however, use them when trying to remove a hair from the tip of their tongue. It is possible to use the velaric air stream mechanism simultaneously with a pulmonic air stream mechanism. Try saying a string of *tsk-tsk-tsk* [| | |], simultaneously breathing in and out through the nose; you can easily observe that the two events are independent of each other.

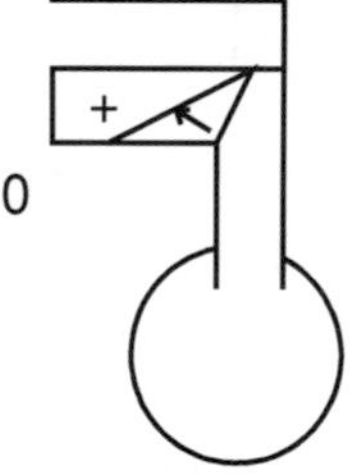

Figure 13.10 Velaric egressive stop. The body of the tongue is raised, decreasing the oral cavity

Bagpipes are constructed so that an inflated bag is pressed to act as the initiator of the air mechanism forming the sound. Since the bag is the initiator, the player is free to breathe at will, blowing through a tube to inflate the bag as required. Bagpipe music, thus, is written without any pauses for breathing. Bagpipe players often practise with a chanter, a special instrument without a bag, similar to a recorder or clarinet. Ordinarily, of course, the chanter is played with pulmonic egressive air. To produce the sustained notes of bagpipe music, however, and to breathe as well, the musician learns to use a velaric egressive air stream to keep the music going, while simultaneously using a pulmonic ingressive air stream through the nasal passage to replenish the air supply in the lungs (Figure 13.11). The same combination of air stream mechanisms is used in glass-blowing to produce a long steady air-flow.

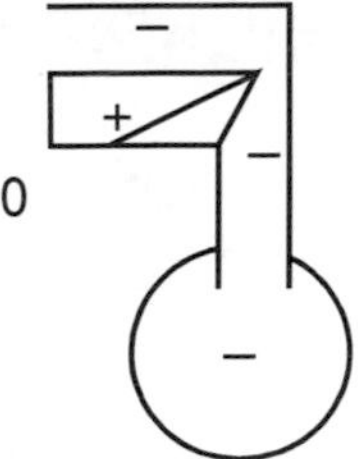

Figure 13.11 A velaric egressive air stream simultaneous with an ingressive pulmonic air stream with velic opening

Œsophagic air stream mechanism

Individuals with cancer or other ailments in their larynx sometimes require surgery which restructures the air tract so that they breathe through a hole in the neck. Such people obviously cannot use the pulmonic air stream mechanism to produce sounds. Sometimes they learn to swallow air partially and then to belch in a controlled fashion using this air for speech (Figure 13.12). This air stream mechanism is known as **œsophagic** /ˌɛsəˈfejdʒɪk/ because it uses the **œsophagus** /əˈsɒfəgəs/ GA /-ˈsɑf-/, the tube from the mouth to the stomach.

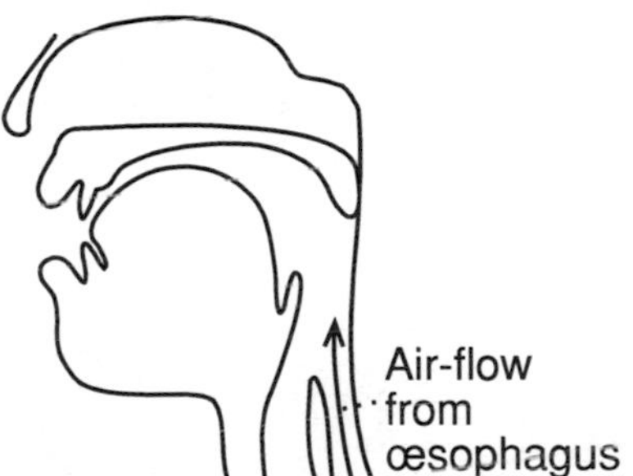

Figure 13.12 Œsophagic air stream

The œsophagus is a soft tube lying behind the trachea. It is normally flat when not in use carrying food to the stomach. The top of the tube is just above and behind the larynx. Any air coming from the stomach misses the vocal folds, but passes through the oral and nasal cavities. In œsophagic speech, voicing is missing, but normal articulations can take place in the upper vocal tract, which acts as a resonating chamber, as in normal speech. Obviously, this sort of speech lacks a good deal in quality, but it may be the best alternative available.

Technical terms

abdominal
air pressure
air stream
  air stream mechanism
Boyle's Law
bronchus
cartilages
click
diaphragm
egressive
ejective
external intercostals
glottalic
implosive
ingressive
initiator
internal intercostals
œsophagus
  œsophagic
plosive
pulmonic
subglottal pressure
trachea
velaric

Symbols

	Pulmonic	**Glottalic**	**Velaric**
Egressive	Plosives p t k	Ejectives p′ t′ k′	–
Ingressive	–	*Implosives ɓ ɗ ɠ	Clicks ʘ | ! ǂ ‖

* As described in the text, implosives are not made with a glottalic ingressive mechanism; it is convenient and traditional, however, to show them on a chart in this slot.

Exercises

Basic

1 Review

pʌzɛ	bɛxo	ŋotʊ	geθaw	ɲiɹ̥aj	ʃɑtʒej
hɪvɔ	dʒil̥e	keʒɔ	mowɸaw	ɣɒɾæ	ɹænɔ
ʔɒd̪ʊ	ɹ̥ejɣɛ	n̪ʊʃɑ	ðajʔi	d̪owm	ðɒl̥ʊ

2 Take a slow breath in and then a slow breath out. Most people find it fairly easy to speak with an ingressive air stream, although voicing does not work well. Try saying the following while breathing in:

[ˈtɹajɪŋ tə ˈtɔk wajl ˈbɹiðɪŋ ɪn ɪz bɪˈzɑ(ɹ)].

3 Ejectives are made by lowering the larynx, closing the vocal folds, forming the articulatory closure, and raising the larynx, creating a higher pressure between the vocal folds and the articulatory closure. Perhaps this description worked for you; it sure doesn't for most people. It is, however, quite useful once you start to get the basic feel of an ejective. Ejectives are not difficult to produce, but they involve a number of activities which are hard to coordinate at first. Be patient, eventually you'll get there.

Hints:

a. Pretend you have a hair on the tip of your tongue. Extend the tip of your tongue just beyond the lips and try to spit the hair off. With luck, you may be using the glottalic egressive air stream. Now, try this without extending your tongue to produce [p' p' p'].

b. To feel your larynx move, touch your adam's apple lightly and swallow. You will feel your larynx go up and down. Now try to get the same effect without swallowing.

c. Now:

i. Start to make a [k].
ii. Hold your breath.
iii. Try to get the adam's apple up. Thinking that you are about to swallow may help.
iv. Push the [k'] out.

d. Some children use an ejective [p'] to imitate a gunshot as in [p'aw]. Notice that the ejective makes a noticeable pop.

Once you have some success with an ejective, try different places of articulation.

p' p' p'   t' t' t'   c' c' c'   k' k' k'

Now try to put a vowel with the ejective:

p'ɑ   t'ɑ   c'ɑ   k'ɑ

Try these:

ɑp'ɛ	ot'u	ik'ɑ	nut'u
k'ele	p'ɔk'i tʊk'	p'oc'u	

Try an ejective fricative:

f' f' f'   s' s' s'   ʃ' ʃ' ʃ'   ç' ç' ç'

f'ʊ	f'ɪ	f'ə	s'i	s'ɑ	s'ɛ
ʃ'o	ʃ'u	ʃ'æ	ç'ɛ	ç'ɑ	ç'ɔ

4 Try the following ejectives from Bearlake Slave (Canada, Northwest Territories; Rice, p.c.). The acute accent ['] indicates high tone; low tone is unmarked.

/pet^{h}á/	*his/her father*	/petá/	*his/her eye*	/pet'álé/	*its wing*
/k^{h}ő/	*fire*	/kõ/	*reeds*	/k'ʊ/	*cloud*
/ts^{h}ẽ/	*dirt*	/tsine/	*day*	/ts'éré/	*blanket*
/tʃ^{h}õ/	*rain*	/tʃõ/	*here*	/tʃ'õ/	*porcupine*
/k^{wh}a/	*carrot*	/nak^{w}e/	*he/she lives*	/k^{w}'a/	*diaper*
/tɬ^{h}e/	*grease, lard*	/tɬa/	*water plant*	/tɬ'a/	*grass*

5 Implosives involve lowering the larynx. They have special symbols: [ɓ ɗ ɠ].

Hints:

a. If possible, listen to someone who can make ejectives.

b. Some people use [ɠ] when imitating frogs, pouring water, or just when acting silly.

c. Try to make a [b] with extra heavy voicing. Many people make an implosive [ɓ] when trying this.

d. Most learners raise their eyebrows while making implosives. Do not interfere with any supercilious activity; it may be crucial.

When you finally get a bit of an implosive going, try practising these:

ɓ ɓ ɓ ɓ ɓ   ɗ ɗ ɗ ɗ ɗ   ɠ ɠ ɠ ɠ ɠ
ɓɑ ɗɑ ɠɑ   ɓu ɗe ɠo   ɠɛ ɗi ɓæ
ɓɑɓɛ   bɑɓɛ   ɓɑbɛ   duɗɑ   ɗudɑ
tɛɓu   lɑɠe   ɹiɗo   ɗegi   goɠu
ɠlɑ   ɗɹib   ɑɓnu   ɑnɓu   poɓe

6 Clicks are not particularly difficult. The trick is to integrate them smoothly in a string of other sounds. Slow and steady practice is the only method for success.

a. Bilabial. A bilabial click is essentially a kiss. The symbol is [ʘ]. Place your forefinger (either hand) horizontally, just touching your lips and kiss your finger. This is a bilabial click. Now remove your finger and try several of these clicks in a row.

ʘ ʘ ʘ ʘ ʘ
ʘi   ʘe   ʘɛ   ʘa   ʘɑ   ʘɔ   ʘo   ʘu
ɑʘu   oʘe   eʘɑ   ɔʘɛ   ʘiʘu   ʘɛʘɔ   ʘaʘɑ   ʘoʘeʘ

If you are practising with a partner, you may want to try a few quadrilabial clicks.

b. The dental click is symbolised as [|]. In its reduplicated form, it is used in English as a sign of disapproval or regret, often written *tsk-tsk*.

c. The alveolar lateral click is made by putting the tip of the tongue at the alveolar ridge with a velaric ingressive air stream mechanism with a lateral release; in English, its reduplicated form is frequently written *gitty-up*. The symbol is [||].

|| || || || ||
||i ||e ||ɛ ||a ||ɑ ||ɔ ||o ||u
i||ɑ   ɑ||o   e||i   a||ɛ ||ɔ||o ||a||ɑ ||u||ɛ ||i||e||

d. Lateral clicks can be made with central, alveolar, or postalveolar tongue positions. A postalveolar or palatal click is written [!]. The tongue tip is at the back of the alveolar ridge.

! ! ! ! !
!i   !e   !ɛ   !a   !ɑ   !ɔ   !o   !u
e!o   ɔ!o   ɑ!i   u!ɛ   !o!ɔ   !ɛ!a   !o!ɛ   !u!e!

Try these:

|itɔ   !ɑko   ʘole   nɛ||u   ŋɑ!o |aʘu
!e|ɑ ||e!o   ʘɔ||ɛ |i!a ||oʘu   ʘɑ||ɔ
ɑʘɑ|ɑ|| ɔ!ekuʘ   o||ɑŋiʘa   u|i||o   ʘɛ!ɑ ||eʘi

e. Clicks can be combined with various other phonetic phenomena such as voicing, breathy voice, nasalisation. We will look at nasal clicks here.

Try saying a sequence of [ʘ ʘ ʘ ʘ ʘ | | | | | || || || || || ! ! ! ! !] while simultaneously slowly breathing in and out. It is clear that both pulmonic and velaric air streams can occur at the same time.

Now say a long [ŋŋŋŋŋŋ].

Say a long [ŋŋŋŋŋ] and a series of clicks [|||||] at the same time. Each of these is a nasal click and can be written [ŋ̂|].

Now try a series of these:

ŋ̂|ɛ   ŋ̂|u   ŋ̂|ɑ   ŋ̂||a   ŋ̂||i   ŋ̂||o
ŋ̂!u   ŋ̂!ɑ   ŋ̂!e   ŋ̂ʘɔ   ŋ̂ʘɛ   ŋ̂ʘa
ŋ̂||eta   ŋ̂|okɑ   ŋ̂||ɑŋi   oŋ̂ʘaŋu   iŋ̂||a!o   uŋ̂!oʘe

Advanced

7 Try the following ejectives from Amharic (Ethiopia):

/t'ɨl/	*quarrel*	/tɨl/	*warm*	/dɨl/	*victory*
/k'ɨr/	*stay away*	/kɨr/	*thread*	/gərr/	*innocent*
/mətʃ'/	*one who comes*	/mətʃ/	*when*	/mədʒ/	*grinding stone*
/s'əggɑ/	*grace*	/səggɑ/	*to worry*	/zəggɑ/	*to close*

8 The double articulation [ɡ̂b] is a common sound in many languages. The [g] and the [b] are simultaneous, and the whole sound is often an implosive. Practise distinguishing [ɡ̂b], [g], and [b].

ɡ̂bi   ɡ̂be   ɡ̂bɑ   ɡ̂bo   gɛɡ̂bu   ɡ̂beɡ̂bo
baɠbu   ɡ̂bɑbɛ   giɠɔ   ɓɛɡ̂bu   ɡ̂bɛɓɪ   ɡ̂boɠu

9 Vietnamese has implosives. Pay particular attention to the back unrounded vowels; [ɯ] and [ɤ] are the unrounded equivalents of [u] and [o]. (Tone is not marked.)

/ɓɛn/	*side*	/bɤ/	*shore*	/ɓæn/	*to shoot*	/ba/	*three*
/ɗi/	*go*	/ɗa/	*stone*	/ɗo/	*be red*	/ɗɤn/	*application*
/ŋɯi/	*sniff*	/ɯa/	*to like*	/ɗɯt/	*to break*	/ɗɯŋ/	*don't*
/mɤi/	*invite*	/xɤp/	*joint*	/sɤm/	*be early*	/ɯɤt/	*be wet*

10 Chilcotin (Canada, British Columbia). Practise the labialised consonants:

/kʷixkʷix/ *Steller's Jay*
/sɛkʷ′ɛ̃t/ *my kidney*
/tʃɛkʷix/ *blouse*
/gʷɛdɛðk′æn/ *it is burning*
/hʷɛθ/ *cactus, thorn*
/nɛntʰasgweθ/ *I will tickle you*
/nosgʷɛθ/ *I want to tickle you*
/næts′ɛtɛtʰɛlkʷix/ *whooping cough*
/dɛtʃɛntɛɬkʷ′ɛð/ *woodpecker*
/ɛkʷɛ̃ð/ *back the same way*
/tɛnahʷɛð/ *gooseberry*
/xʷɔstɛstæðt′e/ *suspenders*
/sɛgʷɛð/ *my leg muscle*
/ɛgiðgʷɛt/ *eggshell*

11 Practise the lateral affricates in Rae Dogrib (Canada, Northwest Territories):

/ɬo/ *smoke* /ɬo/ *much* /kˀaɬa/ *still, yet* /natɬa/ *he walks*
/tlĩa/ *mouse* /tɬĩ/ *dog* /tla/ *water-grass* /ĩdle/ *one*

Chapter 14

Syllables and suprasegmentals

The **segments** of a language are the consonants and vowels. The **suprasegmentals** comprise several linguistically important phenomena which are not segmental, such as length, stress, pitch, and intonation. The term suprasegmental derives from the fact that these elements often extend over a string of segments. Suprasegmentals are often defined in terms of syllables, so we will begin with a general consideration of the syllable.

In this chapter you will learn about:

- the nature of the syllable;
- long vowels and consonants;
- the use of pitch in speech;
- metrical theory of stress.

Syllable

The **syllable** is a phonological unit of organisation containing one or more segments. Syllables are found in all languages; that is, all languages organise sounds in terms of syllables. They are usually easy to count. Almost everyone will agree that the words *book, table, carnation, particular, lackadaisical,* and *compatibility* have one to six syllables, respectively. Even in a language which you do not know, you can often count the syllables in a word.

Although it may be easy to count syllables, it is not always easy to divide a word into syllables. The word *kidnap* has two syllables. Almost all English speakers will divide those syllables as /kɪd – næp/. The word *very* also has two syllables, but it is difficult to know where to divide it. Neither /vɛ – ɹi/ nor /vɛɹ – i/ seems satisfactory, or, in another sense, both seem satisfactory.

Structure of the syllable

In Chapter 5, we learned the basic terms for parts of the syllable; they are shown here again in Figure 14.1. A lower-case Greek sigma [σ] is often used as a symbol for a syllable. Typically, the **nucleus** of a syllable is the vowel; the **onset** is the preceding consonant, and the **coda** is the consonant after the vowel. Together, the nucleus and the coda form the **rhyme**.

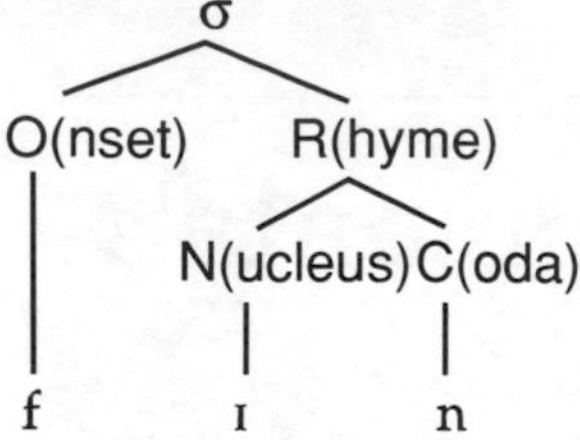

Figure 14.1 Structure of the syllable

Any of these elements may branch, that is, have more than one unit. In *fling,* the onset branches; in *belt,* the coda branches (Figure 14.2).

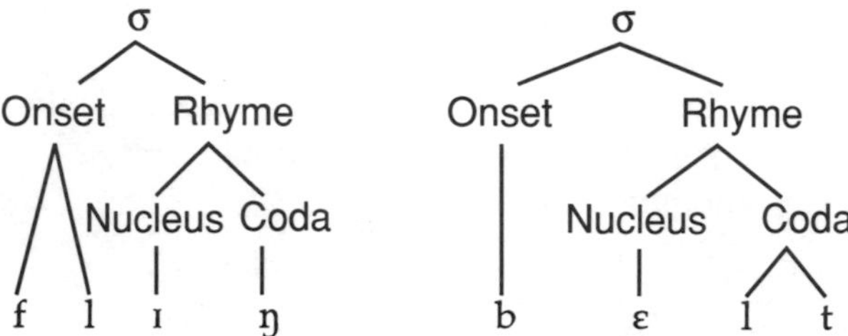

Figure 14.2 Branching onset and coda

In a syllable containing a diphthong, such as *bite* /bajt/, the nucleus branches (Figure 14.3). In languages with contrastive long and short vowels, a long vowel such as in German /raːt/ 'advice', is often analysed as having a branching nucleus with a sequence of two identical vowels /raat/. Two adjacent identical segments are called **geminates**.

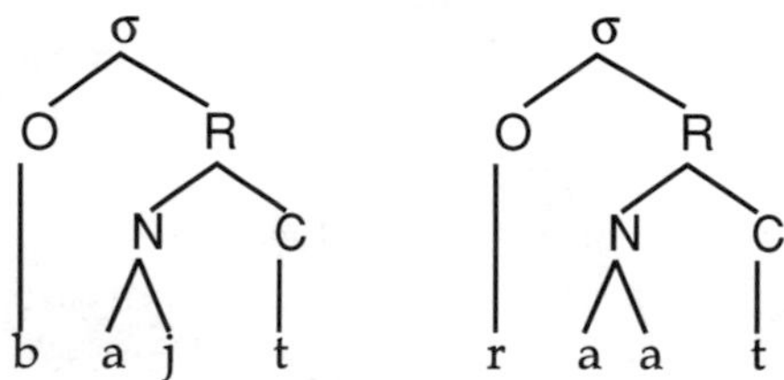

Figure 14.3 Branching nuclei

The nucleus of a syllable is ordinarily a vowel or diphthong. However, sonorant consonants sometimes form the nucleus and are then known as **syllabic consonants** (Figure 14.4). These are indicated by a short stroke under the consonant, as in [l̩]. Quiotepec Chinantec (Suárez, 1983) makes extensive use of syllabic nasals. The superscript numerals indicate tones.

/m̩ʔ^{1}/	*ant*	/m̩ː^{23}/	*sandal*
/m̩ʔ^{3}/	*tomato*	/ʔm̩^{3}m̩ː^{4}/	*you pinch (pl)*

Quiotepec Chinantec

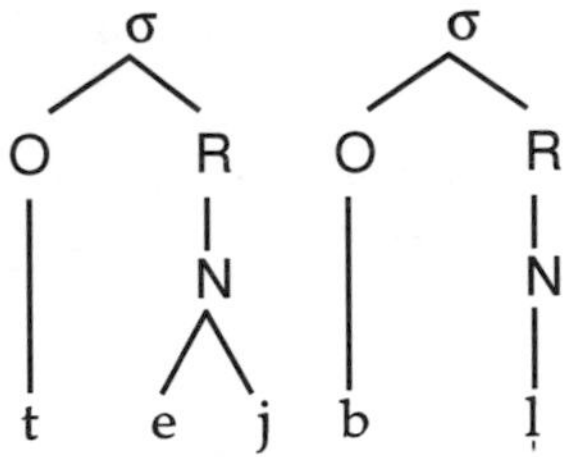

Figure 14.4 Syllabic consonant in English *table*

An **open** syllable is one that has an empty coda, that is, no final consonant: e.g., [ʌ], [tu], [splæ]. A **closed** syllable has one or more final consonants: e.g., [ik], [nʊdʒ], [dɛlps]. The terms **light** and **heavy** syllables are common, although their definition varies slightly depending on what language is being analysed. A syllable with a branching nucleus or with a branching coda is heavy. A syllable with an unbranched nucleus and no coda is light. A syllable with an unbranched nucleus and a single consonant in the coda, for example [lʌg], functions as a heavy syllable in some languages and as a light syllable in others (Figure 14.5). The onset is irrelevant to the distinction of heavy and light.

light	**heavy**
V	VV
CV	CVV
	CVCC
	CVVCC

← (CVC) →

Figure 14.5 Light and heavy syllables. C represents a consonant; V, a vowel. CVC syllables may be heavy or light, depending on the language

The last syllable of a word is known as the **ultimate syllable** or **ultima**. The second last is the **penultimate syllable** or **penult**. The third last syllable is known as the **antepenultimate syllable** or **antepenult**.

detectable /də –	ˈtɛk –	tə –	bl̩/
	antepenult	**penult**	**ultima**

Production of the syllable

We would like to be able to state just how a syllable is produced. Unfortunately, there is no satisfactory, general explanation of how syllables are produced. Clearly, however, the production of syllables involves at least in part the way in which the lungs move air out of the body.

Some years ago, Stetson (1951) put forward a theory that syllables were formed by a **chest pulse**. By this, he meant a single contraction of muscles in the rib cage acts to pull the rib cage down, thereby pushing air out of the lungs. Stetson suggested that each chest pulse pushes a bit of air out which forms the air-flow used for a single syllable. Later work (for example, Draper, Ladefoged and Whitteridge, 1957, 1958, 1960), however, showed that Stetson's chest pulse theory was unworkable.

Perception of the syllable

Sonority refers to the relative loudness of sounds. If we look at the waveform of the word *loving* (Figure 14.6), we can easily see that the intensity (which we perceive as loudness) of the vowels is much greater than that of the neighbouring consonants.

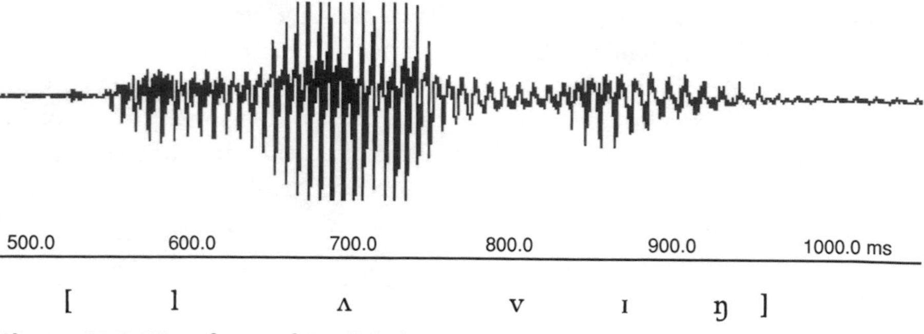

Figure 14.6 Waveform of English *loving*

Phonologists have proposed the notion of a sonority hierarchy (Table 14.1, modified from Selkirk, 1984). This hierarchy categorises groups of sounds by their relative sonority. The values in the index are relative. Two articulatory factors generally contribute to sonority: an open vocal tract and voicing. We perceive greater sonority as greater **prominence**. More sonorant sounds stand out and are perceptually more prominent than their neighbours.

Table 14.1 Sonority hierarchy

Sound	Sonority index
Low vowels	10
Mid vowels	9
High vowels	8
glides	7
ɹ, l	6
Nasals	5
s	4
Voiced fricatives	3
Voiceless fricatives (not [s])	2
Voiced stops	1
Voiceless stops	0.5

In Figure 14.7, the sonority values for the word *loving* have been predicted. Sonority is the vertical dimension. When the individual lines of relative sonority are joined, the resulting pattern is called a **sonority curve**. From these sonorities, we would predict that *loving* would have a sonority curve as shown in Figure 14.8. This curve is, in fact, fairly close to the intensities shown in the waveform of Figure 14.6.

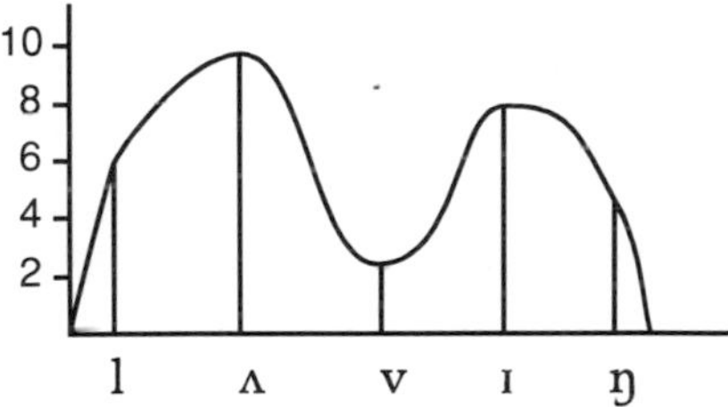

Figure 14.7 Sonority curve of English *loving*

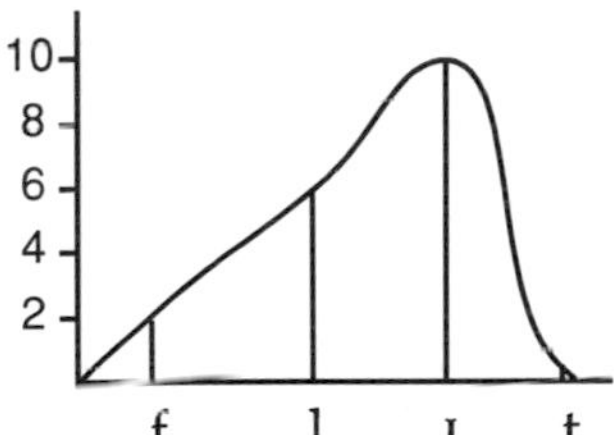

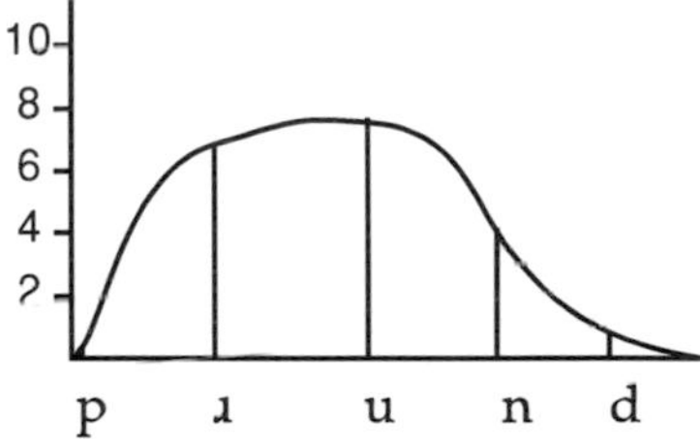

Figure 14.8 Sonority curves for *flit* and *pruned*

The sonority theory holds that a peak of sonority defines a syllable. In Figure 14.7, there are two peaks, so the theory correctly predicts that we will perceive *loving* as having two syllables.

This theory generally works, with peaks of sonority corresponding to the nuclei of syllables, and troughs of sonority corresponding to the onsets and codas of syllables. Figure 14.8 shows sonority curves for *flit* and *pruned*. In *flit*, the /l/ is more sonorous than the /f/; the peak of sonority is in the vowel; and the final /t/ has very little sonority at all. In *pruned*, the greatest peak of sonority is in the vowel, the consonants surrounding the vowel, /ɹ/ and /n/, are less sonorous, and the consonants at the extreme edges of the word, /p/ and /d/, are least sonorous of all. These words have a complex syllable structure, but the sonority theory agrees with the position of each segment in the syllable.

If we plot the sonority curve for a word like *split*, however, we see that the curve (Figure 14.9) has two peaks of sonority: one for the [s], and one for the vowel; yet *split* clearly consists of only one syllable.

The sonority theory thus does not work for syllables beginning with /s/–stop clusters. There is no obvious explanation for this; we can only note

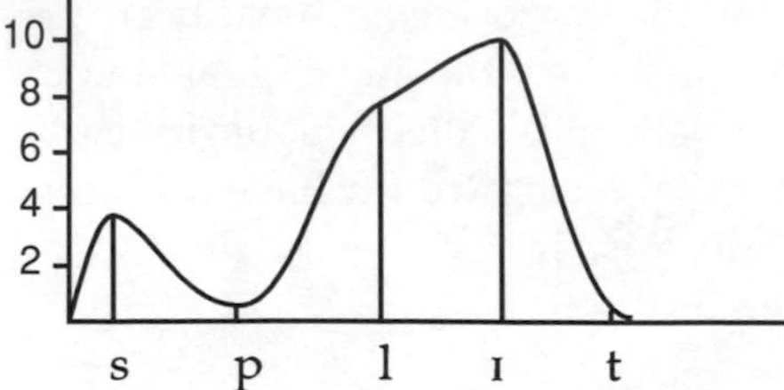

Figure 14.9 Predicted sonority of English *split*

that in many languages there seems to be something special about the ability of /s/ to form consonant clusters without creating a peak of sonority.

A second problem for the sonorant theory appears if we examine the syllabic structure for English and French *table*. English *table* has two syllables with its syllabic [l̩], but French *table* has only one syllable, as the [l] is not syllabic. The sonority theory gives the same sonority curve (Figure 14.10) for both languages and predicts two syllables for both.

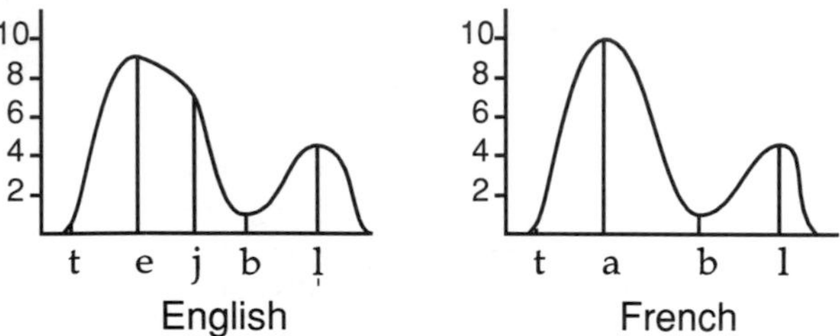

Figure 14.10 Predicted sonority of English *table* and French *table*

Although the sonority theory meets with very wide success in explaining how syllables are perceived, it needs to be refined further to cover certain cases.

Syllables and moræ

If we apply our notions of sonority to Japanese, we can readily divide words into syllables. Syllables have the general pattern of consonant – vowel, with an optional consonant in the coda.

/ha-ʃi/	*edge*	/kek-koŋ/	*marriage*
/ʃoo-kai/	*introduction*	/mu-ra-sa-kii-ro/	*purple*

Japanese

Note that /ŋ/ and a homorganic obstruent are the only permissible syllable codas. A syllable nucleus may branch: /oo/, /ai/, /ii/.

Japanese has traditionally recognised a unit called the **mora**, in addition to the syllable. The difference between syllables and moræ is that a consonant in the coda of a syllable forms a mora of its own, and a branching nucleus forms two moræ. The words from the list above are given again below, this time divided into moræ.

ha-ʃi	ke-k-ko-ŋ
ʃo-o-ka-i	mu-ra-sa-ki-i-ro

The traditional **moraic** analysis for Japanese (e.g., Bloch, 1950) has been that each mora takes about the same amount of time to be pronounced. Thus, /kekkoŋ/ and /ʃookai/ take twice as long as /haʃi/, and /murasakiiro/ with six moræ takes three times as long. In Chapter 5 we described English as **stress-timed** and French as **syllable-timed**. The Japanese system could be called **mora-timed**.

Japanese speakers are clearly aware of the mora as a phonological unit. Japanese poetic rhythm is defined by the number of moræ. A *haiku* poem, for example, is written in 17 moræ.

/ha-ru ta-tsu ja	*Spring starts;*
ʃi-n-ne-n fu-ru-ki	*new year; old rice;*
ko-me go ʃo-o/	*five quarts*

(Matsuo Bashō, 1684)

Beckman (1982) found evidence contradicting the traditional view; her study showed no convincing evidence for the existence of the mora as a unit of timing. In written Japanese, each mora is written with a separate *kana* symbol. Beckman suggests that the ability to conceptualise Japanese in terms of moræ is due in large part to familiarity with the writing system. The mora, in any case, seems to play a part in the phonological behaviour of Japanese (Vance, 1987; also below in this chapter under *pitch accent*).

Length

Length refers to the duration of a sound. We saw in Chapter 4 that English has non-contrastive variation of length: English vowels are longer before a voiced consonant than before a voiceless one. Other languages have contrastive distinctions of vowel length. Length is transcribed, occasionally by a double vowel /ee/, but more commonly with a colon [:] following the long segment: /e:/. A single raised dot [·] can be used for an intermediate length between short (unmarked) and long [:].

/ba/	*mud*	/ba:/	*wide open*
/bi/	*bend*	/bi:/	*narrow*
/bliba/	*make dirty*	/bliba:/	*dirty, soiled*
/bala/	*climb*	/bala:/	*moving quietly*

Ewe

Contrasts of length are often accompanied by small alternations of quality. In German, the long vowels have a different articulation from the short vowels, generally higher and more peripheral.

biete	/biːtə/	'offer (impv)'	*Bitte*	/bɪtə/	'request'
Beet	/beːt/	'(flower) bed'	*Bett*	/bɛt/	'(sleeping) bed'
fühlen	/fyːlən/	'feel'	*füllen*	/fʏlən/	'fill'
Höhle	/høːlə/	'cave'	*Hölle*	/hœlə/	'hell'
Fuß	/fuːs/	'foot'	*Fluß*	/flʊs/	'river'
Schoß	/ʃoːs/	'lap'	*schoß*	/ʃɔs/	'shot (past)'
Staat	/ʃtɑːt/	'state'	*Stadt*	/ʃtɑt/	'city'

German

Consonants may also be long. Phonetically, in the English word *penknife,* we find a long /n/. On closer examination, however, we discover that the first /n/ belongs to one morpheme *pen,* and the second /n/ belongs to a different morpheme *knife.* In fact, in English, we can find no geminates (i.e., long) consonants *within* a morpheme.

Italian is a language which has contrastive long and short consonants within morphemes.

/fato/	*fate*	/fatto/	*done*
/akanto/	*acanthus*	/akkanto/	*alongside*
/ara/	*altar*	/arra/	*guarantee*
/kolo/	*sieve*	/kollo/	*neck*

Italian

Pitch and tone

All languages use pitch and stress to some degree. Some languages make very extensive use of pitch or stress. In the following sections, we will look at some of the ways in which these properties are used in language.

We perceive changes in the fundamental frequency as changes in **pitch**. In phonetics, pitch is often referred to as **tone**, particularly when it distinguishes different words in a language. Languages which contrast lexical items with tone alone are called **tone languages**. For example, in Sherbro, a West African language, [ná] spoken with a high tone means 'cow', whereas [nà] with a low tone means 'spider'. English speakers are usually somewhat surprised to learn that most languages in the world are tone languages.

Note that *high* and *low* are relative terms. A high tone for an adult man may have the same pitch as a low tone for a child. Apparently, listeners identify the pitch range of a speaker quickly and adjust their notion of high and low for that speaker accordingly.

We have already noted in Chapter 12 that the fundamental frequency of a phonetic sound is determined by the vibration rate of the vocal folds, and we examined the ways in which the larynx acts to vary this vibration rate. Every sound with vibrating vocal folds has a pitch. Most commonly, a pitch pattern extends over a syllable.

The Mandarin dialect of Chinese has four distinctive tones which can be illustrated with the segments /ma/. With a high level tone, /mā/ means 'mother'. With a high rising tone, /má/ means 'hemp'. With a tone that first falls and then rises, /mǎ/ means 'horse', and with a low falling tone, /mà/ means 'scold'. Figure 14.11 below shows different ways that have been used to transcribe the tones of this dialect.

One way to indicate tone (Figure 14.11a) uses a vertical mark to indicate the vocal range and places a second line next to this to show the tone, something like musical notation. Although clumsy to write, this system gives a clear visual image of the tone pattern. Superscript numerals (Figure 14.11b) are occasionally used to mark tone. This system, known as the *Wade-Giles* system, was commonly used in the past with Chinese. Unfortunately, such marks have little mnemonic value and are often omitted. Another scheme (Figure 14.11c) indicates the tones of Chinese using extra consonants and vowels. In 1958, China officially adopted the transcription system known as *Pinyin* /ˌpin ˈjin/, which uses accents (Figure 14.11d); the shape of the accents suggests the tonal pattern.

	a	b	c	d
'mother' /ma/ *high level*	˥	ma¹	mha	mā
'hemp' /ma/ *high rising*	˧˥	ma²	ma	má
'horse' /ma/ *low falling-rising*	˨˩˦	ma³	maa	mǎ
'scold' /ma/ *low falling*	˥˩	ma⁴	mah	mà

Figure 14.11 Mandarin Chinese tone

In general, the notation of Figure 14.11a above is useful when first analysing the language. After the tonal system of a language is determined, other marks such as accents are more convenient. In a two-tone system with high and low, an **acute accent** [´] marks a high tone, and a **grave accent** [`] marks a low tone. In a three-tone system, a **macron** [¯] is used for a mid-tone. A **circumflex accent** [ˆ] is often used to mark a falling tone, and a **haček** [ˇ] is used to mark a rising tone. (In the Pinyin system for Chinese, a **breve** [˘] with a rounded bottom, is used instead of a haček.) Often (H) and (L) are used to indicate high and low tones. Usage in transcribing tone varies, so when you find accent marks, you will have to determine whether they represent tone, stress, or something else, and then determine what value each accent is used for.

Allophonically, low vowels tend to be spoken with lower fundamental frequency than high vowels. When the tongue is lifted to produce the higher vowel, the larynx is also pulled upwards, thus tensing the vocal folds slightly, producing a higher vibration rate.

Register and contour tone languages

In Chinese, the tones have a specific shape at a particular point on the musical scale: high level, low falling, etc. Such tones are called **contour tones**. Vietnamese has a contour system with six tones, as shown in Figure 14.12 (Thompson, 1965). Note that laryngeal quality and glottal stops are associated with certain tones.

a. Mid level, with falling final [ɗɤm]'stab', [tɯ] 'fourth', [ma] 'ghost'	˧˨
b. Long low falling breathy voic [gɤm] 'near', [ɗɯŋ] 'do not', [ma] 'that'	˨˩
c. High rising [rɤt] 'very', [sɯk] 'strength', [ma] 'cheek'	˧˥
d. Short low falling, ending in glottal stop [ŋɤp] 'flooded', [ŋɯə] 'horse', [ma] 'rice seedling'	˨˩
e. falling rising [fɤj]'comma', [tʰɯ] 'try', [ma] 'grae'	˨˩˦
f. High rising, broken by glottal stop [ɗɤj] 'be fat', [cɯ] 'written word', [ɗa] 'anterior tense marker'	˧˥

Figure 14.12 Tones in Vietnamese

In contrast to contour tones, **register tones** are always level. Languages with register tone typically distinguish only two or three levels. Sherbro is a register tone language with two levels. In Figure 14.13 we see a typical utterance. Note the allophonic variation which causes a final high tone to be mid after a low tone.

Nupe (Nigeria) is a register tone language with three tones (Figure 14.14):

High		—	—	—		—			—
Low	—				—		—		
	jà	mɔ́	kí	já	jèn	dʒó	ì	-	ʃɔ́
	I	you	fut.	cook-for	something	eat	morning		
	'I will cook something for you eat this morning.'								

Figure 14.13 Register tones in Sherbro

MH	LL	LM	MM	ML
| |	| |	| |	| |	| |
ē dú	è dù	è dū	ē dū	ē dù
'kind of fish'	'Niger River'	'kind of yam'	'thigh'	'deer'

Figure 14.14 Tones in Nupe

Phonetic rising tones (marked as [ˇ]) occur in some words. In such cases, phonologists argue that the correct representation for these rising tones is to have a low–high sequence associated with the same syllable (Figure 14.15). In the same manner, falling tones [ˆ] can be associated with a high–low sequence.

L LH	L LH	L LH
| V	| V	| V
è bč	è bǔ	è lě
'pumpkin'	'cross'	'past'

Figure 14.15 Rising tones in Nupe

Drift and step

A phenomenon found in some register tone languages is **downdrift**. For example, Igbo (Ghana, West Africa; Hyman, 1975) has two tones: high and low. The first syllable is high (H), and the second is low (L). The third syllable is high, but not quite so high as the first syllable. With downdrift, the level of *high* is reset just a little lower after a low tone. The result is that the actual value of high drifts downwards (Figure 14.16). The level of the low tone may drift lower as well.

In Hausa (Nigeria, West Africa), a high tone can actually drift phonetically lower than a low tone which occurs early in the sentence (Figure 14.17).

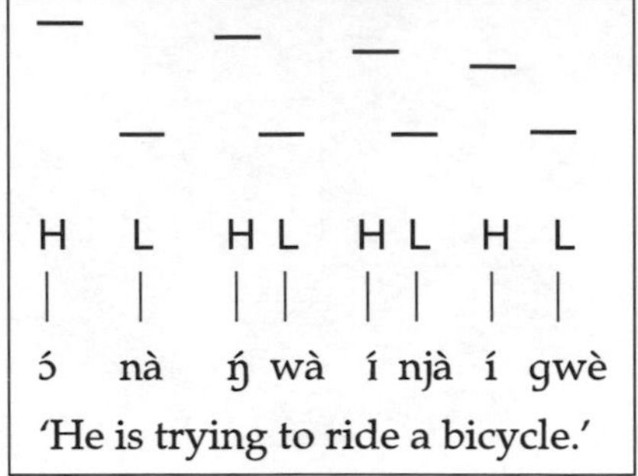

Figure 14.16 Downdrift in Igbo

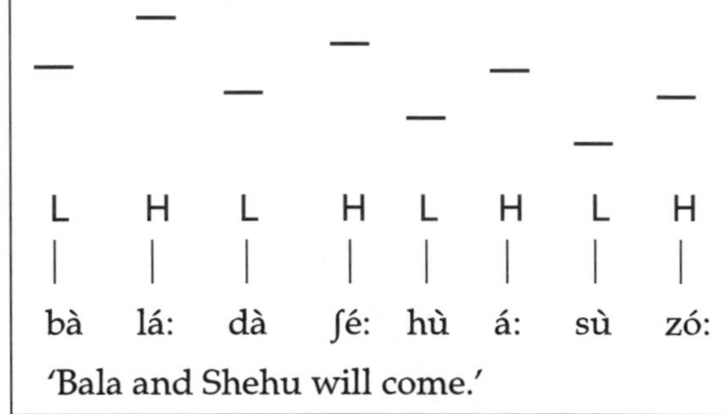

Figure 14.17 Downdrift in Hausa

Downstep and upstep

Some languages, such as Coatzospan Mixtec (Figure 14.18), exhibit **downstep** (Suárez, 1983). In such languages, the high-tone level becomes increasingly lower, but the mechanism is different from that of downdrift. Each syllable is lexically specified as *high, low,* or *downstep* [↓]. After a high tone, a syllable with downstep is slightly lower in pitch than the previous high tone, and this level becomes the new level for later high tones. Note in Figure 14.18 that the high-tone level drops after every occurrence of downstep. Acatlán

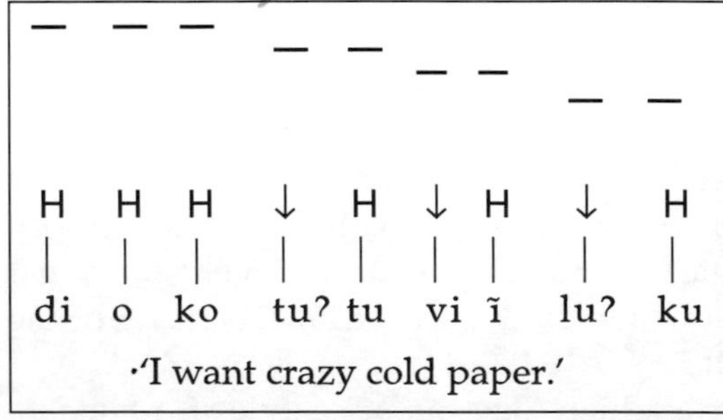

Figure 14.18 Downstep in Coatzospan Mixtec

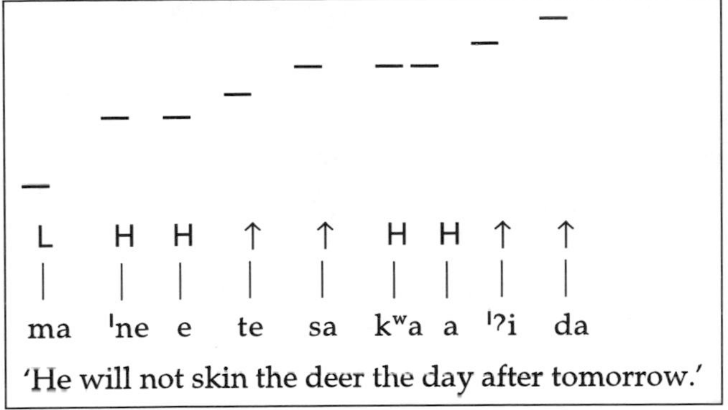

Figure 14.19 Upstep in Acatlán Mixtec

Mixtec (Súarez, 1983) has **upstep**, the reverse of downstep (Figure 14.19). Here, certain syllables, marked [ꜛ], are higher after a previous unstepped tone.

Pitch accent

In terms of tone, Japanese words are either 'accented' or 'unaccented'. Unaccented words have a low tone on the first mora and a high tone on subsequent moræ; a one-mora word has a high tone (McCawley, 1968; Vance, 1987). In the examples below, a word is given in its basic form and then with a suffix added – /wa/ (marking the topic of a clause); the relevance of the suffix will become clear shortly. Tone is indicated with H for high tone, and L for low tone; the hyphens divide moræ.

/ki/	H	*spirit*	/ki-wa/	LH
/ha-ʃi/	LH	*edge*	/ha-ʃi-wa/	LHH
/to-mo-da-ti/	LHHH	*friend*	/to-mo-da-ti-wa/	LHHHH
/mu-ra-sa-ki-i-ro/	LHHHHH	*purple*	/mu-ra-sa-ki-i-ro-wa/	LHHHHHH

With the 'accented' words, there is a fall from high to low tone. This fall, traditionally known in Japanese as **pitch accent**, is phonologically unpredictable and is marked here with /˺/. The basic tone pattern prevails (the first mora has low tone, and subsequent moræ have high tone), except that the mora immediately preceding /˺/ has high tone, and all moræ following /˺/ have low tone.

/ki˺/	H	*tree*	/ki˺-wa/	HL
/ha˺-ʃi/	HL	*chopsticks*	/ha˺-ʃi-wa/	HLL
/o-ka˺-a-sa-ma/	LHLLL	*mother*	/o-ka˺-a-sa-ma-wa/	LHLLLL
/ja-ma-za˺-ku-ra/	LHHLL	*wild cherry tree*	/ja-ma-za˺-ku-ra-wa/	LHHLLL
/ta-n-sa-ŋ-ga˺-su/	LHHHHL	*carbon dioxide*	/ta-n-sa-ŋ-ga˺-su-wa/	LHHHHLL

The forms for *edge, bridge,* and *chopsticks* below show three possibilities. *Edge* with no pitch accent and *bridge* with pitch accent on the first mora both have a low–high tone pattern in isolation. They can only be distinguished when a suffix is added since the pitch accent in *bridge* causes the suffix to have low tone. The word for *chopsticks* has the same segments but with pitch accent on the first mora giving it a different tone pattern from the other two in all environments.

/ha-ʃi/	LH	*edge*	/ha-ʃi-wa/	LHH
/ha-ʃi˺/	LH	*bridge*	/ha-ʃi˺-wa/	LHL
/ha˺-ʃi/	HL	*chopsticks*	/ha˺-ʃi-wa/	HLL

Japanese is not a tone language in the sense that each mora can independently have a high tone or a low tone. Rather, there is an overall tonal pattern for words and a linguistically determined lexical accent /˺/ which overrides the pattern with a fall from high to low. Languages with tonal patterns like that of Japanese have been called **pitch-accent** languages.

Tone in Swedish

Swedish intonation often strikes English ears as 'musical' or 'lilting'. We could easily imagine that pitch might play a distinctive role in Swedish. Indeed, we do find a few hundred pairs of words which contrast by means of pitch. The two pitch patterns are shown in Figure 14.20 with examples below. Both patterns have a relatively level pitch at the beginning of the word. Pattern I simply falls at the end. Pattern II falls somewhat, rises, and then falls again.

Pattern I		**Pattern II**	
re:gel	*rule*	re:gel	*bolt*
anden	*the duck*	anden	*the spirit*
vi:ken	*the bay*	vi:ken	*folded*
taŋken	*the tank*	taŋken	*the thought*

Swedish

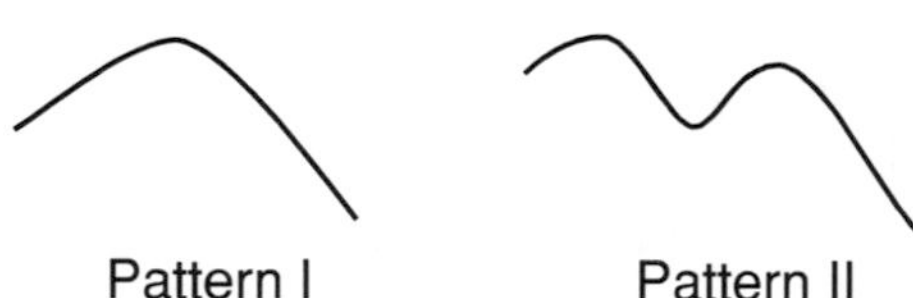

Figure 14.20 Contrastive tones in Swedish

Does this type of contrast make Swedish a tone language? Not really. The basic suprasegmental pattern of Swedish is intonational, like English, although the intonational patterns are phonetically quite different from those of English. The contrastive use of tone is only a very small part of a much larger pattern. Compare Chinese, where tone forms a crucial part of every lexical item. Swedish is also the native language of a small minority of people living in Finland. Interestingly, the Finnish dialect of Swedish does not have the tone pattern typical of Swedish and does not distinguish the pairs shown above.

Whistling and drumming

Some societies speaking tone languages use whistling and drumming to communicate under certain conditions. The pitch of the whistling or drumming imitates the tonal pattern of normal speech. Context is obviously an important element in distinguishing similar utterances. In English, we do this to a very limited extent. We can often understand an utterance such as 'I don't know' even when only the intonation is heard through a mouth full of food, when this is a reasonable answer to a question.

Stress

Phonetically, **stress** is the perceived prominence of one syllable over another; the prominence is due to an interplay of loudness, pitch, and duration. At the phonetic level, we can measure the factors contributing to the prominence and rank syllables in terms of levels of stress as we did for English in Chapter 5. Generally greater loudness or duration produce greater prominence. In most English accents, higher pitch also conveys prominence, but in the English of Northern Ireland and in Danish, lower pitch conveys prominence.

In the last decade, phonologists have explored the patterning of stress in many languages and have revealed a very rich and intricate part of certain languages. This section gives an introduction to some of this work. Our concern here is to show some of the basic ways in which stress patterns vary in languages and how linguists have attempted to account for that patterning. The approach taken here is somewhat similar to that of Halle and Vergnaud (1987).

Typically, in a word, one syllable stands out as more prominent than the others. This is true for all languages. Some languages have only one stress per word with the location determined by a general principle. In French stress falls on the ultima, with little variation in the relative prominence of the other syllables:

culture	/kylˈtyr/	'culture'
agrafer	/agraˈfe/	'staple'
epouvantable	/epuvɑ̃ˈtabl/	'terrible'
prononciation	/prɔnɔ̃sjaˈsjɔ̃/	'pronunciation'
electrocardiogramme	/elɛktrokardjɔˈgram/	'electrocardiogram'

In other languages, such as English, we find a pattern of alternating stresses. In *propaganda*, for example, the primary stress is on the penultimate syllable; there is, however, as well, a secondary stress on the first syllable /ˌpɹɑpəˈgændə/. In a longer word, such as *unreliability* [ˈʌnɹɪˌlajəˈbɪlɪti], there are two secondary stresses, on the first and third syllables as well. We observe then that in many words, English has a pattern of alternating stress, with some sort of stress on every other syllable.

In many languages, the position of stress is predictable and need not be indicated in the lexicon. In French, we can automatically stress the final syllable in every word. In Scots Gaelic, stress always falls on the first syllable of a word:

/ˈʃɛxəd̪/	*past*	/ˈmɔːn̪ʲə/	*peat*
/ˈbðebəd̪að/	*weaver*	/ˈpiːbəðɔxg/	*piping*
/ˈðʒixən̪ʲixəɣ/	*forgetting*	/ˈahəraxəɣ/	*changing*
/ˈʃaramɔnəxəɣ/	*preaching*		

Scots Gaelic

The patterning of stress, however, is frequently more complex than that found in French or Scots Gaelic. In many languages, a word has more than one stress. In Weri, a language of New Guinea, stress falls on odd-numbered syllables counting from the right. The rightmost stress is primary [ˈ]; the other stresses are secondary [ˌ].

ʊˌlʊaˈmit *mist* ˌakʊˌneteˈpal *times*

Weri

We can see that Weri has an alternating stress pattern – one syllable with stress, the next unstressed. Phonologists have analysed such patterns by dividing words into constituents called **feet**, each consisting of two syllables. In Weri, the feet are constructed by dividing the word into two-syllable units, starting at the right edge of the word and moving to the left. The division into feet is shown below by parentheses. The stressed syllable, or **head**, of each foot is indicated by an asterisk in the line above, called the **foot line**. Note that in words with an odd number of syllables (e.g., /ˌakʊˌneteˈpal/), the remaining syllable [a] (at the beginning of the word) forms a foot of its own. Such a foot, with fewer than the normal number of syllables, is said to be **degenerate**.

```
(     *) (     * )    (*) (    *) (    * )  foot
 ʊ – ˌlʊ – a – ˈmit   ˈa – kʊ-ˌne – te-ˈpal
```

We still have to account for the fact that the last stress is primary, but the preceding ones are secondary. We do this by constructing another line, the **word line**, above the foot line. The word line combines all the feet into a single unit and thus has only one set of parentheses. In order to make the stress of the last foot stronger than the others, we place an asterisk above the asterisk of the last foot. We can now interpret our analysis phonetically. A syllable with two asterisks receives primary stress, a syllable with one asterisk receives secondary stress, and a syllable with no asterisk is unstressed.

```
(               *)     (                  * )  word
(     *) (      *)     (*)  (     *) (    * )  foot
ʊ – ˌlʊ – a – ˈmit     ˈa – kʊ-ˌne – te-ˈpal
```

Comparing our analyses of Weri, French, and Scots Gaelic, we see that the feet of Weri have a fixed number of syllables (in our examples two); such feet are called **bounded**. We can also apply our system of analysis to French or to Scots Gaelic. In both languages, all the syllables of a word belong to a single foot. In French, the rightmost syllable receives an asterisk; in Scots Gaelic the leftmost syllable receives an asterisk. The feet of French and Scots Gaelic are **unbounded** in that they can have any number of syllables. In this book, we use the term *bounded* only to describe feet of two syllables.

```
(               *)     (  *              )  foot
e – pu – vɑ̃ – ˈtabl     ˈbɔ̃e – bə – dað
```

French **Scots Gaelic**

In both French and Weri, the rightmost syllable of a foot is the head, receiving stress; in Scots Gaelic, the leftmost syllable is the head. In Weri, we need a separate word line to distinguish between different levels of stress. In French and Scots Gaelic, the word line adds no new information.

If we now look at Maranungku, an Australian language, we find a pattern like Weri, but reversed; in Maranungku, stress falls on odd-numbered syllables counting from the left.

```
(*                    )    (*                           )  word
(*        )(*    )  (*)    (*       )  ( *      )  ( *    )  foot
1        2  3    4   5     1      2      3    4       5  6
ˈlaŋ – ka-ˌra -te – ˌti    ˈwe – le – ˌpe -ne – ˌman-ta
```

prawn *kind of duck*

Maranungku

We see that the foot in Maranungku is bounded, left-headed, and formed from left to right. Since primary stress is on the leftmost foot, the word is left-headed.

The observations that we just stated for Maranungku are called **stress parameters**; they govern the placement of stress. For each language, we have to establish the parameters. We have to determine if the feet are bounded or unbounded. Are the feet right-headed or left-headed? If the feet are bounded, we further have to determine the direction: are they established from left to right or right to left? And finally, is the word right- or left-headed? For the languages we have examined so far in this section, the parameters are shown in Table 14.2.

Table 14.2 Metrical parameters

	French	**Scots Gaelic**	**Weri**	**Maranungku**
bounded or **unbounded**	unbounded	unbounded	bounded	bounded
head of foot	right	left	right	left
direction	—	—	r → l	l → r
head of word	—	—	right	left

Extrametricality

In Polish, a word has only one stress falling on the penultimate syllable. The following examples show that stress moves as more syllables are added after the root:

hippopotamus	/hi-po-ˈpo-tam/	nominative singular
	/hi-po-po-ˈta-ma/	genitive singular
	/hi-po-po-ta-ˈma-mi/	instrumental plural

Polish

In Polish, we find only one unbounded foot, but it is not right-headed; rather, the stress falls one syllable back from the right end. Phonologists have introduced a parameter, called **extrametricality**, to account for such phenomena. We say that in Polish, the final syllable of a word is extrametrical and does not form part of a foot. We enclose an extrametrical syllable in angled brackets – < >.

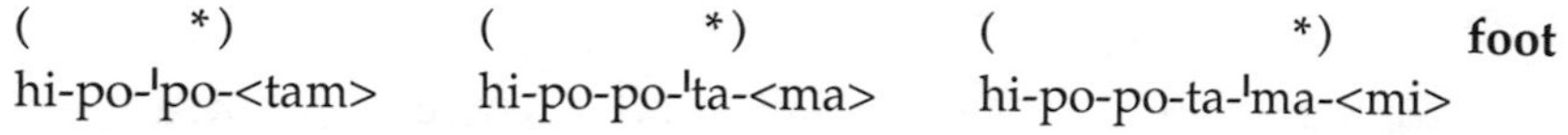

We can now state the parameters of Polish as:

a. The final syllable is extrametrical.
b. Feet are unbounded.
c. Feet are right-headed.

Extrametricality may look like a trick to get us out of a hard spot, but phonologists have found that extrametricality is an important concept in many languages. Note that only one syllable in a word may be extrametrical. Only the first or last syllable of a word can be extrametrical. Further, in a particular language, the extrametrical syllable is always the first syllable or the last one; it cannot be the first for some words and the last for others. Note that a degenerate foot arises when an extra syllable is left over at the end of foot-formation, whereas an extrametrical syllable is one that is overlooked at the beginning of foot-formation.

Koya (India; Tyler, 1969) is a language in which the internal nature of the syllable is important. In Koya, primary stress falls on the first syllable and secondary stress is found on every subsequent heavy syllable (i.e., having either a long vowel or a consonant in the coda). In the examples below, unbounded feet are constructed in the foot line. The leftmost syllable is given an asterisk, as is every heavy syllable. On the word level, an asterisk is added for the leftmost syllable. Thus, syllables with two asterisks receive primary stress; syllables with one asterisk receive secondary stress; and the others are unstressed.

(*)	(*)	(*)	**word**
(*)	(* *)	(* *)	**foot**
ˈnu – du – ru	ˈnu – ˌdur – ku	ˈee – ˌlaa – ɖi	
forehead	*foreheads*	*younger sister*	

(*)	(*)	(*)	**word**
(* *)	(* *)	(* *)	**foot**
ˈnaa – ˌtoɳ – te	ˈle – ˌdʒooɳ – ɖu	ˈmut – tʃa – ˌtoɳ – ɖu	
along with me	*young man*	*leper*	

(*)	(*)	(*)	**word**
(* * *)	(* * * *)	(* * *)	**foot**
ˈmeʈ -ˌtaat – ˌpor – ro	ˈpee – ˌtʃoo – ˌmin – ˌnaa – na	ˌken – ja – ˌkon – ˌtaa – na	
on the mountain	*I am starting*	*I will hear for myself*	

Koya

We can now state the parameters of Koya:

a. No extrametricality.
b. Unbounded feet.
c. Left-headed; heavy syllables are stressed.
d. Left to right.
e. Word: left-headed.

Emphatic and contrastive stress

Emphatic stress is often used to draw attention to a word or utterance. In the utterance *Mary has* two *cars*, by placing extra stress on *two*, a speaker can express surprise or definiteness. **Contrastive stress** is used to avoid a misinterpretation. Extra stress on *two* would then be used to avoid any confusion as to the number of cars Mary has. In English, the words *effect* and *affect* as nouns are both traditionally pronounced /əˈfɛkt/. To distinguish them, the pronunciations /ˈiˌfɛkt/ and /ˈæˌfɛkt/ are used; in fact these pronunciations are so commonly used, that for some speakers they have become used even in non-contrastive situations.

Intonation

Intonation is the use of pitch distinctively over a phrase. Whereas tone languages distinguish two lexical items by tone, such as /ná/ 'cow' and /nà/ 'spider' in Sherbro, intonation generally conveys different sorts of meaning. Intonational differences may distinguish statements from questions or commands; intonation may add a meaning such as doubt, politeness, or boredom.

Even in a language as widely studied as English, research into intonation has not produced a clear understanding of how it works. Nevertheless, Cruttenden (1986) showed that various intonational languages use intonations that have an overall falling pattern for certain purposes and intonations with an overall rising pattern for others.

Falling	*Rising*
Neutral statement	Tentative statement
Wh-question	Yes–No question
Command	Request

Try to find a native speaker of German, an intonational language, and compare the intonational patterns of the following English and German sentences.

Falling intonation

Neutral statement
My parents won't arrive until Monday.
Meine Eltern kommen erst am Montag an.

Wh-question
Where are you going now?
Wo gehen Sie jetzt hin?

Command
Be nice to each other!
Seid nett zueinander!

Rising intonation

Tentative statement

She's leaving today?
Reist sie heute vielleicht ab?

Yes–no question

Did the dog bite your leg?
Hat der Hund dir ins Bein gebißen?

Request

Would you please accompany us.
Möchten Sie bitte mitkommen.

(Wh-questions ask for a blank to be filled in; in English, they generally begin with words in *wh: who, what, where,* etc. Yes–no questions ask for a response of 'yes' or 'no'.) For me, although a falling intonation pattern with yes–no questions is common, a rising intonation is possible, particularly with contrastive meaning: 'Did the dog bite your *leg*?' (not your hand). See Chapter 5.

The attitudinal meaning of intonation can be exceedingly subtle. Very often, you will find various intonation patterns with slightly different nuances.

Intonation and tone languages

A tone language can have intonation just as a non-tonal language does. Consider the following utterances (Figure 14.21) from Hausa (Schuh, 1986). We see that Hausa has two register tones with downdrift. In the statement, the tones generally move from the middle to the lower portion of the speaker's pitch range (shown by the brackets). In the question form, two

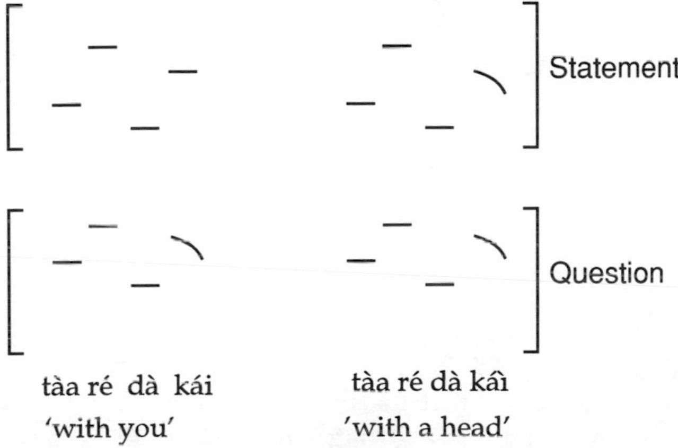

Figure 14.21 Statement and question in Hausa

things happen: (1) the final high syllable falls; and (2) the entire utterance is in the upper part of the range with downdrift suspended. The second utterance is similar, except that the final syllable falls even in the statement.

Rhythm and rate

We have already mentioned three tendencies in rhythm. Some languages, such as French, tend to pronounce syllables with approximately the same duration; these are called **syllable-timed**. Others, such as English, tend to space the stresses at approximately even intervals; these are called **stress-timed**. Still other languages, such as Japanese, can be called **mora-timed**. For all of these types, it must be understood that these terms describe tendencies. Many other factors complicate the situation. Contrastive and emphatic stress may provide extra length to certain elements. There is a tendency in many languages to lengthen the first and/or last syllable of an utterance.

People obviously vary the rate of speech as they speak. The average is about five syllables per second (Laver, 1994). A rapid rate often suggests excitement or impatience. Slower speech is used when the speaker is tired, uncertain, or deliberate. In gathering our thoughts, we often pause. We can leave the pause empty or, particularly if we are concerned not to lose our turn in the conversation, we insert a hesitation noise such as [mː] or [ʌː].

In speaking faster, we do not necessarily speed everything up evenly. There is a tendency to shorten the voiced portions more than the voiceless portions. Further, there is some evidence that languages vary in how faster rates of speech are produced (Rogers, 1992): Mongolian tends primarily to shorten the voiced portions, whereas Turkish has more general shortening. Maintaining contrastive cues may also be a factor in shortening.

Speaking faster often involves certain changes in style. Compare the following differences in the sentence *I do not know*. In most of these further variations could be found with different stress patterns. The accent here is GA.

[¬aj ˌdu¬nɑt ˈnow]
[¬aj də ˌnɑt ˈnow]
[¬aj ˌdownt ˈnow]
[¬aj ˌdown ˈnow]
[¬aj ˌdõw ˈnow]
[ˌaj də̃ ˈnow]
[ˌaj ¬õw ˈnow]
[ˌaj ə̃ ˈnow]
[ˌãw̃ ˈnow]

In this particular sentence, we see that the main verb [now] maintains its basic form throughout, and there is a strong tendency for the subject pronoun [aj] to do so as well. The stylistic shortening takes place in the auxiliary verb *do* and the negative particle. The negative particle tends to maintain either a phoneme /n/ or nasalisation.

Note that this type of variation does not represent carelessness; if anything, it can be produced only by paying considerable attention to linguistic rules. More formal situations call for forms higher on the list; more casual situations call for forms lower on the list. People often object when someone uses a socially inappropriate form. In school, a relatively formal situation, to reply [ˌãw̃ ˈnow] to a question may be interpreted as rude or slovenly. On the other hand, if, in a movie, someone is telephoned in the middle of the night and replies in a sleepy voice [ˍaj ˌdu ˍnɑt ˈnow], this pronunciation is likely to be interpreted as annoyance at being awakened or bad acting.

Technical terms

- acute accent
- antepenult
  - antepenultimate syllable
- bounded
- breve
- chest pulse
- circumflex accent
- closed syllable
- coda
- contour tone
- degenerate
- downdrift
- downstep
- external intercostals
- extrametrical
- head
- foot
  - foot line
- geminate
- grave accent
- haček
- heavy syllable
- intonation
- length
- light syllable
- macron
- mora (moræ)
  - moraic
- nucleus
- onset
- open syllable
- parameter
- penult
  - penultimate syllable
- pitch
- pitch accent
- register tone
- rhyme
- segment
- sonority
  - sonority curve
- stress
  - stress languages
  - stress parameter
- suprasegmental
- syllabic consonants
- syllable
- timing
  - stress-timed
  - syllable-timed
  - mora-timed
- tone
  - tone language
- ultima
  - ultimate syllable
- unbounded
- upstep
- word line
  - word stress

Exercises

Basic

1 Tone. Practise these.

bàbá	sósò	fìfí	gúgù	nèlé	θázà
ʒɔ̀kɔ̀	xɛ̀ŋú	ɸéʔɔ̀	hàðɛ̀	ɹòdʒí	jáʃú

Now try these. Try each form with the various tone patterns.

fʊlikɑ   dɔɣiɸu   naʃeðɛ

e.g.: fʊ̀lìkɑ́ fʊ́líkɑ̀ fʊ́lìkɑ́ fʊ̀líkɑ̀ etc.

ˋ ˋ ˊ   ˊ ˊ ˋ   ˊ ˋ ˊ   ˋ ˊ ˋ   ˋ ˊ ˊ   ˊ ˋ ˋ

ˋ ˋ ˋ   ˋ ˊ ˋ   ˋ ˊ ˊ   ˊ ˊ ˊ   ˊ ˋ ˊ   ˋ ˊ ˋ

Now try saying these:

nɯilùdʒà   ɣɛ̀ʃɔ́@ɹi   wɛ̀ˀàtʃú   ɹ̥ɛ́kázɔ́

ɣɑ̀hèɸò   ŋèpóˀɑ̀   βàfì@ɔ̀   ɡóðéxɑ̀

2 The mid tone is a level tone half way between a high tone and a low one; it is marked [¯]. Pronounce [lafiku] with each of the tone patterns below.

e.g.: [láfíkú – láfīkú], etc.

ˊ ˊ ˊ   ˊ – ˊ   ˊ – –   ˊ – ˊ   ˊ – –   ˊ ˊ –

ˋ ˋ ˋ   ˋ – ˊ   ˋ – –   ˋ – ˋ   ˋ – –   ˋ ˋ –

ˊ – ˋ   ˋ – ˊ   – – ˊ   – – –   – – ˋ   – – –

– ˋ –   – ˋ ˊ   ˋ – ˊ   ˊ – ˋ   – ˋ ˊ   – ˊ ˋ

Similarly, pronounce [bomeˀikʌ] with each of the tone patterns below:

e.g.: [bómēˀìkʌ̀ – bōméˀíkʌ́], etc.

ˊ – ˋ ˋ   – ˊ ˊ ˊ   ˋ ˋ ˋ ˋ   – ˋ ˊ ˋ   ˋ – ˊ ˊ

ˊ ˊ ˋ ˋ   – ˊ – ˋ   – ˊ – ˋ   ˊ ˊ ˊ –   ˋ – – ˊ

ˊ – – ˋ   ˋ ˊ – –   – ˊ – ˊ   – ˊ – ˊ   ˊ ˋ – ˊ

– ˊ ˊ ˋ   ˋ – ˋ ˊ   – – ˋ ˋ   ˋ ˊ ˋ –   – ˊ – ˋ

Take your time in practising. Ability with tone is not developed overnight. Your progress will be gradual, not dramatic. Just try to improve; don't try to compete with others. Some rather annoying people seem naturally better at tone than the rest of us – maybe they have ingrown toenails as compensation.

3 Practise saying [fomekinɑ] with the following tones:

e.g.: fómèkínɑ̀

ˊ ˋ ˊ ˋ   ˊ ˊ ˊ ˋ   ˊ ˊ ˋ ˊ   ˊ ˊ ˋ ˋ

ˊ ˋ ˊ ˊ   ˊ ˋ ˊ ˋ   ˊ ˋ ˋ ˊ   ˊ ˋ ˋ ˋ

ˋ ˊ ˊ ˊ   ˋ ˊ ˊ ˋ   ˋ ˊ ˋ ˊ   ˋ ˊ ˋ ˋ

ˋ ˋ ˊ ˊ   ˋ ˋ ˊ ˋ   ˋ ˋ ˋ ˊ   ˋ ˋ ˋ ˋ

Try these:

tíɣáɸɛ̀s̠ù   tʒɔ́l̥éɟjɔ̀dɔ̀   sɑ̀ðɛ̀l̠ɔ́ŋɑ̀   vòpɸìçáɹ̥ú

jɛ̀ˀéçódé   ɡáɟɛ̀bvùxɔ́   hèʃít̠s̠ɛ́ɹ̥ɑ̀   hjúd̠ðíʒóβè

4 Moving tones fall from high to low or rise from low to high. Falling tones are shown with [ˆ] over the vowel, and rising tones with [ˇ].

First practise a long fall [ɑ̂]:

ɑ̂   ɑ̂   ɑ̂   ɑ̂

î   ê   ɛ̂   â   ɑ̂   ɔ̂   ô   û

bî   bê   bɛ̂   bâ   bɑ̂   bɔ̂   bô   bû

And now a long rise [ǎ]:

ǎ	ǎ	ǎ	ǎ				
ǐ	ě	ɛ̌	ǎ	ɑ̌	ɔ̌	ǒ	ǔ
bǐ	bě	bɛ̌	bǎ	bɑ̌	bɔ̌	bǒ	bǔ

Now try:

ɹékɛ̂	ɲɔ̀ɸǒ	wàsǐ	fɛ́lǔ
ɱ̥ɔ̀z̠ǎ	çòkɛ̂	fɑ̀ɣɯ́	βɛ́ʝɔ̂

Now try [dolifu] with each of the following tone patterns:

e.g.: dòlǐfú dólífú dólífû

´ ˇ `	´ ´ ´	´ ´ ^	´ ^ ˇ	^ ˇ ´
` ˇ ´	ˇ ´ `	ˇ ` ´	ˇ ´ `	ˇ ´ ^
^ ` ˇ	´ ` ^	ˇ ^ ˇ	` ` ^	´ ´ ˇ
^ ^ `	` ˇ ˇ	^ ^ ^	ˇ ˇ ˇ	` ˇ ˇ

Advanced

5 Vowel length

a aː	o oː	u uː	ɛ ɛː	iː i	uː u	ɑː ɑ	eː e
ɔpɔː	akaː	oːdo	efeː	eːfe	ɛʃɛː	ɑːbɑ	idiː
bɛːvɔ	pufaː	tɑːθɛː	dɑðaː	tiːsɔː	dizuː	kaxe	goːɣeː

6 Long consonants. How do you pronounce *fourteen* and *eighteen*? Consider the length of the [t] in these words carefully. Practise the following:

nː	lː	ɹː	sː	mː
ɑnɑ	ɑnːɑ	olːo	oːloː	ɛɹɛː
ibːu	ɑːgo	ɛkːa	esːu	ɤɣːo

Try the following pairs of short and long consonants in Italian:

/fato/	*fate*	/fatto/	*done*
/kade/	*he falls*	/kadde/	*he fell*
/fola/	*fable*	/folla/	*crowd*
/nono/	*ninth*	/nonno/	*grandfather*

7 Yoruba (Nigeria; Bamgbose, 1966) is a register tone language with three levels. High tone is marked by [´], low tone by [`], and mid tone is unmarked. Practise the single words first, and then the sentences. Be sure to take your time; speak slowly at first, exaggerating the tones. A useful exercise is to tape record yourself, and then to transcribe the tones of your speech. Then compare your transcription with the original below. After doing this a few times, you should improve in both your ability and your confidence at producing and transcribing tones.

/iʃɛ́/	*work*	/ìʃɛ́/	*poverty*
/awo/	*cult*	/àwo/	*plate*
/ɔwɔ̀/	*broom*	/ɔ̀wɔ̀/	*respect*

àwɔn èǹjɔn wa àɡ͡bɛ̀ ni wɔ́n	*Our people are farmers*
wɔ́n raʃɔ tó pɔ̀ ʃùɡ͡bɔ́n wɔn	*They bought many cloths,*
ɔ̀ rówó sɔn	*but they could not pay for them.*
ilé tó tóbi tó lɛ́wà tó sì dára	*A big, fine and good house*
wɔ́n rɛja ɛrɔn àtɛ̀fɔ́	*They bought fish, meat, and vegetables.*
wɔn ɔ̀ fɛ́kó ʃòfò	*They do not want it; let it be wasted.*

8 In the following words, try to control stress and pitch separately. The accents indicate tone.

ˈlómè	ˈfákìsɛ̀	fàˈkísɛ̀	ˈlòmé	ˈfàkísɛ̀	fàˈkìsɛ
lòˈmé	ˈfàkísɛ́	fáˈkísɛ̀	lóˈmè	ˈfàkísɛ́	fáˈkìsɛ́

9 Given the following parameters, construct foot and word lines for the words below, and assign the proper stress.

bounded (two syllables to a foot) *ultima extrametrical*
right-headed foot *right to left*
left-headed word

lamikɛ defoniʃupanikɔ tozɛ makɔɲizu

10 From the forms below, describe the parameters necessary to account for stress in this language.

dɔnífuŋ lemnókɔnne sɔné rizɛ́nomvusʌŋ

11 From the forms below, describe the parameters necessary to account for stress in this language.

lɛ́ʒupàŋ ŋɔfúlzimtɛ̀ tídʒolèðultɛ̀ fumé

12 Practise aspiration and retroflex consonants in Bengali:

/kal/	*tomorrow*	/kʰal/	*canal*
/gal/	*cheek*	/gʰal/	*wounded*
/bag/	*behind part*	/bagʰ/	*tiger*
/ʃap/	*snake*	/ʃapʰ/	*clean*
/sɒtʰa/	*proposition*	/ʃudʰu/	*only*
/dɔpʰtor/	*office*	/skʰlɔlon/	*fault*
/stʰir/	*quiet*	/spʰuliŋgo/	*sport*
/ʈat/	*mat*	/tat/	*heat*
/ɖan/	*right side*	/dan/	*gift*
/beɖ/	*flower bed*	/bed/	*Vedas*

13 The tonal system of Cantonese (a dialect of Chinese spoken in southern China, including Hong Kong) is very complex. It has at least six tones. Practise the following words.

a. 53		**b.** 35		**c.** 33	
/ka/	*home*	/ka/	*false*	/ka/	*marry*
/saj/	*west*	/saj/	*wash*	/saj/	*small*
/kaw/	*ditch*	/kaw/	*nine*	/kaw/	*enough*
/kam/	*present*	/kam/	*so (manner)*	/kam/	*so (degree)*
/pin/	*border*	/pin/	*flat, thin*	/pin/	*change*
/fan/	*divide*	/fan/	*powder*	/fan/	*advise*

d. 21		**e.** 23		**f.** 22	
/ma/	*hemp*	/ma/	*horse*	/ma/	*scold*
/laj/	*come*	/laj/	*propriety*	/laj/	*example*
/lam/	*blue*	/lam/	*behold*	/lam/	*warship*
/jyn/	*round*	/jyn/	*far*	/jyn/	*court*
/fan/	*grave*	/fan/	*excited*	/fan/	*share*

14 Thai distinguishes voiced, plain voiceless, and aspirated voiceless stops and fricatives:

/p^{h}àa/	*split*	/t^{h}am/	*do*	/k^{h}àt/	*interrupt*
/pàa/	*forest*	/tam/	*pound*	/kàt/	*bite*
/bàa/	*shoulder*	/dam/	*black*		
/zãn/	*levitation*	/zauŋ/	*edge*		
/sãn/	*example*	/sauŋ/	*harp*		
/s^{h}ãn/	*rice*	/s^{h}auŋ/	*winter*		

15 Prenasalised consonants. Practise saying the following words from Central Carrier (an Athabaskan language, spoken in British Columbia in Canada) with nasal onset. At first, make the nasal a separate syllable: [m – bət]. Then try to make the nasal a part of the same syllable as the following oral stop: [mbət].

/mbət/	*your stomach*	/ndaj/	*what*
/ntʃa/	*big*	/ŋgan/	*your arm*
/ŋgeni/	*that*	/ŋ^{w}g^{w}ət/	*your knee*

Try the following words from Gbeya (Central African Republic; Samarin, 1966).

/ba/	*to take*	/mba/	*to greet*
/dak/	*to extract*	/ndak/	*to chase*
/guri/	*to smoke meat*	/ŋguti/	*to burst (intr)*
/nɔ/	*to drink*	/ndɔ/	*to have sexual intercourse*
/ŋ͡mãj/	*to split*	/ŋ͡mg͡ban/	*to uproot*

Appendix A

English consonantal allophones

The following list of English allophones, although extensive, describes only the more common variations in RP and GA English. Speakers of other accents will obviously have allophonic variations different from those shown here. As well, even within a single accent area, individuals often have personal variations.

For more details on the production and occurrence of the various allophones, consult the relevant section in Chapter 3. Unless noted, the descriptions below apply to both RP and GA.

/p/ voiceless bilabial stop

aspirated	[pʰ]	initially in stressed syllables;	*pay, appear*
		finally	*stop*
unaspirated	[p]	after syllable-initial /s/;	*spy, spot*
		initially in weakly stressed syllables;	*upper, pyjamas*
		finally	*stop*
no release	[p˺]	before /b p/	*chipboard, rippoint*
inaudible release	[p˺]	finally;	*stop*
		before other stop	*apt, ripcord*
nasal release	[pm]	before /m/	*topmast*
nasal onset	[mp]	after /m/	*ramp, lumpy*

Some RP speakers reinforce syllable final /p/ with a glottal stop as [ˀ͡p].

/b/ voiced bilabial stop

partially voiceless	[#b̥b], [bb̥#]	at edge of phrase	*bun, bet, boat*
			cob, ebb, robe
voiced	[b]	medially	*lobby*
no release	[b˺]	before /b p/	*ribpoint, scrubboard*
inaudible release	[b˺]	before other stop	*rubbed, tubeguard*
nasal release	[bm]	before /m/	*submarine*
nasal onset	[mb]	after /m/	*lumber*

/t/ voiceless alveolar stop

aspirated	[tʰ]	initially in stressed syllables; finally	*toy, entire* *write*
unaspirated	[t]	after syllable-initial /s/; finally	*sty* *write*
GA		syllable-initial in unstressed syllables, initially and after obstruents	*tobacco, actor*
RP		initially in weakly stressed syllables	*tobacco, actor, dirty, winter, bottom, metal*
RP glottalised	[ʔ͡t]	medially and finally	*mat, hitting, city, sent*
no release	[t̚]	before /t d/	*eight times, hot dog*
GA: inaudible release	[t̚]	finally; before other stop	*write* *Atkins, at best*
nasal release	[tn tn̩]	before /n/	*Bittner, button*
nasal onset	[nt]	after/n/	*went*
lateral release	[tl]	before /l/	*butler*
lateral onset	[lt]	after /l/	*belt, faulty*
GA tap	[ɾ]	at beginning of non-initial unstressed syllables after vowels and /ɹ/	*city, writer, dirty, barter*
GA tap with nasal release	[ɾm̩]	before syllabic [m̩]	*bottom*
GA nasal tap	[ɾ̃]	after /n/, at beginning of unstressed syllable	*winter, flinty*
GA tap with lateral release	[ɾl̩]	before syllabic [ɫ̩]	*rattle, metal*
glottalised	[ʔ͡t]	before syllabic [n̩]	*button*
dental	[t̪]	before [θ ð]	*eighth, at three*
GA slightly retroflexed	[ʈ]	after /ɹ/	*hurt, cart*

Speakers show a fair bit of variation in the allophones of /t/. Some RP speakers reinforce non-initial /t/ with a glottal stop as [ʔ͡t]. Some GA speakers replace taps with voiced stops.

/d/ voiced alveolar stop

partially voiceless	[#d̥d], [dd̥#]	at edge of phrase	*debt, dog, do* *add, odd, Ed*
voiced	[d]	medially	*ready*
no release	[d̚]	before /d t/	*Ed did, add two*
inaudible release	[d̚]	before other stops	*redcap, Edgar*
nasal release	[dn dn̩]	before /n/	*Sidney, sudden*
nasal onset	[nd]	after /n/	*bend*
lateral release	[dl dl̩]	before /l/	*bedlam, curdle*
lateral onset	[ld]	after /l/	*weld*
dental	[d̪]	before / θ ð/	*width, add them*
slightly retroflexed	[ɖ]	after /ɹ/	*bird, card*

/k/ voiceless velar stop

aspirated		initially in stressed syllables	
. . . advanced	[k̟ʰ]	. . . before front vowels	*keep, kin, cane*
. . . not advanced	[kʰ]	. . . before other vowels;	*cook, cot, cone, cut*
		finally	*lack, luck*
unaspirated		after /s/ in same syllable; medially, in weakly stressed syllables	
. . . advanced	[k̟]	. . . before front vowels	*skin, lucky*
. . . not advanced	[k]	. . . before back vowels; finally	*scan, luck*
no release	[k̚]	before /g k/	*sick girl, stoke coal*
inaudible release	[k̚]	finally;	*stack*
		before other stops	*deck post, sock drawer*
nasal release	[kŋ̍]	before nasals, particularly in casual speech	*bacon*
nasal onset	[ŋk]	after /ŋ/	*drink*

Some RP speakers reinforce syllable final /k/ with a glottal stop as [ʔ͡k].

/g/ voiced velar stop

partially voiceless		initially	
. . . advanced	[#g̟̊g]	before front vowels	*gear, geld, gale*
. . . not advanced	[#g̊g]	before other vowels	*good, got, gum, go*
	[gg̊#]	finally	*egg, dog, rug*

voiced		medially	
. . . advanced	[g̟]	before front vowels	*muggy*
. . . not advanced	[g]	before other vowels	*rugger*
no release	[g˺]	before /g k/	*big game, eggcup*
inaudible release	[g˺]	before other stops	*nagged, bagpipes*

/f/ voiceless labiodental fricative

	[f]	in all positions	*foul, suffer, enough*

/v/ voiced labiodental fricative

partially voiceless	[#v̥v]	at edge of word	*van, vote, Vince*
	[vv̥#]		*love, sieve, salve*
voiced	[v]	medially	*having, grovel*

/θ/ voiceless dental fricative

	[θ]	in all positions	*thin, ether, smith*

/ð/ voiced dental fricative

partially voiceless	[#ð̥ð]	at edge of word	*then, that, those*
	[ðð̥#]		*seethe, writhe*
voiced	[ð]	medially	*father, southern*

/s/ voiceless alveolar fricative

alveolar	[s]	in all positions	*see, lesser, fuss*

/z/ voiced alveolar fricative

partially voiceless	[#z̥z]	at edge of word	*zeal, zip, zoo*
	[zz̥#]		*ease, close, raise*
voiced	[z]	medially	*gazing, easy*

/ʃ/ voiceless postalveolar fricative

rounded	[ʃʷ]	in all positions	*shin, fissure, mesh*

/ʒ/ voiced postalveolar fricative

partially voiceless	[#ʒ̊ʷʒʷ]	at edge of word;	*gigue, genre, Giles*
rounded	[ʒʷʒ̊ʷ#]		*beige, rouge, garage*
voiced rounded	[ʒʷ]	medially	*vision, pleasure*

The degree of rounding of /ʃ/ and /ʒ/ varies among speakers.

/h/ voiceless vowel

voiceless vowel, same quality as following vowel	[h]	initially	*hello, hot, hip, hung*
breathy voiced, same quality as following vowel	[ɦ]	medially	*ahead, anyhow, ahoy*
voiceless palatal glide	[ç]	/hj/	*huge, Hugh*

/tʃ/ voiceless postalveolar affricate

rounded	[tʃʷ]	all positions	*chin, watch, nature*

Some RP speakers reinforce syllable final /tʃ/ with a glottal stop as [ʔ͡tʃ].

/dʒ/ voiced postalveolar affricate

rounded	[dʒʷ]	in all positions	
partially voiceless	[#d̥ʒ]	at edge of word	*gem, jug, Jones*
	[d#]		*edge, age, gouge*
voiced	[dʒʷ]	medially	*logic, fragile*

The degree of rounding of /tʃ/ and /dʒ/ varies among speakers.

/m/ bilabial nasal

voiced	[m]	in all positions	*much, simmer, ram*
unreleased	[m̚]	before bilabials	*number, simper, some more*

/n/ alveolar nasal

voiced	[n]	in all positions	*nut, sinner, ran*
unreleased	[n̚]	before /d, n/	*sander, run now, some more*
syllabic	[n̩]	after consonant	*sudden, button, prison*
dental	[n̪]	before /θ, ð/	*tenth, in the night*

/ŋ/ velar nasal

voiced	[ŋ]	medially and finally	*singer, rang*
unreleased	[ŋ̚]	before /k, g/	*sinker, finger*
syllabic	[ŋ̍]	after /k, g/ in casual speech	*bacon, Fagan*

/l/ alveolar lateral

Prevocalically, the phoneme /l/ has two major classes of allophones: clear [l] before front vowels, and dark [ɫ] before back vowels.

Clear [l]

voiceless	[l̥]	after aspirated stops	*play, clay, complain, incline*
partially voiceless	[l̥l]	after syllable-initial /s f θ ʃ/	*slip, athlete, Schlitz*
voiced	[l]	initially; medially, in weakly stressed syllables after a stop	*lie, litre, supplement, *settler, *circling, *fondling*

**Some words vary as to whether the /l/ is syllabic or not:*

[fɒnd-lɪŋ ~ fɒn-dl̩-lɪŋ ~ fɒn-də-ɫɪŋ] GA [fand-].

Dark [ɫ]

partially voiceless	[ɫ̥]	finally; before a voiceless consonant	*well, pile, fool milk, dealt, elf*
voiced	[ɫ]	after a vowel, before voiced consonant	*feels, twelve, weld*
syllabic	[ɫ̩]	finally, after a consonant	*table, chisel, fondle*
dental	[ɫ̪]	before /θ ð/	*filth, well then*

/ɹ/ retroflex approximant

rounded voiced	[ɹʷ]	prevocalic, syllable-initial	*red, rotten*
voiced postalveolar with retroflexion	[ʒʷ]	after syllable-initial /d/	*dream, Andrew*
voiceless	[ɹ̥ʷ]	after aspirated /p k/	*pray, tray, crawl*
postalveolar with retroflexion	[ʃ̰ʷ]	after syllable-initial /t/	*tree, sentry*
GA unrounded voiced	[ɹ]	postvocalic	*car, purring*

/j/ palatal glide

voiceless	[j̊]	after aspirated /p k/	*pure, cute*
voiced	[j]	all other positions	*yes, beauty, bay*

See also /hj/ under /h/.

/w/ voiced labial-velar glide

voiceless	[ʍ]	after aspirated /p t k/	*pueblo, twin, quick*
voiced	[w]	all other positions	*wet, dwell, Gwen, know, now*

/ʍ/ voiceless labial-velar glide GA only

voiceless	[ʍ]	initially and medially	*when, anywhere*

Appendix B

Glossary

Abdominal muscles *n.* Muscles of the lower trunk used in expelling air from the lungs.

Accent *n.* (1) Stress: *The accent is on the second syllable.* (2) A phonetic dialect: *an Australian accent.* (3) A diacritic, particularly a grave, acute, or circumflex accent [´ ` ˆ].

Accidental gap *n.* See **gap.**

Acoustic *adj.* Referring to the physical nature of sound. —**Acoustics** *n.* The study of sound. —**Acoustic phonetics** *n.* The study of the physical properties of sounds used in human language.

Active theory *n.* A theory of hearing which holds that perception involves active participation of the hearer's brain and knowledge of the language.

Acute accent *n.* The superscript diacritic [´], used to indicate a high tone or a primary stress.

Adam's apple *n.* The forward protrusion of the neck just below the chin, formed by the angle of the thyroid cartilage.

Advanced *adj.* Referring to a sound made farther to the front of the vocal tract than another or than usual: *an advanced [g].* Diacritic is [̟]. Cf. **retracted.**

Affricate /ˈæfɹikət/ *n.* A sound consisting of a stop followed by a homorganic fricative, often considered a single phonological unit; e.g., [pf tʃ gɣ]. —**Affrication** *n.* —**Affricated** *adj.*

Air pressure *n.* The force exerted by air on a surface.

Air stream *n.* A flow of air used to produce sounds. —**Air stream mechanism** *n.* The mechanism producing the air stream, e.g., **pulmonic, glottalic, velaric.**

Allophone /ˈæləˌfəwn/ GA /ˈæləˌfown/ *n.* A variant of a phoneme. —**Allophonic** *adj.*

Alveolar /ˌælˈviələ/ GA /-ləɹ/ *adj.* Having an articulation with the tip or blade of the tongue at the alveolar ridge. —**Alveolar ridge** *n.* The bony ridge immediately behind the upper teeth. —**Alveolo-** *combining form.*

Alveolo-palatal *adj.* Having an articulation with the blade of the tongue at the very forward portion of the palate.

Alveolus /ˌælˈviələs/, *pl.* **alveoli** /ˌælˈviəli/ *n.* An air sac in the lungs.

Ambisyllabicity principle *n.* A principle of syllabification whereby, in an unstressed syllable, the first consonant of the onset also serves as the coda of the preceding syllable. —**Ambisyllabic** *adj.*

Amplitude *n.* A property of a wave; in acoustics, normally measured as variation in the air pressure. Variations in amplitude are perceived as changes in loudness. Cf. **intensity**.

Antepenultimate syllable *n.* The third-last syllable of a word; same as **antepenult**.

Anticipatory *adj.* Referring to changes in which a later element influences an earlier one; commonly applied to **assimilation** and **dissimilation**. Same as **regressive**. —**Anticipatory** (or **regressive**) **assimilation** *n.* The assimilation of an earlier sound to a later one; e.g., in a sequence XY, X changes to become more like Y. Cf. **progressive**.

Apex /ˈejpɛks/ *n.* The tip of the tongue. —**Apical** /ˈæpikəl/ *adj.* —**Apico-** *combining form*: **apico-dental, apico-alveolar**.

Apico-alveolar *adj.* Having an articulation involving the tip of the tongue and the alveolar ridge.

Apico-dental *adj.* Having an articulation involving the tip of the tongue and the upper teeth.

Approximant *n.* A manner of articulation with an opening less than that of a vowel and greater than that of a fricative. Approximants are made without a turbulent air stream; they include **liquids** and **glides**.

Arrhotic /əˈɹəwtik/ GA /əˈɹowɾik/ *adj.* In English, referring to accents, such as RP, which have lost codal /ɹ/. See **rhotic**.

Articulation *n.* The movement of the organs, especially of the upper vocal tract, so as to form different sounds. —**Articulate** *v.* —**Articulator** *n.* An organ involved in articulation. The **upper articulators** are the upper lip, upper teeth, palate, velum, uvula, and posterior pharyngeal wall. The **lower articulators** are the lower lip and the various parts of the tongue. —**Articulatory** *adj.* —**Articulatory phonetics** *n.* The branch of phonetics dealing with how sounds are made. See **auditory** and **acoustic phonetics**. —**Primary articulation** *n.* The closest constriction in a consonant. —**Secondary articulation** *n.* The second closest constriction in a consonant: e.g., **palatalised, velarised.** —**Double articulation** *n.* An articulation with two equally closed constrictions: e.g., [k͡p].

Arytenoid cartilages RP /ˌæɹɪˈtinɔjd/, GA /ˌɛɹɪˈtinɔjd/ also /əˈɹɪtənɔjd/ *n.* Two pyramid-shaped cartilages of the larynx situated on the cricoid cartilage, and forming the rear point of attachment for the vocal folds.

Ascender *n.* A symbol extending above the x-height line.

Aspiration *n.* A period of voicelessness following a consonant, usually accompanied by a greater air pressure; written as [ʰ]: e.g., [pʰ tʰ kʰ]. —**Aspirate** /ˈæspɪˌɹejt/ *v.* —**Aspirated** *adj.* —**Aspirate** /ˈæspɪrət/ *n.* An aspirated consonant.

Assimilation /əˌsɪməˈlejʃən/ *n.* A process whereby one sound becomes more like another. See **anticipatory assimilation** and **progressive assimilation**. —**Assimilate** /əˈsɪməˌlejt/ *v.* To become more like another sound.

Auditory *adj.* Referring to hearing. —**Auditory phonetics** *n.* The branch of phonetics dealing with hearing and perception.

Back *n.* The dorsum of the tongue; the rear portion of the horizontal surface of the tongue. —*adj.* (1) **Retracted**: *a back [k].* (2) Referring to a vowel or glide made in the back portion of the vowel area: e.g., [ɑ ʌ ɯ w]. Cf. **front** and **central**.

Base line *n.* The imaginary line along the lower edge of symbols such as [x e s f].

Bernoulli Principle /bəˈnuli/ GA /bəɹ-/ *n.* An observation of physics that objects at the edge of a moving stream tend to move to the centre of the stream; the faster the flow of the stream, the faster the objects move to the centre. More precisely, the pressure perpendicular to the mid-line of a moving stream is inversely proportional to the velocity of the stream.

Bilabial *adj.* Having an articulation involving both lips, as in the sounds [p b m ɸ ɓ].

Blade *n.* The surface of the tongue just behind the tip, also called the *lamina.*

Bounded foot *n.* In metrical theory, a foot having a constraint on the number of syllables allowed. Typically, a bounded foot has two syllables.

Boyle's Law *n.* A principle of physics that, in a closed container, the pressure of a gas varies inversely with the volume.

Breathy voice *n.* An adjustment of the glottis, occasionally used in language, made with the vocal folds vibrating, but with considerable escape of air. —**Breathy voiced** *adj.*

Breve /bɹiv/ *n.* The superscript diacritic [˘], occasionally used to mark (1) short vowels, (2) unstressed vowels, or (3) a falling-rising tone.

Broad transcription *n.* A transcription with little or no phonetic detail. A **phonemic transcription** is a broad transcription. See **narrow transcription**.

Bronchus /ˈbɹɒŋkəs/ GA /ˈbɹɑŋkəs/, *pl.* **bronchi** *n.* A tube leading from the trachea to the lungs.

Bunched-[ɹ] *n.* In English, an /ɹ/ made with the tongue tip down and the body of the tongue drawn up and back. Cf. **retroflexed-/ɹ/**.

C *n.* An abbreviation for **consonant**.

Canadian raising *n.* The occurrence of the diphthongs [ʌw] and [ʌj] before voiceless consonants, rather than [aw] or [aj]; typical of most Canadian accents.

Cardinal vowel. *n.* An arbitrary reference point for describing vowel quality. —**Cardinal vowel theory** *n.* A theory of describing vowels by locating them in relation to the cardinal vowels.

Cartilage *n.* A firm, flexible type of tissue such as that found in the larynx or outer ear. —**Cartilagenous glottis** *n.* The portion of the glottis found between the arytenoid cartilages. See **ligamental glottis**.

Central *adj.* (1) Referring to a vowel made in the central portion of the vowel area: e.g., [ə ɨ ʉ]. (2) Referring to a vowel made more to the centre of the vowel area than another or than usual: *a central [e]*. See **front**, **back**, and **mid**. (3) Not lateral; referring to a manner of articulation with the air passing out through the centre of the vocal tract.

Chest pulse *n.* According to R. H. Stetson, a contraction of the rib cage expelling air from the lungs and responsible for the production of a syllable; Stetson's theory is not generally in favour today.

Circumflex accent *n.* The superscript diacritic [ˆ], sometimes used to mark a falling tone.

Clear [l] *n.* A type of [l] with the quality of a front vowel. See **dark** [ɫ].

Click *n.* An ingressive velaric stop; e.g., [ʘ | ! ǂ ||].

Close *adj.* Having a narrow opening; cf. **open**. —**Close vowel** *n.* A high vowel.

Closed syllable *n.* A syllable ending in a consonant.

Cluster *n.* A sequence of sounds, e.g., [ks] is a consonant cluster.

Coda *n.* A part of a syllable, consisting of the consonants following the nucleus. —**Codal** *adj.*

Complementary distribution *n.* In phonological theory, two sounds are in complementary distribution if neither occurs in any environments in which the other occurs. Cf. **contrastive distribution** and **free variation**.

Complex repetitive wave *n.* A wave with a repeating waveform and a more complex shape than that of a simple **sine wave**.

Consonant *n.* A sound with an opening less than that of a vowel. Consonants include **obstruents**, **approximants**, and **nasals**; they typically function as the onset or coda of a syllable.

Contextual length *n.* Length which is dependent on the context. See **inherent length**.

Continuant *adj.* A distinctive feature defining the class of sounds in which air flows out of the oral cavity. **Vowels**, **approximants**, and **fricatives** are continuant sounds.

Contour tone language *n.* A language with a system of moving tones.

Contrastive distribution *n.* In phonological theory, two sounds are in contrastive distribution if they occur in the same environment, potentially forming a difference of meaning. Cf. **complementary distribution** and **free variation**. —**Contrast** *v.* To be in contrastive distribution, to form a distinction of meaning.

Coronal RP /ˈkɔɹənəl/ GA also /kəˈɹownəl/*adj.* A class of sounds made with the tip or blade: dental, alveolar, alveolo-palatal, postalveolar, retroflex.

Creaky voice *n.* An adjustment of the glottis, occasionally used in language.

Creole *n.* A language which originated as a pidgin, but which has become a native language.

Cricoid cartilage /ˈkɹajˌkɔjd/ *n.* A ring-shaped cartilage at the bottom of the larynx, just above the trachea.

Cycle *n.* A single repetition of a wave pattern.

Dark [ɫ] *n.* A type of [l] with the quality of a high back vowel. See **clear [l]**.

Decibel RP /ˈdɛsɪˌbɛl/ GA also /ˈdɛsɪbəl/ *n.* A measurement comparing the power of two sounds. In common usage, the decibel level is a measure of the loudness of a sound. Abbreviated **dB**.

Degenerate foot *n.* In metrical theory, a foot having only one syllable. A degenerate foot results when a syllable is left over after dividing the form into bounded feet.

Dental *adj.* Having an articulation involving the tip or blade of the tongue and the upper teeth. —**Denti-** *combining form.*

Descender *n.* A symbol extending below the base line.

Devoicing *n.* A process whereby a sound changes from voiced to voiceless.

Diacritic *n.* A mark which modifies the value of a symbol; for example a basic symbol [r] might be written with various diacritics: [r̃ r̥ rʷ].

Dialect *n.* A variety of language, particularly a geographical one.

Diaphragm *n.* A large dome-shaped muscle below the lungs used in breathing. —**Diaphragmatic** /ˌdajəˌfɹægˈmætɪk/ GA /-ɾɪk/ *adj.*

Diphthong RP /ˈdɪfˌθɒŋ/ GA /ˈdɪfˌθɔŋ/ *n.* A vowel articulation with a noticeable change in quality, commonly analysed as a cluster of a vowel and a glide; e.g., [aj] or [ju]. (Note especially the spelling and pronunciation of *diphthong*.) —**Diphthongal** *adj.* —**Diphthongisation** *n.* The process whereby a simple vowel becomes a diphthong. See also **falling** and **rising diphthong**.

Discrete *adj.* Having definite boundaries with no overlapping.

Dissimilation *n.* A process whereby one sound becomes less like another. —**Dissimilate** *v.*

Dorsal *adj.* A class of sounds made with the front or back of the tongue: palatal, velar, uvular.

Dorso-uvular *adj.* Having an articulation with the back of the tongue articulating with the uvula.

Dorsovelar *adj.* Having an articulation with the back of the tongue articulating with the velum.

Dorsum /ˈdɔsəm/ GA /ˈdɔɹsəm/ *n.* The back part of the tongue, which articulates with the velum and uvula. —**Dorsal** *adj.* —**Dorso-** *combining form*: **dorso-velar, dorso-uvular**.

Double articulation *n.* See **articulation**.

Downdrift *n.* In tone languages, the gradual lowering of the pitch range.

Downstep *n.* In tone languages, the linguistically determined lowering of the pitch level used for high tone.

Egressive *adj.* Referring to an airstream with the air flowing outwards.

Ejective *n.* A consonant, typically a stop, made with a glottalic airstream mechanism; e.g., [p', t', k', s'].

Encoding *n.* The process of using language to convert meaning to sound.

Environment *n.* The linguistic situation in which a sound occurs; e.g., in *pin,* the environment of [ɪ] is [p–n].

Epenthesis /əˈpɛnθəsɪs/ *n.* The insertion of a sound in a word: e.g., in *film* [ˈfiləm] the [ə] is epenthetic. —**Epenthetic** /ˌɛpənˈθɛtɪk/ GA /-ɾɪk/ *adj.*

Epiglottis /ˌɛpɪˈglɒtɪs/ GA /ˌɛpɪˈglɑɾɪs/ *n.* A cartilage of the larynx, rising up and back from the adam's apple, partially obscuring the vocal folds from above. —**Epiglottal** *adj.*

Esophagus *n.* See **œsophagus**.

Expanded *adj.* A distinctive feature defining the class of vowels made with the tongue root advanced and with the larynx lowered.

External intercostals *n.* Muscles located between the ribs, used in breathing.

Extrametrical *adj.* In metrical theory, referring to a syllable which is overlooked in establishing the metrical structure of a word. —**Extrametricality** /ˌɛkstɹəˌmɛtɹɪˈkælɪti/ GA /-ɾi/ *n.*

F_0 *n.* **Fundamental frequency**.

F1, F2, F3, etc. *n.* **First formant**, **second formant**, **third formant**, etc.

Falling diphthong *n.* A diphthong with a falling prominence, with the vowel preceding the glide; e.g., [aj, ɔj, ɛɥ].

False vocal folds *n.* Bands of tissue located above the vocal folds, not ordinarily used in speech.

Falsetto *n.* An adjustment of the glottis with a portion of the vocal folds vibrating; not ordinarily used in speech, but found in singing, especially yodelling.

Faucal pillars *n.* Two pairs of muscular arches at the rear of the mouth; also called **faucial**.

Filter *n.* A **resonator** thought of as a device for altering the spectrum of a wave.

Final *adj.* At the end of a unit; typically, of a word.

Flap *n.* A manner of articulation in which the lower articulator strikes the upper articulator in passing. See also **tap**.

Foot *n.* In phonological theory, an organisational unit comprising one or more syllables; used especially in describing the stress pattern. —**Foot line** *n.* The line in a metrical description describing the placement of stress in the feet.

Formant /ˈfɔmənt/ GA /ˈfɔɹmənt/ *n.* In acoustic phonetics, a concentration of energy at specific frequencies. Formants are apparent in broadband spectrograms.

Fortis *adj.* **Tense**; cf. **lenis**.

Fourier analysis /ˈfʊɹɪˌə/ GA /ˈfʊɹiej/ *n.* A mathematical analysis of a complex repetitive wave as a sequence of sine waves.

Free variation *n.* In phonological theory, two sounds are in free variation if they occur in the same environment without forming a difference of meaning; e.g., [t tʰ t̚] are in free variation word-finally in English, in that any of the three may occur with no difference in meaning. See **complementary distribution** and **contrastive distribution**.

Frequency *n.* An acoustic property of a wave, corresponding to the number of cycles per second; measured in Hertz (Hz). Variations in frequency are perceived as changes in pitch.

Frication *n.* The noise of a turbulent airstream, typical of fricatives.

Fricative *n.* A manner of articulation in which the opening is sufficiently narrow to cause a turbulent air stream; also called **spirant**.

Front *n.* (1) The part of the tongue between the blade and the back, articulating with the palate. (2) Referring to a vowel or glide made in the forward part of the vowel area: e.g., [i y j]. See **back** and **central**. —**Fronted** *adj.* **Advanced**.

Fry, vocal *n.* See **creaky voice**.

Fundamental frequency *n.* The frequency of the fundamental harmonic; abbreviated $\mathbf{F_0}$. —**Fundamental (harmonic)** *n.* The lowest harmonic; abbreviated $\mathbf{F_0}$. The fundamental frequency determines the pitch of a sound.

GA See **General American**.

Gap *n.* (1) A non-occurring sequence of sounds. An **accidental gap** is potentially a word, but does not actually occur; a **nonsense word**: e.g., Eng. /glɪg/. A **systematic gap** is a sequence of sounds not allowed in a language: e.g., Eng. initial /tl–/. (2) The absence of energy in a spectrogram, typically indicating a stop.

Geminate /ˈdʒɛmɪnət/ *n.* One of two identical, adjacent sounds: e.g., [p] in [appu].

General American *n.* A standard accent in the United States, spoken widely, especially outside the East and South, abbreviated **GA**.

Glide *n.* A short, rapidly moving vowel sound. In the diphthong [aj], the vowel sound [a] is relatively steady, but the tongue moves rapidly during the [j] glide. Same as **semivowel**.

Glottis /ˈglɒtɪs/ GA /ˈglɑɾɪs/*n.* The space between the vocal folds. —**Glottal** *adj.* —**Glottal stop** *n.* A stop formed by a complete closure of the vocal folds, written [ʔ]. —**Glottalic** *adj.* Referring to an air stream mechanism having the closed glottis as initiator.

Grave accent RP /gɹɑv/ GA /gɹejv/ *n.* The superscript diacritic [̀], used to indicate a low tone or a secondary stress.

Haček /ˈhɑ̝ˌtʃɛk/ *n.* (1) The superscript diacritic [ˇ], used to indicate a rising tone. (2) In non-IPA transcriptions, a haček is sometimes used to modify certain consonantal symbols:

š = ʃ č = tʃ ž = ʒ ǰ = dʒ.

Harmonic *n.* A component of a complex wave having the form of a sine wave.

Head *n.* (1) The central or crucial part of an element. (2) In metrical theory, the stressed syllable of a foot.

Heavy syllable *n.* A syllable typically with a coda or with a long vowel in the nucleus.

Hertz /hɜts/ GA /həɹts/ *n.* A unit of frequency equal to one cycle per second, abbreviated **Hz**, named for the German physicist Heinrich Hertz.

High *adj.* (1) Referring to a vowel or glide made in the high portion of the vowel area: e.g., [i ɯ j]. (2) Referring to a vowel or glide made higher than another or than usual: e.g., *a high [e]*. (3) Referring to a tone with a greater frequency than another or than usual. See **low** and **mid**. —**Height** *n.* (1) The vertical position of the tongue, used in describing vowels. (2) A distinctive feature describing vowel height. (3) The pitch level of a tone.

Hold *n.* The mid portion of a consonant when the articulators are together in maximum constriction.

Homorganic *adj.* Having the same place of articulation; e.g., in [mp nt ŋk], the nasal is homorganic with the following stop.

Hyoid bone /ˈhajˌɔjd/ *n.* A horseshoe-shaped bone located behind the chin.

Implosive *n.* (1) A stop made with the vocal folds vibrating as the larynx is lowered. (2) A stop made with an ingressive glottalic air stream mechanism.

Inaudible release *n.* An unheard release, as in the [p] in English *apt*.

Ingressive *adj.* Referring to an air stream with air flowing inwards. See **egressive**.

Inherent length *n.* Length which is independent of the context. See **contextual length**.

Initial *adj.* At the beginning of unit; typically, of a word.

Initiator *n.* The vocal organ which sets the air stream in motion.

Intensity *n.* An acoustic property of a sound related to amplitude and frequency. Variations in intensity are perceived as changes in loudness.

Interdental *adj.* Having an articulation in which the tip or blade of the tongue is between the teeth.

Internal intercostals *n.* Muscles located between the ribs, used in breathing.

International Phonetic Alphabet *n.* The official phonetic transcription system of the **International Phonetic Association** and the one used in this book. Both the alphabet and the association are abbreviated **IPA**.

Intervocalic *adj.* Between vowels; e.g., the [n] in *any*.

Intonation *n.* A distinctive pattern of pitch. —**Intonation contour** *n.* A pattern of intonation.

IPA See **International Phonetic Alphabet** and **International Phonetic Association**.

Kinæsthesia /ˌkɪnəsˈθiziə/ GA /-ˈθiʒə/ *n.* The sensations associated with physical movement. —**Kinæsthetic** /ˌkɪnəsˈθɛtɪk/ GA /-ɾɪk/ *adj.*

Labial *adj.* (1) Referring to the lips. (2) A class of sounds made with the lips: bilabial, labiodental, linguo-labial.

Labialisation *n.* A secondary articulation involving lip rounding. —**Labialised** *adj.* —**Labio-** *combining form*: **labiodental**.

Labial-velar *adj.* Having a double articulation which is simultaneously labial and velar.

Labiodental *adj.* Having an articulation involving the lower lip and the upper teeth.

Lallans /ˈlælənz/ *n.* A traditional dialect of English spoken in the lowlands of Scotland.

Lamina /ˈlæminə/ *n.* The surface of the tongue between the apex and the front. Same as **blade**. —**Laminal** *adj.* —**Lamino-** *combining form*: **laminoalveolar, laminodental**.

Laminoalveolar *adj.* Having an articulation involving the blade of the tongue and the alveolar ridge.

Laminodental *adj.* Having an articulation involving the blade of the tongue and the upper teeth.

Larynx /ˈlæɹɪŋks/ GA /ˈlɛɹ-/, *pl.* **larynges** /ləˈɹɪndʒiz/ *n.* The voice box, a structure of cartilage and muscle above the windpipe and below the throat, containing the vocal folds. —**Laryngeal** /ləˈɹɪndʒəl/ *adj.*

Lateral *adj.* Referring to a manner of articulation in which the centre of the vocal tract is closed but the sides are open allowing air to escape; the opposite of **central**. —*n.* A sound made with a lateral articulation: e.g., [l ʎ ɫ]. —**Lateral onset** *n.* A lateral followed by a homorganic stop, with a transition consisting only of raising the sides of the tongue: e.g., [ld]. —**Lateral release** *n.* A stop followed by a homorganic lateral, with a transition consisting only of lowering the sides of the tongue: e.g., [dl].

Lax *adj.* In English, *lax* is used to refer to the vowels [ɪ ɛ æ ʌ ʊ]. *Lax* refers to a classification of English sounds, rather than to a measurable phonetic property. Cf. **tense**.

Length *n.* The duration of a segment.

Lenis *adj.* **Lax**; cf. **fortis**.

Level *n.* A type of representation: e.g., **broad, narrow, phonemic, phonetic**. —*adj.* Not moving; e.g., *a level tone.*

Ligamental glottis *n.* The portion of the glottis lying between the vocal folds.

Light syllable *n.* A syllable with a short vowel in the nucleus.

Line drawing *n.* A type of graphic representation showing articulatory activities. The labial, coronal, dorsal, velic, and glottal activities are shown on separate lines.

Linguistics *n.* The study of language.

Linguo-labial *adj.* Having an articulation involving the tip or blade of the tongue and the upper lip.

Linking -/ɹ/ *n.* In RP and other accents, the presence of [ɹ] in phrases and words such as *the idea(r) of it, saw(r)ing.*

Liquid *n.* A term referring to the class of **laterals** and **rhotics**.

Lisp *n.* A speech problem, involving the substitution of an incorrect coronal fricative; e.g., [lɪθp] for [lɪsp].

Locus /ˈləwkəs/ GA /low-/, *pl.* **loci** /-ˌsaj/ *n.* On a spectrogram, the point to which the transition of the second formant appears to be pointing.

Long *adj.* Referring to a segment of greater duration than another or than usual. Length is usually marked with a colon or a raised dot: [ɑː eˑ].

Loudness *n.* A perceptual quality of a sound, corresponding generally to its intensity.

Low *adj.* (1) Referring to a vowel made in the lower portion of the vowel area: e.g., [a ɑ ɒ]. (2) Referring to a vowel made lower than another or than usual: e.g., *a low [i].* (3) Referring to a tone with a lower frequency than another or than usual. See **high** and **mid**. —**Lowering** *n.* The process whereby a vowel moves to a lower position: e.g., [u]₊ [o].

Lower articulator *n.* The articulators of the lower jaw and tongue: i.e., lower lip, lower teeth, apex, lamina, front, dorsum, root.

Macron /ˈmejkɹən/ also /ˈmæk-/ *n.* The superscript diacritic [¯] used to indicate (1) a mid tone or (2) sometimes a long vowel.

Manner of articulation *n.* The kind of articulation, particularly the degree of opening, nasality, and laterality.

Maximisation of onset *n.* A principle of syllabification whereby the onset is made as large as possible, consistent with the phonotactics of a word-initial onset.

Medial *adj.* In the middle of a unit; typically, of a word.

Mel /mɛl/ *n.* A unit of pitch. —**Mel scale** *n.* A scale for measuring pitch, as opposed to frequency.

Mid *adj.* Between **high** and **low**; used with vowels and tones. See **central**.

Millisecond *n.* One one-thousandth of a second; 1 ms = 0.001 sec.

Minimal pair *n.* Two forms which differ only by one sound, as *pair, care.*

Monophthong /ˈmɒnəfˌθɒŋ/ GA /ˈmɑnəfˌθɔŋ/ *n.* A steady vowel; see **diphthong**.

Mora /ˈmɔɹə/, *pl.* **moræ** /ˈmɔɹi/ *n.* A unit of time, used in describing certain languages, such as Japanese. —**Moraic** /ˌmɔˈɹejɪk/ *adj.*

Mora-timed *adj.* Referring to languages in which each mora of an utterance takes about the same amount of time. See **stress-timed, syllable-timed**.

Morpheme *n.* The smallest meaningful unit of a word. —**Morphology** *n.* The study of morphemes.

Moving tone *adj.* Referring to non-level tones.

Narrow transcription *n.* A transcription showing phonetic detail. An **allophonic transcription** is an example of a narrow transcription. See **broad transcription.**

Narrow-band spectrogram *n.* A type of spectrogram, useful for seeing harmonics.

Nasal *adj.* Referring to sounds, both consonants and vowels, with velic opening and air flowing out through the nasal passage. —*n.* A nasal stop: *Scots Gaelic has four nasals.* (i.e., nasal stops) —**Nasal cavity** *n.* The air cavity leading from the top of the pharynx to the nostrils. —**Nasal onset** *n.* A nasal followed by a homorganic stop, with a transition consisting only of raising the velum to make a velic closure: e.g., [nd]. —**Nasal release** *n.* A stop followed by a homorganic nasal, with a transition consisting only of lowering the velum, making a velic opening, e.g., [dn]. —**Nasalisation** *n.* The process whereby a sound becomes **nasalised.** —**Nasalised** *adj.* Same as **nasal.**

Noise *n.* Sound resulting from vibration without a regular repeated cycle, typical of fricatives.

Nonsense word *n.* A word in a language which is phonologically possible, but which does not happen actually to occur in that language; an **accidental gap**, e.g., in RP English /ˈbɹɪlɪg, ˈslajðɪ, təwvz, ˌawtˈgɹejb/.

Nucleus /ˈnjukliəs/, *pl.* **nuclei** /ˈnjukliˌaj/ *n.* The part of the syllable with the greatest sonority; typically, the vowel of a syllable.

Obstruent /ˈɒbstɹʊənt//ˈɑbstɹʊənt/ *n.* A class of sounds which includes stops, fricatives, and affricates.

Œsophagus /əˈsɒfəgəs/ GA /-ˈsɑf-/ *n.* The tube which carries food from the throat to the stomach. —**Œsophagic** /ˌɛsəˈfejdʒɪk/ *adj.* Referring to an air stream mechanism with the œsophagus as initiator, using **œsophageal** /əˌsɒfəˈdʒiəl/ GA /-ˌsɑf-/ air. [All of these are sometimes spelled *eso-*].

Onset *n.* (1) The elements in a syllable preceding the nucleus. (2) The initial phase of a consonant, during which the articulators are coming together. See also **lateral onset** and **nasal onset**; see **hold** and **release**.

Open *adj.* Having a wide opening; cf. **close.** —**Open vowel** *n.* A low vowel.

Open syllable *n.* A syllable with no final consonant. See **closed syllable**.

Oral *adj.* (1) Referring to the mouth. (2) Not nasal: e.g., an oral stop. —**Oral cavity** *n.* The air cavity leading from the throat to the lips; the mouth.

Organ of Corti /ˈkɔɹti/ *n.* A part of the inner ear, containing the auditory nerve endings.

Orthography *n.* The ordinary way of writing a language, as opposed to a phonological or phonetic transcription.

Oscillation *n.* A repeated alternation.

Overlapping *n.* A situation in which the articulations of two sequential phonemes are realised phonetically as (partially) simultaneous; e.g., the articulations of /pt/ in English *apt* partially overlap phonetically.

Overtone *n.* Harmonic.

Palatal *adj.* Having an articulation involving the front of the tongue and the hard palate. —**Palate** *n.* The hard palate; the rigid upper surface of the mouth lying behind the alveolar ridge. —**Palatalisation** *n.* (1) The process whereby an articulation moves more towards the palate. (2) A secondary articulation with the quality of a high front unrounded vowel. —**Palatalised** *adj.*

Parameter *n.* In metrical theory, a dimension used for specifying variation in stress placement.

Penultimate syllable *n.* The second-last syllable of a word; same as **penult**.

Pharynx /ˈfæɹɪŋks/ GA /ˈfɛɹɪŋks/, *pl.* **pharynges** /fəˈɹɪndʒiz/ *n.* The vertical tube leading from the larynx (**laryngeal pharynx**) past the oral cavity (**oral pharynx**) to the nasal cavity (**nasal pharynx**). —**Pharyngeal** /ˈfəˈɹɪndʒəl/ *adj.* Having an articulation involving the root of the tongue and the **pharyngeal wall**, the rear wall of the pharynx. Same as **radico-pharyngeal**. —**Pharyngealisation** *n.* A secondary articulation involving the quality of a pharyngeal constriction. —**Pharyngealised** *adj.*

Phonation *n.* The phonetic activities of the vocal folds.

Phoneme *n.* A contrastive segment in a language. —**Phonemic** *adj.*

Phonetic *adj.* (1) Referring to phonetics. (2) Emphasising detail and variation in speech; **allophonic**.

Phonetics *n.* The study of the sounds of human language. —**Articulatory phonetics** *n.* The branch of phonetics having to do with the production of sounds. —**Acoustic phonetics** *n.* The branch of phonetics having to do with the physical properties of sound. —**Auditory phonetics** *n.* The branch of phonetics having to do with hearing and perception. —**Phonetician** *n.* A specialist in phonetics; a nice sort of person.

Phonology *n.* The study of the sound systems of human language. —**Phonological** *adj.* Emphasising the internal structure of a sound system as opposed to **phonetic** detail.

Phonotactics *n.* The description of the arrangement of sounds in a language with respect to each other; e.g., in English, initial clusters of stop–approximant occur, except /tl/ and /dl/.

Pitch *n.* The perceptual property of sound which distinguishes, for example, notes on a piano; pitch corresponds generally to the physical property of frequency.

Pitch accent *n.* A type of tone system in which a lexically determined syllable alters the otherwise predictable tone pattern of an utterance.

Place of articulation *n.* For a particular sound, the place of greatest closure in the vocal tract.

Plosive /ˈpləwsɪv/ GA /plow-/ *n.* An egressive pulmonic stop.

Point of articulation *n.* Same as **place of articulation**.

Post- A prefix used to indicate a more retracted place of articulation, e.g., postalveolar.

Postalveolar *adj.* Having an articulation involving the tip or blade of the tongue and the area bordering the alveolar ridge and the palate.

Postvocalic *adj.* After a vowel.

Pre- A prefix used to indicate a more advanced articulation, e.g., pre-alveolar.

Prenasalised *adj.* A stop preceded by a homorganic nasal in the syllable onset: e.g., [mba, ŋge]

Primary articulation *n.* See **articulation**.

Primary cardinal vowels *n.* A term sometimes used for the cardinal vowels [i e ɛ a ɑ ɔ o u].

Primary stress *n.* The strongest level of stress.

Progressive *adj.* Referring to changes in which a later element is influenced by an earlier one. Cf. **anticipatory**, and also **assimilation, dissimilation**. **—Progressive assimilation** *n.* The assimilation of a later sound to an earlier one; e.g., in a sequence XY, Y changes to become more like X.

Prominence *n.* The degree to which a sound or group of sounds stands out from its neighbours in length, loudness, stress, or pitch.

Propagation *n.* The method by which a sound wave is propelled through the air.

Pulmonic *adj.* Referring to an air stream mechanism having the lungs as initiator.

Radix /ˈɹejdɪks/ *n.* The root of the tongue. **—Radical** *adj.* **—Radico-** *combining form*: **radico-pharyngeal** *adj.* Having an articulation involving the root of the tongue and the pharyngeal wall.

Received Pronunciation *n.* The standard English accent in England, abbreviated **RP**.

Reduced vowel *n.* In English, a vowel which has undergone reduction, changing to [ə] or [ɪ].

Register tone language *n.* A language with a system of level tones.

Regressive See **anticipatory**.

Release *n.* (1) The final portion of a consonant when the articulators move away from each other. (2) The manner in which the closure of a stop opens; see **lateral release** and **nasal release**.

Resonance *n.* The property of an object allowing it to vibrate in response to outside vibrations. In speech, the vocal tract resonates selectively to the vibrations of the vocal folds, altering the spectrum of the original wave. **—Resonance curve** *n.* A curve showing the natural vibrating tendency of an object. **—Resonator** *n.*

Retracted *adj.* Referring to a sound made farther to the back of the vocal tract than another or than usual: *a retracted [g]*. The diacritic is [_]. Cf. **advanced**.

Retroflex(ed) *adj.* (1) Having an articulation with the tip or blade of the tongue curled back and articulating with the back of the alveolar ridge. (2) Referring to a vowel with the tongue curled back towards the retroflexed position, producing an [ɹ]-quality; see **rhotic**.

Retroflex-[ɹ] *n.* In English, an /ɹ/ made with the tongue tip curled up and back. Cf. **bunched-/ɹ/**.

Rhotic /ˈɹəwtɪk/ GA /ˈɹowɾɪk/ *n.* An r-like sound: e.g., [r ɹ ɾ ɽ ʀ]. —*adj.* (1) Referring to a vowel with a retroflexed articulation. (2) In English, referring to an accent such as GA, which has retained historic codal /ɹ/, as in *car, harden*. —**Rhotacised** *adj.*

Rhyme *n.* The portion of the syllable after the onset, containing the nucleus and coda, i.e., the vowel and any following consonants. Occasionally spelled **rime**.

Rhythm *n.* The metrical cadence of a language; the pattern of prominent elements.

Rising diphthong *n.* A diphthong with a rising prominence; i.e., with the vowel following the glide: e.g., [ju wɔ].

Root *n.* The rear vertical surface of the tongue; see **radix**.

Round(ed) *adj.* Made with rounded lips; **labialised**: e.g., [o u tʷ]. —**Rounding** *n.* (1) The quality of being rounded. (2) The process whereby a sound becomes rounded. —**Unrounded**. See **labialisation**.

RP See **Received Pronunciation**.

Rule *n.* A formal statement of a linguistic relationship. **Phonological rules** state the relationship between **phonemes** and **allophones**.

Sagittal section *n.* A diagram showing the head, or other part of the body, as though cut in two from front to back.

Schwa /ʃwɑ/ *n.* A mid-central vowel, symbolised [ə].

Scots *n.* The dialects of English historically spoken in the lowlands of Scotland. See **Lallans**.

Secondary articulation *n.* See **articulation**, and also **labialisation**, **palatalisation**, **velarisation**, **pharyngealisation**.

Secondary cardinal vowels *n.* A term sometimes used for the cardinal vowels [y ø œ ɶ ɒ ʌ ɤ ɯ].

Secondary stress *n.* A level of stress weaker than a **primary stress** (but stronger than a **tertiary stress** or that of an **unstressed** syllable), as in the first syllable of *telegraphic* /ˌtɛləˈɡɹæfɪk/.

Segment *n.* A consonant or a vowel. —**Segmentation** *n.* The division of a stream of speech into segments.

Serif /ˈsɛɹɪf/ *n.* A short horizontal stroke at the top or bottom of symbol.

Semivowel *n.* See **Glide**.

Sibilant *n.* The sounds [s] or [z] and sometimes [ʃ] or [ʒ].

Sine wave *n.* A specific type of simple repetitive wave; same as **sinusoidal wave.**

Slant lines *n.* See **solidi**.

Smoothing *n.* In casual or rapid RP, the process whereby the glide is lost in diphthongs preceding /ə/, as when *fire* [fajə] becomes [faə].

Solidi /ˈsɒlɪdi/ GA /ˌsɑl-/, *sg.* **solidus** *n.* The symbols //, used to enclose phonemic transcriptions; also known as **virgules**, or most commonly **slant lines**. See **square brackets**.

Sonorant /ˈsɒnəɹənt/ GA /ˈsɑn-/ or /ˈsown-/ *n.* (1) A class of sounds including **nasals**, **liquids**, **glides**, and **vowels**; the sounds which are not **obstruents**. —*adj.* A distinctive feature.

Sonority *n.* The overall loudness of a sound in comparison to others of the same length, stress, and pitch. —**Sonority curve** *n.* A curve showing the sonority for each segment of a word.

Sound system *n.* The inventory and interrelationships of the sounds of a language.

Spectrogram *n.* A representation of the sound spectrum of a stretch of speech. **Spectrograph** *n.* A machine which produces spectrograms.

Spectrum, *pl.* **spectra** *n.* A representation of the harmonic components of a sound, showing their frequency and amplitude (or intensity).

Spike *n.* In a spectrogram, a vertical stroke, typically showing the release of a stop.

Spirant *n.* A **fricative.**

Square brackets *n.* The brackets [ ], used to enclose phonetic transcriptions: e.g., [fəˈnɛtɪk]. See **solidi**.

Stop *n.* A manner of articulation involving a complete closure so that no air exits through the mouth. The use of 'stop' alone implies an **oral stop**, as opposed to a **nasal stop**.

Stress *n.* A property of a syllable, generally related to the syllable's prominence in relation to its neighbours.

Stress language *n.* A language which uses stress to contrast different lexical items; e.g., English *survey* noun – verb RP [ˈsɜˌvej – səˈvej] GA [ˈsəɹˌvej – səɹˈvej].

Stress parameter *n.* A constraint governing the placement of stress in a language.

Stress-timed *adj.* Referring to languages in which major stresses tend to occur at even intervals of time. Cf. **syllable-timed, mora-timed**.

Stricture *n.* A closure, complete or partial, involved in an articulation.

Strong form *n.* In English, the form of certain words (e.g., /ˈhæv/) occurring in a stressed position, as opposed to a **weak** form (e.g., /əv/) occurring without stress.

Subglottal *n.* Below the glottis. Subglottal air-pressure refers to pressure in the lungs.

Supraglottal *adj.* Above the glottis. Same as **supralaryngeal**.

Supralaryngeal *adj.* Above the glottis; i.e., including the pharyngeal, oral, and nasal portions of the vocal tract.

Suprasegmental *adj.* Referring to various phenomena which may extend over more than one segment: i.e., tone, stress, length, rhythm.

Syllable *n.* A unit of phonological organisation, typically larger than a segment and smaller than a word. Every syllable has a nucleus, consisting of a vowel or syllabic consonant. —**Syllabic** *adj.* (1) Referring to syllables. (2) Referring to the element of a syllable forming the nucleus. —**Syllabic consonant** *n.* A consonant which forms the nucleus of a syllable. —**Syllabicity** *n.* The property of forming, or potentially forming, a syllable. —**Syllabification** *n.* The division of a form into syllables. —**Syllabified** *adj.* Divided into syllables.

Syllable-timed *adj.* Referring to languages in which each syllable of an utterance takes about the same amount of time. See **stress-timed**, **mora-timed**.

Symbol *n.* A graphic mark representing a phonetic element, particularly a segment.

Systematic gap See **gap**.

Tap *n.* A manner of articulation in which the lower articulator strikes the upper articulator in a brief, ballistic fashion. The [ɾ] of GA English is a tap.

Tense *adj.* In English, *tense* is used to refer to the diphthongs and the vowels [i e ɑ o u]. *Tense* refers to a classification of English sounds, rather than to a measurable phonetic property. Cf. **lax**.

Tertiary stress *n.* A level of stress weaker than **secondary stress**, but stronger than that of **unstressed** syllables.

Thyroid cartilage /ˈθajˌɹɔjd/ *n.* The plough-shaped cartilage at the front of the larynx.

Tilde /ˈtɪldə/ *n.* A diacritic [˜] written (1) above a symbol [ẽ] to indicate nasalisation, (2) below a symbol [ḛ] to indicate creaky voice or (3) through a symbol [ɫ ɗ] to indicate velarisation or pharyngealisation.

Tip *n.* The foremost point of the tongue; same as **apex**.

Tone *n.* The phonological use of **pitch**. —**Tone language** *n.* A language which distinguishes words using pitch.

Tonic syllable *n.* In English, the syllable of a phrase with the major pitch change.

Trachea /tɹəˈkiə/ GA /ˈtɹejkiə/ *n.* The tube leading from the **bronchi** to the **larynx**.

Transcription *n.* The written representation of speech sounds. A very abstract transcription of an utterance is a **broad** or **phonemic transcription**; a **narrow** or **phonetic transcription** shows a great deal of detail. —**Transcribe** *v.*

Transient *n.* In acoustics, a very brief noise.

Transition *n.* A change; particularly, the change in shape of a formant at the edge of a segment.

Tree *n.* A diagram showing the internal, hierarchical structure of a linguistic unit, such as a segment.

Trill *n.* A manner of articulation in which one organ vibrates against another in a rapid series of articulations.

Ultima *n.* The last syllable of an utterance. —**Ultimate** *adj.*

Umlaut *n.* (1) The process whereby a back vowel becomes a front vowel. (2) The diacritic [¨].

Unbounded foot *n.* In metrical theory, a foot with no upper limit on the number of syllables it may contain.

Unilateral *adj.* A lateral manner of articulation with air-flow only on one side of the vocal tract.

Unstressed *adj.* Having the weakest level of stress.

Upper articulator *n.* The articulators of the upper jaw: i.e., upper lip, upper teeth, alveolar ridge, palate, velum, uvula, pharyngeal wall.

Upper vocal tract *n.* The **supralaryngeal vocal tract**, i.e., the vocal tract above the larynx, consisting of the mouth, the nasal passage, and the pharynx.

Upstep *n.* In tone languages, the linguistically determined raising of the pitch level used for high tone.

Utterance *n.* A stretch of speech.

Uvula /ˈjuvjʊlə/ *n.* The small appendage hanging down at the back of the velum. —**Uvular** *adj.* Having an articulation with the dorsum of the tongue articulating with the uvula.

V *n.* An abbreviation for **vowel**.

Velaric /ˌviˈlæɹɪk/ GA /vəˈlɛɹɪk/ *adj.* Referring to an air stream mechanism having the velum as initiator.

Velic /ˈvɪlɪk/ *adj.* Referring to the upper surface of the velum. With a **velic closure**, air-flow through the nose is cut off, producing an oral sound; with a **velic opening**, nasal sounds are produced.

Velum /ˈviləm/ *n.* The soft palate. —**Velar** /ˈvilə/ GA /-əɹ/ *adj.* Having an articulation with the dorsum of the tongue articulating with the velum. —**Velarisation** *n.* A secondary articulation with the quality of a high back unrounded vowel. —**Velarised** *adj.*

Ventricle of Morgagni /ˌvɛntɹɪkəl əv ˌmɔˈgɑnji/ GA /ˌmɔɹˈgɑnji/ *n.* The cavity between the false and true vocal folds. —**Ventricular** *adj.*

Vertical striation *n.* A vertical line in a broad-band spectrogram, corresponding to a vocal fold vibration.

Vibration *n.* A rapid movement back and forth.

Virgules See **solidi**.

Vocal folds *n.* Two bands of muscle and other tissue extending from a single point at the **thyroid cartilage** backwards to each of the **arytenoid cartilages**. The space between the vocal folds is known as the **glottis**. Often referred to as vocal cords.

Vocal organs *n.* The parts of the body used in speech.

Vocal tract *n.* Generally, the air passages used in speech production; especially, the supralaryngeal vocal tract; i.e., the pharynx and the oral and nasal cavities.

Vocalic *adj.* Referring to vowels.

Voice, voicing *n.* A glottal adjustment involving vibration of the vocal folds. —**Voiced** *adj.* Referring to a sound made with voicing. —**Voiceless** *adj.* Referring to an adjustment of the glottis with the vocal folds not vibrating. —**Devoice** *v.* To change from voiced to voiceless.

Voice bar *n.* A dark bar sometimes found at low frequencies in a spectrogram, indicating voice.

Voice onset time *n.* In a consonant–vowel sequence, the time between the release of the closure and the beginning of voicing. Abbreviated **VOT**.

VOT See **voice onset time**.

Vowel *n.* A sound made with the vocal tract quite open; vowels typically function as the nucleus of a syllable. —**Vowel colour** *n.* Vowel quality; i.e., [i] not [e].

Wave *n.* In phonetics, the alternations of air pressure which convey sound. —**Waveform** *n.* The graphic representation of a sound wave, showing the variation in amplitude (or intensity) over time.

Weak form *n.* In English, the form of certain words (e.g., /əv/) occurring in an unstressed position, as opposed to a **strong** form (e.g., /ˈhæv/) occurring with stress.

Wh-question *n.* A question which asks for information other than 'yes' or 'no'; in English, typically beginning with *wh–*: *who, what, when, where, how*. Cf. **yes–no question**.

Whisper *n.* An adjustment of the vocal folds used in whispering. —**Whispering** *n.* A quiet way of speaking using **voicelessness** and **whisper**.

Wide-band spectrogram *n.* A type of spectogram; useful for seeing formats.

Word line *n.* The line in a metrical description describing the placement of stress in the word.

X-height line *n.* The imaginary line along the upper edge of symbols such as [x e s ɑ].

Yes–no question *n.* A question answered by 'yes' or 'no'; cf. **wh-question**.

Appendix C

Calligraphy

Writing transcriptions clearly and legibly is important. Most transcriptions have very little redundancy. If you make a mistake, there is little to indicate that you did so. This appendix shows you how to write the symbols introduced in this book. If you write your transcriptions carefully, according to the examples in this appendix, you (and others) will be able to read them in years to come. If you are handing in assignments in a course, clear writing will keep your work from being marked down for being unreadable.

- Phonetic writing is usually clearer if each symbol is written separately and not joined together cursively.
- Ordinary capital letters are not used, although some 'small capitals' are used. Small capitals look like capital letters, but are the same height as ordinary lower-case letters: [ɴ *r* ɢ]. Do not use lower-case letters where small capitals are required.
- Do not capitalise proper nouns or adjectives: e.g., [ˈkænədə], [ˈsuzən]. The only capital letters used are the small capitals which are special phonetic symbols.
- Keep punctuation to an absolute minimum. Periods are easily confused with diacritics.

Look at the word *drop* in Figure C.1. Notice the **base line**. The letters [d r o] sit on the base line, and the bowl of the [p] rests on the base line. Almost all phonetic symbols either sit or hang from the base line.

Figure C.1 Lines used in writing symbols

The line at the top of the [r] and the [o] is called the **x-height line**. It shows the height of many lower-case letters, such as [x]. Many symbols are written totally between the x-height line and the base line (Figure C.2).

Some symbols, such as [d], are written partially above the x-height line (Figure C.3). Such symbols are said to have **ascenders**.

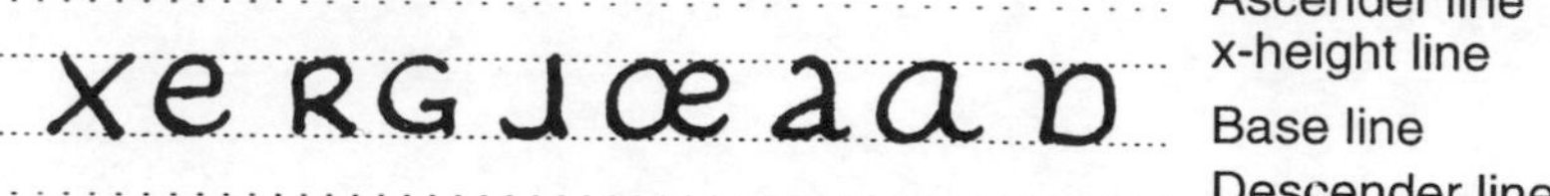

Figure C.2 Symbols written between base-line and x-height line

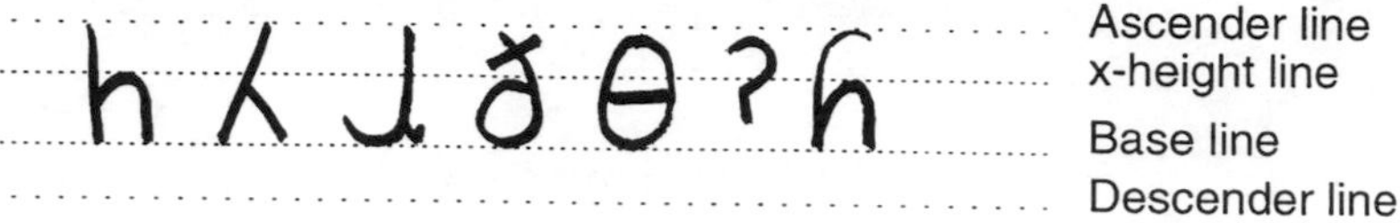

Figure C.3 Symbols with ascenders

Similarly, some symbols, such as [p], are written partially below the base line (Figure C.4); such symbols are said to have **descenders**.

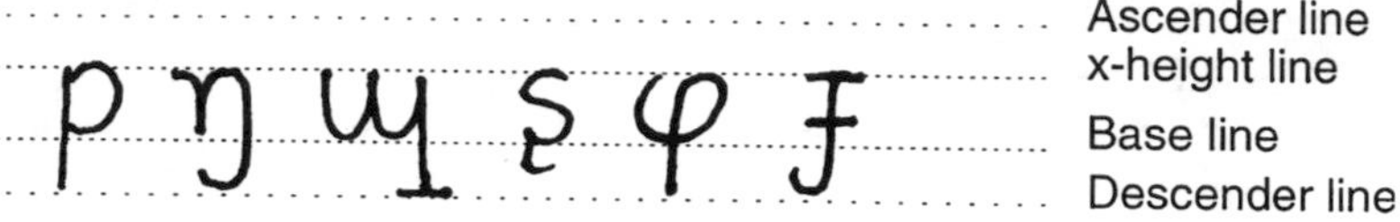

Figure C.4 Symbols with descenders

A few symbols have both ascenders and descenders (Figure C.5):

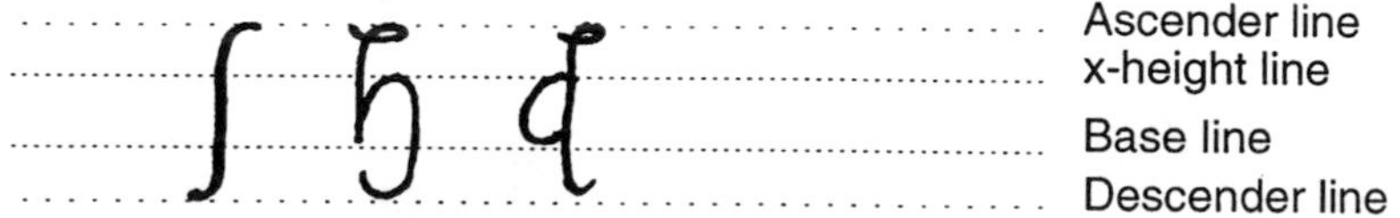

Figure C.5 Symbols with both ascenders and descenders

In looking at the examples, notice the height of the symbol, paying particular attention to any ascenders and descenders. Many symbols are somewhat similar to each other (Figure C.6). Often small matters, such as ascenders and descenders, are crucial.

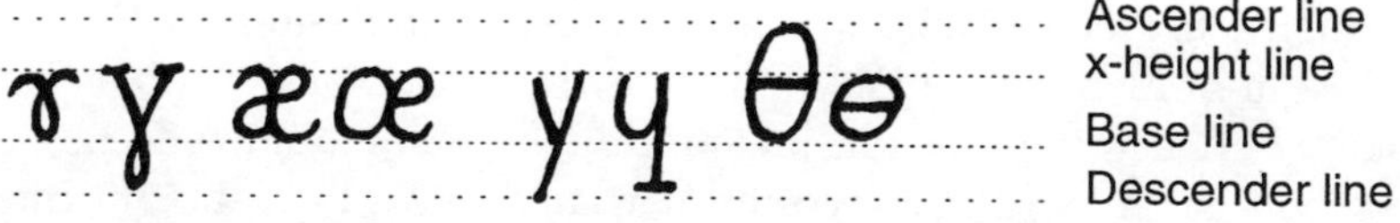

Figure C.6 Some confusing symbols

Many symbols have **serifs**; these are the small lines often found at the tops and bottoms of strokes in printed type. In handwriting, serifs are generally absent. In hand-written phonetic transcriptions, serifs are occasionally useful in distinguishing similar symbols: e.g., [ɤ ɣ], [y ɥ].

Many people have made serious efforts to develop an interesting writing style for themselves and find the conventions of phonetic transcription confining. Phonetic calligraphy does not exclude individuality, but its main purpose is conveying information clearly, not looking interesting or impressive. You are certainly free to develop your own style, provided your writing is legible. Perhaps you will become one of the great calligraphic masters of phonetics that future generations will strive to emulate.

In the examples in this appendix, only symbols other than those in the ordinary Roman alphabet are given. Common names for symbols are given, where they exist. Sometimes notes on particular points are added, often when a similar symbol exists. Pullum and Ladusaw (1996) is an excellent compendium of phonetic symbols and their usage. It gives not only the IPA transcription practice, but a variety of other traditions as well. The current IPA chart (1996) is included in Appendix E.

Vowels

Symbols for unrounded vowels are presented first, then rounded vowels.

ɪ **Small capital i**. Extra symbol for a vowel in the high front unrounded region. Make sure that it is the same height as [e].

ɛ **Epsilon** RP /ˌɛpˈsajlən/, GA /ˈɛpsɪˌlɑn/. Lower mid front unrounded vowel. Mathematicians sometimes write epsilon as ε; this shape is not used in phonetics.

æ **Ash** /æʃ/. Extra symbol for a vowel in the low front unrounded region. Take special care in writing this symbol. It is made with one stroke. The backs of each half should touch. Make sure that it is distinct from [œ].

a **Front a**. Low front unrounded vowel. It is best written with two strokes. Be very careful not to write [ɑ] by mistake, nor to confuse [a] with [ə].

ɑ **Back a**. Low back unrounded vowel. This must be kept distinct from [a].

ʌ **Caret** RP /ˈkæɹɪt/, GA /ˈkɛɹət/. A lower mid back unrounded vowel. A turned [v].

ɤ **Ram's horns**. A higher mid back unrounded vowel. Keep distinct from gamma [ɣ] (a velar fricative). Ram's horns is the same height as [e];

gamma goes below the base line. Sloping shoulders for ram's horns help distinguish it from gamma which has straight serifs.

ɯ **Turned m**. A high back unrounded vowel. Keep distinct from [w] and [ɰ].

ɨ **Barred i**. High central unrounded vowel. An ordinary [i] with a short stroke through the middle. It must be distinct from [i] and [ɪ].

ə **Schwa** /ʃwɑ/. A mid central unrounded vowel. A turned [e]. Be careful to keep this symbol distinct from [a].

ɚ **Rhotic schwa, r-coloured schwa**. A mid central unrounded vowel with retroflexion; the symbol is the vowel [ə] combined with the rhotic diacritic [˞]. Must be distinct from [ə].

ɜ **Reversed epsilon**. Extra symbol for a vowel in the mid central unrounded region. Be sure not to confuse this with [ɛ].

ɐ **Turned a**. Extra symbol for a vowel in the low central unrounded region.

ʏ **Small capital y**. Extra symbol for a vowel in the high front rounded region. Be sure to make all small capital letters no higher than a lowercase e. Serifs help to distinguish this symbol from the ordinary [y].

ø **Barred o**. Higher mid front rounded vowel. It is important to keep this vowel symbol distinct from the symbol for null – Ø, and from phi [φ]. In handwriting, I usually write the null symbol with a backwards slash.

œ **O-E digraph**. Lower mid front rounded vowel. This symbol must be kept distinct from capital o-e digraph [ɶ] and from ash [æ].

ɶ **Capital o-e digraph**. Low front rounded vowel. This symbol must be kept distinct from o-e digraph [œ], and from ash [æ].

ɒ **Turned back a**. A low back rounded vowel. A rounded [ɑ].

ɔ **Open o**. Lower mid back rounded vowel.

ʊ **Small capital u**. Extra symbol for a vowel in the high back rounded region. Make sure that it is the same height as [e].

ʉ **Barred u**. High central rounded vowel. An ordinary [u] with a short stroke through the middle.

ɵ **Barred o**. Extra symbol for a vowel in the mid central rounded region. Must be distinct from [θ]. Barred o [ɵ] does not rise above the x-height line; [θ] does.

ɞ **Closed reversed epsilon**. Lower mid central rounded vowel.

Vowel examples

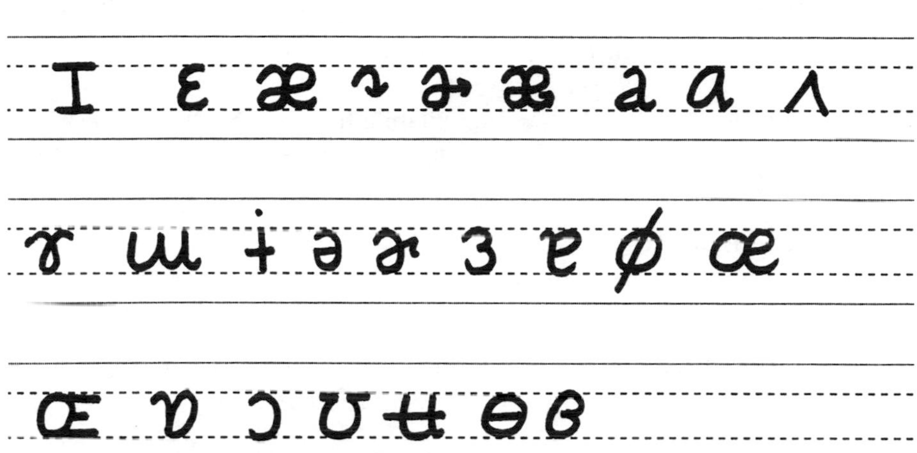

Figure C.7 Examples of vowel symbols

Consonants

Consonant symbols are presented in the order: stops, fricatives, nasals, laterals, rhotics, other approximants, other consonants. Within each of these categories, the consonants are ordered by place of articulation, moving from front to back.

ɖ **Voiced retroflex stop**. A [d] with a retroflex hook, pointing to the right.

ʈ **Voiceless retroflex stop**. A long [t] with a retroflex hook, pointing to the right.

ɟ **Barred dotless j**. A voiced palatal stop. This symbol can be made as a turned [f]. Note that the curled tail is a descender; the top serif is common.

ɡ **G**. A voiced velar stop. The cursive form [ɡ] is much more common in phonetic transcription than the printed form [g].

ɢ **Small capital g**. A voiced uvular stop. Make sure that this small capital symbol is the same height as [e]. Keep it clearly distinct from [c].

ʔ **Glottal stop**. A dotless question mark. This symbol must not have a dot. The bottom horizontal serif is optional.

ɸ **Phi** /faj/. A voiceless bilabial fricative. This symbol must be kept distinct from the vowel [ø] and from the null sign Ø. An alternative version of phi exists [ϕ], which in handwriting is unfortunately easily confused with [ø] and Ø.

β **Beta** /ˈbejtə/ GA /-ɾə/. A voiced bilabial fricative. Note that the upper bowl is above the x-height line, and the lower stem extends below the base line.

θ **Theta** /ˈθejtə/ GA /-ɾə/. A voiceless dental fricative. This symbol extends above the x-height line. It must be kept distinct from the vowel [ɵ], which is the same height as *e*.

ð **Eth** /ɛð/. A voiced dental fricative. The stem leans to the left. A mathematician's delta δ is not correct. The curls on the crossbar are optional.

ʃ **Esh** /ɛʃ/. A voiceless palato-alveolar fricative. It has both an ascender and a descender.

ʒ **Ezh** /ɛʒ/. A voiced palato-alveolar fricative. A [z] with a lower tail.

ɕ **Curly tailed c**. A voiceless alveolo-palatal fricative. The tail extends slightly below the base line. This symbol must be kept distinct from [ç].

ʑ **Curly tailed z**. A voiced alveolo-palatal fricative. The tail extends slightly below the base line.

ʂ **Voiceless retroflex fricative**. An [s] with a retroflex hook. Note that the hook attaches at the left and points to the right.

ʐ **Voiced retroflex fricative**. A [z] with a retroflex hook. Note that the hook attaches at the right and points to the right.

ç **C-cedilla** /ˌsi səˈdɪlə/. A voiceless palatal fricative. A [c] with a small hook underneath, as used in French. This symbol must be kept distinct from [ɕ].

ʝ **Curly j**. A voiced palatal fricative. Take care to keep this symbol distinct from an ordinary [j].

ɣ **Gamma** /ˈgæmə/. A voiced velar fricative. The bowl is made below the base line. This symbol must be kept distinct from the vowel [ɤ] (ram's horns). Flat serifs for gamma and sloping shoulders for ram's horns help to keep them distinct.

χ **Chi** /kaj/. A voiceless uvular fricative. This symbol must be kept distinct from the velar fricative [x]; a lengthened stroke from top left to bottom right helps. Curling the ends of this stroke adds distinctiveness as well.

ʁ **Inverted small capital r**. A uvular approximant. Make sure that this symbol is the same height as [e]. Make sure not to reverse this symbol; keep the straight vertical line on the left.

ħ **Crossed h**. A voiceless pharyngeal fricative.

ʕ **Reversed glottal stop**. A voiced pharyngeal fricative. Be careful not to write an ordinary glottal stop [ʔ] by mistake.

ɧ **Hooktop h with tail**. A voiceless postalveolar-velar fricative. Keep distinct from [ɦ] and from [ŋ].

ɱ **Labiodental nasal**. An m with a long tail.

ɳ **Retroflex nasal**. An [n] with a retroflex hook, pointing to the right.

ɲ **Palatal n**. A palatal nasal. Be sure that the tail is on the left side, pointing to the left.

ŋ **Ing** /ɪŋ/. A velar nasal. Make sure that the tail is on the right side, pointing to the left.

ɴ **Small capital n**. A uvular nasal. Make sure that this small capital symbol is the same height as [e].

ɬ **Belted l**. A voiceless alveolar lateral fricative. The crossbar has a loop on the left side; this symbol must be kept distinct from dark [ɫ], with a curled crossbar without the loop.

ɫ **Tilde l**. A velarised alveolar lateral. Keep distinct from [ɬ].

ɮ **L-ezh ligature**. A voiced alveolar lateral fricative. The [l] and [ʒ] are written together as one symbol.

ɭ **Retroflex lateral**. A long [l] with a retroflex hook pointing to the right.

ʎ **Turned y**. A palatal lateral approximant. Note that this is a *y*, turned upside-down, not a Greek lambda λ.

ʟ **Small capital l**. A velar lateral approximant. Make sure that it is the same height as an [e].

ʀ **Small capital r**. A uvular trill. Make sure that this symbol is the same height as [e].

ɾ **Fish-hook r**. An alveolar flap. This symbol is an [r] with the upper left serif missing. The lower horizontal is usually present.

ɽ **R with right tail**. A retroflex flap. Keep this distinct from [ɺ].

ɺ **Turned long-legged r**. An alveolar lateral flap. Keep this distinct from [ɹ].

ɹ **Turned r**. A retroflex approximant. Keep the stem vertical; if the legs get too splayed, it looks like a [ʌ].

ʋ **Curly v**. A labiodental approximant. Keep distinct from [v] and [u]; a loop on the right stem helps maintain the distinction.

ɰ **Turned m with long right leg**. A high back unrounded semivowel; a velar approximant. Keep distinct from [ɯ].

ɥ **Turned h**. A high front rounded semivowel; a labial-palatal approximant. Keep this symbol clearly distinct from [y]. The lower horizontal serif is helpful in maintaining the distinction.

ʍ **Inverted w**. A voiceless high back rounded semivowel; a voiceless labial-velar approximant. Keep this symbol clearly distinct from [m].

ɦ **Hooktop h**. A breathy voiced vowel. A curl on the top helps keep it distinct from ordinary [h].

ɓ **Hooktop b**. An implosive bilabial stop. A curl on the top helps keep it distinct from ordinary [b].

ʄ **Hooktop barred dotless j**. An implosive palatal stop. A curl on the top helps keep it distinct from ordinary [ɟ].

ɗ **Hooktop d**. An implosive alveolar stop. A curl on the top helps keep it distinct from ordinary [d].

ɠ **Hooktop g**. An implosive velar stop. A curl on the top helps keep it distinct from ordinary [g].

ʘ **Bullseye**. A bilabial click.

ǀ **Pipe**. A dental click. Making this symbol with a descender keeps it distinct from a lower case [l]. Be sure not to slant it and confuse it with a virgule; use to enclose phonemic transcriptions.

ǃ **Exclamation point**. A (post)alveolar click.

ǂ **Double barred pipe**. A palato-alveolar click.

ǁ **Double pipe**. An alveolar lateral click.

Consonant examples

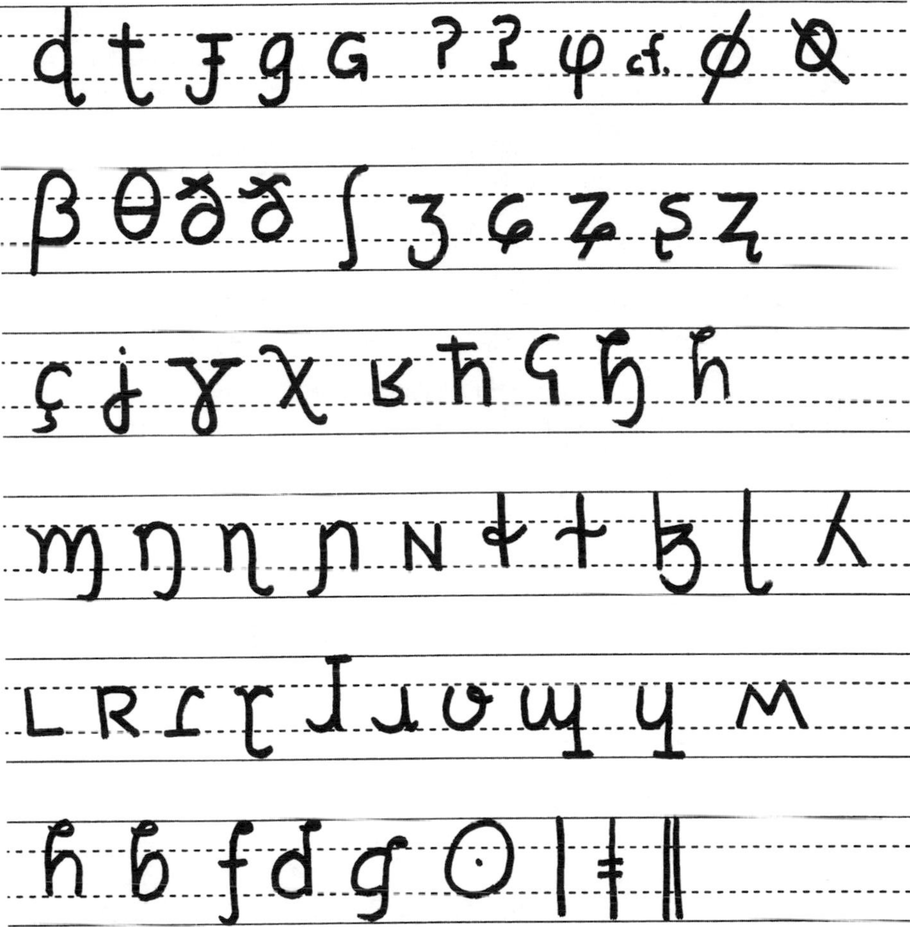

Figure C.8 Examples of consonant symbols

Diacritics

Diacritics are marks added to the main symbol to alter its value. Their placement in relation to the main symbol is important. Most are placed above, below, or after the main symbol. In the following presentation, an [x] is used to show the position of the main symbol in relation to the diacritic. Only the most common diacritics are shown; others can be seen on the IPA charts. The diacritics are presented in the order superscript, subscript, postposed, other.

x̃ **Tilde** /ˈtɪldə/. Nasalisation. Note that the left side is low, and the right side is high.

x́ **Acute** /əˈkjut/. A high tone; a strong stress.

x̄ **Macron** /ˈmækˌɹɒn/, GA /ˈmækˌɹɑn/ ~ /ˈmejkɹən/. A level tone; occasionally used for a long vowel.

x̀ **Grave** /gɹɑv/, GA also /gɹejv/. A low tone; a secondary stress.

x̂ **Circumflex** /ˈsɜkəmˌflɛks/ GA /ˈsəɹ-/. A falling tone. Note that this diacritic has a pointed top; do not use a rounded top.

x̌ **Haček** /ˈhɑˌtʃɛk/. A rising tone. This diacritic must have a pointed bottom. Keep it distinct from a breve [˘] with a rounded bottom.

x̆ **Breve** /bɹiv/. A syllable with weak stress; in Pinyin transcription of Chinese used for falling-rising tone. Note that this diacritic has a rounded bottom. Keep it distinct from a haček with a pointed posterior.

x̪ **Subscript bridge**. Dental. This diacritic converts an alveolar symbol to a dental one.

x̺ **Subscript turned bridge**. Apical.

x̻ **Subscript bridge**. Laminal.

x̥ **Under-ring**. Voiceless. A subscript ring; keep distinct from subscript dot.

x̤ **Subscript umlaut** /ˈumˌlawt/. Breathy voice.

x̰ **Subscript tilde**. Creaky voice.

x⁝ **Three subscript dots**. Whisper. Make sure that the individual dots are clear; keep distinct from subscript umlaut [̤]. Not an official IPA symbol.

x̩ **Syllabic mark**. Used to make a consonant syllabic. A vertical subscript stroke. Keep distinct from a subscript dot and from the mark for secondary stress, which precedes a symbol.

x̯ **Subscript arch**. Non-syllabic. Converts a vowel to the corresponding semivowel.

x̞ **Subscript t**. Shows a pronunciation lower or more open than usual.

x̝ **Inverted subscript t**. Shows a pronunciation higher or more closed than usual.

x̟ **Subscript plus**. Shows a pronunciation more advanced (farther towards the lips) than usual.

x̠ **Understroke**. Shows a pronunciation more retracted (farther towards the glottis) than usual.

xʰ **Raised h**. Aspiration.

xʷ **Raised w**. Labialisation.

xʲ **Raised j**. Palatalisation.

xˠ **Raised gamma**. Velarisation. See also mid tilde.

xˤ **Raised reversed glottal stop**. Pharyngealisation. See also mid tilde.

xʼ **Apostrophe**. Ejective. This symbol must be curved to the left and not straight.

x˞ **Rhotic hook**. A raised hook attached to the right side of the main symbol. With [ə], often combined as a single symbol [ɚ].

x̚ **Corner**. Inaudible release or unreleased.

xː **Length**. In handwriting, this symbol is normally a colon; in careful transcription it is made of two triangles.

xˑ **Half length**. In handwriting, this symbol is normally a raised dot; in careful transcription it is made of a triangle.

xꜛ **Upstep**. A superscript upwards arrow.

xꜜ **Downstep**. A superscript shafted arrow pointing down.

x̴ **Mid tilde**. A diacritic indicating either velarisation or pharyngealisation. Drawn horizontally through the middle of a symbol. Care must be taken that the basic symbol is clear. See superscript ram's horns and superscript reversed glottal stop.

ˈx **Primary stress**. Precedes a syllable with primary stress.

ˌx **Secondary stress**. Precedes a syllable with secondary stress.

‿x **Tertiary stress**. Precedes a syllable with tertiary stress. Not an official IPA symbol.

Diacritic examples

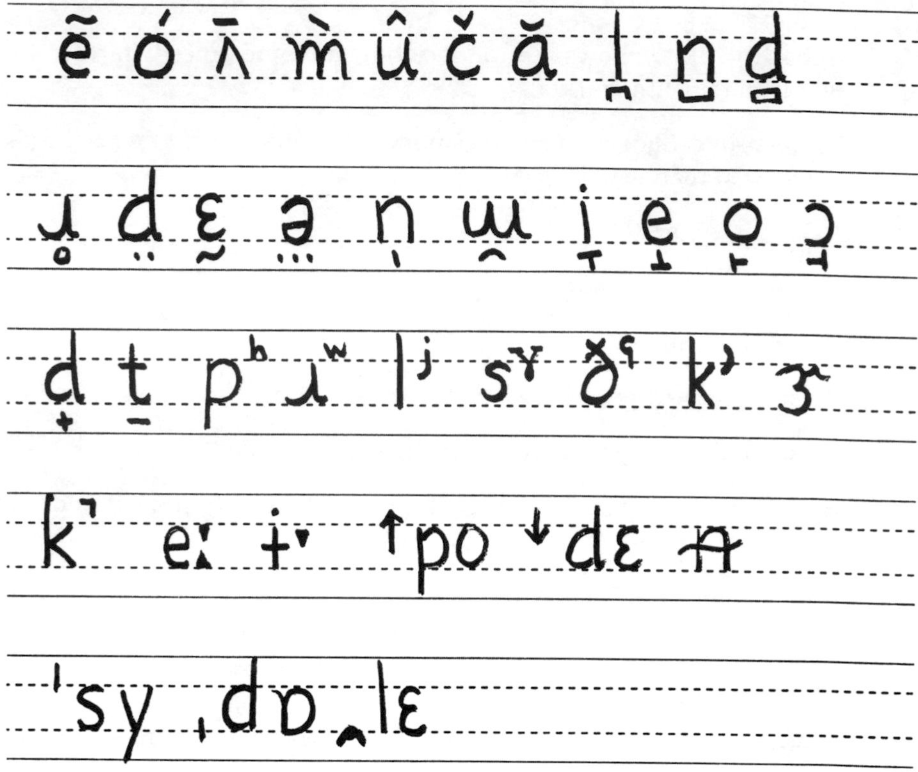

Figure C.9 Examples of diacritic symbols

Miscellaneous symbols

x͡x **Top ligature**. Written above two symbols to indicate that they are pronounced simultaneously (e.g., [k͡p]) or that they form a single phonological unit (e.g., an affricate [t͡ʃ]).

[XXX] **Square brackets**. Used in pairs to enclose phonetic transcriptions.

/XXX/ **Solidus** /ˈsɒlɪdəs/ (*pl.* **solidi** /ˈsɒlɪˌdi/ GA /ˈsɑl-/). Also known as **virgule** /ˈvɜˌgjul/ GA /ˈvəɹ-/ and **slant line**. Used in pairs to enclose phonemic transcriptions.

Miscellaneous examples

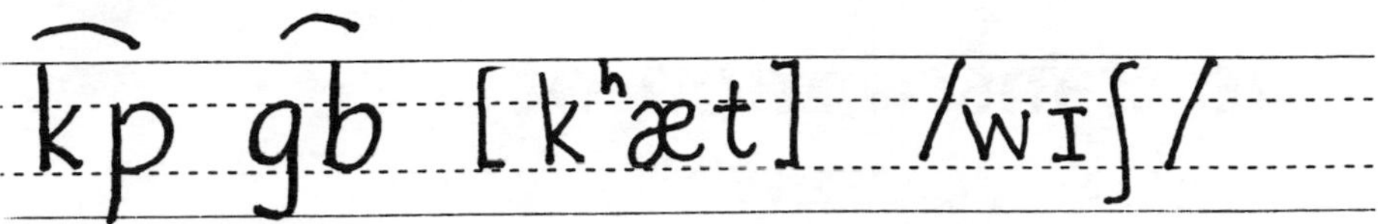

Figure C.10 Miscellaneous symbols

Appendix D

The transcription of English vowels

Students are understandably frustrated by the existence of different transcription systems for English. They often ask 'Why can't linguists and phoneticians just get together and agree on a single transcription scheme for English?' Clearly this has not happened, nor does it appear to be a likely development. An investigation of the transcription of English vowels is thus useful, both in considering why the variety of transcription schemes exists and in familiarising you with the variations in use. The aim of any transcription scheme is to provide an unambiguous way of recording pronunciation. Transcription schemes, however, for the same accent of the same language may differ considerably according to level, purpose, and scope.

Level

A broad transcription is one which records only phonemic contrasts; whereas a narrow transcription includes phonetic detail. In constructing a completely broad transcription, we remove all predictable detail. For example, in both RP and GA, there are many variations of length; in neither accent, however, is length phonemically contrastive. Therefore, it would not be indicated, since it can always be predicted. Other examples of predictable phenomena which we have considered are VOT, Canadian raising, smoothing. Smoothing is slightly different from the others in that it is optional; however, if a speaker uses smoothing, the results are predictable.

A completely narrow transcription is only theoretically imaginable. It would include all observable phonetic detail. The amount of such detail that could be recorded by reliable and careful observation would be overwhelming. Consider the following example found in Laver (1994).

[k̠ʰɑ̰̃˖ːɫ̺̃ˀ ɾi̠̞ʃ] 'with him' (Scots Gaelic, Skye)

The recording of this two-syllable word requires 20 symbols: 6 basic symbols and 14 diacritics. Only the final [ʃ] is unremarkable. Making such a transcription is obviously onerous, and reading a page or two of it well-nigh unmanageable. A transcription such as this is obviously not intended for regular reading purposes, but for the investigation of phonetic detail. Most of this detail is predictable and would not be needed in a completely broad transcription.

Thus, for our purposes, producing a workable transcription for a language, a broad transcription, or at least a fairly broad one, is necessary. At the same time, we need to make narrow transcriptions of selected portions of speech for detailed study.

Purpose

Transcriptions are made for various purposes. A broad transcription may be academically satisfying in its simplicity to the specialist, but its conciseness may be a deterrent for someone wanting to learn a foreign language. For example, someone learning GA may find it useful to have the tap [ɾ] represented explicitly. A strictly broad transcription would only indicate this as /t/ since taps are predictable in GA; however, a teaching transcription or a dictionary such as Wells (1990) might show taps to emphasise certain differences between RP and GA.

Dictionaries generally indicate pronunciation; however, they face the problem that their users rarely consult or learn how to use the pronunciation key provided. As a result, they try to provide transcriptions which a linguistically naive reader will tend to understand correctly. To this end, English dictionaries have often followed a tradition of transcription which tried to look as much like ordinary spelling as possible. For example, one might find /ə/ represented variously as [ă ĕ ĭ ŏ ŭ] depending on the spelling of the word; such a scheme misleadingly suggests that there are five distinct vowels. Fortunately, dictionaries in recent years have tended to use transcription schemes more like those in academic use.

Scope

The simplest situation for transcription is of one single accent. Speakers, however, are not uniform. In virtually all accents of English, *either* and *neither* have two acceptable pronunciations in the first syllable: [i] or [aj]. RP is relatively uniform, but Wells (1990) nevertheless had a large number of items where he was aware of variation and which he submitted to an opinion poll to determine preferences within RP speakers. GA represents an example of accent variation where it is one standard accent in the United States, but not the only one. Any English dictionary lists alternative pronunciations on virtually every page.

Table D.1 Variation between RP and GA in the low back vowels

	RP	GA	Possible vowel symbol
calm	ɑ	ɑ	ɑ
cot	ɒ	ɑ	ɒ
caught	ɔ	ɔ	ɔ
long	ɒ	ɔ	ɔ̇

Some transcription schemes are intended to be valid for more than one accent. For example, we could transcribe both the RP [əw] and GA [ow] diphthongs the same way, perhaps as /ow/. For the GA speaker, the transcription is transparent, but the RP speaker must remember that /ow/ means [əw]. This would likely work quite well.

A more complicated example is shown in the variation of vowels between RP and GA (Table D.1 above), where we can develop a transcription system which unambiguously represents these possibilities by having a separate symbol for each different pair of vowels.

Here we have used a superscript dot diacritic to create a fourth vowel. Such a system requires learning on the part of the user. RP speakers must learn that words with [ɔ̇] sound are just like the ones with [ɒ]; GA speakers must learn that [ɔ̇] is just like [ɔ]; the use of two symbols suggests that there is a subtle difference between the two vowels, which is not so for GA speakers. This system is slightly harder for RP speakers to learn, but we can easily turn the tables by substituting [ɒ̇] for [ɔ̇], making the system harder for GA speakers. The point here is that we can create an unambiguous transcription system for two accents by employing different symbols for each pair of contrasts. For two accents, this approach is fairly workable, but for several accents the number of contrastive sets is usually too large to work easily.

In a similar vein, we might include the post-vocalic /ɹ/ needed for GA and understand that it is not present in RP; thus, we could transcribe *car* as /kɑɹ/ for both accents. The situation is complicated by the fact that /ɹ/ after a vowel in GA corresponds to an RP /ə/ in words like *pure, pour, pair*. A word like *purr* is different still. We could transcribe *purr* as /pəɹ/, and the RP speaker would have to learn that /əɹ/ = [ɜ]. Or, we could compromise a bit and transcribe it as /ɜɹ/ so that the GA speaker has to live with a vowel that is not quite right and the RP speaker has to drop the /ɹ/. The point here is that the situation is complex and that generally whatever we do to simplify things for one accent complicates things for the other. Note also that in this sort of transcription, we have to include the /ɹ/. Its loss is predictable, but it is not possible to predict its insertion: /ˈfɑðə/ could be interpreted by a GA speaker as either *father* or *farther*.

Comparison of schemes

The *Longman Pronunciation Dictionary* by J. C. Wells (1990) gives pronunciations for RP and GA. The transcriptions used in this book and in Wells are shown below, both for RP and GA, and are later compared to point out some of the problems which one faces in devising a transcription scheme for English.

Analysis of differences

One major difference between Wells and this book is that he uses a length mark. This is a broad–narrow difference. In this respect, I have opted for a broader transcription which leaves vowel length to be predicted; Wells's

Table D.2 Two transcription systems for RP and GA: this book and Wells's dictionary

	SLIP		Wells	
	RP	GA	RP	GA
beat	i	i	iː	iː
bit	ɪ	ɪ	ɪ	ɪ
bait	ej	ej	eɪ	eɪ
bet	ɛ	ɛ	ɛ	ɛ
bat	æ	æ	æ	æ
boot	u	u	uː	uː
good	ʊ	ʊ	ʊ	ʊ
boat	əw	ow	əw	ow
bought	ɔ	ɔ	ɔː	ɒː
butt	ʌ	ʌ	ʌ	ʌ
cot	ɒ		ɒ	
calm	ɑ	ɑ	ɑː	ɑː
sofa	ə	ə	ə	ə
burr	ɜ	ə	ɜː	ɜ˞ː
buy	aj	aj	aɪ	aɪ
bough	aw	aw	aʊ	aʊ
boy	ɔj	ɔj	ɔɪ	ɔɪ
peer	ɪə		ɪə	
pair	ɛə		eə	
pure	ʊə		ʊə	
butter	əɹ		ᵊɹ	

system explicitly states length. My reasoning is that, as a textbook of phonetics, I want this book to focus on the parts where students have the most trouble. Length is usually quite easy and apparent to students. Some authors indicate length, but with a glide: writing the vowel of *beat* and *boot* as /ij uw/.

The glides in *bait* and *boat* are predictable; they could have been omitted. I have included them because native speakers of English generally have difficulty in hearing these glides, and I want them to become aware of their presence. Many authors have transcribed the RP vowel in *boat* as /ow/. This would, of course, have simplified the overall scheme, but at the expense of phonetic accuracy. Becoming more aware of different vowel qualities in different accents is a very effective way of mastering vowel production.

The use of the symbol [æ] for the vowel in *pat* is so commonplace that linguists rarely think about it. It does, however, violate a principle of using cardinal vowels whenever possible. There is no reason why [a] could not be used for this vowel, and indeed earlier authors, such as Jones (1975) did. However, [æ] has become thoroughly entrenched in English phonetics as the symbol for this vowel. I suspect that the use of [æ] was originally an artefact of technology: typewriters did not have different symbols for [a ɑ], so authors typed [a] for the back vowel and [ae] with a half backspace to get [æ] for the front vowel.

Wells uses different symbols for the vowels in the two syllables of GA *further* [ˈfɝðᵊr], and again different symbols for GA *caught* [ɒ] and *force* [ɔ]; I have transcribed these as [ˈfəɹðəɹ], [kɔt], and [fɔɹs]. The choice of symbols is not significant, nor is his use of a right-side-up [r]; however, distinguishing the vowel sounds [ɝ ᵊ] and [ɒ ɔ] does have some significance. The GA accent is not uniform: some speakers have different vowels in these situations and others do not. The history of science talks about lumpers and splitters. Some people tend to look for uniformity, whereas others look for diversity. In this case, at least, Wells has split, and I have lumped.

Advice

At the beginning, you should simply endeavour to master the transcription of the book you are using. As you move on to other books with different transcription schemes, you need to focus on the specifics of their system and also learn to translate between the new system and the familiar one. At some point, when you have learned several different systems, the confusion and frustration will disappear; you will feel comfortable with the different systems, and you will be able to appreciate the advantages of each.

Appendix E

The International Phonetic Alphabet

The **International Phonetic Association (IPA)** was founded in 1886 and for the past century has recommended an alphabet of phonetic symbols suitable for the transcription of any language. The **International Phonetic Alphabet (IPA)** has been occasionally revised over the decades, with a major revision in 1989 and minor ones in 1993 and 1996. The latest version of the Alphabet is reproduced below.

Although phonetic transcription in practice has steadily moved towards the official IPA, phoneticians and linguists have often introduced their own symbols and usages. In particular, linguists and, less often, phoneticians trained or practising in the United States have followed a slightly different tradition. *Phonetic Symbol Guide* (Pullum and Ladusaw, 1996) provides an excellent survey of transcription practice although it contains revisions of the IPA only through 1993.

CONSONANTS (PULMONIC)

	Bilabial	Labiodental	Dental	Alveolar	Postalveolar	Retroflex	Palatal	Velar	Uvular	Pharyngeal	Glottal
Plosive	p b			t d		ʈ ɖ	c ɟ	k g	q ɢ		ʔ
Nasal	m	ɱ		n		ɳ	ɲ	ŋ	ɴ		
Trill	ʙ			r					ʀ		
Tap or Flap				ɾ		ɽ					
Fricative	ɸ β	f v	θ ð	s z	ʃ ʒ	ʂ ʐ	ç ʝ	x ɣ	χ ʁ	ħ ʕ	h ɦ
Lateral fricative				ɬ ɮ							
Approximant		ʋ		ɹ		ɻ	j	ɰ			
Lateral approximant				l		ɭ	ʎ	ʟ			

Where symbols appear in pairs, the one to the right represents a voiced consonant. Shaded areas denote articulations judged impossible.

CONSONANTS (NON-PULMONIC)

Clicks	Voiced implosives	Ejectives
ʘ Bilabial	ɓ Bilabial	ʼ Examples:
ǀ Dental	ɗ Dental/alveolar	pʼ Bilabial
! (Post)alveolar	ʄ Palatal	tʼ Dental/alveolar
ǂ Palatoalveolar	ɠ Velar	kʼ Velar
ǁ Alveolar lateral	ʛ Uvular	sʼ Alveolar fricative

VOWELS

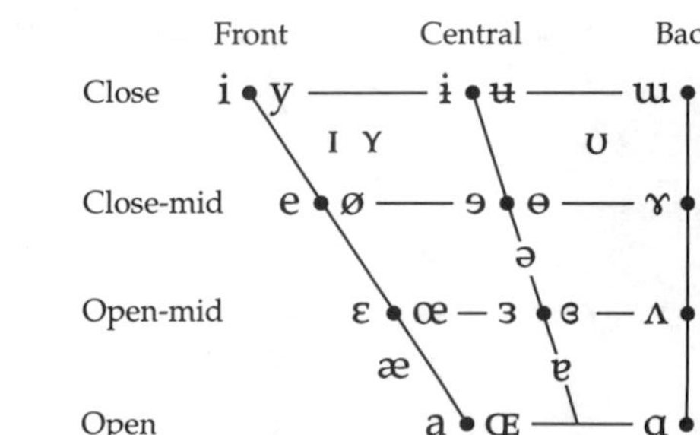

Where symbols appear in pairs, the one to the right represents a rounded vowel.

OTHER SYMBOLS

ʍ	Voiceless labial-velar fricative	ɕ ʑ	Alveolo-palatal fricatives
w	Voiced labial-velar approximant	ɺ	Alveolar lateral flap
ɥ	Voiced labial-palatal approximant	ɧ	Simultaneous ʃ and x
ʜ	Voiceless epiglottal fricative		
ʢ	Voiced epiglottal fricative		Affricates and double articulations can be represented by two symbols joined by a tie bar if necessary. k͡p t͡s
ʡ	Epiglottal plosive		

DIACRITICS Diacritics may be placed above a symbol with a descender, e.g. ŋ̊

̥ Voiceless	n̥ d̥	̤ Breathy voiced	b̤ a̤	̪ Dental	t̪ d̪
̬ Voiced	s̬ t̬	̰ Creaky voiced	b̰ a̰	̺ Apical	t̺ d̺
ʰ Aspirated	tʰ dʰ	̼ Linguolabial	t̼ d̼	̻ Laminal	t̻ d̻
̹ More rounded	ɔ̹	ʷ Labialized	tʷ dʷ	̃ Nasalized	ẽ
̜ Less rounded	ɔ̜	ʲ Palatalized	tʲ dʲ	ⁿ Nasal release	dⁿ
̟ Advanced	u̟	ˠ Velarized	tˠ dˠ	ˡ Lateral release	dˡ
̠ Retracted	e̠	ˤ Pharyngealized	tˤ dˤ	̚ No audible release	d̚
̈ Centralized	ë	~ Velarized or pharyngealized ɫ			
̽ Mid-centralized	e̽	̝ Raised	e̝	(ɹ̝ = voiced alveolar fricative)	
̩ Syllabic	n̩	̞ Lowered	e̞	(β̞ = voiced bilabial approximant)	
̯ Non-syllabic	e̯	̘ Advanced Tongue Root	e̘		
˞ Rhoticity	ɚ a˞	̙ Retracted Tongue Root	e̙		

SUPRASEGMENTALS

ˈ Primary stress

ˌ Secondary stress

ˌfoʊnəˈtɪʃən

ː Long eː

ˑ Half-long eˑ

̆ Extra-short ĕ

| Minor (foot) group

‖ Major (intonation) group

. Syllable break ɹi.ækt

‿ Linking (absence of a break)

TONES AND WORD ACCENTS

LEVEL		CONTOUR	
e̋ or ˥	Extra high	ě or ˩˥	Rising
é ˦	High	ê ˥˩	Falling
ē ˧	Mid	e᷄ ˧˥	High rising
è ˨	Low	e᷅ ˩˧	Low rising
ȅ ˩	Extra low	e᷈ ˧˦˧	Rising-falling
↓	Downstep	↗	Global rise
↑	Upstep	↘	Global fall

Figure E.1 The International Phonetic Alphabet (revised to 1993, updated 1996)

Bibliography

Abercrombie, D. (1991) *Fifty years in phonetics*. Edinburgh: Edinburgh University Press.

Al-Ani, S. H. (1970) *Arabic phonology: an acoustical and physiological investigation*. The Hague: Mouton.

Allen, W. S. (1947) 'Notes on the phonetics of an Eastern Armenian speaker', *Transactions of the Philological Society*, 50: 810–20.

Aronoff, M. and Oehrle, R. T. (eds) (1984) *Language sound structure*. Cambridge, MA: MIT Press.

Bailey, C.-J. N. (1985) *English phonetic transcription*. Dallas, TX: Summer Institute of Linguistics.

Baken, R. J. (1987) *Clinical measurement of speech and voice*. Boston, MA: College Hill.

Ball, M. J. (1989) *Phonetics for speech pathology*. London: Taylor and Francis.

Bamgboṣe, A. (1966) *A grammar of Yoruba*. West African Language Monographs, 5. Cambridge: Cambridge University Press.

Beckman, M. E. (1982) 'Segment duration and the "mora" in Japanese', *Phonetica*, 39: 113–35.

Beckman, M. (1988) 'Phonetic theory', in F. J. Newmeyer (ed.), *Linguistics: the Cambridge survey*. Cambridge: Cambridge University Press, 1: 216–38.

Berg, R. E. and Stork, D. G. (1982) *The physics of sound*. Englewood Cliffs, NJ: Prentice-Hall.

Berry, J. (n.d.) *The pronunciation of Ewe*. Cambridge: Heffer.

Berry, J. (n.d.) *The pronunciation of Gã*. Cambridge: Heffer.

Bills, G. D., Vallejo, B. and Troike, R. C. (1969) *An introduction to spoken Bolivian Quechua*. Austin: University of Texas Press.

Bloch, B. (1950) 'Studies in colloquial Japanese IV: Phonemics', *Language*, 26: 86–125.

Borden, G. J., Harris, K. S. and Raphael, L. (1994) *Speech science primer*, Baltimore MD.: Williams and Wilkins.

Bouhuys, A. (1974) *Breathing*. New York: Grune and Stratton.

Browman, C. P. and Goldstein, L. (1985) 'Dynamic modelling of phonetic structure', in V. A. Fromkin (ed.), *Phonetic linguistics: essays in honor of Peter Ladefoged*. Orlando, FL: Academic Press, pp. 35–53.

Browman, C. P. and Goldstein, L. (1986) 'Towards an articulatory phonology', *Phonology Yearbook*, 3: 219–52.

Browman, C. P. and Goldstein, L. (1989) 'Articulatory gestures as phonological units', *Phonology*, 6: 201–52.

Butcher, A. and Ahmad, K. (1987) 'Some acoustic and aerodynamic characteristics of pharyngeal consonants in Iraqi Arabic', *Phonetica*, 44: 156–72.

van Buuren, L. (1988) 'Margaret Thatcher's pronunciation: an exercise in ear-training', *Journal of the International Phonetic Association*, 18: 26–38.

Campbell, L. (1973) 'On glottalic consonants', *International Journal of American Linguistics*, 39: 44–6.

Carnochan, J. (1948) 'A study in the phonology of an Igbo speaker', *Bulletin of the School of Oriental and African Studies*, 12: 415–30.

Catford, J. C. (1977) *Fundamental problems in phonetics*. Bloomington, IN: Indiana University Press.

Catford, J. C. (1988) *A practical introduction to phonetics*. Oxford: Oxford University Press.

Catford, J. C. and Pisoni, D. B. (1970) 'Auditory vs. articulatory training in exotic sounds', *Modern Language Journal*, 54: 477–81.

Chambers, J. K. (1973) 'Canadian raising', *Canadian Journal of Linguistics*, 18: 113–35.

Chao, Y.-R. (1947) *Cantonese primer*. New York: Greenwood Press.

Chatterji, S. K. (1921) 'Bengali phonetics', *Bulletin of the School of Oriental and African Studies*, 2: 1–25.

Chayen, M. J. (1973) *The phonetics of Hebrew*. The Hague: Mouton.

Cho, S.-B. (1967) *A phonological study of Korean*. Uppsala: Uppsala University Press.

Chomsky, N. and Halle, M. (1968) *The sound pattern of English*. New York: Harper and Row.

Clark, J. and Yallop, C. (1990) *An introduction to phonetics and phonology*. Cambridge: Basil Blackwell.

Clarke, S. (1997) 'The role of Irish English in the formation of new world Englishes', in Jeffrey Kallen (ed.), *Focus on Ireland*. Amsterdam: John Benjamins, pp. 207–25.

Clements, G. N. (1985) 'The geometry of phonological features', *Phonology Yearbook* 2: 223–50.

Clements, G. N. and Hume, E. (1995) 'The internal organization of speech sounds', in J. A. Goldsmith (ed.), *The handbook of phonological theory*. Oxford: Blackwell, pp. 245–306.

Cruttenden, A. (1986) *Intonation*. Cambridge: Cambridge University Press.

Crystal, D. (1995) *The Cambridge encyclopedia of the English language*. Cambridge: Cambridge University Press.

Crystal, T. H. and House, A. S. (1988a) 'The duration of American–English stop consonants', *Journal of Phonetics*, 16: 285–94.

Crystal, T. H. and House, A. S. (1988b) 'The duration of American–English vowels: an overview', *Journal of Phonetics*, 16: 263–84.

Delattre, P. and Freeman, D. C. (1968) 'A dialect study of American *r*'s by x-ray motion picture', *Linguistics*, 44: 29–68.

Dickson, D. R. and Maue-Dickson, W. (1982) *Anatomical and physiological bases of speech*. Boston, MA: Little, Brown.

Dieth, E. (1950) *Vademecum der Phonetik*. Bern: Francke.

Docherty, G. J. (1992) *The timing of voicing in British English obstruents*. New York: Foris Publications.

Doke, C. (1926) *Phonetics of the Zulu language*. Special number *Bantu Studies*.

Doke, C. M. (1927) *Textbook of Zulu grammar*. Capetown: Longmans Southern Africa.

Dow, F. D. M. (1972) *An outline of Mandarin phonetics*. Canberra: Faculty of Asian Studies in association with the Australian National University Press.

Draper, M. H., Ladefoged, P. and Whitteridge, D. (1957) 'Expiratory muscles involved in speech', *Journal of Physiology*, 138: 17–18.

Draper, M. H., Ladefoged, P. and Whitteridge, D. (1958) 'Respiratory muscles in speech', *Journal of Speech and Hearing Research*, 2: 16–27.

Draper, M. H., Ladefoged, P. and Whitteridge, D. (1960) 'Expiratory muscles and airflow during speech', *British Medical Journal*, 18 June: 1837–43.
Dulong, G. and Bergeron, G. (1980) *Le parler populaire du Québec et de ses régions voisines. Atlas linguistique de l'est du Canada*. Québec: L'Editeur officiel du Québec.

von Essen, O. (1964) *Grundzüge der hochdeutschen Satzintonation*. Ratingen: A. Henn.

Fennell, T. G. and Gelsen, H. (1980) *A grammar of modern Latvian*. The Hague: Mouton.
Ferguson, C. A. and Chowdhury, M. (1960) 'The phonemes of Bengali', *Language*, 36: 22–59.
Fink, B. R. and Demarest, R. J. (1978) *Laryngeal biomechanics*. Cambridge, MA: Harvard University Press.
Fok, C. Y.-Y. (1974) *A perceptual study of tones in Cantonese*. Hong Kong: University of Hong Kong.
Fox, A. (1984) *German intonation: an outline*. Oxford: Oxford University Press.
Friðjónsson, J. (1981) *Phonetics of modern Icelandic*. Reykjavik.
Fry, D. B. (1979) *The physics of speech*. Cambridge: Cambridge University Press.
Fuller, M. (1990) 'Pulmonic ingressive fricatives in Tsou', *Journal of the International Phonetic Association*, 20: 9–14.

Gairdner, W. H. T. (1925) *The phonetics of Arabic*. London: Humphrey Milford.
Gendron, J.-D. (1966) *Tendances phonétiques du français parlé au Canada*. Paris: Klincksieck.
Gimson, A. C. (1980) *An introduction to the pronunciation of English*. London: Edward Arnold.
Grant, W. (1913) *The pronunciation of English in Scotland*. Cambridge: Cambridge University Press.
Gregg, R. J. (1960) *A student's manual of French pronunciation*. Toronto: Macmillan.
Gussenhoven, C. and Jacobs, H. (1998) *Understanding phonology*. London: Edward Arnold.

Halle, M. (1983) 'On distinctive features and their articulatory implementation', *Natural Language and Linguistic Theory*, 1: 91–105.
Halle, M. and Stevens, K. N. (1969) 'On the feature "Advanced tongue root"', *Quarterly Progress Report*, MIT Research Laboratory of Electronics, 94: 209–15.
Halle, M. and Stevens, K. N. (1979) 'Some reflections on the theoretical bases of phonetics', in B. Lindblom and S. Ohman (eds), *Frontiers of speech communication*. London: Academic Press, pp. 335–49.
Halle, M. and Vergnaud, J.-R. (1987) *An essay on stress*. Cambridge, MA: MIT Press.
Handel, S. (1989) *Listening: an introduction to the perception of auditory events*. Cambridge, MA: MIT Press.
Hanna, S. A. and Greis, N. (1976) *Writing Arabic*. Leiden: E. J. Brill.
Hardcastle, W. J. (1976) *Physiology of speech production: an introduction for speech scientists*. London: Academic Press.
Hardcastle, W. J. and Laver, J. (eds) (1997) *Handbook of phonetics*. Oxford: Blackwell.
Henderson, J. B. and Repp, B. H. (1982) 'Is a stop consonant released when followed by another stop consonant?', *Phonetica*, 39: 71–82.
Hixon, T. J. (1987) 'Respiratory functions in speech', in T. J. Hixon (ed.), *Respiratory function in speech and song*. Boston, MA: College Hill Press, pp. 1–54.

Hoffman, C. F. (1963) *A grammar of the Margi language*. Oxford: Oxford University Press.

Holm, J. (1988) *Pidgins and creoles*. Cambridge: Cambridge University Press.

Howie, J. M. (1976) *Acoustical studies of Mandarin vowels and tones*. Cambridge: Cambridge University Press.

Howren, R. (1979) 'The phonology of Rae Dogrib', in *Contributions to Canadian linguistics*. Mercury Series, Canadian Ethnology Service Paper No. 50. Ottawa: National Museum of Canada, pp. 1–6.

Hughes, A. and Trudgill, P. (1996) *English accents and dialects: an introduction to social and regional varieties of British English*. London: Edward Arnold.

van der Hulst, H. and Smith, N. (1988) 'The variety of pitch accent systems: introduction', in H. van der Hulst and N. Smith (eds), *Autosegmental studies on pitch accent*. Dordrecht: Foris, pp. ix–xxiv.

Hyman, L. M. (1975) *Phonology: theory and analysis*. New York: Holt, Rinehart and Winston.

Jakobson, R., Fant, G. and Halle, M. (1952) *Preliminaries to speech analysis*. Cambridge, MA: MIT Press.

Jassem, W. (1976) 'The acoustics of consonants', in D. B. Fry (ed.), *Acoustic phonetics*. Cambridge: Cambridge University Press, pp. 124–31.

Johnson, K. (1997) *Acoustic and auditory phonetics*. Oxford: Blackwell.

Jones, D. (1975) *An outline of English phonetics*. Cambridge: Cambridge University Press.

Jones, D. and Ward, D. (1969) *The phonetics of Russian*. Cambridge: Cambridge University Press.

Kahane, J. C. and Folkins, J. W. (1984) *Atlas of speech and hearing anatomy*. Columbus, OH: Charles E. Merrill.

Kálmán, B. (1972) 'Hungarian historical phonology', in L. Benko and S. Imre (eds), *The Hungarian language*. The Hague: Mouton, pp. 49–84.

Kao, D. L. (1971) *Structure of the syllable in Cantonese*. The Hague: Mouton.

Keating, P. (1987) 'A survey of phonological features', *UCLA Working Papers in Phonetics*, 66: 124–50.

Kent, R. D. and Read, C. (1992) *The acoustic analysis of speech*. San Diego, CA: Singular.

Killingley, S.-Y. (1985) *A new look at Cantonese tones: five or six*. Newcastle upon Tyne: S.-Y. Killingley.

Kim, C. W. (1965) 'On the autonomy of the tensity features in stop classification (with special reference to Korean stops)', *Word*, 21: 339–59.

Kim, C. W. (1970) 'A theory of aspiration', *Phonetica*, 21: 107–16.

King, Q. (1979) 'Chilcotin phonology and vocabulary', in *Contributions to Canadian linguistics*. Mercury Series, Canadian Ethnology Service Paper No. 50. Ottawa: National Museum of Canada, pp. 7–41.

Kökeritz, H. (1953) *Shakespeare's pronunciation*. New Haven, CT: Yale University Press.

Kökeritz, H. (1978) *A guide to Chaucer's pronunciation*. Toronto: University of Toronto Press.

Kostić, D. and Das, R. H. (1972) *A short outline of Bengali phonetics*. Calcutta: Statistical Publishing Society.

Kreidler, C. W. (1989) *The pronunciation of English*. Oxford: Basil Blackwell.

Labov, W. (1991) *Sociolinguistic patterns*. Philadelphia, PA: University of Pennsylvania Press.

Ladefoged, P. (1964) *A phonetic study of West African languages*. Cambridge: Cambridge University Press.

Ladefoged, P. (1967) *Three areas of experimental phonetics*. London: Oxford University Press.

Ladefoged, P. (1971) *Preliminaries to linguistic phonetics*. Chicago: University of Chicago Press.

Ladefoged, P. (1983) 'Cross-linguistics studies of speech production', in P. F. MacNeilage (ed.), *The production of speech*. New York: Springer-Verlag, pp. 177–88.

Ladefoged, P. (1993) *A course in phonetics* (3rd edn). Fort Worth, TX: Harcourt Brace Jovanovich.

Ladefoged, P. (1996) *Elements of acoustic phonetics* (2nd edn). Chicago: University of Chicago Press.

Ladefoged, P. and Bhaskararao, P. (1983) 'Non-quantal aspects of consonant production: a study of retroflex consonants', *Journal of Phonetics*, 11: 291–302.

Ladefoged, P. and Halle, H. (1988) 'Some major features of the International Phonetic Alphabet', *Language*, 64: 577–82.

Ladefoged, P. and Maddiesen, I. (1996) *The sounds of the world's languages*. Oxford: Blackwell.

Ladefoged, P. and Traill, A. (1984) 'Linguistic phonetic description of clicks', *Language*, 60: 1–20.

Ladefoged, P., Cochrane, A. and Disner, S. (1977) 'Laterals and trills', *Journal of the International Phonetic Association*, 7: 46–54.

Laufer, A. and Condax, I. D. (1979) 'The epiglottis as an articulator', *Journal of the International Phonetic Association*, 9: 50–6.

Laver, J. (1980) *The phonetic quality of voice description*. Cambridge: Cambridge University Press.

Laver, J. (1994) *Principles of phonetics*. Cambridge: Cambridge University Press.

Léon, P. R. (1966) *Prononciation du français standard*. Montréal: Didier.

Léon, P. R. (ed.) (1968) *Recherches sur la structure phonique du français canadien*. Montréal: Didier.

Lieberman, P. and Blumstein, S. E. (1988) *Speech physiology, speech perception, and acoustic phonetics*. Cambridge: Cambridge University Press.

Lindau, M. (1974) 'The feature advanced tongue root', in E. Voeltz (ed.), *Third annual conference on African languages*. Bloomington, IN: Indiana University Press, pp. 127–34.

Lindau, M. (1978) 'Vowel features', *Language*, 54: 541–63.

Lindau, M. (1979) 'The feature expanded', *Journal of Phonetics*, 7: 163–76.

Lindau, M. (1985) 'The story of /r/', in V. A. Fromkin (ed.), *Phonetic linguistics: essays in honor of Peter Ladefoged*. Orlando, FL: Academic Press, pp. 157–68.

Lindau, M., Norlin, K. and Svantesson, J. (1990) 'Some cross-linguistic differences in diphthongs', *Journal of the International Phonetic Association*, 35: 173–81.

Lisker, L. and Abramson, A. S. (1957) 'Linguistic segments, acoustic segments, and synthetic speech', *Language*, 33: 370–40.

Lisker, L. and Abramson, A. S. (1964) 'A cross-language study of voicing in initial stops', *Word*, 20: 384–422.

Lisker, L. and Abramson, A. S. (1971) 'Distinctive features and laryngeal control', *Language*, 47: 767–85.

Lowery, B. M. (1979) 'The phonological system of Blackfoot', in *Contributions to Canadian Linguistics*. Mercury Series, Canadian Ethnology Service Paper No. 50. Ottawa: National Museum of Canada, pp. 41–66.

MacNeilage, P. F. (ed.) (1983) *The production of speech*. New York: Springer-Verlag.

Maddieson, I. (1984) *Patterns of sounds*. Cambridge: Cambridge University Press.

Maddieson, I. (1985) 'Phonetic cues to syllabification', in V. A. Fromkin (ed.), *Phonetic linguistics: essays in honor of Peter Ladefoged*. Orlando, FL: Academic Press, pp. 203–21.

Maddieson, I. (1989) 'Linguo-labials', in R. Harlow and R. Cooper (eds), *VICAL 1: Oceanic languages*, Part 2. Auckland: Linguistic Society of New Zealand, pp. 349–76.

Maddieson, I. and Emmorey, K. (1984) 'Is there a valid distinction between voiceless lateral approximants and fricatives?', *Phonetica*, 41: 181–90.

Malmberg, B. (1970) *Svensk fonetik*. Lund: Gleerups.

McAlpin, D. W. (1975) 'The morphophonology of the Dravidian Noun', in H. F. Schiffman and C. M. Eastman (eds), *Dravidian phonological systems*. Seattle, WA: University of Washington, pp. 206–23.

McCarthy, J. J. (1988) 'Feature geometry and dependency: a review', *Phonetica*, 43: 84–108.

McCawley, J. D. (1968) *The phonological component of a grammar of Japanese*. The Hague: Mouton.

Merrifield, W. R. (1963) 'Palantla Chinantec syllable types', *Anthropological Linguistics*, 5: 1–16.

Minifie, Fred, Hixon, Thomas J. and Williams, Frederick (1973) *Normal aspects of speech, hearing, and language*. Englewood Cliffs, NJ: Prentice-Hall.

Mitchell, A. G. and Delbridge, A. (1965) *The speech of Australian adolescents: a survey*. Sydney: Angus and Robertson.

Mougeon, R. and Beniak, E. (1989) *Le français canadien parlé hors Québec*. Québec: Presses de l'Université Laval.

Norlin, K. (1987) *A phonetic study of emphasis and vowels in Egyptian Arabic*. Working Papers No. 30. Lund: Lund University, Department of Linguistics.

Obrecht, D. H. (1969) *Effects of the second formant on the perception of velarization consonants in Arabic*. The Hague: Mouton.

Okell, J. (1969) *A reference grammar of colloquial Burmese*. Oxford: Oxford University Press.

Olive, J., Greenwood, A. and Coleman, J. (1993) *Acoustics of American English speech: a dynamic approach*. New York: Springer-Verlag.

Paddock, H. (1974) 'Some variations in the phonology and grammar of Newfoundland English'. ms.

Paddock, H. (1981) *A dialect survey of Carbonear, Newfoundland*. Publication of the American Dialect Society, 68. University, AL: University of Alabama Press.

Painter, C. (1973) 'Cineradiographic data on the feature "covered" in Twi vowel harmony', *Phonetica*, 28: 97–120.

Perkell, J. (1971) 'Physiology of speech production: a preliminary study of two suggested revisions of the features specifying vowels', *Quarterly progress report*, MIT Research Laboratory of Electronics, 102: 123–39.

Peterson, G. E. and Barney, H. L. (1952) 'Control methods used in a study of the vowels', *Journal of the Acoustical Society of America*, 24: 175–84.
Picard, M. (1987) *An introduction to the comparative phonetics of English and French in North America*. Amsterdam: John Benjamins.
Pickett, J. M. (1999) *The acoustics of speech communication*. Boston, MA: Allyn and Bacon.
Pierrehumbert, J. and Beckman, M. (1988) *Japanese tone structure*. Cambridge, MA: MIT Press.
Pike, K. L. (1963) *Phonetics*. Ann Arbor, MI: University of Michigan.
Pike, K. L. (1967) 'Tongue-root position in practical phonetics', *Phonetica*, 17: 129–40.
Pullum G, K. and Ladusaw, W. A. (1996) *Phonetic symbol guide* (2nd edn). Chicago: University of Chicago Press.

Ramos, T. V. (1971) *Tagalog structures*. Honolulu: University of Hawaii Press.
Roberts, P. A. (1988) *West Indians and their language*. Cambridge: Cambridge University Press.
Rogers, H. (1992) 'Laryngeal timing in Mongolian', *Proceedings of the 1992 annual conference of the Canadian Linguistic Association*. pp. 241–8. Toronto: Canadian Linguistics Association.
Romaine, S. (1988) *Pidgin and creole languages*. London: Longman.

Sagey, E. (1991) 'The representation of features and relations in nonlinear phonology', Ph.D dissertation, MIT. New York: Garland Press.
Samarin, W. J. (1966) *The Gbeya language: grammar, texts, and vocabularies*. Publications in Linguistics, 44. Berkeley, CA: University of California Press.
Schuh, W. R. (1986) 'The phonology of intonation in Hausa', *Northeast Linguistic Society*, 17: 327–41.
Selkirk, E. (1984) 'On the major class features and syllable theory', in Mark Aronoff and Richard T. Oehrle (eds), *Language sound structure*. Cambridge, MA: MIT Press, pp. 107–36.
Shearer, W. M. (1979) *Illustrated speech anatomy*. Springfield, IL: Charles C. Thomas.
Shorrocks, G. (1997) 'Celtic influences on the English of Newfoundland and Labrador', in H. L. C. Tristam (ed.), *The Celtic Englishes*. Heidelberg: Universitatsverlag C. Winter, pp. 320–61.
Solá, D. F. (1972) *Spoken Cuzco Quechua*. Lima: Yachay-Wasi Academy of Quechua.
Stetson, R. H. (1951) *Motor phonetics*. Amsterdam: North Holland Publishing Co.
Stewart, J. M. (1967) 'Tongue root position in Akan vowel harmony', *Phonetica*, 16: 185–204.
Strevens, P. (1976) 'Spectra of fricative noise in human speech', in D. B. Fry (ed.), *Acoustic phonetics*. Cambridge: Cambridge University Press, pp. 132–50.
Suárez, J. A. (1983) *The Mesoamerican Indian languages*. Cambridge: Cambridge University Press.
Syamala, K. B. (1972) *Malayalam phonetic reader*. Mysore: Central Institute of Indian Languages.

Thomas, A. (1987) *La variation phontiqué: cas du franco-ontarien*. Montréal: Didier.
Thompson, L. C. (1965) *A Vietnamese grammar*. Seattle, WA: University of Washington Press.
Tranel, B. (1987) *The sounds of French*. Cambridge: Cambridge University Press.
Trubetzkoy, N. S. (1939) *Grundzüge der Phonologie*. Gottingen: Vandenhoeck and Ruprecht.

Trudgill, P. and Hannah, J. (1994) *International English.* London: Edward Arnold.

Tyler, S. A. (1969) *Koya: an outline grammar*. Publications in Linguistics, 54. Berkeley, CA: University of California Press.

Vance, T. J. (1987) *An introduction to Japanese phonology*. Albany, NY: State University of New York Press.

Vinay, J.-P. (1950) 'Bout de la langue ou fond de la gorge', *French Review*, 23: 489–98.

Walker, D. C. (1984) *The pronunciation of Canadian French.* Ottawa: University of Ottawa Press.

Walker, R. (1979) 'Central Carrier phonemics', in *Contributions to Canadian linguistics.* Mercury Series, Canadian Ethnology Service Paper No. 50. Ottawa: National Museum of Canada, pp. 93–118.

Wardhaugh, R. (1986) *An introduction to sociolinguistics*. Oxford: Basil Blackwell.

Wells, J. C. (1982) *Accents of English* (3 vols). Cambridge: Cambridge University Press.

Wells, J. C. (1990) *Longman pronunciation dictionary*. Harlow: Longman.

Westerman, D. and Ward, I. (1957) *Practical phonetics for students of African languages.* Oxford: Oxford University Press.

Witting, C. (1977) *Studies in Swedish generative phonology*. Uppsala: Uppsala University Press.

Wolfram, W. and Schilling-Estes, N. (1998) *American English*. Oxford: Blackwell.

Zemlin, W. R. (1988) *Speech and hearing science*. Englewood Cliffs, NJ: Prentice-Hall.

Index